A BRIEF HISTORY
OF SAUDI ARABIA

A BRIEF HISTORY OF SAUDI ARABIA

JAMES WYNBRANDT

Foreword by Fawaz A. Gerges

Checkmark Books®

An imprint of Facts On File, Inc.

A Brief History of Saudi Arabia

Text Copyright © 2004 by James Wynbrandt; Foreword by Fawaz A. Gerges

All rights reserved. No part of this book may be reproduced or utilized in any form or by any means, electronic or mechanical, including photocopying, recording, or by any information storage or retrieval systems, without permission in writing from the publisher. For information contact:

Checkmark Books
An imprint of Facts On File, Inc.
132 West 31st Street
New York NY 10001

Library of Congress Cataloging-in-Publication Data

Wynbrandt, James
  A brief history of Saudi Arabia / James Wynbrandt; foreword by Fawaz A. Gerges.
      p. cm.
  Includes bibliographical references and index.
  Contents: The land and its pre-Islamic history—The birth of Islam (571–632)—The Islamic Empire and Arabia (632–1258)—The golden age of Islam (c. 750–1258)—The Mamluks, Ottomans, and the Wahhabi-Al Saud alliance (1258–1745)—The first Saudi state (1745–1818)—Roots of modern Arabia (1818–1891)—Unity and independence (1891–1932)—Birth of a kingdom (1932–1953)—A path to world power (1953–1973)—Oil and arms (1973–1990)—The Gulf crisis and its aftermath (1990–2001)—The challenges ahead.
      ISBN 0-8160-5203-4 (hc: alk. paper)—ISBN 0-8160-5795-8 (pbk.)
  1. Saudi Arabia. [1. Saudi Arabia—History.] I. Title.
      DS204.25.W96 2004
      953.8—dc22

                                                                                    2003019231

Checkmark Books are available at special discounts when purchased in bulk quantities for businesses, associations, institutions, or sales promotions. Please call our Special Sales Department in New York at (212) 967-8800 or (800) 322-8755.

You can find Facts On File on the World Wide Web at http://www.factsonfile.com

Cover design by Semadar Megged
Maps and charts by Dale Williams

Printed in the United States of America

MP Hermitage 10 9 8 7 6 5 4 3 2 1

This book is printed on acid-free paper.

CONTENTS

Appendixes

LIST OF ILLUSTRATIONS

LIST OF MAPS

LIST OF CHARTS

FOREWORD

Before 9/11, to many Americans Saudi Arabia was a distant, alien place shrouded in mystery. Beyond anecdotes and stereotypes, little was known about either the complexity of Saudi culture and society or its polity. Two encounters shaped Americans' perceptions of the Arabian kingdom. The early 1970s oil embargo unraveled Americans' sense of economic invincibility and left its negative imprint on how they viewed this small country that exercised power over their economy and affected their quality of life. Also important was the 1991 Gulf War, which brought hundreds of thousands of U.S. troops into Saudi Arabia, giving Americans a glimpse of life in a different, closed society.

In the Western imagination, the Arabian kingdom became synonymous with oil monopoly; decadent, wealthy princes whose tales and adventures captivated tabloid readers; and veiled, hapless women, forbidden to drive, let alone travel, on their own. An exotic portrait of Saudi Arabia, partly real and partly surreal, prevailed. But on the whole, Saudi Arabia was not on the radar screen of most Americans, who seemed to show no intellectual interest in discovering either the secrets of this distant land or its impact on their checkbooks.

This changed with the events of 9/11. The ruling royal family found itself in a very unenviable position on the morning after the events. The fact that 15 of the 19 hijackers involved were from Saudi Arabia—and that some financing and planning for the attacks allegedly occurred on Saudi soil—brought outrage and recrimination against the conservative kingdom by U.S. opinion makers and serious accusations about its alleged role in financing militancy and terrorism. Critics of the royal family accused the kingdom of financing and harboring terrorists and advocated a dramatic shift in U.S. foreign policy toward it. Some analysts and commentators went further and called for the toppling of the royal family and its replacement with a friendlier regime.

In the eyes of many Americans, Saudi Arabia was swiftly transformed from an "ambivalent ally" to an "enemy." No concrete, solid evidence was produced regarding the kingdom's support of terrorists, but the Saudi establishment's strategy of using religion as a legitimizing device and its channeling of hundreds of millions of U.S. dollars to various Islamic movements proved to be damning in the eyes of many Americans.

The Saudis positively, albeit slowly, responded to Washington's requests to confirm the identities of the 15 Saudi hijackers, block some accounts with links to terrorist groups, and arrest some of bin Laden's associates and sympathizers. Yet they were criticized not only for not doing enough and not fully joining the U.S.-led war against terrorism but also for collusion with al-Qaeda.

The royal family was found guilty without a proper trial. A stream of TV commentators and politicians supplied plenty of ammunition to use against the highly conservative kingdom. Americans were told that the sources of evil reside in the unholy alliance between reactionary Wahhabism and the House of Saud. Advocacy and simplification replaced critical analysis and rich historical narrative.

Saudi Arabia is the birthplace of Islam and its prophet whereto Muslims the world over journey to experience the sacred. The *umma*— the Muslim community worldwide—faces Mecca, the birthplace of the Prophet, during daily prayers. It is this sense of uniqueness that shapes Saudis' religious sensibilities and inspires them with a missionary zeal. Both the religious and ruling establishments share this deep sense of commitment to spreading their puritan form of Islam—one that was born and nourished in the Arabian desert.

Thus it is misleading to reduce the kingdom's structure to that of the social contract that exists between the House of Saud and Wahhabism that has assured domestic peace for more than a century. In the eyes of Saudis, the birth of their kingdom is synonymous with the birth of Islam, and only to Islam it owes its existence. Early Islam supplied the ideological foundation for the founding fathers of Saudi Arabia and also enabled the latter to subdue and unite disparate, warring tribes into a relatively functioning polity.

Although Saudi leaders have recently cracked down on religious hard-liners, they must recognize that their social contract with the conservative Wahhabi movement that sustained the kingdom for more than a century has long expired. After all, it is important to recognize that bin Laden's revolt has deep roots in the Saudi reality. Tales of rampant corruption, coupled with exploding population statistics and diminishing opportunities, particularly for young people (a constituency that represents more than 60 percent of the population), inflamed religious sensibilities against the royal family and its patron, the United States. In the eyes of many Saudis, the United States is seen as an internal player that helps sustain the harsh status quo.

Furthermore, the 1991 stationing of U.S. military forces in Saudi Arabia, home to the holiest Muslim shrines, Mecca and Medina, estranged not only the Wahhabi conservative establishment but also the pious public. This development was used as a lightning rod to ignite bin Laden's onslaught against his royal benefactors and their super-power ally.

The anti-American rhetoric by the religious hard-liners masks a more practical agenda—toppling the pro-Western monarchy that is seen to have forfeited its mandate as a guardian of the ethos of Islam. Both the hard-liners' rhetoric and their agenda resonate with the alienated Saudi youths (burdened with 25 percent unemployment) who readily accept Washington's culpability in perpetuating their predicament.

The terrorist attacks in Riyadh in 2003—which killed 35, including eight Americans—were aimed not just at Western targets but also at the symbolic links between the West and the ruling House of Saud. The goal is to replace the pro-American monarchy with a more authentic, Islamist government similar to that of the Taliban in Afghanistan.

Initially, instead of confronting the threat head on, the royal family attempted to walk a tight rope between maintaining its alliance with the United States and trying to placate the religious establishment. That dichotomy partially explained the reluctance of the Saudi government to crack down harder on the militants and their spiritual gurus.

But the House of Saud appears to be steadily recognizing that the religious hard-liners can no longer be mollified or persuaded to stop their incitement of the youths. They are waging jihad (total war) for the heart and soul of Islam, for the control of the Saudi state, with no com-promise. The official Saudi-American connection is just one in their litany of grievances. Neither the withdrawal of American troops from the kingdom nor even the severance of the Saudi-American connection will appease the religious hard-liners: Nothing short of a change of leadership in Riyadh will do.

Although in the short term the tough security measures imple-mented seem to have preempted and disrupted terrorist cells and attacks, on their own they cannot resolve the deepening crisis and mis-trust between those who govern and the governed. The challenge fac-ing the Saudi royal family, as a young former Saudi judge and Islamic scholar said, revolves around its willingness to "disregard the Wahhabi teachings" and to tackle the root causes of social grievances that nour-ish extremism and threaten its very survival. This ambitious project will take time and resources and it involves risks. But the alternative is more militancy and political decay.

As a counterweight to the religious hard-liners, the Saudi regime must expand its social base by empowering the professional, enlightened classes and making their voices heard in civil society. Reforming conservative Saudi society will not be easy or risk-free, but the royal family cannot bury its head in the sand in the face of the gathering storm. It must do away with old habits and old ways and begin the arduous process of genuine institution building and of conceding the existence of an autonomous civil society beholden neither to the religious or ruling establishments.

Given the importance of Saudi Arabia and the outcome of the current internal struggle, there has never been such a need for scholarly revisiting of the country, its history, culture, and politics. Such an intellectual exercise must shed light on the nature and character of the Saudi polity, the complex relationship between the ruling class and the religious establishment, the sources of political legitimacy, its political economy, and its regional and international alliance.

Fortunately, James Wynbrandt's *A Brief History of Saudi Arabia* comes at an auspicious time and fills an important gap in the scholarly literature. The title—*A Brief History of Saudi Arabia*—does not do justice to the book's historical richness and broad scope. Wynbrandt contextualizes the history of Saudi Arabia within the rise of Islam in the Arabian Peninsula, the starting point and the departure point for any critical understanding of the role of religious sensibilities in the formation of political and popular culture in Saudi Arabia.

A Brief History of Saudi Arabia chronologically and systematically examines the evolution and development of the sociopolitical and economic structure of Arabia as well as the subsequent formation of modern Saudi Arabia. General readers and undergraduates, in particular, will find the book highly accessible and informative. Historical episodes, leading actors, and complex terms are explained and made intelligible. Given its introductory character, the chronological method adopted by the author clarifies and simplifies the narrative further.

Another strength of the book lies in its timeliness and comprehensiveness. It takes the narrative from the birth of Islam until the 9/11 events. The author devotes a solid chapter to the oil revolution that made the country a power to be reckoned with and another chapter to the first 1991 Gulf War and its aftershocks. The last chapter focuses on the current challenges facing the kingdom in the aftermath of 9/11 and the social turmoil and terrorism that threaten to unravel internal stability.

—Fawaz A. Gerges

ACKNOWLEDGMENTS

The author is deeply indebted to Dr. Fawaz A. Gerges for his invaluable insights and generous contribution of the foreword to this work. Many thanks also to Ambassador Richard Murphy at the Council on Foreign Relations and Dr. Gregory Gause of the University of Vermont for their review of the manuscript and their many comments and suggestions regarding its content. Nancy Dishaw and the staff at the Middle Eastern Studies Association provided tremendous assistance in helping the author contact the many academic specialists whose knowledge and expertise were invaluable in addressing a subject of this complexity in a condensed format. The scholars include Dr. Abbas Amanat of Yale University, Professor Bernard Haykal of New York University, Dr. Cemal Kafadar at Harvard University, and Dr. Eleanor Doumato of Brown University. Thanks also to Dr. Michael Crocker for his help and generous use of his photographs. For their assistance in locating photographs and images, the author wishes to thank Jeffrey Spurr and the staff of the Fine Arts Library at the Harvard College Library, Rima Hassan and the staff of the Royal Saudi Embassy, and Richard Doughty and the staff of Saudi Aramco. The author also owes a deep debt of gratitude to Claudia Schaab for her guidance and helpful advice throughout the work on this book.

NOTE ON PHOTOS

Many of the photographs used in this book are old, historical images whose quality is not always up to modern standards. In these cases, however, their content was deemed to make their inclusion important, despite problems in reproduction.

NOTE ON ARABIC TRANSLITERATION AND SPELLING

Spoken Arabic incorporates several sounds not produced in the English language, and no standard system exists for transliterating these vocalizations into English. Some texts use diacriticals, or accent marks, to indicate where and which such sounds should be voiced in a transliterated word. But without familiarity with spoken Arabic, such markings can be more confusing than helpful. In the interests of simplicity and accessibility, even some scholarly works have dispensed with the use of diacriticals (e.g., *Saud* rather than *Sa'ud*), an approach this book observes as well.

Likewise, no standardized English spelling exists for many Arabic proper nouns, and variations in their transliteration are common. Where such choices exist, the author has attempted to balance the demands of historical usage and evolving standards.

Within the text, Arabic words are rendered in italics; those that have been accepted into English, as determined by inclusion in *Merriam-Webster's Collegiate Dictionary, Tenth Edition*, are rendered without italics. In Arabic, the article *al*, meaning "the," is frequently appended to proper nouns by a hyphen. It is written in lowercase unless it begins a sentence. In many spellings of place-names, the *al* can be dropped (e.g., al-Medina, or Medina; al-Hasa, or Hasa). This *al* is distinct from *Al*, which is appended to family names (Al Saud, Al Sabah), where it means "house of" or "family of."

Names of tribes are often preceded by *Bani* or *Banu*. The word *ibn* or *bin* means "son of" or "descendant of" and is frequently appended to names; *bint* means "daughter of." *Abu* means "father of," and *Abd*, found in common names (Abduallah, Abd al- . . .) means "servant of."

INTRODUCTION

Forming the heart of the Arabian Peninsula, the Kingdom of Saudi Arabia lies at the nexus of three continents: Africa, Asia, and Europe. Its geographic position made the peninsula a crossroads of early civilizations, traversed by trade routes that linked Mesopotamia and Egypt and connected the Greek and Roman Empires with those of India and China. Yet apart from a few trading communities, the peninsula and its inhabitants remained largely unknown to these early societies, a terra incognita that defied the explorations and conquests that opened the rest of the ancient world. Its harsh geography and climate have kept the land that is now Saudi Arabia isolated into modern times, as they forged the unique character and culture of its fiercely independent people.

Yet, throughout history, Arabia, as the homeland of the Kingdom of Saudi Arabia has traditionally been known, has played a prominent role in human events, first due to its strategic location, then as the land from which Islam and the Islamic Empire spread, and more recently as the world's largest source of petroleum. In the last half-century Saudi Arabia has taken on new roles of world importance: as a strategic military ally of the West, a major player in the world's financial markets, and as a linchpin in the resolution of Middle East conflict.

The tragic events of September 11, 2001, planned and perpetrated in the main by Saudi-born terrorists, have raised questions about what role the kingdom plays in the spread of international terrorism, and whether Saudi Arabia is a friend or foe of the West, and in particular the United States. The ensuing debate has often revealed misperceptions and lack of understanding of the complexities of the social, cultural, and political realities of the kingdom and its policies. These realities have been directly shaped by the tribal society and the Islamic roots upon which the kingdom is built. Therefore, answering these questions requires an understanding of Arabia's history.

The goal of this work is to provide a basic historical framework for attempting to understand contemporary Saudi Arabia, as well as providing an accessible account of the people and events that have given rise to the modern Saudi state. It surveys the natural history and pre-Islamic civilizations of the peninsula, the coming of Muhammad, his message, and the spread of the Islamic Empire. It recounts the battles for control of Islam's holiest land waged by a succession of empires, and the religious reform movement that reshaped the peninsula two and a half centuries ago. It follows that movement and its champions as it begat a religious and military campaign that eventually led to the founding of Saudi Arabia. It surveys the transformation of the kingdom in the last century into a global power, and finally summarizes and addresses primary issues confronting the kingdom's future, including social and economic challenges, the stability of the monarchy, regional conflicts, and the ongoing battle by conservative and progressive elements within Saudi Arabia for the soul of the kingdom.

At the beginning of the 21st century, Saudi Arabia is at a crossroads: Will it continue to cling to the traditions of its conservative religious roots, or become more open to the changing realities beyond its borders? Can the state survive as an absolute monarchy, or will accommodations need to be made to the growing calls for freedoms and rights that many of its citizens demand? Will it be part of the solution or a source of problems for international peace and stability in years to come? It is hoped that this book will provide a solid foundation from which readers may address such questions regarding the Kingdom of Saudi Arabia and its future role on the world stage.

1

ARABIA: THE LAND AND ITS PRE-ISLAMIC HISTORY

For most of its history, what is now Saudi Arabia and the Arabian Peninsula were part of Africa. Hundreds of millions of years ago, portions of its eastern boundaries were periodically submerged by seas that eventually became the Persian Gulf. The sediments from the marine plant and animal life of these waters became the source of the region's petroleum deposits. The peninsula itself is a relatively recent creation, formed 20 million to 25 million years ago when tectonic forces split the Arabian plate, or shield, from the African plate. The massive rift valley that formed where Arabia separated from Africa is filled by the Red Sea, and the fissure continues through the African continent. Adjoining the south end of the Red Sea, the Gulf of Aden separates the Arabian Peninsula from the Horn of Africa and opens into the Arabian Sea to the east. At the peninsula's southeast corner, the Arabian sea narrows into the Gulf of Oman, which connects with the Persian Gulf at the Strait of Hormuz to the north. These latter two gulfs separate the peninsula from Iran.

Before meeting the peoples who first inhabited this land, let us survey the stage upon which their drama unfolded.

Geology and Geography

The upthrust activity associated with the peninsula's formation raised the western and southern ends of the crystalline bedrock underlying the peninsula, so that the land mass exhibits a general and gradual downward slope to the east. The same geologic forces that split the land from Africa are slowly rotating it counterclockwise in a motion that will, in about 10 million years, close off the Persian Gulf and transform that body of water into a lake.

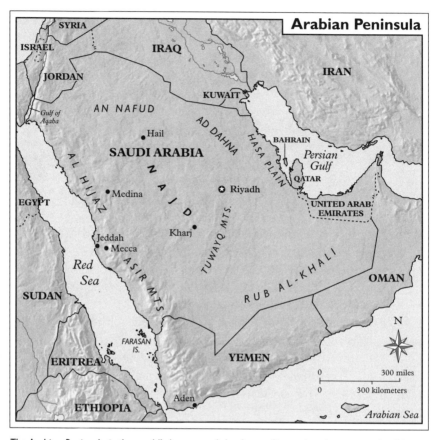

The Arabian Peninsula is the world's largest such landmass. Situated at the crossroads of Asia, Africa, and Europe, it has long played a large role in human history, though its inhospitable geography and climate kept Arabia isolated.

The Arabian Peninsula is the world's largest, at some 865,000 square miles (2,240,000 sq km), or about the size of Europe or India. Saudi Arabia occupies about 80 percent of the peninsula and is about one-quarter of the area of the continental United States. Seven sovereign states border the kingdom. Along its northern frontier, from west to east, are Jordan, Iraq, and Kuwait. To the south and east are Yemen, Oman, the United Arab Emirates, and Qatar. The island nation of Bahrain lies off Saudi Arabia's coast north of Qatar.

The land of Arabia, as the area now occupied by the kingdom and the peninsula as a whole has historically been called, has several distinct geographic regions. Overall, its features are characterized by various types of desert, barren and inhospitable. Along the west coast lie Hijaz

2

and Asir. Najd, which means "plateau," occupies the north-central area of the kingdom. The Eastern Province (traditionally known as Hasa) extends from Najd to the Persian Gulf. The vast Rub al-Khali desert dominates the kingdom's south-central region.

Hijaz and Asir

The western portion of Saudi Arabia consists of Hijaz in the north and Asir in the south. These regions have traditionally been associated with Arabia's more sedentary, as opposed to nomadic, populations. Today, the cities of Mecca and Medina and the port of Jiddah are found here. The Red Sea Escarpment, a range of steep mountains, parallels the length of the peninsula's west coast from the Gulf of Aqaba in the north to the Gulf of Aden in the south. These mountains are divided by a gap at about the midpoint of the peninsula, in the vicinity of Mecca. This gap marks the dividing line between Hijaz and Asir. The coastal mountains of Hijaz drop sharply to the Red Sea. Few natural harbors exist in this region, and the coastal plain (Tihamah) is much narrower in the north than it is to the south. In Hijaz, the mountains range from about 7,000 feet (2,133 m) in the north to about 1,800 feet (550 m) near Mecca. Their eastern slopes are scored by dry river beds (wadis) and

Asir, in southwest Saudi Arabia, is a region of rugged highlands. (Courtesy of Tor Eigeland/ Aramco World/PADIA)

areas of large lava beds (*harrat*) left by fairly recent volcanic activity. Scattered spring- or well-fed oases dot the region. These have historically supported settlements and agriculture.

To the south, in the more rugged Asir, the mountain range widens and climbs higher, rising to more than 10,000 feet (3,048 m). The upper slopes receive enough rainfall to support agriculture, and crops are grown on terraced plots. The western slopes are steep, as in the north, but not as near to the sea. The Tihamah lowlands, about 40 miles wide on average (65 km), spread from the mountains to a salty tidal plain that runs along the coast of Asir. The mountains' eastern slope descends gently to a plateau marked by numerous wadis, which support relatively large-scale oasis-based agriculture. Farther east, the plateau gradually drops to the vast desert sands of the Rub al-Khali. South of Asir are the mountainous highlands of Yemen, whose highest elevations reach about 12,000 feet (3,660 m).

Najd

East of Hijaz and Asir lies Najd, which forms the center of Arabia, a great, rocky plateau dotted with small sand deserts and mountains. Its border with the western coastal provinces is undefined. This was long the heart-

The *Tuwayq Escarpment* curves through the central Najd region in the heartland of the Arabian Peninsula. (Courtesy Tor Eigeland/Aramco World/PADIA)

land of the Bedouin, nomadic tribes, with its relatively few settled inhabitants living in scattered oasis-based towns and villages. The plateau, about 200 miles (320 km) wide, slopes downward from west to east, descending from about 4,000 feet (1,360 m) to about 2,200 feet (750 m). A low limestone escarpment in the vicinity of Riyadh, the Jebel Tuwayq, one of several such formations in the region, forms the heart of Najd. Marked by many oases and large salt marshes, the escarpment swings north to south in an arc some 500 miles (800 km) long. Its western face rises steeply some 300 to 750 feet (90–225 m) above the plateau, the result of gradual erosion of softer rock and terrain around it.

Parallel and just east of Jebel Tuwayq is Ad Dahna, an 800-mile-long (1,300 km), narrow desert, extending from the Great Nufud desert in the north to the Rub al-Khali in the south. The sand's high iron oxide content gives it a reddish orange tint. Ad Dahna is bordered on the east by the As Summan Plateau. The barren and rocky plateau, some 50 to 150 miles (80–240 km) wide, is marked by ancient river gorges and isolated buttes bearing the signs of eons of erosion. The plateau drops from an elevation of about 1,300 feet to about 750 feet (400–225 m).

Persian Gulf Coast

Flat lowlands and coastal plain extend east from the As Summan Plateau for some 35 miles (60 km). The desolate landscape is generally featureless and covered with gravel or sand. The northern portion is the Ad Dibdibah Plain. To the south lies the Eastern Province, or Hasa. One of the most fertile areas in Saudi Arabia, it includes the largest oasis in the country. The capital of Hasa is the town of Hufuf. From here the land descends toward the sandy shores of the Persian Gulf.

In the south of the Eastern Province the Al Jafurah sand desert, which reaches the gulf near Dhahran, merges with the Rub al-Khali at its southern end. The Persian Gulf coast is extremely irregular, merging sandy plains, marshes, and salt flats (sabkhahs) almost imperceptibly with the sea. The sea itself is shallow, with shoals and reefs extending far offshore.

The Deserts

Most of Saudi Arabia is desert. Average annual precipitation is about 4 inches (100 mm). Prevailing winds such as the southerly kauf and the northwesterly shamal kick up severe dust storms. During the summer season (mid-April–mid-October) daytime temperatures routinely reach 113 degrees Fahrenheit (45 degrees Celsius). In coastal regions, humidity is high, amplifying the effects of the heat. During December and

Most of Saudi Arabia's land is composed of various forms of desert. This area, south of Riyadh, borders on the Rub al-Khali, one of the world's great sand deserts. (Courtesy of Dr. Michael Crocker/King Abdul Aziz Foundation)

January daytime temperatures reach about 59 degrees F (15 degrees C), with nighttime temperatures in high elevations sometimes dipping below freezing. Three great deserts dominate the landscape. North of Najd lies the Great Nufud, or An Nafud. Encompassing more than 20,000 square miles (52,000 sq. km), An Nafud dominates the heart of the peninsula. Extending to the steppes of northern Arabia, it is characterized by sand dunes dozens of miles in length. The area to its north is part of the Syrian Desert, an upland plateau with numerous wadis and extensive grass and scrub vegetation. At Wadi as Sirhan, the land drops 1,000 feet (300 m) below the surrounding plateau. Caravans have passed through this area for thousands of years. Ad Dahna, cited above, borders Najd to the east. To the south is one of the largest sand deserts in the world, the Rub al-Khali. More than 212,000 square miles (550,000 sq. km) in size, it contains sand mountains towering some 1,000 feet (300 m), and is mostly waterless and uninhabited.

Natural History

Saudi Arabia contains some of the harshest environments on Earth. However, for most of its history the peninsula enjoyed a less extreme climate. Large river systems with deltas and marshes flowed through

Arabia in prehistoric times. Fossilized remains of ancestors of elephants, giraffes, and rhinoceros dating to 19 million years ago have been found in eastern Saudi Arabia, as have fossils of primitive horses and elephants from the late Miocene period, 6 million to 8 million years ago. Fossil evidence found in Abu Dhabi, on the Persian Gulf, also shows that freshwater mussels, catfish, turtles, crocodiles, and hippopotamus thrived here. The surrounding area was composed of grass and woodlands, where vast herds of wildlife roamed in more recent times, including several species of antelope, giraffes, and carnivores, including saber-toothed cats. (Thus far, such remains have not been found elsewhere in the Arabian Peninsula.) As it would prove to be throughout its human history, the peninsula served as a crossroads for the spread of species between Africa and southwestern Asia during the Miocene period. It is thought that animals used an isthmus across what is now the mouth of the Red Sea to expand or move their habitat between these continents.

Over time, a combination of factors altered the area's climate. The formation of mountains in the Middle East and changes in ocean currents and the pattern of the monsoon are all thought to have contributed to a gradual desertification. With the ending of the last Ice Age, some 15,000 years ago, the peninsula's climate turned drier, with the associated global warming playing a role, as well. Grasslands and bush that once covered its plains turned to scrub and then desert.

Pre-Islamic History

The first inhabitants are estimated to have arrived in the peninsula between 15,000 and 20,000 years ago, near the end of the last Ice Age. Evidence of human habitation throughout the Stone Age has been found, though little archaeological work has been conducted in the kingdom. During its early human history, Arabia was populated by a diverse Neolithic population who survived as hunters and gatherers, most unrelated to the Arabs who later came to dominate the region. Little is known about these first inhabitants. Prehistoric artists left a record in the vast number of petroglyphs, or drawings on rocks, found throughout the Arabian Peninsula. They depicted human figures, wildlife, and other renderings dating back thousands of years before writing was created.

As the climate became drier, the land could no longer support their way of life. The Neolithic nomads retreated and settled in the few fertile areas around oases. They may have been displaced by Semitic tribes who had first settled in southern Arabia. These tribes shared the same

7

Petroglyphs, or rock drawings, dating to Neolithic times are found throughout Saudi Arabia, bearing witness to the abundance of the land before desertification occurred. This example at Shuwaymas, near Jubbah, includes images of long- and short-horned cattle, cheetahs, hyenas, oryx, ibex, ostriches, horses, mules and camels, and human figures. (Courtesy of Lars Bjurstrom/*Saudi Aramco World*/PADIA)

root language rather than an ethnic identity and included, along with the Arabs, Hebrews and Assyrians.

Inscriptions were carved on rocks in more recent times, but very little of the translatable material provides historical information.

Some 10,000 years ago agriculture and permanent settlements developed, preceding the beginning of the last major wet period, which lasted from 8000 to 4000 B.C. The isolation and variation of the peninsula's population began to change during the first millennium B.C. Circumnavigation of the peninsula was mastered by the Phoenicians during this time, enabling increased trade that helped foster interactions within the peninsula and with other lands.

Early Civilizations

While conditions became more harsh in the interior of the peninsula, the south and east, corresponding to present-day Yemen, Oman, and Bahrain, were largely unaffected. Monsoon rains provided Yemen with sufficient water for agricultural cultivation, and the lands to the east had plentiful groundwater. Additionally, all enjoyed strategic locations

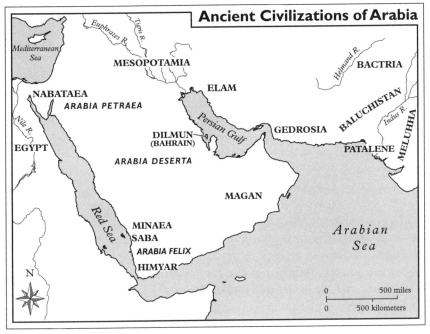

Several civilizations arose on the Arabian Peninsula.

on the trade routes. Several civilizations flourished around the perimeter of the peninsula, deriving their power from their position along these mercantile routes.

Dilmun and Magan

The Dilmun civilization arose on the islands that now make up Bahrain and adjacent coastal areas. Due to its strategic position between the civilizations of the Middle East and Persia and India, Dilmun became a major supply stop, providing water and provisions to ships and a thriving market for their cargo. As early as 3200 B.C., during the Bronze Age, trade flourished between Dilmun, Magan (present-day Oman), Babylonia, and the Indus River Valley. Many items from other cultures dating to the late third and early second millennium B.C. have been found at Dilmun. Its bounty was celebrated in Mesopotamian literature. A tablet dated to 3100 B.C. proclaimed Dilmun an "Elysium," with eternally youthful and healthy citizens. Ancient myths proclaimed the place so pure that wolves and lions abandoned their predatory ways there.

Dilmun was also well known throughout the ancient world for its pearls, according to the Roman historian Pliny, who reported that pearls had been harvested there since the early second millennium B.C. In *Deipnosophistai* (the learned banquet, or banquet of the sophists), Greek writer Athenaeus (ca. A.D. 200) of Egypt wrote of the culinary treasure Dilmun's mollusks yielded: "... there is an island in the Persian Gulf where pearls are found in abundance, wherefore the island is surrounded with bamboo rafts from which the natives dive in 20 fathoms of water and bring up bivalves" (Athenaeus 1993, 403).

Investigations of nearby oases reveal that by 3000 B.C., crops were cultivated and animals had been domesticated for both food and as draft animals, a way of life that would define these settlements, so typical of Arabia, for the next 5,000 years.

One of the great creation tales of ancient mythology, the Mesopotamian story of Enki and Gilgamesh (also known as "Enki and Ninhursag") is set in Dilmun. Enki was the god of wisdom and water and Gilgamesh the king of Uruk in Mesopotamia. This saga recounts a wondrous tale: "... fresh waters shall run out of the ground for you. . . . Your pools of salt water shall become pools of fresh water. . . . Dilmun shall become an emporium on the quay for the land" (Hoyland 2001, 14).

Scholars have asserted that the Saga of Gilgamesh is one of the first preserved works of literature in world history, considerably predating the Iliad and the Odyssey. It is thought to have originated perhaps as early as the 13th century B.C., and the oldest written evidence dates to the seventh century B.C. The biblical account of Noah and the Great Flood, a similar though not as complete narrative, is said to have been influenced by it.

Dilmun, which reached its pinnacle from 2200 to 1600 B.C., controlled trading routes and built fortified cities and magnificent temples. Adjacent mainland areas were also under its rule. Considered a holy land, Dilmun also became a necropolis, where the dead from surrounding areas were brought for interment. Today, tens of thousands of burial mounds still exist. The empire survived for some 2,000 years. When the Indus Valley civilization fell for unknown reasons in the middle of the second millennium B.C., so did that of Dilmun and Magan.

Magan, whose wealth was based on copper, was replaced by alternative copper sources in Anatolia and Cyprus, beginning at the latest by 1745 B.C. Between 1000 and 330 B.C. the copper trade gradually declined.

Dilmun is recorded as a vassal of Assyria in the eighth century B.C. The flourishing incense and spice trade bypassed it. By 600 B.C. Dilmun had been absorbed into the Babylonian Empire. Two hundred years later, Nearchus, one of Alexander the Great's generals, established a colony on the island of Falaika off the coast of what is now Kuwait, from which he explored the area surrounding the Persian Gulf. From this time until the rise of the Islamic Empire, the main island of Bahrain was known by its Greek name, Tylos.

Saba

Present-day Yemen was the site of Saba, established sometime between 1000 and 750 B.C. This is the biblical land of Sheba, presided over at one time by the famed queen of Sheba. The earliest reference indeed comes from the Hebrew Bible, recounting her visit to King Solomon, written about 950 B.C. This tale was initially regarded as apocryphal due to beliefs that civilization did not exist in southern Arabia at that early date. But recent archaeological evidence indicates that Saba was flourishing by the late second and early first millennium B.C. Evidence of the civilization's existence dates to the Bronze Age.

More definitive accounts of Saba or Sabaeans start in the mid-eighth century B.C., and the earliest identified official reports from the kingdom are from about 600 B.C. The Sabaeans are referred to in the annual Assyrian war chronicles made during the reign of King Sargon II (722–705 B.C.), when the Assyrians controlled northern Arabia. The chronicle refers to a king of Saba, Yithi-amara. Additionally, inscriptions made during the reign of one of the last kings of Ur, about 2500 B.C., refer to "Sabam," thought to mean "the country of Saba," which would indicate its existence at this early date.

Saba retained its importance because it was the source of aromatics, such as frankincense and myrrh, which were used in religious ceremonies throughout the ancient world. The rich trade in these homegrown commodities supported several kingdoms in addition to Saba between the fourth century B.C. and the middle of the first millennium A.D., the major ones being the Minaean (ca. fourth to second centuries B.C.), Qataban (ca. fourth to first centuries B.C.), Hadramite (ca. third century B.C. to A.D. third century), and Himyarite (ca. second century B.C. to A.D. sixth century). (The ruins of frankincense trading centers marked on maps of Claudius Ptolemy from the second century A.D. have been found in present-day Yemen by archaeologists.) However, Saba remained the dominant power.

The Sabaean civilization was technologically and socially advanced and had one of the region's strongest armies. The crowning achievement of the civilization was the construction of the Marib Dam, said to have measured some 50 feet (16 m) high, almost 200 feet (60 m) wide, and some 2,000 feet (620 m) long. It included a sluice system, diversion wall, and settling basin. It may have been constructed as early as

11

the middle of the first millennium B.C. Holding back the River Adhannah near its nexus with Jebel Balaq, the lake that the dam created irrigated an area of 9,600 hectares or more, or about 37.5 square miles. Nearby was the capital city of Marib. Pliny, who traveled in the area, wrote of its lush vegetation and rich agriculture.

The Romans called the area Arabia Felix, "happy or fortunate Arabia," as the goods that came from there showed it to be a land of plenty. For centuries Saba's control extended from the territory of the Old Qataban into Africa.

During the first century B.C., the mastery of sailing allowed traders to use the monsoon winds to sail nonstop from Arabia and Africa to India. The first to do so was Eudoxus of Cyzicus, who made the voyage three times between 117 and 109 B.C. The expanding maritime trade spelled the decline of the caravan trade and the cities along the land routes, and this led the kingdoms of southern Arabia to develop ports. Rome's attempted invasion in 24 B.C., following its conquest of Egypt, may also have played a role in the cities' ebbing fortunes. The Roman army attacked under Marcus Aelius Gallus, governor of Egypt, at the command of the emperor Augustus.

Strabo, the Roman scholar, wrote of Augustus's purpose for targeting southern Arabia: ". . . they were very wealthy, and they sold aromatics and the most valuable stones for gold and silver, but never expended with outsiders any part of what they received in exchange. For (Augustus) expected either to deal with the Arabs as wealthy friends or to master wealthy enemies" (Strabo 1930, 355).

An official of Nabataea, in northern Arabia, who had promised to guide and provision Gallus's forces, proved duplicitous, taking him by the most circuitous and treacherous path, a journey lasting two years, from 26 to 24 B.C. Gallus was forced to retreat after taking several cities and was ultimately defeated by the Sabaeans. He returned with accounts of the people and customs of the lands, According to Pliny, Gallus recounted that "nomads live on milk and the flesh of wild animals" and that "the Arabs wear turbans or else go with their hair unshorn; they shave their beards but wear a mustache."

The Marib Dam underwent extensive repairs in the fifth and sixth centuries A.D., an undertaking requiring at least 20,000 craftsmen and laborers gathered from surrounding tribes. But the dam collapsed in A.D. 542, causing the Flood of Arim, which is referred to in the Quran, Sura 34: "'Eat of what your Lord has given you and render thanks to Him; a territory fair and happy and a Lord oft-forgiving.' But they gave no heed. So we unloosed upon them the waters of the dams and replaced their gardens by two others bearing bitter fruit, tamarisks, and a few nettle shrubs. Thus we punished them for their ingratitude."

The collapse of the dam led to the end of the Sabaean civilization. Without irrigation, crops could no longer be grown. Inhabitants gradually abandoned the area.

Nabataea

In the northwestern corner of the peninsula, in what is now southern Jordan, the Nabataean civilization arose. Its exact origin is unknown, but its founders appear to have been nomads from the Naqab Desert of Palestine and northern Arabia who settled in the area sometime in the third century B.C. These nomads became traders and merchants and established trading links extending from India, China, and the Far East to Greece, Rome, and Egypt. Incense, spices, gold, iron, copper, ivory, animals, sugar, medicines, fabric, and perfume were among the goods that passed through their territory. In the fourth century B.C., the Nabataeans made the hidden fortress-city of Petra (rock) their capital. Its buildings, temples, and tombs were carved into the sandstone rock mountains. Petra may have had 20,000 to 30,000 inhabitants at one time.

Strabo wrote that "The Nabataeans are a sensible people, and are so much inclined to acquire possessions that they publicly fine anyone who has diminished his possessions and also confer honours on anyone who has increased them. Since they have but few slaves, they are served by their kinfolk for the most part, or by one another, or by themselves, so that the custom extends even to their kings" (Strabo 1930, 367).

A pantheon of deities was ruled by the sun god, Dushara, and the goddess Allat. (As we will see, in pre-Islamic Arabia the goddess al-Lat was worshipped.) Nabataeans spoke an Arabic dialect but later adopted Aramaic. They were also greatly influenced by Hellenistic (Greek) culture. Highly skilled in hydrology, they constructed an elaborate system of dams, canals, and reservoirs to irrigate their lands in the midst of the harsh desert. The empire's wealth made it a target of nearby powers. The Seleucid king Antigonus, to the north, who came to power when Alexander's empire was divided, attacked Petra in 312 B.C. and easily conquered the city, plundering its riches. But the amount of plunder slowed the conquerors' withdrawal, and the Nabataeans counterattacked, annihilating the Seleucids in the desert. Yet the Nabataeans managed to maintain good relations with the Seleucids, due to their mutual trade interests.

In the first century B.C. the Sicilian historian Diodorus Siculus wrote in his *Bibliotheca Historica,* "While there are many Arabian tribes who use the desert as pasture, the Nabataeans far surpass the others in wealth although they are not much more than ten thousand in number. For not a few of them are accustomed to bring down to the sea frankincense and myrrh and the most valuable kinds of spices, which they procure from those who convey them from what is called Arabia Felix" (Diodorus, 19.94).

While the Seleucids and the Ptolemies of Egypt battled over Jordan for most of the third century B.C., Nabataea remained independent. The empire began to expand, taking control of Damascus around 150 B.C. Ultimately, their growing power concerned the Romans, who arrived in Damascus in 65 B.C. and ordered the Nabataeans to withdraw. Two years later, General Pompey sent a force to attack Petra, but the city remained independent. Whether this outcome was gained through military victory or tribute payment is unclear.

Julius Caesar's assassination in 44 B.C. precipitated a period of chaos in Rome's Jordanian territories, which encouraged attacks on these outposts of the empire by the Parthian rulers of Mesopotamia and Persia. The Nabataeans supported the Parthians, and after Rome defeated their allies, Nabataea was forced to pay tribute to the victors. Failure to pay led to two invasions by the Roman vassal, King Herod the Great. After his second attack in 31 B.C., Herod took control of a large area of Nabataea, including its lucrative trading routes into Syria. Yet Nabataea still retained its independence. Under King Aretas IV (r. 9 B.C. to A.D. 40), settlements were built along the caravan routes to develop the incense trade.

Nabataea allied itself with Rome to help put down the Jewish uprising in A.D. 70. Rome finally took direct control of the kingdom following the death of Rabbel II in A.D. 106. Rabbel had made a pact with the Romans: as long as they did not attack during his lifetime, they could have the kingdom after his death. The Romans renamed it Arabia Petraea, or "rocky Arabia," and redesigned the city of Petra with traditional Roman architecture. Between Arabia Petraea in the north and Arabia Felix in the south lay the vast expanse of Arabia Deserta. A period of peace and prosperity followed during the Pax Romana. With this annexation of the kingdom, direct Roman contact with the nomads increased. A brief confrontation with Arabs east of the Euphrates occurred during Trajan's Parthian War. In the mid-second century A.D. Rome apparently garrisoned troops at Palmyra, in Syria, which previously policed the desert caravan routes on its own.

Gradually, trade activity dwindled. Palmyra surpassed Nabataea as an overland trading center and seaborne trade around the peninsula increasingly diminished the importance of the overland routes. Petra was slowly abandoned, becoming uninhabited probably in the fourth century A.D.

The Arabs of the Interior

Independent of the civilizations at its peripheries, a vibrant culture arose in the interior of the peninsula. The indigenous people inhabiting the peninsula have long called their land Jazirate Al-Arab: "Island of the Arabs." Most surviving accounts of these people come from Assyrians, Babylonians, Egyptians, Israelites, and other civilizations of the era who came in contact with them. The designation "Arab" first appears in biblical and Assyrian texts written between the ninth and fifth centuries B.C., where the people are described as desert nomads. Since accounts from both cultures refer to them as Arabs, it is likely this was the name they gave themselves, though its origin is unknown. Thereafter, "Arab" came to mean a nomadic desert dweller. The Hebrew Bible refers to "all the Arab kings" bringing tribute to King Solomon (ca. 970–931 B.C.), though the date of this writing is unknown. An inscription dated to 853 B.C. records a victory the Assyrian king Shalmaneser III achieved over a coalition that included "Gindibu the Arab" and his force of 1,000 camels. The Assyrians possibly were interested in the territory because of the increase in the trade of aromatics between southern Arabia and the Mediterranean. They sought to control the northern end of the trade routes, which was mostly run by Arabs and adjoined their empire.

The Arabs developed both sedentary and nomadic populations. The former resided in villages and towns, often associated with oases, wells, or other permanent water sources, and made their living in agriculture, craftwork, and trade. The nomadic populations were primarily breeders of livestock. The lines between sedentary and nomadic populations sometimes blurred, as some desert dwellers might spend part of the year in a permanent settlement and part of it as migrant shepherds.

Whether sedentary or nomadic, the structure of pre-Islamic society in Arabia was based on the clan; a clan is composed of several related families that form a group. In the absence of recognized government in Arabia, the clan determined the code of conduct and provided protection for its members. Without a clan for protection, an individual had no one to appeal to for redress of any act committed against him by another person, whether robbery, mischief, or murder.

Slavery, an ancient Semitic institution, was practiced by the Arabs. Captives taken prisoner in battle, or women and children of those conquered in battle, could be made slaves. (However, often such captives were ransomed rather than kept in servitude.) Captives taken in raids could also be made slaves. Slavery continued after the coming of Islam and is recognized in the Quran, though Muhammad promulgated rules designed to assure humane treatment of those held in bondage.

Arabic Writing

Writing originated some 5,000 years ago in Mesopotamia (Gk., land between the rivers) and possibly concurrently in Egypt. The first forms used symbolic characters, evolving into phonetic systems. Arabia, situated between the two civilizations, was doubtless exposed to these writing systems. Some evidence points to the development of early Sinaitic script, Arabia's first form of writing, dating to around 2000–1500 B.C. By 1000 B.C. two writing systems were in use in the peninsula: in the north Musnad al-Shamali, and in the south Musnad al-Janubi. Use of the former expanded throughout northern Arabia, becoming the root of the Lihyanite, Safaitic, and Aramaic writing systems, which flourished around the middle of the first millennium B.C. From Aramaic, Nabataean script developed, and from Nabataean, Arabic writing developed. Meanwhile, in the south, the use of Musnad al-Janubi likewise expanded, developing into the Sabaean, Qatabani, Hadrami, and Hassanean scripts.

Spoken Arabic is a Semitic language. The first surviving evidence of written Arabic dates to the early fourth century A.D., found in an inscription also bearing Syriac and Greek text. With the rise of Islam in the seventh century, Arabic, the language of the Quran, spread throughout the peninsula, and the more ancient writing forms vanished. In the eighth and ninth centuries, written Arabic evolved into the standardized form of the language used today.

The development of letter-based writing, as opposed to pictographic forms, played a large role in the spread of culture and growth of economies. Alphabets did not require the lengthy training of earlier writing forms, enabling virtually anyone to learn. Now traders could place orders, enter contracts, and conduct business much more easily.

The Bedouin

During the first and second centuries of the Common Era, evidence indicates that nomadic society began to flourish in northern Arabia, a process now referred to as "Bedouinization." It is thought to have been spurred by the economic and social deterioration of the region's settled

DOMESTICATION OF THE CAMEL

One of the major factors in the development of the overland trade was the domestication of the camel, which likely began in the third millennium B.C. Camels were hunted for food prior to domestication. Perhaps sometime between 1500 and 800 B.C., they were first used as pack animals after a method of saddling them was developed. Before their use for transport, trade with Greek and Roman civilizations was limited. Arabian dhows plied the waters all around and across the Indian Ocean, but until the camel was harnessed for trade, crossing more than 1,200 miles of inhospitable Arabian desert was impossible. Domestication of the camel allowed both nomadic life and trade for the sedentary populations to flourish. Caravan cities, like Petra and Palmyra, developed to service the camel caravans.

Camelus dromedarius, or dromedary, the Arabian camel, has a single hump, distinguishing it from its double-humped Asian cousin, the Bactrian camel. It subsists on thorny plants, dry grasses, and saltbush, yet can eat almost anything. Besides providing efficient transportation, camels were used for food and shelter. Camel's milk was used in place of water and its hair used in tents. They could be eaten in times of need, and potable water in sufficient quantities for sustenance remained in their stomachs for two days after drinking.

Bedouin life was made possible by the camel, as was Arabia's overland trade; no other animal was capable of traversing the desert. (Courtesy of the Fine Arts Library, Harvard College Library)

population centers, shifting the balance of power to its migratory people. Bedouin society and its code of conduct, with its penchant for raiding and blood feuds, developed. A tradition of hospitality was also part of this code. If an outsider managed to penetrate the perimeter of a Bedouin encampment and touch a tent before being intercepted, it was incumbent on the tribal leader to receive him with hospitality and guarantee his safety. The name of the Arab nomads, Bedouin, is taken from the French version of the Arabic word *badawi* (pl. *bedu*), "desert dweller." The Bedouin refer to themselves simply as Arabs.

The Bedouin believed that agriculture and trade were inferior occupations. Instead, they raised sheep, goats, and camels, bred horses, raided, and hunted. Game in the area included oryx, gazelles, cheetahs, panthers, and most prized of all, the ibex. In addition to supplying food, hunting provided an outlet to display skills and gain honor.

Bedouin life was driven by the need for water. They migrated in search of pasture land, moving between winter and summer grazing areas. Though the nomads left no structures to evidence their former presence, remnants of encampments dating to this era are widespread, as are thousands of graffiti they scratched on rocks.

About the beginning of the Common Era, accounts of desert tribes were first recorded by scribes of Rome's Severan dynasty, who reported them as a troublesome element on the frontiers. Much of the land along the desert fringe was under the rule of local Arab chiefs allied with Rome, who were primarily responsible for controlling the nomadic populations in their regions. In the first century A.D., Rome removed most native rulers and replaced them with Roman officials, exposing the tribes to Romans directly. A handful of references in the first and second centuries A.D. refer to generals (*strategos*) or tribal chiefs (*phylarchos*) of the nomads.

By the third century, large tribal confederations had formed, an arrangement that gave tribal chiefs more power. Contemporary accounts cite nomad rulers and tribal groups by name. These rulers appear to have played off the struggle between the Byzantine and Persian empires, offering their services and seeking recognition. Over the succeeding centuries they played a growing role in the warfare between Rome and Persia that was waged on Arabia's doorstep.

From the late fourth century A.D., the Romans began to give up some forts along the frontier, possibly giving responsibility for security to local tribes allied with Rome. References to Saracen (derived from a word meaning "confederation") raids are found throughout this period. During this time the Roman emperor Constantine made Byzantium his capital and renamed it Constantinople (today, Istanbul). Though the Byzantines considered themselves Romans, they spoke Greek rather than Latin and were Christians rather than pagans. Their efforts to control and tax the nomads in northern and central Arabia were unsuccessful. The Bedouin refused to submit to outside authority, and their nomadic life and uncertain location at any time made it difficult for Roman forces to find and subdue them.

In A.D. 500 Bedouin invaded Syria and Palestine and raided Jerusalem. The warring dynasties whose lands bordered Bedouin territory (Byzantium, Sassanid Persia, and southern Arabia) tried to enlist them as allies against the dynasties' enemies. Byzantium formed alliances with tribes on the Syrian border, the Salih and Bani Ghassan, at the beginning of the sixth century. This marked the establishment of the Ghassanid confederation, which supported the Byzantines. The Lakhmid dynasty settled near Iraq's border and allied itself with the Sassanians.

Bedouin Life

In the Bedouin encampment, each tent represents one family, and tents of clan families are pitched together in a group known as a *hayy*. A tribe is composed of several kindred clans joined together. The leader of the tribe or clan is the sheikh. The sheikh was depended on for wise counsel. He ruled by the consent of his group, and decisions were made with the input of the tribal council, composed of individual clan leaders. Tribes observed no higher authority and were dependent on their prowess as warriors and raiders to survive and prosper. Less able tribes could buy the protection of more powerful tribes. Each tribe had its own area, called *dirahs* or ranges, within which they claimed exclusive rights to pasturage and use of all wells. Though isolated most of the year from the sedentary Arabs of the towns, the Bedouin benefited from the trade routes when trade flourished. Some even gave up their nomadic existence for sedentary life.

Bedouin tents (*beit al-sha'r,* or "house of hair") are made primarily from goat's wool, though that of camel and sheep can also be used. The wool is woven into strips (*fala'if*) that are then sewn together. The resulting rectangle is raised on tent poles, with ropes used to create tension and secure the structure from the outside. Another piece of fabric hangs like a flap at the back of the tent, long enough so that it can be wrapped around the entire tent at night or during storms. The coloring of streaked black and brown comes from the natural color of the animal hair. The loose weave allows for dissipation of heat, and despite its dark

POETRY

Poetry was Arabia's principal form of literary expression in pre-Islamic times. Beyond simply an art form, it served as the basis of the oral tradition by which news was transmitted and tribal and clan traditions and history were passed on. The Bedouin developed a highly stylized and formalized form for poetry that followed strict rules of form and content. They might be elegy, eulogy, or satire. Their verse celebrated courage, loyalty, love, and retribution. The principal form was the *qasidah*, or ode, a tale of a search for lost love. About 60 lines long, each ending in rhyme, the *qasidah* begins with a preface about love, proceeds to a description of the beloved's now-deserted encampment, recounts the great hardships of the poet's search for her, before ending with an appeal to the listener for generosity. Within the constraints of this form, poets exercised endless invention and originality.

The poetry is virtually impossible to appreciate fully in translation, but its flavor was captured by Reynold A. Nicholson in *A Literary History of the Arabs,* in his translation of "Song of Vengeance" by Taabbata Sharran, a noted robber-poet.

> *O'er the fallen of Hudhail stands screaming*
> *The hyena; see the wolf's teeth gleaming!*
> *Dawn will hear the flap of wings, will discover*
> *Vultures treading corpses, too gorged to hover*
> *(Nicholson 1969, 100).*

Poetry contests were popular in some areas of pre-Islamic Arabia, and winners of these competitions brought great honor to their tribes. Religious pilgrimages to Mecca took place even before Islam appeared. Poetry and literary contests were also staged in that city. One of the traditions of the time in Mecca, after the introduction of written Arabic, was the *muallaquat,* or the hangings, so known because poets and writers would hang their writings, typically eulogizing their tribe, on a wall set aside for the purpose.

Most of the pre-Islamic poetry and prose that was transmitted orally and survives today was written down during the Umayyad period (A.D. 661–750), a time when increasing urbanization of society led to efforts to preserve its more unfettered past. But the pre-Islamic poetry that forms the majority of the peninsula's earliest literary heritage is limited in both its place and time of origin within Arabia, going back only to the fifth century A.D. and originating in north-central Najd. Whatever can be gleaned of society and custom from these verses may have been far from universal among Arabs of the era.

color, it is typically 10–15°F cooler inside than outside during the day. When it rains, the moisture expands the yarn, closing the gaps in the weave and keeping out water. The fabric lasts about five years, and sections are replaced as they wear out. The size of the tent reflects the importance of the owner or the size of his family. Inside, a decorated curtain divides the tent into sections, typically one for men, one for the family, and a cooking area.

Commerce and Caravans

Maritime trade has been of vital interest to the Arabian Peninsula from antiquity to the present. Though the peninsula's coastal states and kingdoms have, for the most part, retained their independence throughout

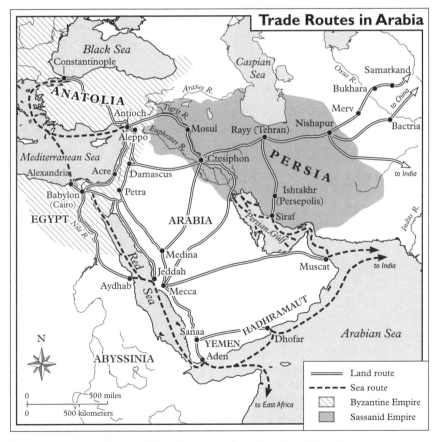

Trade routes stretched across Arabia, allowing the flow of goods and ideas between ancient civilizations and bringing Arabia's interior into contact with the outside world.

history, they nonetheless have had a large impact on Arabia by providing portals through which goods and ideas from throughout the world entered the peninsula, enriching the isolated interior.

Goods were brought across the desert from Oman and Saba in huge caravans. Their routes followed natural pathways along the interior of the peninsula. One of the most heavily traveled pathways ran up the western side of the peninsula, through Asir and Hijaz, about 100 miles inland from the Red Sea, to Gaza, bound for the Mediterranean civilizations. Caravan cities sprang up to service the trading commerce.

By ship, spices and fabrics came from India; silk from China; and gold, ivory, and ostrich feathers from Africa. From the desert of the interior came dates and almonds. But some of the most valuable commodities shipped from Saba were grown in Arabia: frankincense, myrrh, and other aromatics. The Greek historian Herodotus (d. ca. 430 B.C.), in his *Histories*, Book III, wrote of this trade: "Arabia is the last inhabited land toward the south; and it is the only country which produces frankincense, myrrh, cassia, cinnamon, and gum-mastik. All these but myrrh are difficult for the Arabians to get . . . for the spice-bearing trees are guarded by small winged snakes of varied colour, many around each tree . . ." (Herodotus 1995, 135).

By the time of the Persian Empire, more about the peninsula was known, primarily from the sailing expedition of Scylax of Caryanda

---

FRANKINCENSE AND MYRRH

Myrrh is the resin of the commiphora myrrh tree, which grows wild in groves. Tapped twice a year, the thick trunks yield a clear resin that hardens into a reddish or yellowish brown gum. Myrrh was used in cosmetics and perfumes and as a medicinal applied in poultices and unguents. Frankincense is the gum of bushy trees of the genus *Boswellia* (named for James Boswell, biographer of the English writer and critic Dr. Samuel Johnson). The trees likely were found in the Qara Mountains on the coast of Oman, at the southeastern tip of the peninsula. Frankincense was used in religious ceremonies and cremations throughout the civilized ancient world. Egyptians used it in embalming and believed burning it enabled one to commune with the gods. The relative value and universal demand for the aromatics among the ancients is illustrated in the biblical account of the birth of Jesus, when frankincense and myrrh joined gold as the precious gifts the three Wise Men gave the newborn child.

sent by Darius and especially the explorations ordered by Alexander the Great (d. 323 B.C.) during his conquest of Persia. Throughout the Roman Empire's days of glory, demand for the aromatics remained strong. A year's harvest of myrrh was burned at the funeral of Nero's wife in Rome, according to Pliny the Elder.

The importance of the Sabaean trading empire that brought vitality to the rest of the peninsula began to decline in the fourth century A.D. A Greek, Hippalus, discovered that the monsoon winds of the Indian Ocean blew west to east for six months and then reversed, blowing east to west for six months. He set sail straight across the ocean from the peninsula and returned on the monsoon. Now the traders could bypass the Arabian trading centers and go right to the Far East themselves. The collapse of the frankincense market dates to the early fourth century as well, as Rome's pagan rites increasingly gave way to Christian worship. In 313, Emperor Constantine signed the Edict of Milan, legitimizing Christianity, and himself converted to the faith on his deathbed in 327. The elaborate cremations and funerary displays that used pyres of frankincense were replaced by simple burials.

The decline in trade had a calamitous impact in Arabia. The economic downturn caused some sedentary Arabs to revert to nomadism, which again became the predominant lifestyle in the peninsula. Tribal warfare and female infanticide were widespread. Muslims call the period before the coming of Islam Jahiliyya, the Age of Ignorance, in contrast to the Age of Light that followed. And if the darkest hour is just before the dawn, surely this was Arabia's. As Abdallah ibn Abd al-Rahman al-Darimi (d. 877) wrote in the introduction to his sunnah, a compilation of the words and deeds of the prophet Muhammad:

> *Hearts had become hard. Every day a pit was dug in the corner of the desert for an innocent girl to be buried. Human beings were more brutal and cruel than hyenas. The powerful crushed the weak. It was a time when brutality was taken for humanity, cruelty received approval, the bloodthirsty were exalted, bloodshed considered a virtue, adultery and fornication were more common than legal marriages. Family structure had been destroyed.*

Yet within some 20 years after Muhammad first proclaimed his message, almost the entire peninsula would be united in its dedication to one God, and Arabia would launch an empire that would transform the world.

2

THE BIRTH OF ISLAM
(571–632)

At the dawn of the seventh century, Arabia's fortunes were in decline. The Red Sea supplanted overland caravan routes as a conduit for trade. Changes in religious practices in the Roman Empire ended the already diminished use of frankincense and myrrh in religious services, and thus the lucrative trade in these aromatics. For the sedentary populations, the declines meant less margin for survival during the plagues of locusts, desiccating droughts, epidemics, flash floods, and other calamitous visitations that periodically befell the land. For the nomadic Bedouin, the deprivations also led to an increase in raiding and warfare, as tribes became desperate in the face of want. Yet within a generation, Islam, the religion brought forth by Muhammad, revered as the Messenger of God by his followers, would transform Arabia, bringing social order and unity to the fractious and isolated population.

Pre-Islamic Religious Communities

Palestine, Arabia's neighbor to the north, had already given birth to two of the world's major religions, Judaism and Christianity. These faiths were likely predated by other monotheistic faiths. By the middle of the first millennium, both religions had established thriving, if isolated, communities in Arabia. Arabic-speaking Jewish tribes were found throughout the peninsula, and a considerable population had settled at the oasis of Yathrib (later renamed Medina), where Muhammad would settle with his followers to escape persecution in Mecca. A good number of the peninsula's Jews from this era are thought to have been Arabs who converted to Judaism, rather than members of Jewish tribes that migrated southward from Palestine. More than a century before Islam's rise, a Jewish kingdom had been established in southern Arabia. It was

24

destroyed by Ethiopian Christians, during conflict between the Byzantine Empire (with which the Ethiopians were allied) and the Persian Empire (with which the Jews and pagans were allied). A Christian community was well established at Najran, southeast of Mecca, but in 523 it was slaughtered by Dhu Nuwas, the ruler of Himyar, in what is now Yemen. Dhu Nuwas was concerned about their threat to his power, given the rise of a Christian kingdom in Abyssinia.

The presence of Christian and Jewish communities exposed the people in settlements and towns to the concept of monotheism. Both religions were represented in Mecca, and debates on religious topics among Arabs, Christians, and Jews enlivened the marketplace of Ukaz, near Mecca. Numerous other religious groups existed in Arabia. The Hanifs were monotheists noted for devoutness and virtue, claiming spiritual lineage with Abraham. Muhammad identified himself as a Hanif before he received the calling, which later reinforced his aura of religious purity. Nestorians, a Christian sect, were also active. But most Arabs were polytheists. The Bedouin practiced an animistic, pagan religion. They worshipped spirits associated with springs, trees, rocks, and other inanimate objects. Shrines and holy places were found throughout the peninsula. Among the thousands of inscriptions discovered within the peninsula, invocation of various deities is the most common subject. The Bedouin also incorporated beliefs of Semitic astral religions, recognizing deities associated with heavenly bodies. Several goddesses (al-Lat, al-Uzzah, al-Manat) were revered above all. Some animistic religions also recognized a superior deity, Allah, though this figure's powers seem vaguely defined and the veneration accorded it weak.

Mecca

The history of Mecca, Islam's most important city, before the time of Muhammad is largely unknown. The earliest Muslim accounts of its past relate that Adam built a house of worship in Mecca that was destroyed in the Great Flood. Wedged between two high mountain ridges in a valley oriented roughly north to south, accounts of its early days tell of crude mud buildings, stifling heat, and clouds of flies. Yet whoever controlled Mecca held a position of power and importance, for it included guardianship of the sacred shrine as well as the rights to water and feed the pilgrims, along with whatever taxes or other revenues could be extracted from visitors or those who profited from them.

THE PILGRIMAGE IN PRE-ISLAMIC ARABIA

Even before the time of Muhammad, making a religious pilgrimage was a venerable tradition in Arabia. The Bedouin made pilgrimages to shrines throughout Arabia to honor their gods. The most important of these sites was in Mecca. The principal religious and commercial center of Hijaz since the middle of the first millennium, Mecca's name comes from the Sabaean word for "sanctuary." One of Mecca's sustaining features was its well, known as "Zamzam." According to Islamic tradition, Abraham, ancestral patriarch of both the Arabs and Jews, brought his wife Hagar and son Ishmael here, at God's command, and then returned to his wife Sarah. Hagar, having exhausted the water they brought, set off to search for a source in the area. Fearing he was being abandoned, Ishmael stamped his foot in the sand. A spring appeared. This is said to be the origin of the well. Upon Abraham's return, he and Ishmael are said to have built the shrine that would become the Kaaba.

Today the Kaaba is Islam's holiest shrine, or *haram* (sacred place). It is in the direction of the Kaaba, in Mecca, that Muslims face during their prayers. At the time of Muhammad, the Kaaba was a rough rectangular stone building, or possibly simply an enclosure. Within its walls, more than 300 idols representing what has been termed a "pagan pantheon" were enshrined. Among them was the patron deity of each clan. The principal god was Hubal. The Kaaba also housed a sacred black stone, believed to be a meteorite.

Pilgrimages to the Kaaba were made during Dhu al-Hijja, a month of the lunar calendar. During this time, fighting among the warring tribes and clans—who were usually engaged in some form of warfare—was forbidden. It was a time for poetry contests and other competitions and activities. The cessation of hostilities also facilitated trade, for caravans could travel without fear of raids. For some, its foundation in religious obeisance was forgotten. By the time of Muhammad the pilgrimage had degenerated into what one account called "a rendezvous of unspeakable vice," as pilgrims indulged their tastes for alcohol and debauchery (Nutting 1964, 25).

The Kaaba in Mecca's Grand Mosque is Islam's most sacred shrine. It was a site of religious pilgrimages and veneration even before the coming of Islam. (Courtesy of S. M. Amin/*Aramco World*/PADIA)

The Quraysh was Mecca's dominant tribe. They are thought to have arrived in Mecca sometime early in the fifth century and took control of it shortly thereafter when Qusayy, one of its members, became Mecca's ruler, possibly through marriage to the daughter of the king he succeeded.

By the time of Muhammad's birth in the latter sixth century, ongoing warfare between the Byzantine Empire and Persia's Sassanid dynasty had severed the caravan route from the Mediterranean to the mouth of the Persian Gulf. It was replaced by an alternative overland route from the Mediterranean along the western coastal plain of Arabia to Yemen, where goods came and went to India and Africa by ship. Mecca was situated near the intersection of this north-south trade route and a major route that went east to Iraq. Thus, Mecca has traditionally been portrayed as a wealthy caravan city. Yet recent scholarship suggests its economy may have been more locally oriented, its trade based on regional agriculture, crafts, and other goods and services. But it is clear that Meccans themselves engaged in trading with distant markets via caravan, and the pilgrimage traffic accounted for additional economic activity. Whatever the provenance of its economic growth, while Arabia's fortunes were in decline, Mecca's were ascending. Its success created a growing disparity between the merchant and the artisan and trade classes in the city. As relationships became more mercantile, a consequent weakening of the tribal and clan ties that had previously created the strongest social bonds ensued.

Muhammad

Only a few undisputed facts about Muhammad's early life are known. Many of the details of his life that have passed down through history are considered unsubstantiated and even unreliable. Saudis, however, and indeed all Muslims, accept it as truth. Almost everything said about Muhammad comes from two major sources, both written more than 200 years after his death: the *Expeditions of Muhammad* by Muhammad ibn Umar Al-Waqidi (d. 822) and *The Biography of the Messenger of God* by Muhammad ibn Ishaq ibn Yasar (d. ca. 768) and edited by Ibn Hisham (d. 833). The latter was the first organized narrative of Muhammad's life, a compilation of all the author could ascertain about Muhammad. The author, known as Ibn Ishaq, sought to legitimize Muhammad's claim and place as the last prophet of God. Some of the stories are miraculous and apocryphal, akin to those of Jesus in the New Testament. Nevertheless, Muslims view Muhammad as a human rather than godly being.

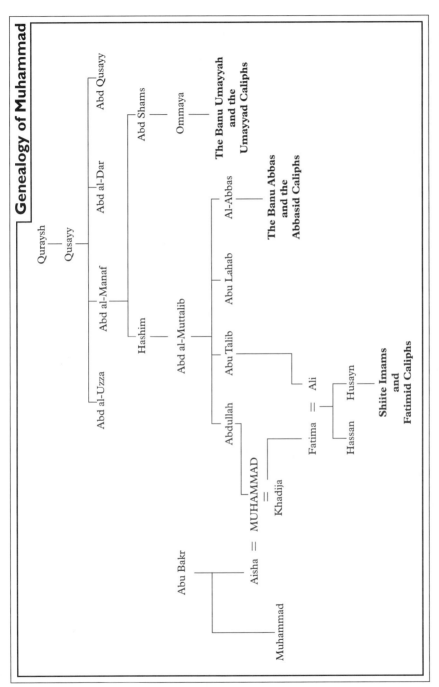

Genealogy of Muhammad

Quraysh
Qusayy

Abd al-Uzza — Abd al-Manaf — Abd al-Dar — Abd Qusayy

Hashim

Abd Shams

Ommaya

The Banu Umayyah and the Umayyad Caliphs

Abd al-Muttalib

Abdullah — Abu Talib — Abu Lahab — Al-Abbas

The Banu Abbas and the Abbasid Caliphs

MUHAMMAD
=
Khadija

Aisha = MUHAMMAD

Abu Bakr

Muhammad

Fatima = Ali

Hassan   Husayn

Shiite Imams and Fatimid Caliphs

In the patriarchal society of Arabia, ancestry became critical in legitimizing the leadership of the Islamic community. This chart depicts the genealogy of Muhammad's ancestors and his early descendants.

29

The Quran also provides some insight into Muhammad, and aspects of the man and his life can also be gleaned from the Traditions of Muhammad (al Hadith), collected anecdotes about Muhammad's words and actions accepted as authentic by religious scholars, first published in 833.

Muhammad was born in Mecca in approximately the year 570. He was a member of the Quraysh tribe and of the Hashim clan that was founded by Qusayy's grandson, Hashim (ca. 440–500), Muhammad's great-grandfather. The Hashim was a noble clan, but their power was second to that of the Umayyad clan. Ommaya, eponymous founder of the Umayyads, was Qusayy's great-grandson. The Umayyads would later found Islam's first dynastic caliphate. Thereafter, empires throughout the Islamic world would be ruled by familial dynasties, some of whom, such as the Abbasids who succeeded the Umayyads, claimed the right to rule by virtue of lineage to the prophet Muhammad's family; Muhammad's uncle, Al-Abbas, also a descendant of Hashim, was the progenitor of the Abbasid caliphate. Through Muhammad, the Hashim line also produced the Alid dynasty of Shia imams (that is, hereditary leaders of the Islamic community believed by Shia to be divinely chosen) and the Hashemite monarchs, King Abdullah and his successors, who began rule of Jordan in the 20th century.

Muhammad's father, Abdullah, died soon after his birth, and his mother died when he was six, leaving him an orphan. Accounts of Muhammad's childhood hold that prior to his mother's death he was raised by a wet nurse, Halima, in the desert, as was the custom of the day. He was said to have exhibited fits that have been attributed to epilepsy in his childhood and as an adult. This affliction has been cited by some as an explanation for accounts of the agitated states Muhammad sometimes exhibited while receiving the revelations that became the Quran. But others dispute that there is evidence that Muhammad suffered epileptic seizures.

After his mother's death, Muhammad's grandfather, Abdul Muttalib, a leader of the community, cared for him. When his grandfather died two years later, an uncle, Abu Talib, a merchant and collector of the poor tax, raised him.

As a youth Muhammad worked as a shepherd and caravan attendant, and at age 12 he accompanied his uncle on a trade caravan to Syria. A meeting with a monk in a monastery had a profound impact on young Muhammad, awakening him to monotheism. In Mecca he developed a reputation as a peacemaker and arbitrator. He worked in the employ of a wealthy widow, Khadijah, who was engaged in trade. His integrity and demeanor won him her respect and love. She is said to have proposed to him. Muhammad was 25 when they married, and Khadija was 15 years his senior. She bore him six children, two of them boys. Neither of the males survived infancy, and only Fatima, his most beloved daughter, had children. (Fatima's progeny would become one branch of Muhammad's descendants claiming legitimacy for leadership of Islam.) Muhammad's work in the caravan trade took him to Syria and Palestine, where he came in closer contact with monotheistic religions, giving him a basic, though imperfect, knowledge of Christianity and Judaism.

An indication of the respect Muhammad was reputed to enjoy can be inferred from one of the traditions of an event said to have occurred when he was 35 years old, or around the year 605. The Kaaba was undergoing renovations under the hands of the four leading clans of the city, each working on individual areas. This reflected Mecca's own division into quarters, each occupied by one of the clans. Work on the Kaaba had progressed to the point that called for resetting the black stone in its proper position. Each clan sought the honor, and the dispute almost provoked a civil war. Finally the clans decided they would randomly select the next person who walked into the sacred place to replace the stone. Muhammad was the next to enter, and because of his reputation for honesty and integrity, he was universally approved for the honor. Informed of the task and the decision, Muhammad said, "Give me a cloak," according to Ibn Ishaq, who recounted the episode in the *Biography of the Messenger of God*: ". . . and when they brought it to him, he took the Black Stone and put it inside it and said that each tribe should take hold of an end of the cloak and they should lift it together. They did this so that when they got it into position he placed it with his own hand, and then building went on above it" (Ibn Ishaq 1955, 85).

The Calling/The Quran

Muhammad developed an antipathy for the pagan practices that drew the crowds of pilgrims to Mecca. A contemplative, spiritually curious man, he spent considerable time in prayer, meditation, and fasting. A cave in Mount Hira, a few miles north of Mecca, served as his retreat for some of these spiritual journeys. When Muhammad was 40, sometime around 610, he told Khadija of a vision he had received during one of his retreats:

> He came to me while I was asleep, with a coverlet of brocade whereon was some writing, and said, 'Read!' I said, 'What shall I read?' He pressed me with it so tightly that I thought it was death; then he let me go and said, 'Read! . . . Read in the name

31

of thy Lord who created . . .' So I read it, and he departed from me. And I awoke from my sleep, and it was as though these words were written on my heart . . . when I was midway on the mountain, I heard a voice from heaven saying, 'O Muhummad! Thou art the apostle of God and I am Gabriel.' I raised my head towards heaven to see [who was speaking], and lo, Gabriel in the form of a man with feet astride the horizon saying, 'O Muhammad! Thou art the apostle of God and I am Gabriel'" (Guillaume 1955, 106).

Muhammad's revelation marked the beginning of Islam. The message that Muhammad said Gabriel had directed him to spread came from an eternal, heavenly tome. This is the Quran, the holy book of Islam. *Quran*

A contemplative man, Muhammad sought refuge for meditation at a cave on Mount Hira, near Mecca. It is said that here he received his first revelation designating him as the prophet of God. This painting by an anonymous artist depicts the cave, one of Mecca's most famous sites. (Courtesy of Norman MacDonald/Art Resource, NY)

means to read or recite, and the Quran is a recitation of the heavenly book. Muslims regard Arabic, the language of the Quran, as the language of God. The beauty and lyricism of the Quran has often been cited as proof of its divine provenance. Part of the tradition of its validity is the argument that Muhammad, said to be illiterate, could not have created the perfect Arabic of the Quran. However, his illiteracy is not universally accepted by scholars. Whatever its provenance, the Quran has elements and traditions from both the Old and New Testaments, as well as from other religions of the time, including Sabaism (worship of the stars), Zoroastrianism, Hanifism, and Arabian pagan beliefs.

The God of the Quran was not unknown to Meccans, who were proud of their reputed descent from Abraham and the recognition of monotheism that was implied by this lineage. But they also preferred worshipping their idols—representing their polytheistic pantheon—to the worship of Allah. They also regarded the idea of resurrection with skepticism. When Muhammad began preaching, he did not have to convince Meccans of the supremacy of Allah; he had to get them to stop turning their back on Him.

Islam

Islam, the name of the religion based on the teachings of Muhammad and the Quran, means "submission." The submission is to Allah, the supreme being; an adherent refers to him or herself as a *Muslim,* or one who submits to the will of God. The word *Islam* comes from *salam,* which means peace. Despite the military campaigns that fostered its spread, the teachings of the Quran were fairly liberal for the time and were interpreted and practiced with great tolerance.

Rather than deny the validity of other monotheistic religions of the time (Christianity and Judaism), Islam built upon them. Muhammad accepted Abraham and Moses as prophets of God, and he placed Jesus in the same position: a chosen messenger rather than a divine being. Muhammad preached that he himself was the last of the four prophets chosen to bring the word of God to the people, following Abraham, Moses, and Jesus. Islam also shared the beliefs of these religions in the Day of Judgment, Resurrection, heaven, hell, and the eternal life of the soul. Thus, Muhammad considered Muslims to be brothers of Christians and Jews, as well as Zoroastrians, referring to all as *ahlu al khitab,* or "People of the Book," and proclaiming the Old and New Testaments of the Bible as inspired by the same divine revelations that yielded the Quran.

33

THE FIVE PILLARS:
THE TENETS OF ISLAM

The tenets of Islam are simple and consist of five devotional duties, or *ibadat*. These are called the Five Pillars of Islam: the affirmation of faith *(shahada)*; daily prayer *(salat)*; almsgiving *(zakat)*; fasting during the month of Ramadan *(sawm)*; and making the pilgrimage (hajj). The methods of performing these religious obligations are prescribed.

Testimony—*Shahada* expresses the core tenet of Islam: "There is no God but God (Allah), Muhammad is his Messenger." As noted, Allah was not an unfamiliar being when Muhammad spoke of him. Allah was Arabic for "the God," though often translated as simply "God," and He had already been an object of worship, though the pagans of the era gave more obeisance to a pantheon of minor deities and spirits. To be a Muslim required not only exalting God, but also disavowing other powers beyond his.

Prayer—Muslims pray five times daily: at dawn, noon, mid-afternoon, sundown, and night. In Islamic communities, a call to prayer *(adhan)* is made from the top of a minaret, a mosque's tower. The one who summons the worshipers is called a muezzin. The faithful, after a ritual cleansing *(wudu)*, unfurl a prayer rug facing the *qibla*, or direction toward Mecca. Prostrating themselves, prayers, which usually follow an established series of steps and devotionals, are offered. Muslims usually pray communally every Friday afternoon at the community mosque. Men and women pray in separate areas.

Alms—The giving of alms, or *zakat*, is incumbent on all well-off Muslims. Islam mandates that these alms first go to the poor of one's own clan

Spreading the Word

Khadija was Muhammad's first convert, and she convinced him to tell others about his vision. In 613 he began publicly preaching his message. As he began to spread word of his revelation, Muhammad was treated benignly, considered mad for his obsession with an impending judgment day. He said nothing to question the polytheism on which Mecca thrived. But then Muhammad's preaching turned against idolatry. To the tribal leaders, this endangered all their people; a tribal member known to repudiate sacred idols would be a grave insult to all tribes who came to Mecca to worship them.

and then to others in the community. Sharing one's own blessings is seen as God's will. Later in Islamic history, *zakat* would be instituted as a form of taxation by some Islamic regimes.

Fasting—Ramadan, the ninth month of the Muslim calendar, commemorates Muhammad's reception of God's revelation. During this month, fasting during daylight is required. This is meant as a display of piety, a commitment to God, and an affirmation of the equality of all Muslims. The sick and weak, pregnant or nursing women, soldiers on duty, people undertaking essential travel, and children are exempt from the prohibition, but all others must refrain from eating, drinking, or smoking during daylight. The fast may end when light is deemed insufficient to distinguish a black thread from a white one. The time of the year when Ramadan falls changes, as it is marked by the lunar calendar, which is eleven days shorter than the solar calendar. When it falls in the summer, longer daylight hours make observing the fast more difficult. The month of Ramadan ends with the holiday of Id al Fitr, a three-day feast and holiday.

Pilgrimage—The pilgrimage to Mecca, or hajj, should be made by every Muslim who is able at least once in his or her lifetime. Muhammad may not have anticipated the hardships and demands this would entail when Islam spread thousands of miles in all directions from Arabia. Nonetheless, for almost 1,500 years, Muslims from around the world have performed this last of the Five Pillars. In Mecca, they perform special rites observed during the 12th month of the lunar calendar. Over the years the enormous numbers of the hajjis, as those making or who have made the pilgrimage are known, have brought an infusion of wealth, new ideas, and sometimes problems.

Islam's message of unity also ran contrary to the structure of Arabian society. Tribe and clan were the defining social units. Allegiances to outside institutions were unknown. In contrast, Islam taught that all believers were brothers, a revolutionary concept. This threatened established order by transferring allegiance from the tribal and clan leaders to a commonly revered deity. (The faith itself had no earthly leader, though such an office would be created and filled by the caliph during the Islamic Empire.) And by condemning the idolatrous pagan practices that brought pilgrims to Mecca, Islam threatened the economic lifeblood of Mecca's leading citizens, who profited from the pilgrimage.

The Quraysh, Muhammad's own tribe, as the guardian of the holy site, stood to lose the most. They could be driven from their position as caretakers of the sacred shrine, or even exterminated.

Muhammad's first followers, in addition to his wife, included his daughter, Fatima, father-in-law Abu Bakr, adopted son Ali Omar, and his slave Zayd ibn Haritha. At first, his preaching was ignored by almost all others. But as he attracted more converts, Muhammad became an object of ridicule, derision, and finally hostility. The Meccans used both persecution and debate to confront Muhammad. They belittled his assertions of prophethood, asked for demonstrations of miracles, and encouraged him to work the imminent destruction he warned of. Muhammad was ordered to desist his denunciation of idolatry, but he continued preaching his message in marketplaces and in Mecca's public square. Only his connection to his clan and tribe shielded him.

Muhammad's message of universal brotherhood, threatening to the established powers, found appeal among the lower classes, and they comprised the majority of early adherents, numbering some 40 believers. Many were slaves. However, he also attracted some of Mecca's leading citizens. Umar, from the powerful Umayyad clan, and the aforementioned Abu Bakr, a respected merchant, both of whom would play a large role in the spread of Islam, were among them. His young cousin Umar, son of the uncle who raised Muhammad, Abu Talib, was also an early adherent. Later, Umar ibn al-Khattab, a respected young man who had previously been one of the faith's staunchest enemies, joined their cause. These were among the Companions of the Prophet, the circle of his trusted early followers, whose accounts of Muhammad's life are recorded in the hadith (literally, "traditions"). A complement to the Quran, the hadith became one of the cornerstones of Islamic law as the words and deeds of Muhammad that it recounted became one of the keys to defining what constituted lawful and unlawful conduct.

Mecca Turns Hostile

As Muhammad gained yet more adherents, the Meccan establishment, fearful of his growing power, began to persecute his lower-class followers. Unlike Muhammad, they had no protection from a clan and were thus vulnerable to harm. Muhammad sent some followers, said to number a little more than 80, to Abyssinia, in present-day Ethiopia, where they received protection from the Christian king Negus. The Quraysh dispatched a pair of emissaries bearing gifts to prevail upon

Negus to expel the Muslims, but the Abyssinian ruler demurred. Though few of Muhammad's clan converted, they nonetheless continued to assure his safety, as tribal custom demanded. The Quraysh tried to pressure the Hashim clan to end its protection of Muhammad, and in 616 Meccans called for a boycott against Muhammad and his followers, vowing that no commerce or marriages would be conducted with the Muslims. By this time Muhammad had attracted some of Mecca's leading citizens, who were spiritually unsatisfied with popular polytheism.

Muhammad also sought converts among Christians and Jews of Mecca, the "People of the Book," whom he saw as his natural constituency, as his God was their God. Rebuffed by Christians, to whom Jesus was more than one in a line of prophets, Muhammad focused on attracting followers among Jews.

In 619 Muhammad's wife Khadijah died, and shortly thereafter so did his uncle, Abu Talib, weakening Muhammad's protection. His other uncle Abu Lahad, who assumed leadership of the clan, was among those most opposed to Muhammad. Muhammad looked for a place to move with his growing community. He contacted the citizens of Taif, a town in the hills some 50 miles southeast of Mecca. His request to move his community infuriated Meccans already opposed to him, and when Taif refused, his position became even more precarious.

It was shortly after this that Muhammad reported to his followers of a miraculous journey he experienced one night. This has become one of the most well known and theologically important episodes of his life, known as his Night Journey (Isra) and referred to in the Quran (17:1). The account is accepted by many as having been embellished and altered from its original retelling. But as tradition relates, Muhammad reported that while asleep the previous night, the angel Gabriel had taken him, astride a winged horselike animal named Buraq, to Jerusalem, where he met Abraham, Moses, Jesus, Adam, Joseph, and other biblical figures. After leading them in prayer, Muhammad was taken to the seven spheres of heaven, where his mission on Earth was affirmed. From here, he also saw the suffering of those damned to hell and the paradise awaiting those who followed God's will. It was during this journey that he received instructions that Muslims should pray five times each day.

As recorded in the Quran, Muhammad said he had been taken from the "sacred" or "inviolable place of worship," which was interpreted as the mosque at the holy shrine of Mecca, to the "remote" or "farthest place of worship." This latter reference was originally thought to mean heaven. But after the capital of Islam moved to Damascus under the Umayyad caliphs, the phrase "farthest place of worship" was reinterpreted as Jerusalem, former site of the Temple of Solomon. (It was on the spot of Muhammad's supposed ascension that the Umayyads built the Dome of the Rock, Islam's holiest site in Jerusalem.) Later, the two interpretations were combined, with the prophet traveling first to Jerusalem and then to heaven. Whatever his destination or route, Islamic scholars and the faithful have also debated over the years whether Muhammad's nocturnal excursion was a physical or spiritual journey. (After his death, his widow Aisha declared that "Muhammad was transported only in his spirit.")

The allusion to Jerusalem has been taken to signify Muhammad's recognition that Islam was a continuation of the holy injunctions delivered by prophets of the past. It was no secret that Muhammad sought the support of Mecca's Jews, hoping that they would accept him as the messiah their religion told them to expect.

The account of his journey only increased the scorn and ridicule from his opponents, and the Jews of Mecca neither followed him nor recognized the mantle of divine prophet that he claimed. (Later, after moving to Yathrib, he chose Jerusalem as the *qibla,* the direction to face while conducting prayers, as Jews traditionally did. After disagreements with the Jews in his adopted city, Muhammad would receive a revelation directing him to reorient the *qibla* to Mecca. It has been suggested that this reorientation was useful in ascertaining whether Jewish converts were sincere, by seeing if they turned away from Judaism's holy city while praying.) Muhammad continued preaching to his tribesmen, as well as others. Delivering God's message in the Kaaba one day, his recitation invoked the names of three of the chief idols, Lat, Uzza, and Manat (Quran 53:1–20). He then uttered a verse:

> *"These are the exalted Gharaniq (possibly demigods) whose mediation is accepted."*

Thus, the revelation accepted the legitimacy of these idols' powers. The Quraysh heard this as Muhammad's repudiation of his damning pronouncements about idolatry. Among his followers, it caused profound disillusion. This last verse was later repudiated in the Quran (22:51, 52), with Muhammad reciting that the words came not from God but from the devil. These were the Satanic Verses. They are recorded in Muhammad's biography by Ibn Ishaq, but they are not in the Quran. Through the ages, they have represented a theological dilemma for the faithful, as the episode suggests a fallibility on the part of Muhammad, who is considered infallible. His disavowal of those verses strained relations with the Quraysh further.

The Hegira

At this time, the oasis city of Yathrib, a cultural center some 250 miles northeast of Mecca, was roiled by Arab tribal disputes between the Aws and the Khazraj. Meanwhile, Jewish tribes prospered with their control over most of the trade routes passing through the town. The most powerful of the Jewish tribes were the Banu Qurayza, Banu Nadir, and Banu Quynuqa. Seeking to end their conflict with the Aws, representatives of the Khazraj met with Muhammad in 621 to ask for his assistance as an arbitrator. It was common practice in Arabian communities to bring in a respected outsider to resolve otherwise intractable problems. Muhammad explained that as Muslims, their tribal affiliations would be moot, because they would all be one community. The following year a dozen leaders representing most of the Arab clans met with Muhammad to find out more about his faith. All 12 are said to have accepted his message immediately. The 12 returned to Yathrib to serve as apostles, spreading the word of Islam. Muhammad also sent a trusted follower who had memorized large portions of the Quran to spread its word in Yathrib. Within a short time, most of the Arabs had converted. During the pilgrimage of 622, a delegation of 73 converts representing all the Arab clans in Yathrib came to meet Muhammad and report on the spread of Islam. They invited him to immigrate to Yathrib, promising allegiance and protection, and Muhammad accepted.

It reportedly took Muhammad six months to travel from Mecca to Yathrib, a journey known as the Hegira, or "Emigration." The trip had to be conducted in secrecy, as the leaders of Mecca, fearing his alliance with Yathrib, had launched a plan to have Muhammad killed. He arrived on September 22, 622. This marks the beginning of the Muslim calendar. Seventy men followed him. Yathrib became known as the City of the Prophet (in Arabic, "Medina't al Nabi)" or simply Medina, the name by which it is known today.

Muhammad and the leaders of Yathrib signed an agreement, the Constitution of Medina, which defined the structure of the community, or *ummah*. Jewish tribes as well as Arabs were in the *ummah*, though most of the Jews retained their faith, which Muhammad permitted under a covenant they reached:

> "To the Jew who follows us belong help and equality. He shall not be wronged nor shall his enemies be aided. . . . The Jews . . .

> *are one community with the believers (the Jews have their religion and the Muslims have theirs). . . . The Jews must bear their expenses and the Muslims their expenses. Each must help the other against anyone who attacks the people of this document. They must seek mutual advice and consultation, and loyalty is a protection against treachery. . . . God approves of this document" (Guillaume 1955, 231-233).*

While his years in Mecca were marked by the development of his message, in Medina the focus became the consolidation of power for the faith in the name of God. Muhammad set about establishing a community, its institutions, and promulgating the tenets of the faith that had by now all been expressed and codified. Rules governing marriage, concubinage, divorce, and slavery were set. Yet his overriding goal was to return to Mecca and cleanse the holy site of the pagan idolatry he preached against.

The Community in Medina

From the beginning, tensions arose within the *ummah* and with the larger community of Medina. Within the *ummah,* divisions grew between his followers from Medina (Ansar, or "helpers") and those who had emi-

Medina, the adopted city of the prophet Muhammad. His emigration, known as Hegira, to Yathrib (later renamed Medina) in 622 is a milestone in the history of Islam and marks the beginning of the Islamic calendar. (Courtesy of S.M. Amin/*Saudi Aramco World*/PADIA)

grated from Mecca (Muhajirun). The Medinese became resentful of the dependence of the Muhajirun, who brought little besides their faith with them to Medina. To provide for his community, Muhammad ordered raids on the caravans traversing nearby routes between Yemen and Syria. Where before Islam had taught peace and nonviolence, new revelations allowed the faithful to seek out and attack nonbelievers.

> To those against whom war is made, permission is given [to fight] because they are wronged ... [They are] those who have been expelled from their homes in defiance of right [for no cause] except that they say, 'Our Lord is Allah'" (Quran 22:39–40).

As Muhammad began to narrow his view of the *ummah* to include only Muslims, the Jewish tribes who had considered themselves members, though they did not recognize Muhammad as God's prophet, became restive. The Jews' refusal to accord Muhammad divine connection caused more estrangement.

In January of 624 Muhammad changed the orientation of the *qibla* from Jerusalem to Mecca, pointing Islam back toward its Arabian roots, as well as testing the faith of Jewish converts, as noted earlier. In the ongoing struggles between the communities, Muhammad charged that the Jews had gone astray from the true religion of Abraham, which he represented.

Muhammad also faced antipathy from the larger community, composed of Christian and pagan Arabian tribes, the latter deemed "hypocrites" by the fiery words of the Quran. Using the sword where the word of Allah failed to persuade his enemies, Muhammad consolidated power in Medina and was accepted as the Prophet of God. Next he gained support outside of Medina, primarily through alliances with tribal groups. After the death of Khadijah he remarried, taking several wives, some of whom may have been wed to strengthen these ties.

The Quran already promised eternal bliss for the faithful; special dispensation was accorded those who fell in battle fighting for Islam. Muhammad ever reminded his forces of the paradise that awaited them, and his followers fought with that much more boldness, as thoughts of death seemed to carry as much anticipation as fear.

The Campaign for Mecca

With his position in the region solidified, Muhammad began a campaign to conquer Mecca. The first action had been a caravan raid in 623, conducted during a traditionally sacred month, Rajab, when fighting was

HADITH

The hadith, or traditions, reported ear- or eyewitness accounts of Muhammad's words and deeds, passed down orally by an unbroken chain of trustworthy persons. But not all hadith could be taken as gospel truth. Some who promulgated various hadith even admitted to making them up. As the traditions were later used to determine proper courses of action, prescribing what was permissible and what was not, the forgery of Muhammad's words could be valuable. The hadith covered virtually all aspects of life, from the correct way of cutting a watermelon before eating it to the use of a toothpick.

Every perfect hadith has two components: the chain of authenticity (isnad) and the text (matn). The reputations of the authenticators, who are said to have passed it along, were considered in judging the certainty of the hadith. Thus, hadith are classified as genuine (sahih), fair (hasan), and weak (daif).

During the third century of the empire, the hadith were gathered into six now-standard volumes. Their proliferation is evident in the fact that the preeminent cataloger and author of the first volume of the Hadith, Muhammad ibn Isma'il al-Bukhari (810–870), sifted through 600,000 traditions gathered from 1,000 sheikhs during the 16 years of travel he spent while preparing the work. He pared them down to about 7,225 hadith, which he cataloged by subject matter. After the Quran, the Sahih al-Bukhari is the most influential work in Islam. The Hadith of Ibn al Hajaj Al-Nisapuri (d. 875) (Sahih Muslim) has many of the same hadith as al-Bukhari, though the chain of authenticity is sometimes different. These two books are considered by Muslims to contain the most authentic hadith.

prohibited. The Meccans were roused by what they regarded as a violation of tradition. Skirmishes and raids continued.

Early in 624 the Muslims planned a raid on a caravan organized by Abu Sufyan, leader of the Quraysh, and set off with a force of 300. The Meccans heard about the impending raid and set off for Medina with a force of 1,000. The two armies met at an important resting stop on the caravan route, Badr. The Battle of Badr, as the event would be known, began with duels pitting individual Meccan warriors against individual fighters from amongst the Muslims, led by Ali ibn Abu Talib, Muhammad's cousin (and later husband of Fatima). All nine of the Meccans who stepped forward to duel were slain. Pressing the advantage,

Muhammad ordered a charge. In the ensuing fight, several leaders of the Meccan forces were killed, and their troops soon fled the battlefield.

The Battle of Badr was a turning point in the birth of Islam. Muhammad offered it as proof of divine intercession on behalf of the Muslims. The victory gave the Islamic forces a belief in the divine righteousness of Muslims and served to unite the *ummah* as never before. The defeat also united the resolve of the Meccans. The following year, 625, they gathered a force of 3,000 fighters to attack Medina. Muhammad led a force of 500 and met the Quraysh at Uhud, about 5 miles from Medina. As at Badr, the battle began with individual duels, and again Ali quickly dispatched the Meccans' leading banner carriers. But after the Muslims mounted a successful charge, a Meccan counterattack carried the day. Muhammad was wounded, but the Meccans did not press their victory and withdrew toward Mecca.

Once Muhammad had recovered, the raids on caravans and on tribes in the Hijaz and Najd intensified, as did his effort to isolate Mecca. He challenged the Meccans to a battle, which they accepted. But when Muhammad arrived in 626 with a force of 1,500 men on the battlefield near the wells of Badr, the Meccans were nowhere to be seen. The Meccans' failure to fight diminished their stature as it added to that of the Islamic forces and it swayed more tribes to support Muhammad.

Determined to finally deal decisively with Muhammad and his followers, the following year (627) Abu Sufyan, the leader of Mecca, gathered 10,000 men and marched north to attack Medina. Muhammad called them the "army of confederates" because of the Meccan alliance with Bedouin tribes. Muhammad's forces were unprepared for battle. At the suggestion of a Persian who knew about defensive fortifications used in other lands, Muhammad had a trench and earthworks dug across the northern approach to the city, which was surrounded by mountains on the other three sides. Unable to breach the earthworks, the Meccans laid siege to Medina, a campaign subsequently known as the Battle of the Trench. After 20 days, dissension and low morale among the Meccans split their forces apart, and one by one their leaders returned home with their troops. This cemented Muhammad's growing reputation as a power to be reckoned with throughout the peninsula. Tribes began to forge alliances and pledge allegiance to him.

Muhammad's Hajj

In 628, the year after the Battle of the Trench, Muhammad determined to go to Mecca for the pilgrimage and set off with 1,400 men. Camping

The Battle of Badr, at which Muhammad's outnumbered forces defeated the Meccan army, is celebrated as one of Islam's most important victories. This page from an illuminated manuscript of Siyar-e-Nabi (The Life of the Prophet), created in the court of Sultan Murad III in the late 16th century, illustrates the battle. (Courtesy of Erich Lessing/Art Resource, NY)

outside the city, the Muslims sent emissaries stating that they came only to pray peacefully at the Kaaba. After negotiations between Muhammad and Abu Sufyan, the two sides signed the Treaty of Hudaibiyah. The terms called for the Muslims to return to Medina without entering Mecca but gave them permission to make the pilgrimage the following year, and pledged an end to fighting for 10 years. The following year Muhammad led 2,000 Muslims on the pilgrimage and won many new converts. The year after that, 630, after an attack by a tribe allied with the Quraysh on a tribe allied with Muhammad, he declared the treaty void. Muhammad quickly assembled an army of 10,000 and marched on Mecca, making camp just outside the city. His uncle, Al-Abbas, met him on the way and pledged his allegiance. Then Abu Sufyan, the leader of the Quraysh, came and gave his fealty to Muhammad. Mecca fell peacefully. However, not all pledged loyalty, among them Abu Sufyan's son, Muawiyah (r. 661–680) and later his grandson Yazid (642–683). (Paradoxically, they would become the first two caliphs of the Umayyad dynasty.) Muhammad rode into the city upon a camel, triumphant. He then had the idols of the Kaaba gathered and demolished. His lenient treatment of the city with which he had had such bitter relations quickly earned him the respect and loyalty of many of its citizens. After putting down an insurrection by the Hawazin, a Bedouin tribe, in the following weeks, Muhammad could claim Mecca as Islam's. From

MUHAMMAD AND THE JEWS

Muhammad ultimately rid Medina of most of its Jews. Some were assassinated and some banished (the Banu Quynuqa and Banu Nadir tribes). After the battle against the Meccan confederate forces, the last remaining Jewish tribe, the Banu Qurayza was suspected of collaborating with the enemy during the siege. The Quran notes that the Qurayza assisted the confederate forces. After the withdrawal of the Meccans, Muslim forces surrounded their stronghold, and the Qurayza finally surrendered unconditionally. Muhammad left the decision on their fate to the leader of the Aws, the Arab tribe that was their bitter enemy. As decreed by Aws's leader, the men, numbering between 600 and 800, were put to death. The women and children were sold as slaves. Historically, this episode has proved one of the most vexing to scholars in reconciling Muhammad as a man of peace with the actions conducted in the name of the religion he brought forth.

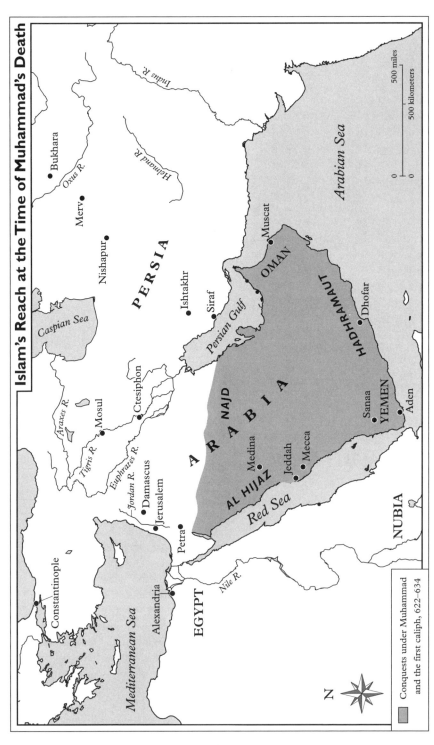

Islam's Reach at the Time of Muhammad's Death

By the end of Muhammad's life, most of Arabia was united under the banner of the religion he proclaimed, Islam.

46

throughout Arabia, tribal leaders and delegations came to pledge their loyalty to Muhammad.

In the following two years the Muslims continued expanding their empire across the peninsula by both force and diplomacy. Muhammad also led campaigns against Christian Arab kingdoms allied with the Byzantine and Sassanian empires in northern Arabia.

In 632 Muhammad made his final pilgrimage to Mecca, leading 40,000 followers, where he delivered the Farewell Sermon, his last speech. Soon after returning to Medina, he developed a violent fever and died at the age of 63. At the time of his death, almost all of Arabia was under his control, and almost all the tribes were unified under the banner of one religion. He had been accepted as the prophet of God, and Islam and Arabia had become as one. The Arab ideal of noble desert warfare, and the Bedouin reality of it, was now a divine mission of conquest. The language in which they took such pride was God's own, and the Arabs saw themselves as his chosen people.

Within one century Islam would claim the largest empire in history, stretching from Spain across India, and would lead the way to a golden age of inquiry and discovery—while Europe was mired in the Dark Ages—that would eventually transform the civilized world.

3

THE ISLAMIC EMPIRE AND ARABIA (632-1258)

By the time of Muhammad's death in 632, almost all of Arabia was united under the banner of the religion he preached. Yet its spread was as much due to Muhammad, his presence and authority, as to the message he brought from God in his recitations. Without Muhammad, Islam's future was precarious. This was demonstrated by the abandonment of the faith by some tribal leaders upon hearing of Muhammad's death. Yet early Muslim leaders surmounted these and other challenges and greatly expanded the empire's reach. The process by which these first successors were selected, however, created enormous strife and left a legacy of division among Muslims that still exists today. As the Islamic empire swiftly expanded, it rapidly lost touch with its Arabian roots, its capital moving to Damascus under the Umayyads and then to Baghdad under the Abbasids. It was during this latter regime that an astonishing confluence of art and science known as the Golden Age occurred, which was extinguished by an onslaught of nomadic tribes from the steppes of Asia, the Mongols.

The Khalifah

Muhammad had appointed no successor to lead the Muslim community, nor had he stated rules for choosing one. The collected verses of his recitations, which would not be gathered into the Quran in its present form for almost 20 years, offered no definitive guidance. Following his death, respected members of the community in Medina met to choose a new leader. Four candidates were considered, all in attendance: Ali ibn Abu Talib (600–661), Muhammad's cousin and husband of his daughter, Fatima; Uthman ibn Affan, an early convert and respected

Muhammad's interment site, the Tomb of the Prophet, in the Prophet's Mosque, Medina.
(Courtesy of S.M. Amin/*Saudi Aramco World*/PADIA)

nobleman from the powerful Umayyad clan of Mecca; Umar ibn al-Khattab, a trusted Companion of Muhammad; and Abu Bakr al-Siddiq, Muhammad's father-in-law, who had accompanied him on the Hegira, or "emigration," from Mecca to Medina. Abu Bakr had also been called on by Muhammad to lead public prayer when Muhammad had been too ill to fulfill the duty in his final days.

During the discussion, Umar is said to have grasped Abu Bakr's hand in a traditional sign of fealty, and after this show of support Abu Bakr was selected as Muhammad's *khalifah,* or "successor." The title, anglicized to "caliph," would henceforth be bestowed upon those who led the Islamic Empire. Each of these four original candidates would serve as caliph in succession, the first three ruling from Medina, and the last, Ali, moving the capital to Kufa in what is now Iraq, even as his leadership was contested. These four subsequently became known as the *rashidun,* or "rightly guided caliphs," for their devotion to Islam and personal connection to the Prophet, qualities that would be lost in future caliphs after their passing.

Abu Bakr's simple, pious ways helped win support for his succession, but he proved a formidable leader in battle as well as in prayer. After several tribes renounced Islam following Muhammad's death, a period known as "the Apostasy" (al-Ridda), Abu Bakr decisively used force to regain their allegiance. He also won the support of tribes in Najd, Central Arabia, enlisting them in campaigns against Persia's Sassanian dynasty and against the Byzantines, heirs to the Roman Empire, in Syria, Palestine, and Egypt. Abu Bakr's brief, two-year reign (632–634) proved the durability of the new faith.

Umar

In a written testament, Abu Bakr appointed Umar as the second caliph, precluding conflict over succession. Umar adopted the title Amir al-Muminin, or "commander of the faithful," and under his leadership (634–644), the Islamic Empire spread rapidly across the Middle East. A major factor behind the successes of the Islamic forces was their tolerance and mercy toward the vanquished. For example, the Muslim general Khalid ibn al-Walid made this offer in writing to the people of Damascus as his forces stood ready to attack their city:

> This is what Khalid ibn al-Walid would grant to the inhabitants of Damascus if he enters therein: he promises to give them security for their lives, property and churches. Their city wall shall not be demolished, neither shall any Muslim be quartered in their houses. Thereunto we give them the pact of Allah and the protection of His

Prophet, the caliphs and the believers. So long as they pay the poll tax [from which Muslims were exempt], nothing but good shall befall them (Nutting 1964, 49).

This tolerance was in contrast to the Byzantines, who helped bring about their own downfall by their persecution of Christian sects in the name of religious orthodoxy. Thus, Syrian Monophysites, Nestorian Christians, and Copts welcomed and in some cases assisted the Muslim invaders. The Byzantines had also raised taxes on local populations to help pay for their ongoing war with the Persians, adding to their unpopularity.

Other factors also helped the Muslim army's astonishing advances. Decades of warfare between the Byzantines and Persians had weakened both empires. Both had failed to build defenses or to garrison troops along their southern flanks because they saw no threat from the disorganized nomadic tribes of Arabia. In battle, the Muslims' camels frightened their enemies' horses. The hit-and-run attacks of their light cavalry could devastate the more heavily armored formations of the Byzantine and Persian forces. And the implacable will of soldiers answering to the call of a God who demanded they wage jihad, or a "holy struggle," against infidels was an invaluable weapon from both a tactical and psychological standpoint.

Following the fall of Damascus in southern Syria in 635, ousted Byzantine officials appealed to Heraclius (575–641), ruler of the Byzantine Empire, to counter the Muslim warriors. Heraclius gathered a large force, and in 636, at Yarmuk, the vaunted Byzantine army under the command of Theodorus was decisively defeated by Arab commander Abu Ubaidah bin Jarrah. Some 100,000 Byzantine soldiers were killed according to one account, while some 3,000 Muslims died. The defeat signaled the beginning of the decline of the Byzantine Empire. Heraclius, who had dismissed a letter from the unknown Prophet of Arabia only a few years before, fled to Constantinople. Jerusalem fell without violence a year later. Its Byzantine ruler sent word to Umar, encamped on the Golan Heights and poised for attack, that he was prepared to surrender. Umar entered Jerusalem alone to accept the city, his simple clothes and lack of retinue startling a populace accustomed to the pomp and ceremony of the Byzantines. Umar pledged to the citizens complete security for their churches.

Along with military victories, Umar's caliphate was marked by bureaucratic efficiency. In conquered lands, the administrative infrastructure of previous regimes was retained where possible. Umar created the financial structure underpinning the empire, instituted an efficient

The Prophet's Mosque in Medina. Today the mosque and its plazas cover an area approximately the size of the town of Yathrib at the time Muhammad arrived on his Hegira from Mecca in 622. (Courtesy of Abdullah Y. Al-Dobais/*Saudi Aramco World*/PADIA)

tax system, and brought the military under state control. He also introduced the Islamic/Muslim calendar, dating it from the Hegira, and began projects to enlarge the holy shrine in Mecca and the mosque in Medina. His 10-year reign was capped by a major victory over the Sassanids at the Battle of Nahavand, called the "Conquest of Conquests," where Muslim cavalry crushed the elephant-led Persian forces in 641, opening Iran to Islam. By the end of Umar's reign most of Sassanian Persia was Islam's, as were the lands of the Fertile Crescent and northern Egypt.

Umar's life ended violently. A recently captured Persian Christian stabbed Umar as he was about to lead prayers in Medina. Mortally wounded, Umar appointed six men to choose his successor. The two candidates were the remaining members of the four Companions of the Prophet first considered as Muhammad's successor: Ali and Uthman. The men chose Uthman as the third caliph (644–656).

Uthman

Under Uthman's leadership, the boundaries of the empire were extended across Persia and Libya and northward into Armenia. He continued the expansion of the holy shrine in Mecca and the mosque in Medina, and he founded the port of Jeddah. But his greatest contribution was the compilation of the Quran as a written text in about the year 650. Muhammad had preached, not written, the message of Islam, and over the years his words had been transcribed, copied, and distributed. Uthman was concerned that the incorrect versions in circulation would distort God's word as relayed by Muhammad. Consequently, he appointed a committee to collect the canonical verses and destroy all others. The result of this effort was the Quran as it appears today, the order of its verses arranged by length, going from the longest to the shortest, as decided by the committee.

Religious Schism: Sunni and Shia

Uthman's reign also marked the first significant dissension in the Muslim community. Uthman was, after all, a member of the Umayya family, the powerful Meccan clan that had persecuted Muhammad and forced his immigration to Medina. Despite his own early conversion, this made Uthman an unpopular caliph for many in the community. Moreover, once in office he was accused of favoritism toward his family and of condoning corrupt governance. Grievances had been registered and efforts to resolve them had collapsed. Anger and resentment grew. In 656, a crowd in Medina threw stones at Uthman. Besieged in his home, Uthman summoned military help, and when word reached

A leaf from the Quran written in Kufic script, dating to the ninth century during the Abbasid dynasty. Kufic was the style of Arabic used to write the first Qurans, which were formalized in about 650 under Caliph Uthman. (Courtesy of Werner Forman/Art Resource, NY)

the rioters, a group led by Muhammad ibn Abu Bakr, the son of the first caliph, broke into Uthman's house and killed him.

Ali ibn Abu Talib, cousin and son-in-law of the prophet Muhammad, and last of the four original Companions considered to lead the community after the Prophet's death, was named caliph in Medina. Some of Ali's supporters believed his selection overdue. Though few in number initially, Ali's supporters claimed Muhammad himself had designated Ali his successor, and that he should have been the first caliph. And while Ali had accepted Uthman's selection, many of his supporters had refused to recognize the Umayyad nobleman as caliph. As unhappiness with Uthman's reign grew, so did the ranks of this so-called party of Ali, or partisans of Ali, in Arabic, *shia 't Ali* or simply *shia* (a designation that has also been anglicized as Shiite). Unlike the Shia, the majority of Muslims supported the election process used to choose the first caliph. They were known as *ahl al-sunna wa-l-jama'ah*: the people of custom and community, or simply Sunni: "people of (the) custom."

Kufa, a garrison town in Iraq founded by Umar, was a stronghold of Shia support, and after his selection as caliph in 656, Ali made his capital there. But Ali's rule was contested. Uthman's cousin Muawiya, the governor of Syria, was Ali's principal adversary and rival for the caliphate. Uthman's murderers had been staunch supporters of Ali, and Ali failed to bring them to justice, feeding opposition against him. Ali was also challenged by Aisha, one of Muhammad's wives, daughter of Abu Bakr, and sister of Uthman's killer. This prompted a civil war, the first armed conflict within the community of believers, lasting from 656 to 661. Ali's forces defeated Aisha's supporters in 656 at the Battle of the Camel, so named because Aisha observed it from her palanquin atop a camel. Aisha was taken prisoner, ending her threat. Ali and Muawiya's forces then fought at the Battle of Siffin, which ended in a stalemate. More bloodshed followed, along with growing dismay at the internecine warfare. Finally Ali and Muawiya agreed to abide by the ruling of a Quranic tribunal on who should be caliph. Some of Ali's supporters were incensed that he would allow an earthly council to decide if he should be caliph, believing only God could make that determination. Known as the Kharijites, or "seceders," this group formed its own caliphate and refused to recognize any other Islamic authority.

The Umayyads

After months of deliberation, the Quranic tribunal ruled that neither Ali nor Muawiya should be the caliph. Ali refused to accept the judgment and relinquish office, which he now exercised from Kufa, in southern Iraq, having been unable to return to Medina or Mecca after the start of hostilities. Civil war resumed, with the Kharijites joining the fight. Ali's Shia forces soundly defeated the Kharijites at the Battle of Nahrawan in 658, but their movement remained alive. Syrian forces loyal to Muawiya attacked Ali's headquarters in Iraq, and in 661 Muawiya, with the support of the governor of Egypt, proclaimed himself caliph and made Damascus his capital. The following year a Kharijite assassinated Ali. Muawiya, who was also an intended victim of the half-successful plot, was now able to consolidate his claim to the caliphate. This marked the beginning of the Umayyad dynasty.

Muawiya controlled the holy sites in Arabia through the governors of Medina and Mecca, both of whom he appointed. Not merely an absentee landlord, he also acquired large homes and other properties in and around Mecca for himself.

Ali was survived by two sons, Hassan and Husayn, grandsons of Muhammad. Ali's followers in Iraq proclaimed Hassan, the older of the two, the new caliph. However, Muawiya paid Hassan and Husayn a stipend not to press claims to the caliphate, assuring peace. Hassan and Husayn believed the caliphate would revert back to them, and thus Muhammad's bloodline, after Muawiya's reign. But the Umayyads had dynastic plans.

The Umayyad caliphate marked an important shift in Islam. The first four, or the "rightly guided" caliphs, had been associates of Muhammad and shared his concern for piety and spiritual matters. They became caliphs by the selection of elders. All came from Mecca and were members of the Quraysh. The assassinations that ended the lives of three resulted in the main from issues of succession, indicative of the passionate divisiveness this issue aroused among the faithful and those who would be caliph. A dynastic line would be less prone to such crises (though familial bloodshed over succession issues would remain a staple of Arabian dynastic politics for centuries).

Whereas the impetus behind the expansion of the empire during the reigns of the first four caliphs had been religious fervor, with the Umayyads, secular concerns came to the fore. The business of the state was given precedence over the state of the religion, as the court devoted itself to administering the vast territories the empire would absorb in less than 30 years.

Muawiya's rule incorporated a *shura* (council of sheiks) with executive powers, giving the tribes a voice in state decisions. As noted, until this time the caliphate had been a designated position, not a blood right. But Muawiya instituted a hereditary rule of succession, one that required the councils' approval of the successor. An account from the ninth century explains how Muawiya made the approval process clear. At a gathering of notables, orators rose to extol Yazid, Muawiya's son, as heir to the empire. When any disapproval was expressed, a tribesman rose in answer, drawing his sword from its scabbard, letting it be known that his blade would provide a swift reply to anyone who objected to Yazid's succession. For his simple but pointed eloquence, Muawiya dubbed the tribesman the prince of orators.

The Martyrdom of Husayn

When Ali's son Hassan died in 669, his brother Husayn became head of the "Alids," those loyal to the house of Ali. Upon Muawiya's death in 680, his son Yazid claimed the title of caliph, as planned. But Husayn refused to recognize Yazid and set out from Medina to Iraq to organize the Alids, though he had virtually no chance of winning back the caliphate. On the way, Husayn and 70 followers and family members were surrounded and eventually slaughtered by an Umayyad force of 4,000 troops at Karbala, in what is now southwestern Iraq. Husayn's head was brought back to Damascus and presented to Yazid.

As a result of Husayn's martyrdom in 680, the schism between Shia and Sunni was suddenly magnified. Husayn's death at Karbala is recognized as the date from which Shiism emerged as an independent sect of Islam. The anniversary of this event, commemorated annually in the Islamic month of Muharram, is the most important religious observance for Shia Muslims around the world.

Husayn's killing precipitated a revolt in Medina. Yazid suppressed the uprising and later laid siege to Mecca. Yazid died during the siege, and the adolescent son who succeeded him, Muawiyah II, soon died as well, his reign lasting but 40 days. The Umayyad forces withdrew from the siege, and competing claims to the caliphate again threatened the stability of the Islamic world.

A New Umayyad Dynasty

Two Arabian tribes based in Syria, the Qays and the Kalb, backed rival candidates for leadership; the Qays backed Abdullah Ibn al-Zubayr, while the Kalb supported Marwan ibn al-Hakam (623–685). Following a bitter war between the tribes, the Kalb and Marwan prevailed, and Marwan was named caliph in 684, founding a new Umayyad dynasty in Damascus. Marwan's title was mainly symbolic, as he held little sway

The Dome of the Rock in Jerusalem, the third holiest shrine in Islam, is built over the site from which Muhammad is said to have ascended to heaven on what is called his Night Journey, or Isra. (Courtesy of the Fine Arts Library, Harvard College Library)

beyond his capital. Indeed, when he died a year later, leaving the caliphate to his son, Abd al-Malik ibn Marwan (r. 685–705), all of Arabia was under the control of Ibn al-Zubayr, who had established a rival caliphate in Mecca. Much of Iraq was ruled by a rebel, al-Mukhtar. Al-Zubayr defeated al-Mukhtar, consolidating his control of the region, which he maintained until 692. In that year Abd al-Malik, the nominal caliph and son of the founder of the new Umayyad dynasty, defeated him at Mecca after unleashing a catapult assault on the city and the Kaaba that reportedly destroyed the shrine. This ended competing claims for control of the Islamic state.

Abd al-Malik's reign was marked by administrative reforms and innovations. He introduced a monetary system, minting coins engraved with the *shahada,* or proclamation of Muslim faith. A postal service was also instituted as well as agencies charged with keeping government records. Abd al-Malik also made Arabic the administrative language of the empire; previously, public records in Damascus had been written in Greek. He also built one of Islam's most sacred edifices, the Dome of the Rock. Built from 687 to 791, it is located on the site of Jerusalem's Temple Mount, where Muhammad is reputed to have ascended to heaven during his Night Journey. At the time of its construction, al-Zubayr still controlled Mecca, and the Dome of the Rock, which is not a mosque but a shrine for pilgrims, was built to drain pilgrimage traffic away from Mecca's Kaaba. (Muslims offer prayer at the adjacent Al-Aqsa Mosque.) Designed by Byzantine architects, the Dome of the Rock was the most monumental building in early Muslim history.

The Islamic conquest resumed during the reign of Abd al-Malik's son and successor, al-Walid I (r. 705–715). Parts of Egypt were retaken from the Byzantines, Carthage was conquered, and in 711 Muslim armies crossed the Strait of Gibraltar and commenced the conquest of Spain, which was completed by 716. To the east, by 710 Muslim forces had advanced as far as the Indus River.

Al-Walid also initiated some of the empire's greatest building projects with the construction of the Umayyad Mosque at Damascus. His policy of levying a tax on nonbelievers while exempting Muslims prompted large-scale conversions to Islam. The many Egyptian Coptics and Persian converts who could not speak the language of God and Islam were seen as a threat to the Arabic character of the religion. Partly in response, al-Walid proclaimed Arabic the official language of the

The Umayyad Mosque in Damascus (Courtesy of the Fine Arts Library, Harvard College Library)

empire (not just of its administration), establishing a universal mode of communication that helped draw its members together.

The secular bent of the Umayyad administrations was reversed under the reign of Umar ibn Abd al-Aziz (r. 717–720), who was born and raised in Medina and pursued policies more in keeping with Islamic principles. Most notably, he abolished the poll tax on converts, which reduced state income but was in keeping with precedent established under the rightly guided caliphs.

After the death of al-Walid, the reigns of all the subsequent Umayyad caliphs were short, with the exception of Hisham (r. 724–743), considered the dynasty's last great ruler. Under Hisham the Islamic Empire achieved its greatest expansion, stopped finally in 732 at the gates of Tours in France.

As Islam spread, many Arabs in positions of authority in far-flung cities amassed large fortunes, which they used to build royal palaces, opulent homes, and grand public buildings and mosques. However, despite the tolerance for the institutions and religions of the conquered peoples shown by the Arab occupiers, anger about the social hierarchy they oversaw rose. In the social and political hierarchy, Arabs occupied the positions of power, half-Arabs were next in standing, followed by native converts. The former Persian elites were among this last group.

After Hisham's death in 743, a series of rebellions led by disaffected non-Arabs, Kharijites, and other dissident groups wracked the Umayyad-led empire. Among them were Sunni purists, Shia, and others who supported hereditary succession through Muhammad's descendants. Ultimately, the regime's secular bent and the Umayyads' reputed dissolute ways, said to include the flouting of Islamic prohibitions against alcohol, fueled a secret movement in support of a claimant descended from Muhammad's paternal uncle and early supporter, Al-Abbas ibn Abd al-Muttalib. The claimant, Abu al-Abbas (r. 749–754), became the progenitor of the next and last Arab dynasty to rule the Islamic Empire, the Abbasids. They would rule in name if not always in authority for 500 years.

The Abbasids

The Abbasids, as the followers of al-Abbas were called, believed the Umayyads were corrupting the sanctity of Islam. As early as the reign of Umar II in 718, a great-grandson of Ibn Abd al-Muttalib, Muhammad ibn Ali, was rallying support in Persia for a restoration of the caliphate to Muhammad's family, the Hashemites. The Abbasids were among the groups supporting this cause in the name of a return to religious purity. Though the Abbasids were Sunni, their support for Abu al-Abbas aligned them with the Alids, descendants of Ali, who were Shia and whose imams were descended from this branch of the Hashemites. Also backing the Abbasids were non-Arab Muslim converts, called client Muslims, or *mawali*. They were so called because converts needed the protection of a clan, and so the converts became clients of the clan providing their protection. *Mawali,* most of whom were Iranian, were treated as second-class citizens, which bred resentment toward the ruling class.

In the mid-eighth century a freed slave led a revolt that began in the former Persia, uniting several otherwise mutually hostile groups in Khorasan and Iraq. The alliance of the Abbasids and Shia, together with these other unlikely allies, ultimately brought down the Umayyads. Their combined armies defeated Marwan II (r. 744–750), last of the Umayyad Marwani caliphs. Marwan II and his family were put to death. One grandson escaped: Abd al-Rahman ibn Muawiya al-Dakhil. After five years of flight across north Africa Abd al-Rahman arrived in Spain in 756, where he was made caliph of Cordoba, home to a large Syrian community. Here he founded a new Umayyad caliphate that made the Iberian peninsula a center of culture and commerce under Islamic rule into the 13th century.

The Abbasid era, which began with the defeat of the Umayyads lasted from 750 to 1258. Following his assumption of the caliphate, the first Abbasid caliph, Abdullah Abu al-Abbas (r. 750–754), eliminated former allies who posed potential threats to his power. He also continued to search out and destroy any vestiges of the Umayyad line. His vigor in these pursuits helped earn him the nickname "the bloodletter," or "blood spiller."

The caliphate was moved to Baghdad in 762, during the reign of the second Abbasid caliph, Abu Jafar al-Mansur (r. 754–775), upon whose orders the new capital was built. Both Abu al-Abbas and al-Mansur consolidated their power at the expense of the Khorasanian Arabs who had helped their cause. Positions of influence and importance, especially in the military, were transferred from Arabs to foreigners; Persians primarily handled state duties, and Turks were given military responsibilities. The Abbasids considered these outsiders more loyal, though the preference accorded them created great resentment among those who had supported the Abbasids and now found themselves shut out of the spheres of power. The Shia had also helped the Abbasids, but the lack of unity among them made ongoing support difficult to assure, and the

Abbasids ultimately severed ties to the Shia community. In 786, Shia in Mecca staged an uprising, which ended in a massacre of many of their group. Survivors fled to the Maghreb (now Morocco), a region of north-western Africa, and founded the independent Idrisid kingdom.

Despite the hopes of a return to Islamic purity among some who welcomed the demise of the Umayyads, the Abbasids were perhaps even more secular, and loyalty to the caliph mattered more than faith in Islam. Under Abdullah al-Mamun (786–833, r. 813–817, restored 819–833), seventh Abbasid caliph, Islam and Western thought came to their closest parallel. Al-Mamun championed the Mutazilite cause. A radical theological movement, Mutazilism held that Muslims should obey a single ruler and that interpretation of religious texts should be consistent with reason. He sought support for this view in the works of Greek philosophers. It was al-Mamun who established the Beit al Hikmah, or "House of Wisdom," in Baghdad in 830, which served as a university, library, and translation bureau to help foster the Mutazilite agenda. Here, Hellenistic and Indian works were translated into Arabic, preserving the knowledge and keeping alive the flame of inquiry that would bring the Renaissance to Europe 500 years hence. Acceptance of this more liberal school of theology upset both orthodox Sunni and Shia, and precipitated more Shia rebellions, all of which were crushed.

The Golden Age

The Islamic Empire was at its height. Baghdad was the richest city in the world. On the seas, the empire's ships were the largest and best. With their highly developed banking system, it was said that an Arab businessman could cash a check in Canton on his bank account in Baghdad and that wealthy women adorned themselves with lavish jewels and pearls, silks and embroidered fabrics. Homes were filled with exquisite carpets and cushions, had sparkling fountains, soft music, and the air was redolent with exotic perfumes of musk, myrtle, and jasmine. The Abbasids collected tribute from some surrounding kingdoms. Unlike the Arab forces of the first Islamic conquests, their armies were professional institutions, able to project the caliph's power throughout the empire.

Such was the grandeur of the reign that, under Caliph al-Muqtadir (907–932), one ceremonial display for envoys from Bzyantium's Constantine VII (r. 913–959) included 160,000 cavalry and footmen, 7,000 black and white eunuchs, and a parade of 100 lions. The envoys were also shown an artificial tree of gold and silver weighing 500,000 drams, or almost 2,000 pounds, whose branches held birds of the same precious metals that chirped by mechanical means.

The Golden Age of Islam, with its wealth and power and intellectual vitality, flourished during the reigns of Harun al-Rashid (764–809, r. 786–809) and his son Abu al-Abbas Abdullah al-Mamun. From here, it would experience a prolonged decline lasting almost 500 years, as territories broke away, and the Abbasid caliphs themselves became puppets of foreign military rulers.

The Decline of the Empire

As the glory of the Abbasid caliphate peaked during the reign of al-Rashid, signs of the empire's decay were already showing. The province of Ifriqiyah—North Africa between what is now Libya and Morocco—fell away from the empire during al-Rashid's reign. Iranian Shia discontent with continued Sunni rule from Baghdad precipitated other revolts, which led to the establishment of minor regional dynasties. Under the rule of al-Rashid's son, al-Mamun, more territories became untethered. When al-Mamun died in 833, succeeded by his brother, al-Mutasim (r. 833–842), the decline continued. No longer able to rely on the loyalty of his army, al-Mutasim recruited an army of slaves, mostly Turks, called Mamluks, to back him. Noted for their horsemanship, the Mamluks soon proved adept at taking the reins of the state, as well. Reliance on this force of foreigners combined with al-Mutasim's abandonment of Baghdad in favor of making his capital at Sumarra created a rift between the caliphate and Muslims that never healed.

From the middle of Caliph al-Wathiq's reign (r. 842–847), the caliphs began to lose control of the caliphate as well as their empire. By the 10th century the Mamluk army had usurped all authority of the Arabian and Persian army. The Mamluks kept the caliph, whom they chose and disposed of at will, as a figurehead. This further eroded the empire's central authority. Independent states proliferated. The Fatimids, Ikhshidids, and Tulunids established themselves in Egypt, while the Hamdanids ruled Syria and northern Mesopotamia. To Baghdad's east were a half-dozen new kingdoms proclaimed by Buwayhids, Ghaznavids, Samanids, Ziyarids, and others.

Though the arts and sciences and culture continued to develop under some of the independent states left by the empire's dissolution, they failed to equal the advances of the Golden Age that preceded them. This marks the beginning of the medieval period of Islam.

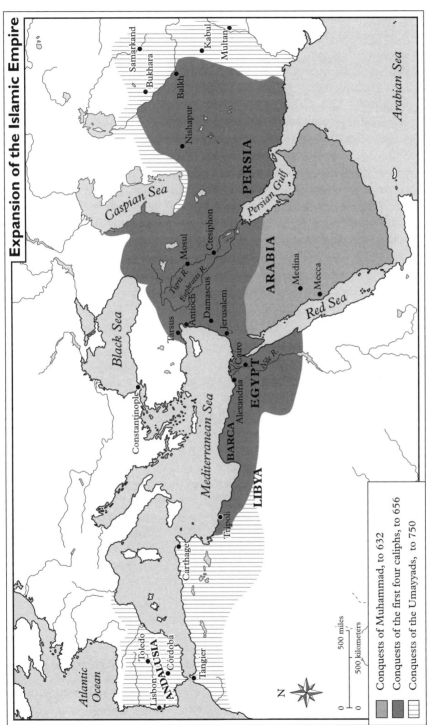

Expansion of the Islamic Empire

Samarkand
Bukhara
Balkh
Kabul
Multan
Nishapur

PERSIA

Caspian Sea

Mosul
Tigris R.
Euphrates R.
Ctresiphon

Persian Gulf

Antioch
Damascus
Jerusalem
Tarsus

ARABIA

Medina
Mecca

Red Sea

Arabian Sea

Black Sea

Constantinople

Cairo
Alexandria

EGYPT

Nile R.

BARCA

Mediterranean Sea

LIBYA

Tripoli

Carthage

Tangier

Toledo
Lisbon
Cordoba

ANDALUSIA

Atlantic
Ocean

N

Conquests of Muhammad, to 632
Conquests of the first four caliphs, to 656
Conquests of the Umayyads, to 750

0   500 miles
0   500 kilometers

At the height of the Golden Age, 100 years after the death of Muhammad, Islam's reach extended from the Atlantic to beyond the Indus River. This map depicts its boundaries and the extent of the territories taken by the first four caliphs and the Umayyads.

SUNNI VS. SHIA

During the turn of the first millennium the Shia developed as a distinct sect. The Shia employed more rituals in their religious ceremonies, similar to pagan practices, than Sunnis displayed. The Shia themselves have numerous sub-sects that have arisen over differences about which of Muhammad's blood lines, propagated through the progeny of his wives, produced legitimate heirs to the caliphate.

The major branch of the Shia is the Imamiyyah, or "Twelvers," so named because they believe there are 12 imams. To the Shia, the imam are divinely chosen hereditary leaders of the Islamic community, the first being Ali, last of the "rightly guided" caliphs. The first four are accepted by all Shia. Ali (d. 661) is considered to have assumed the position upon Muhammad's death. Ali was followed by Hassan (d. 669), Husayn (d. 680), and Ali Zayn al-Abidin (d. 712–713). The imamate passed from father to eldest son, except in the case of Husayn, who became imam after his brother's renunciation of the caliphate. In the times when the imam were alive, various sects arose when they broke off from the Imamiyyah following disputes over succession and the identity of the true imam. More than 40 such Shia sects arose from these disputes.

The religious and ideological differences between the Shia and Sunni sects seem relatively minor to those not of the faith. They have a different set of hadith, or traditions, and practice different forms of sharia, religious law. A key difference is the Shia veneration of the institution of the imam. To Sunnis, the caliph was the spiritual and political leader of the ummah, but his authority was temporal; to the Shia, the authority of the imam was divine, infallible, and without sin. These spiritual qualities made the imam uniquely able to bridge that gap between the visible world and the spiritual world with which every Muslim aspired communion. Through the ages, the Shia have also tended to rely on the imam for guidance in applying Quranic law, while the Sunni have relied more on previous interpretations of the Quran and Hadith laid down by long-established theological and judicial traditions. Sunni Muslims also use

(continues)

(Facing page) The split between Sunni and Shia, the major schism in Islam, arose over disputes about the succession of its rulers. Since Muhammad left no male heirs, Shia believe that only descendants of his cousin Ali are legitimate leaders of the Islamic community. This chart depicts the genealogy of the Alids, as they and their supporters are known. The numbers indicate the succession of rulers.

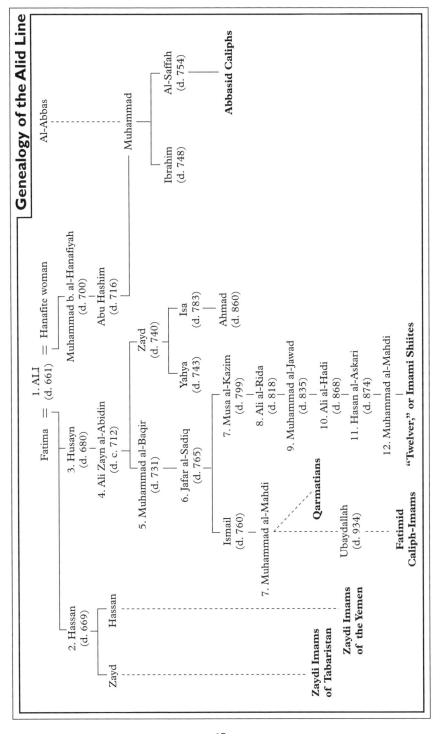

Genealogy of the Alid Line

Al-Abbas

Muhammad

Ibrahim
(d. 748)

Al-Saffah
(d. 754)

Abbasid Caliphs

Fatima = 1. ALI = Hanafite woman
(d. 661)

Muhammad b. al-Hanafiyah
(d. 700)

Abu Hashim
(d. 716)

Zayd
(d. 740)

Yahya
(d. 743)

Isa
(d. 783)

Ahmad
(d. 860)

2. Hassan
(d. 669)

Hassan

Zayd

3. Husayn
(d. 680)

4. Ali Zayn al-Abidin
(d. c. 712)

5. Muhammad al-Baqir
(d. 731)

6. Jafar al-Sadiq
(d. 765)

7. Musa al-Kazim
(d. 799)

8. Ali al-Rida
(d. 818)

9. Muhammad al-Jawad
(d. 835)

10. Ali al-Hadi
(d. 868)

11. Hasan al-Askari
(d. 874)

12. Muhammad al-Mahdi

"Twelver," or Imami Shiites

Ismail
(d. 760)

7. Muhammad al-Mahdi

Qarmatians

Ubaydallah
(d. 934)

**Fatimid
Caliph-Imams**

**Zaydi Imams
of Tabaristan**

**Zaydi Imams
of the Yemen**

SUNNI VS. SHIA *(continued)*

the term imam as an honorific for a holy man. To the Sunni, an imam is also the prayer leader, and any Muslim in good standing who is trained in prayer can be an imam. Usually, however, the position goes to the most respected and religiously knowledgeable congregant. Also, while the Sunni eschew any religious practices that hearken to the idolatry of the pagan past, the Shia, who regard the imams as exalted beings, make pilgrimages to the tombs of the 11 earthly imams, though these journeys are not as important as the pilgrimage to Mecca. (The main branch of the Shia maintains that a 12th imam was born but has remained hidden on Earth to this day.)

Despite what may appear to others as small theological distinctions, ever since the massacre of Husayn in 680, the Shia have reveled in an identification with martyrdom and persecution, a fixation that has been reinforced by their traditional position as outsiders and minorities, ostracized as threats by the temporal leaders whom they refused to recognize due to their Alid allegiance.

The Seljuks

By the 10th century Baghdad, the City of Light, was a decaying shell of a city too weak to defend itself, or halt the hemorrhaging of its borders. By 945, the area around what is now Iraq fell to an Iranian Shia military dynasty, the Buyids. For over a century they wielded the power behind the throne, permitting the caliphate to remain in the Abbasids' Sunni hands.

To the east, a tribe of Turkish warriors from central Asia, the Seljuks, had established a kingdom under the leadership of Tugrul Bey. He initially made Isfahan, in Persia, his capital. The Abbasid caliph, impressed by the tribe's military capability (and heartened by the fact the Seljuks were Sunni), made Tugrul Bey his deputy. Tugrul wanted more, and in 1055 he forced the caliph to appoint him sultan. Tugrul ruled the Abbasid realm until his death in 1063. Again the Abbasids were kept as figureheads to retain the regime's legitimacy.

Tugrul Bey's ascension hastened the dissolution of central authority, and what remained of the empire splintered into regional powers. Territories slipped or broke away, retaining their Islamic character, but under the control of autonomous local rulers.

The Fatimids

The Abbasids were just one of several groups in Islam's history that used claims of Alid lineage to seize the role of hereditary rulers. The Fatimids built an empire centered in Egypt rivaling the Abbasids' own on this very foundation. And as the Abbasids used doubts about the religious rectitude of the Umayyads to undermine and ultimately displace them, so the Fatimids challenged the Abbasids' religious authority as a means of legitimizing their own. But in contrast to the Abbasids, the Fatimids, like the majority of Alids, were Shia. This was the only major Shia-ruled dynasty in Islam. (However, it was not recognized by the Shia in Iran and Iraq.)

Fatima (605–633) was the daughter of Muhammad and his first wife, Khadija. She had married Ali (the fourth and last of the "rightly guided" caliphs) and was the mother of Hassan and Husayn, around whom the Shia movement formed. As the sole progeny of Muhammad to have continued his blood line, she is revered by all Muslims, but most so by the Shia, who ascribe godlike qualities, referring to her as "the virgin" and "the mother of the two Jesuses," reflecting the influence of Christianity on the sect. Today, her birthday and marriage date are celebrated.

The Fatimid dynasty was founded in Tunisia in 909 by Said ibn Husayn (r. 909–934). He claimed descent from Ali and Fatima through the imam Ismail, who was a great-great-grandson of Husayn, martyred at Karbala. This made him an Ismaili, which is a Shia sect. Historians have questioned the validity of ibn-Husayn's proclaimed lineage, and thus the legitimacy of the Fatimid dynasty. But under his rule and that of his descendants, the Fatimids held sway across North Africa and into Arabia.

Ibn Husayn ruled under the title Imam Ubaydullah al-Mahdi. The Aghlabid dynasty he replaced had been Abbasid allies and the last bastion of Sunni dominion in the region. A campaign to sow doubts about the legitimacy of the Abbasids preceded his seizure of power, accomplished with the help of the powerful Kitamah tribe, with whom he had established contact in Mecca during the hajj. The title of "caliph" taken by later Fatimid rulers, rather than "imam" as the ruler of a Shia sect is usually called, is taken as an indication of the depth of their rivalry with the Abbasids. Pursuing a policy of expansion by both land armies and naval power, by 969 the Fatimids ruled all of North Africa, having taken Egypt from the Abbasid-backed Ikhshidid dynasty that year.

The Ikhshidids' brief rule had begun only in the year 935. Since 942 the Ikhshidids had also controlled Mecca and Medina along with western Syria and Palestine under the approval of the Abbasids. Thus, their victory in Egypt earned the Fatimids rule of western Arabia as well. The conqueror of Egypt, Jawhar al-Siqilli (the Sicilian), founded the city of al-Qahirah (City Victorious), or Cairo, which became the Fatimid capital. For the next several centuries, Hijaz, western Arabia, would be under Egyptian influence, if not always their control.

For a time at the peak of its power near the end of the 10th century, the Fatimid empire rivaled and surpassed that of the Abbasids. Among its accomplishments was the founding of Al Azhar, which today is the world's oldest university. Yet its neglected western territories in North Africa began to break away. The seeds of the Fatimids' final decline were planted during the reign of their most able monarch, Abu Mansur Nizar al-Aziz (r. 973–996), with the importation of Turkish and African mercenaries. From

THE CRUSADES

The Fatimid dynasty had historically exercised religious tolerance; most subjects in Egypt were Coptic Christians, Jews, and Sunni Muslims. But some rulers treated Christians and Jews more harshly. One, Caliph al-Hakim (r. 996–1021), ordered the destruction of Jerusalem's Church of the Holy Sepulcher, inflaming Christians. (Al-Hakim, considered to have been mad, is also alleged to have been behind an effort to destroy the sacred Black Stone in the Kaaba, perpetrated by a fanatic who was killed in the midst of his attack.) Likewise, Christian pilgrims visiting the Holy Land often encountered adversity in the Muslim lands they traveled through. These events helped create an antagonistic atmosphere between Christendom and Islam. In 1094 the Byzantine emperor Alexius Comnenus, who was losing Asian territories to the Seljuks, asked Pope Urban II's help in fighting the Islamic forces. A half-century earlier the Seljuk Turks had overrun the western territory of the Abbasid dynasty, before Tugrul Bey established his sultanate in Baghdad in 1055, under which the Abbasid caliph served. The Holy Land itself, at the time of the Crusades, was a disunited region ruled by competing chiefs. The Seljuk Turks controlled the north. In 1095, the year after the Holy Roman Emperor asked for his assistance, Pope Urban II called upon the faithful of Christendom to march on the Holy Land and "wrest it from the wicked race" occupying it.

The First Crusade, so named for the cross under which the men marched, left Constantinople in 1096. Some 30,000 to 35,000 soldiers formed the fighting core of the rag-tag amalgamation of perhaps 150,000 crusaders from across Europe that set off for the Holy Lands in the Levant. A series of crusades followed, lasting until 1291.

these forces came commanders who eventually seized power for themselves. As Fatimid power waned and its territory shrank, western Arabia alone remained faithful to Fatimid rule. Arab tribes such as the Bani Hilal and Bani Sulaym, which had migrated from Najd to Egypt, helped the cause, moving west at the request of the Fatimids in 1052, where they wreaked havoc with their attacks on Tripoli and Tunisia for years.

Salah al-Din and the Ayyubid Dynasty

Salah al-Din ibn-Ayyub (1138–93), a Kurd from Armenia, won glory and renown for driving the Crusaders from Jerusalem as well as for his enlightened leadership. But he was equally committed to restoring Abbasid (and thus Sunni) authority in place of the Fatimids' Shia regime. The dynasty Salah al-Din (anglicized as "Saladin") would lead, the Ayyubids, was named for his father. By 1171 the Ayyubid forces had conquered Egypt and displaced the Fatimids in much of their former territories.

Salah al-Din served under the ruler of Syria, Nur al-Din (r. 1154–74). But after Nur's death in 1174 Salah proclaimed his independence and later defeated Nur's young son, gaining control of Syria. In May of 1175, the Abbasid caliph granted Salah "investiture" over Egypt and western Arabia, as well as much of North Africa, central Syria, and Palestine, giving him at least nominal title to leadership. Turning his attention to the Franks, an ethnonym by which the Crusaders were known, he retook Jerusalem on October 2, 1187. The Franks retained only Antioch, Tyre, and Tripoli, in addition to a few small towns. This defeat provoked what is called the Third Crusade.

Though it affected pilgrimage traffic, the Crusades had little direct impact in Arabia. However, the Muslim holy sites became a target in 1181, when the Crusader Reynaud de Châtillon, a privateer elevated to lord of Montreal and based in Kerac in what is now Jordan, launched a surprise naval attack against Red Sea ports. Some of his forces came close to Medina, where they planned to desecrate Muhammad's tomb. However, all were killed or captured before reaching their objective.

After his death in 1193, the lands that Salah al-Din had conquered gradually were retaken by the Franks. The Ayyubid dynasty ended with a Mamluk coup in 1250, half a century after his passing. The Mamluks continued the battle against the European invaders, and in 1291 Islamic forces under their command drove the last of the Franks from the Holy Land. But by then the Islamic Empire had been brought down by the Mongols, and its glory would never be regained.

The Arabian Peninsula

Whatever independence the peninsula's populations enjoyed, the rulers of the Islamic Empire regarded the territory as theirs. They rarely exercised their authority, particularly avoiding Najd, whose barren lands and fierce tribes offered little incentive for engagement. The foreign hand was felt most heavily in Mecca. The income generated from the hajjis, or "pilgrims," who came by the tens of thousands every year, was one reason for this ongoing interest in Arabia. Additionally, as Islam's temporal leader, it was incumbent upon the empire's ruler to guarantee safe passage for pilgrims on the hajj. Large, guarded caravans and scattered forts along the caravan routes were the primary means of protection in the peninsula's interior, such as the route that traversed Arabia from Baghdad.

CARMATHIANS

The Carmathians, an Ismaili offshoot, appeared around 890, taking their name from the founder of their violent and intolerant breakaway Shia sect, Hamdan Qarmat. Besides repudiating the Syrian leadership of the Ismailis, the Carmathians refused to recognize the legitimacy of the Fatimids when they came to power in North Africa, and they attacked the Abbasids, as well. By the beginning of the 10th century they had established their base in Hasa and had influence throughout Arabia. Their leader, Abu Tahir al-Qarmati, made his headquarters in what is now Bahrain. They and their Bedouin allies became a particular menace to the pilgrimage caravans crossing northern Arabia during the first years of the 10th century. The attacks subsided between 908 and 925, when the destruction of a caravan bound for Mecca from Baghdad signaled the resumption of their depredations. Such was the fear that no pilgrims traveled between Baghdad and Mecca for the next two years.

In 930, the Carmathians attacked Mecca on the first day of the hajj, riding their horses into the *haram,* the holy shrine, and killing the pilgrims praying and circumambulating around the Kaaba. Their victims in the city numbered some 30,000. Zamzam and the other wells of Mecca were despoiled, houses plundered, and finally Abu Tahir had the Black Stone removed from the Kaaba, broke it, and took the pieces away with him. The Carmathians kept the stone for more than 20 years, hoping its possession would elevate their position in the Islamic world and draw pilgrims. They returned the stone in 951, after Abu Tahir's death, held together with what were described as silver bolts due to damage suffered at the Carmathians' hands.

Though from the outside Arabia seemed a uniform, if inhospitable land, its inhabitants recognized a distinct division within it: Hijaz and Najd. The relations between Hijaz, the more settled and traveled region along the west coast, and Najd, the arid interior dominated by Bedouins, were frequently hostile. Hijaz exhibited the influence of a succession of outside rulers: Umayyad, Abbasid, Egyptian, and (later) Ottoman, as well as that of untold numbers of pilgrims. Najd had never come under foreign domination or influence, and its people regarded themselves as the more authentic Arabian culture.

The Sharifs of Mecca

In the midst of the 10th century, about 967, the Quraysh clan reclaimed its hereditary rule in Mecca. The city's leader was known as the sharif. The word generally meant a "noble," or tribal leader, but in this context was used to mean a descendant of the prophet Muhammad, to whom the leaders of Mecca traced their lineage. By the 11th century, this was the ruler's formal title. The sharif was the dominant force in the peninsula, his power often extending beyond Mecca, sometimes east into Najd and to Yemen in the south. The sharifs' authority was exercised in uneasy alliance with western Arabia's ultimate titular ruler, who over the next thousand years included caliphs and sultans (the Ayyubid and Ottoman rulers' title) ruling from Baghdad, Cairo, Damascus, and Constantinople. The sharifs' power fluctuated with the degree of control exerted by the various administrations and rulers claiming the area. It was also subject to forces of nature. Drought and famine that periodically swept the land created political instability capable of toppling the sharif.

It was important for the rulers of the Islamic Empire to foster good relations with the sharifs, both to maintain the legitimacy of their regimes (prominent mention in Friday noon prayers was an important statement of political fealty) and assure access to the holy sites for the empire's citizens. The sharifs' loyalty was ensured primarily by financial rather than military means. Maintaining effective year-round military control over the distant and inhospitable Hijaz was too costly and daunting for the successive regimes that exercised nominal rule over the territory. The hajj became the forum for an annual rite of affirmation of the relationship between sharif and caliph or sultan. The caliph or a representative of the court would lead a procession to the holy sites, bringing gifts and a yearly payment, which constituted a significant amount of the sharif's income. The caliphs also funded renovations of shrines and other public works, and were conduits for large charitable contributions, also delivered during the hajj.

Given the large number of ambitious Quraysh and the wealth and power due the sharif, his rule was often challenged from within, and parricide was an avenue of advancement for more than one future sharif. And because the office wielded more influence than military power, external threats arose as well. Between 1175 and 1200, a series of despots from Mesopotamia, Medina, and Egypt exercised direct control over Mecca, though Amir Mikhtar, the sharif, maintained his office during these years. Weary of his ineffectiveness, the Meccans themselves chose to replace Mikhtar in 1201 with Qatada ibn Idris, who remained as sharif until 1220. He was the first in the line of Hashemites, who ruled Mecca into the 20th century. Qatada expanded his rule to Medina, over portions of Najd, and into Yemen. During the hajj of 1212 a failed assassination attempt on his life prompted Qatada to order an attack on the caravan from Mesopotamia, believing Baghdad's emir had engineered the plot in an effort to halt Qatada's growing power. Sharif Qatada remained in power until age 90, when one of his sons smothered him in bed. Rule of Mecca was subsequently fought over by Qatada's sons and agents of the Ayyubid sultan of Cairo. ("Sultan" was the title used by rulers of the Ayyubid empire.) Control, achieved by military force, passed back and forth between them for the next three decades, near the end of which, in 1250, the Ayyubids were overthrown by the Mamluks, ending Ayyubid involvement in Meccan affairs.

End of the Islamic Empire

The reign of the Abbasids, and the shift in the caliphate from Damascus to Baghdad, had marked a further physical distancing of Arabia from the center of the empire it had launched. It also removed more of the Arab character from Islam, as the Islamic community absorbed the influences of the conquered lands. Yet to a large degree Arabia's ties to the empire's center of power ended with the ascendancy of the Umayyads, who exported the caliphate to Damascus. The Umayyads had even laid siege to Mecca, their former home city, and destroyed the Kaaba late in the eighth century when its ruler, Ibn al-Zubayr, proclaimed himself the rightful caliph and led an insurrection there. The Abbasids who succeeded the Umayyads, though farther away in Baghdad, did more to maintain the links with the empire's Islamic and Arabian roots, primarily through their interest in the two holy cities and the hajj. Yet the glories of the Golden Age that the Abbasids' reign had produced were mostly achieved outside of the peninsula. Many of the era's greatest figures were not even Arabs. The flowering of the empire would not have been possible without a movement away from its birthplace, with its orthodox view of the unity of religious and political power. This change of seat also brought the empire closer to the Persian and Indian empires, which had their own classics and the preserved Hellenic classics.

The Islamic Empire had its roots in the nomadic warrior tradition of Arabia. Now it was threatened by a similar force, the Mongols. These Asiatic peoples had lived a nomadic existence in central Asia on the barren plateau north of the Gobi Desert, plundering caravans on the Silk Route. In the 12th century the warrior chieftain Genghis (Chinggis) Khan (ca. 1162–1227) unified the eastern Mongol tribes into a great confederation and began a westward sweep. In 1256 his grandson, Hulagu Khan (1217–65), conquered Baghdad. After the caliph surrendered, the Mongols destroyed the city and killed all the Abbasids by wrapping them in blankets and trampling them beneath their horses' hooves. In the ensuing slaughter, an estimated 1 million Muslims were killed. Libraries and grand buildings were sacked and burned. Irrigation systems were destroyed. It would take centuries for the society to recover. Though the Mongols never reached Arabia, the power vacuum resulting from the destruction of the Islamic Empire left the peninsula open to other foreign interests.

4

THE GOLDEN AGE OF ISLAM
(CA. 750-1258)

A t the end of the era of Muslim conquest, Islam was embraced from across North Africa and Spain, through Asia Minor, and east to India and China. By the ninth century, the stability the empire brought and the intellectual quest that it fostered had produced a flowering of creativity in the arts, science, and culture. The range and brilliance of its intellectual accomplishments are as astonishing as was the rapid military conquest that enabled its appearance. This was the Golden Age of Islam. It predated Europe's Renaissance (which Islamic learning would play a major role in making possible) by 500 years. At its pinnacle during the reign of the Abbasids in Baghdad, the empire and culture reached a level of sophistication and enlightened governance and public services that would be unequaled for almost 1,000 years. Having recounted the political history of this era, we turn to its artistic and social accomplishments.

Roots of the Golden Age

The strength of the intellectual awakening of the era was in part due to the participation of all cultures within the realm. Inclusiveness was a hallmark of the Golden Age. Christians, Nestorians, Jews, and Zoroastrians, along with their brethren Muslim scholars living across the Islamic world from Spain to Persia added immortal masterpieces to the age's canon. Yet no matter their provenance, the works of the scientists, mathematicians, scholars, poets, and artists from throughout the empire are all considered to be a part of the Arab and Islamic patrimony and therefore hold an important place in Arabian history as well.

Several other factors, in addition to inclusiveness, made the Golden Age possible. First was the political stability resulting from the success of the Islamic conquests. Also, the practice of integrating existing governing institutions in conquered lands into the caliphate's administrative apparatus negated the need to expend energy rebuilding or reorganizing social structures and eased the assimilation of conquered peoples. The absence of borders encouraged trade and the exchange of ideas. The shared language of Arabic, once it became the lingua franca of the realm early in the eighth century, facilitated communication. Moreover, the pursuit of knowledge was a religious imperative, commanded by the Quran. It taught that through an understanding of nature, one could come closer to an understanding of and a oneness with the Creator, which was the goal of a good Muslim. Indeed, much of the intellectual output of this era was produced in the furtherance of Islam. Muhammad's assertion of the value of knowledge was taken to heart, and the wisdom of the learned in conquered territories was sought out by Islamic leaders eager to learn from it. Muhammad had also mandated public education, and schools spread rapidly.

Another important factor was the introduction of paper. Prior to its appearance, writing was done on hides and papyrus, both of which required intensive labor to produce. When papermaking technology arrived in Samarkand, on the eastern border of the empire, from China in the mid-eighth century, mass-production of paper quickly took hold. Pulped rags, hemp, and bark were the raw materials. Fashioned into books, the paper was a major tool in the intellectual explosion. Soon large public libraries—and even personal ones— became commonplace. By the end of the era, knowledge of the most arcane subjects had been accumulated. Al-Nadim's monumental *al-Fihrist* (The catalog) (988), which cataloged works in Arabic, listed manuscripts dealing with hypnotism, juggling, glass-chewing, and sword-swallowing.

The Golden Age reached its high point during the reign of Harun al-Rashid, the Abbasid caliph, and his immediate successors. This was a time, contemporary chroniclers said, "when the world was young," reflecting the age's feeling of growth and possibility. Al-Rashid's son, Abu al-Abbas Abdallah al-Mamum, was perhaps the greatest of all Abbasid caliphs. In 830 he established the Beit al Hikmah, or "house of wisdom," in Baghdad, which served as a university, library, and translation bureau. Large-scale translation and copying projects brought the great works of Greek, Persian, Sanskrit, and Aramaic (Syriac) science and literature to scholars in the Arabic-speaking world. It was through these translations that medieval scholars in Europe were exposed to Hellenic classics, works that would later help make the Renaissance possible. Without this translation effort, many of these works would have been lost forever. In addition to their later influence in Europe, these works sparked thought and discourse within the empire that reverberated for centuries.

Three great thinkers, straddling the 10th and 11th centuries, embodied the intellectual ideals of the time and are considered to be the era's shining lights: Abu Ali al-Hasan ibn al-Haytham (Alhazen), Abu Rayham Muhammad al-Biruni, and Ali al-Hussein ibn Sina (Avicenna). Al-Haytham (b. 965 in present-day Iraq), who experimented with light and vision, is considered the father of the science of optics. He was also among the first to advance the scientific method. Al-Biruni (b. 973 in present-day Uzbekistan) distinguished himself in mathematics, astronomy, and geography. Ibn Sina (b. 981 near Bukhar, now in Uzbekistan) was a physician and philosopher whose medical encyclopedia became a standard medical text in the West.

Mathematics

The study of numbers and mathematics, so important in the quantification and calculation demanded by scientific rationality, saw great advances during the Golden Age. Though "Arabic" numerals were introduced to the empire from India early in the Epoch of Translation, it was the astronomical tables created by al-Khwarizmi (as well as Habash al Hasib, d. ca. 867–874) that made the imported numerology known throughout the empire. Islamic mathematicians also developed trigonometry as a means of measuring distant objects.

Medicine

Islamic physicians transformed medicine from an art based on superstition and conjecture into a science, greatly expanding its scope and reach. This was helped by the translation of writings on medicine from Eastern lands, where its practice was more advanced than in the West. The Islamic Empire treated public health as a state concern. The first free public hospital opened in Damascus 75 years after Muhammad's death. Caliph al-Rashid expanded the system, building Baghdad's first hospital early in the ninth century, with almost three dozen more throughout the empire soon following. The first pharmacies and schools of pharmacology were also established. Examinations were required for pharmacists and physicians seeking to practice their trade as early as the reigns of al-Mamun and al-Mutasim. Asylums throughout the empire cared for the mentally ill, and traveling medical clinics were instituted in the 11th century. Early in the 10th century, a physician in Spain, Abu Bakr Muhammad ibn Zakariya al-Razi (864–930), recognized the connection between bacteria and infection, which led to the introduction of antiseptics in dressing wounds. A prolific author of medical texts, he wrote more than 100 major works in the field and several important treatises on alchemy as well. The intellectual luminary Ali al-Hussein ibn Sina, known in the West as Avicenna (980–1037), was a physician as well as a philosopher, philologist, and poet. His major work among many was *al Qanun fi al Tibb* (*Canon of Medicine*). One of the first Arabic manuscripts translated into Latin, Avicenna's *Canon,* consisting of a million words, became the major medical text of medieval Europe up to the 17th century. Avicenna also recognized the importance of the patients' role in the healing process and the need for rest to allow bodies to heal themselves. Today the pictures of al-Razi and ibn Sina are hung in the School of Medicine at the University of Paris.

The modern study of optics, the science of light and vision, was established by Abu Ali al-Hasan ibn al-Haytham (ca. 965–1040), known as Alhazen to the West, with his *Kitab al-Manazir* (Book of optics), based on Euclid's writings. In the 13th century, Muslim physician Ala-al-Din Abu al-Hasan Ali Ibn Abi al-Hazm al-Qarshi al-Damashqi al-Misri (Ibn al-Nafis, 1213–88) discovered and accurately described the functioning of the human circulatory system. Veterinary medicine also received attention, and Islamic veterinarians led the field for centuries, most notably in their study and practice of equine health care.

Geography

Geography was of interest to the Islamic Empire beyond its use in determining the position of Mecca for prayer and mosque orientation; Arab traders who traversed the empire also drove the science's development. In addition to facilitating communication and travel, the works of the empire's geographers gave its citizens a feeling of being part of something that transcended their own realm of experience,

Al-Khwarizmi used the translation of Ptolemy's *Geography* as a model to create his *Surat al Ard* (image of the Earth), the first map of the Earth and the skies in Islam. Produced with the assistance of 69 other scholars at the direction of al-Mamun, the *Surat* stimulated greater study of geography while remaining a major influence in the field until the 14th century.

THE EPOCH OF TRANSLATION

Early in the Golden Age many of the greatest works of the ancient world were translated into Arabic. India was the first influence, particularly in mathematics and science. In about 771 a traveler from India arrived in Baghdad bearing two important texts: a treatise on mathematics and the *Surya Siddhanta,* a classic Indian treatise on astronomy. The first work introduced what the Arabs called Hindi or Gupta numerals (which the West would subsequently call Arabic numerals) to the Islamic Empire. The empire's own scholars introduced the concept of zero. Both innovations were important in the advance of mathematics.

The astronomical treatise was translated into Arabic by Muhammad ibn Ibrahim al-Fazari at the direction of Al-Mansur, the caliph. The effort took about 10 years (ca. 796–806), and al-Fazari became the empire's first astronomer. The translation was used by the noted astronomer, mathematician, and geographer Abu Jafar Muhammad ibn Musa al-Khwarizmi (ca. 780–850) for his widely used astronomical tables, or *zij.* It is from the title of al-Khwarizmi's mathematics book *Hisab al-jabr w'al Mucabalah,* (The science of reunion and reduction) that the word *algebra (al-jabr),* a branch of mathematics introduced by Egyptian and Greek scholars, is taken. Translated into Latin in the 1100s, it became the standard mathematical textbook in Europe until the 16th century. Al-Khwarizmi also developed the concept of the algorithm.

The stars had always been of interest to Arabians, who used them to navigate across trackless desert. They were needed now to direct them toward Mecca for their prayers. Complying with one of the pillars of Islam, that of facing Mecca when Muslims prayed, required sophisticated knowledge of Earth's size and shape in order to determine the *qibla,* or "sacred directions," from anywhere in the Islamic Empire. Muslim astronomers produced exact tables and diagrams by which the proper direction could be determined.

Translated from Greek, Alexandrian astronomer Ptolemy's (ca. 87–150) *Syntaxis* (Great work), which described a geocentric solar system with the Earth at its center, rather than the correct heliocentric model that Copernicus would propose 500 years later, became

Between the seventh and ninth centuries Arab merchants plied their trade from the Atlantic Ocean to China and from southern Africa to Russia. Many merchants, as well as writers who never left their native cities, wrote accounts of these journeys. (Tales associated with the

the standard astronomical text of the era, known as *Al-Magest* or the *Almagest.*

Greek culture, or Hellenism, became the dominant scientific influence in the Islamic world. Initially, the bulk of the translations were done by Jews and, more commonly, Nestorian Christians from Syria. The latter translated the works into Aramaic (Syriac) and then into Arabic, simply transliterating Greek words with no Arabic equivalent. But little of Greek drama, poetry, or other literary works were translated into Arabic. Instead, Persia became the empire's primary literary influence.

Despite the lyricism of the Quran, poetry's popularity, or at least acceptance, in Arabia had not endured the coming of Islam. The themes of classical Arabic poetry—of sensual pleasures, battle and vengeance, and denial of an afterlife—were incompatible with the message of Islam. Persians, who shared a love of language with the Arabs, developed a modified form of Arabic into their own language, Farsi. It was the tongue of many of the empire's greatest writers, who used it to create verse that became a model for future poets of the empire. Since not all of these Persians converted to Islam, they were free to celebrate earthly delights in verse as Muslims could not. Persian poetry developed its style and reputation in the ninth and 10th centuries in the courts of the Samanids at Bokhara and later at Isfahan, coinciding with the decline of Abbasid power. The most influential of the first court poets were Rudaki and Daqiqi. In the West, the best-known Persian poet today, though he came sometime later, is Umar Khayyam, who wrote the *Rubaiyat.* As we will see, he was also a formidable scientist.

The epoch of translation lasted about a century, from 750 to 850, during which translations continued at an astonishing rate. Within 75 years of Baghdad's founding, the major works of Aristotle (fourth century B.C.), Galen's (A.D. second century) medical texts, and other Greek classics, along with Persian and Indian scientific works were available in Arabic. These works also transformed the character of Islam, from a faith originally identified with Arabian nationalism, into one of Islamic internationalism. The epoch was followed by an era in which Islamic scholars created great works of their own in the fields of science and literature, while Arabic grew into a richly adaptive language capable of expressing both scientific and philosophical concepts.

mythical voyages of Sinbad the Sailor, which would be incorporated into one of the era's most noted literary works, evolved from such accounts.) In the mid-ninth century, "road books," first-person accounts of various countries, began to appear. These were the first works of geography produced independently, without a patron's support. Maps also became common, primarily marking caravan routes, and some were published together in tomes sometimes called the "Atlas of Islam." Geography reached its zenith in the mid-10th century, represented by three great traveling chroniclers of the lands, all of whom borrowed from the maps in the Atlas of Islam in producing narratives of their travels, and whose works included maps of their own creation. Abu Ishaq Ibrahim ibn Muhammad al-Farisi al Istakhri wrote *Kitab al-masalik wa-al-mamalik* (Routes and realms) (ca. 950), which contained maps of each country of the Muslim world. Echoing al-Khwarizmi, Abu al-Qasim Muhammad ibn Hawqal, who traveled the Islamic world throughout the years 943–973, produced a *Kitab surat al-ard* (Picture book of the Earth). And Muhammad ibn Ahmad al-Maqdisi (ca. 946–1000), a traveler and geographer, wrote the *Kitab Al-Aqalim* (Book of countries).

In Arabia, Yemeni geographer and archaeologist Abu Muhammad Al Hasan ibn Ahmad al-Hamdani (d. 945) recorded the history and geography of Arabia, both Islamic and pre-Islamic, in two works: *Sifat Jazirat al Arab Jazirat al-Arab* (Geography of the Arabian Peninsula) and his multivolume *al Iklil* (The crown).

In the waning years of the Abbasid Empire the greatest of the eastern Islamic geographers appeared, Yaqut ibn Abdullah al-Hamawi (1179–1229). Sold to a traveling merchant in Baghdad as a boy, he was educated and then put to work as a clerk, eventually earning his emancipation. To support himself, Yaqut became an itinerant manuscript copier. Having traveled widely, his geographical dictionary, *Mujam al Buldan*, a compilation of toponyms, was a cornucopia of information on the geography, history, ethnography, and natural science of much of the Islamic world.

Astronomy

Deeply interested in the realms of heaven as well as Earth, many Islamic scholars devoted themselves to the study of astronomy and astrology. The same cartographic advances introduced to mapmaking of Earth were applied to the celestial sphere. By the early ninth century Muslim astronomers were making the first celestial observations employing fairly accurate instruments from an observatory in southwest Persia. These instruments included the astrolabe, a versatile pictographic analog computer introduced to the Islamic world from Greek translations and greatly refined during this era. The most widely used type, the planispheric astrolabe, could determine positions of stars, times of sunrise and sunset, current time, and altitude of heavenly bodies in the sky. It was also widely used for astrological purposes, such as fixing the position of stars and planets at the time of birth or conception. Abd al-Rahman (b. Umar al-Sufi; d. 986–987) wrote a treatise on astrolabes describing 1,000 uses for them. Often made of brass, they evolved into elaborate instruments and stunning works of artistry and craftsmanship. The main component was a round brass disk, called a plate, with a map of the celestial sphere, over which smaller disks, set off center, rotated. (The plates were made to be used at specific latitudes.) Other instruments used by astronomers of the era included celestial globes, which displayed the night sky, and quadrants, a quarter-circle marked in degrees from one to 90, with plumb bob attached to form a vertical reference line, for taking the position of celestial objects in reference to the horizon.

Such was their interest and influence in the study of the heavens that Arabs gave us the names of many stars in the night sky, including some of the best known: Sirius ("scorching," the brightest star in the sky); Deneb ("tail of the hen," as in the tail of Cygnus, the Swan); Aldebaran ("follower," as it followed the Pleiades into the sky). Terms such as "azimuth," "nadir," and "zenith" also come from the Arabs.

Astronomers charted celestial bodies with ever greater precision, while still supporting the Ptolemeic model of the geocentric universe, finding ways to explain the discrepancies they discovered. Leading astronomers included Abu Abdullah Muhammad ibn Jabir al Battani (Albatrunius), who worked in al Raqqah between 877 and 918. He refined the calculations on orbits of the moon and planets, the obliquity of the elliptic, and other celestial movements. In Afghanistan, an Arab of Persian descent, Abu al Rayhan Muhammad ibn Ahmad al-Biruni (973–1048), wrote works that discussed Earth's rotation on its axis, correctly determined the positions of latitudes and longitudes, and postulated hydrostatic principles.

Another noted astronomer and mathematician was the poet Umar Khayyam (Omar Khayyam; b. 1038–48; d. 1123–24). He worked as an astronomer at an observatory established by a Seljuk sultan at al Rayy or Naysabur, in Persia. Research by Khayyam and others resulted in refinement of the calendar, making it more accurate than the Gregorian calendar. He also made refinements in the algebra of al-Khwarizmi, introducing novel solutions and classifications of equations.

As part of his House of Wisdom, Caliph al-Mamun built an observatory where celestial movements were systematically tracked and

Islamic astronomers refined the astrolabe, an astronomical calculator, into a versatile instrument. One writer cataloged 1,000 uses for it. This partially transparent model on display in Dhahran illustrates their operation. (Courtesy of S. M. Amin/Aramco World/PADIA)

then compared against the computations of motion in the *Almagest*. Here, measurements of the obliquity of the ecliptic, the precession of the equinoxes, and the length of the solar year were refined. A second observatory was built near Damascus. Al-Mamun's astronomers were able to precisely measure the length of one terrestrial degree, allowing them to calculate the size of Earth and its circumference, accepting as they did that the Earth was round. Their result of 56.66 Arabic miles, or 20,400 miles (and a diameter of 5,600 miles) was respectably close to the actual distance of 25,000 miles. Observatories flourished in several other royal courts, and there was even one in a private home in Baghdad.

The destruction of the Abbasid dynasty and the city of Baghdad did not stop the intellectual advances of the empire. A year after he razed Baghdad in 1258, signaling the end of the Arabic Islamic Empire, Hulagu, the grandson of Genghis Khan, founded the Maraghah Observatory, one of the greatest observatories of the era. Astronomical studies continued into the 14th century and beyond.

Astrologers also added to knowledge. Abu Mashar (d. 886) was among the best known in the realm. Though he believed in the influence of celestial spheres on human events, he also described tidal action, which he connected to the movements of the moon.

Chemistry

The field of chemistry began in the laboratories of Arab alchemists. Alchemy was an ancient art that sought to transmute base substances into gold, the universal elixir. In many ways, this goal was also a metaphorical quest for spiritual perfection, and though these efforts were doomed, they nonetheless greatly expanded knowledge of the properties and reactions of chemicals. They also developed the essential elements of the scientific experiment that—based on observable, reproducible results—replaced the speculative, intuitive methods of the past.

The father of alchemy in the empire was Jabir ibn Hayyam (Geber in the West), from al Kufah, whose heyday was around 776. Today, as many as 100 treatises bearing his name survive in Latin and Arabic, though the great majority are not his. However, he is recognized for his contribution to knowledge about the chemical processes including calcination, reduction, evaporation, sublimation, melting, and crystallization. His ideas on metallurgy survived until the birth of modern chemistry in the 18th century.

Alchemy, the search for an elixir that would turn a base metal into gold, led to the development of chemistry. This manuscript page, from Baghdad in 1222 during the Abbasid caliphate, contains illustrated instructions on producing lead. (Courtesy of Giraudon/Art Resource, NY)

Hydrology

Hydrology, the science of water, so important in the dry lands that composed much of the empire, also received study. Irrigation techniques were developed and helped increase crop yields. The Abbasids also improved the region's ancient waterworks, a network of wells, underground canals, and waterwheels. The improvement in the water supply enhanced the empire's agriculture. New breeds of livestock were developed, and new crops, including cotton, were introduced. Over time, these agricultural changes helped alter diets in medieval Europe by introducing apricots, artichokes, cauliflower, celery, eggplant, fennel, plums, pumpkins, squash, rice, sorghum and new strains of wheat, along with dates and sugarcane.

Zoology

Unlike other natural sciences, the era's zoologists did not distinguish themselves or advance their field. Most works by its scholars were simply catalogs of species, including poems in which the animals were invoked. One animal, however, the horse, received serious attention, no doubt due to the almost mystical hold equines have exerted over the Arabs since history began. One writer on the subject of animals who is remembered is Abu Uthman Amr ibn Babr al-Jahiz, "the goggle-eyed" (d. 868–869), from Basra. Like much of the works on the subject, his *Kitab al Hayawan* (Book of animals) owes more to folklore and theology than biology. Indeed, he had more influence as a radical theologian than a naturalist and founded a Mutazilite sect. He was well known for his writing and his biting wit and, as his nickname implies, for extreme homeliness. What Hitti calls his "repulsive ugliness" made Caliph al-Mutawakkil decide not to hire al-Jahiz as his sons' tutor (Hitti 1953, 382).

Language and Poetry

The Arabs, with their great pride and interest in their language, were ardent students of lexicography, linguistics, and philology. Scholarly works began to appear early in the Abbasid reign and reached their peaks of achievement from the pens of non-Arabs such as the Turk al-Jawhari (d. ca. 1002), whose lexicon, with its alphabetical arrangement by final radical letter of words, became the standard model. Al-Jawhari was emblematic of the interest in language studies that went beyond Islam's Arabs alone. Indeed, what is traditionally termed Arabic literature reflects little Arabian influence. The great Arab historian Abdal Rahman ibn Khaldun (1332–1406) had a chapter in his *Muquddammah* (Introduction to history) entitled "Most of the learned men in Islam were non-Arabians" (Ibn Khaldun, 477). By al-Jawhari's time, the Persian style, with its elegant and affected linguistic flourishes, had supplanted the simple and direct style of Arabian poetry, discussed in chapter 1, whose language was much more succinct and virile.

Yet while Arabian poetry was no longer in style, its influence remained constant. Poets, no matter how urbanized, invoked images of the desert in their verse, a practice that continued into modern times. The Abbasid poets looked to odes of the Umayyads for models for their classic poetry, though as noted earlier, the style they emulated was itself an imitation of the true pre-Islamic poetry of the Jahiliyya.

Literature

New literary genres appeared, such as *adab*. Meaning literally "manners," "good breeding," or "culture," the *adab* includes a large range of literature concerned with social behavior. The stories, often humorous, have a moral, sometimes taking the form of animal fables, similar to Aesop's allegories. Among the most noted *adab* is *Kalilah wa-Dimnah* (Fables of Bidpai), written as a primer for princes in "the laws of polity," translated by Ibn al-Muqaffa (d. 757) from a Pahlavi (pre-Islamic Persian language) version of an Indian work, which itself was based on Buddhist fable books. The translation, with its ornate imagery and flowery language, is another demonstration of the Persian influence in Golden Age literature. Ibn al-Muqaffa was a former Zoroastrian who converted to Islam, but doubts about the sincerity of his belief led to his death by fire in about 757.

Ethics were addressed in works of philosophy that examined mystical and psychological aspects of morality. Another new literary genre, the *maqamah* (assembly) took the form of a dramatic anecdote composed in the rhymed prose style of ancient *saj*. Providing a vehicle for its author to display all his eloquence and learning, it is credited to Badi al-Zaman al-Hamadhani (969–1008), and its definitive example, *Maqamath* (Assemblies, or seances), by al-Hariri of Basra (1054–1122), was considered second only to the Quran as the greatest treasure of the Arabic language for centuries. *Maqamah* itself is regarded as the most perfect form of literary and dramatic expression in Arabic.

The most famous work of Arabic literature in the West, the *Thousand and One Nights (Alf Laylah wa-Laylah)*, first appeared in Mesopotamia in the mid-10th century. Taken mostly from the Persian work *Hazar*

CALLIGRAPHY

Calligraphy evolved into the primary form of the visual arts in Islam. Early Muslims considered it blasphemous to render God in a visual form and forbid creations of His likeness, a prohibition known as *aniconism*. In time, Sunni Muslims expanded the prohibition to include any living thing, as each being contained a kernel of the divine. However, not all Muslim societies espoused aniconism, and thus figurative art was produced in many parts of the Islamic Empire. Persian miniatures are an example of such representational art. Figurative art was also produced under the Umayyads and the Fatimids and, later, under the Ottomans. However, believers who eschew such representations would argue such art is inherently un-Islamic.

Rather than use figurative art to pay homage to their God, as was done in the West, Islamic artists used His language. Written Arabic itself, often in the form of Quranic verses, became their canvas. The flexibility of the letters allowed artists to shape them in many ways, adding another level of meaning to the words themselves.

Two written forms of Arabic existed early in its development. Kufic, named for the town of Kufa in Iraq, though the style predated it, was a thick, blocklike ornamental form with formal flourishes. Naskhi, more rounded, flowing, and less ornamental, was used in letters and business correspondence. Kufic was the calligraphy style used to write the first Qurans. During the Umayyad dynasty, calligraphers transformed the heavy Kufic script into a more flexible, decorative form, developing new styles that brought supple artistry into the writing of words. Naskhi, meanwhile, became the form from which most modern Arabic calligraphy developed.

Under the Abbasids, Kufic script evolved further. Formal rules for the proportion and shape of its characters were codified by the first half of

Afsana (Thousand tales), itself a derivative of an Indian compilation of stories, it was compiled in Arabic by Muhammad ibn Abdus al-Jahshiyari (d. 942), who added local stories that gave it a plot and structure. "Aladdin," "Sinbad the Sailor," and "Ali Baba and the 40 Thieves" are among its many stories. Over centuries, more folk tales from around the world were added. The court of Harun al-Rashid figures prominently as the source of many of its humorous episodes and tales of romance. It appeared in its final form in Arabic in Egypt during the late Mamluk dynasty in the 14th century. Among Arabs, it does not enjoy the same popularity that it does in the West.

---

the 10th century. Yet by the 12th century, Kufic script was no longer in widespread use. The 10th-century Abbasid vizier Ibn Muqlah, an acclaimed calligrapher himself (even after his hand was amputated by one of the three caliphs he served), formalized the rules for Kufic and established the classification of the six styles of Arabic cursive script, Naskhi being the first. The others were: Thuluth, a more flowing cursive form of Naskhi; Rayhani, a more elaborate version of Thuluth; Tawqi, a compressed form of Thuluth in which all letters may be connected together; Muhaqqaq, composed of bold, sweeping lines with diagonal flourishes; and Ruqah, a simple form commonly used throughout the Arab world today.

Calligraphers also molded Arabic script—typically expressions of faith or well-known Quranic verses—into the shape of animals or inanimate objects, a form termed pictorial calligraphy. Kufic script, with its block-like characters, was sometimes rendered in pictographic form to appear like a building, such as a mosque with minarets.

Calligraphy developed into Islam's primary visual art form. This example of pictorial calligraphy, which reads, "In the name of God, the most merciful, the most compassionate," was created in 19th-century India. (Courtesy of Victoria & Albert Museum, London/Art Resource, NY)

Sharia—Law of the Muslims

One area of scientific inquiry was the province of Arab scholars: law, as ascertained by theology. Sharia, as the law is known, provides rules for political and social as well as legal conduct. Quranic study and the need to understand the word of God drove this field. Law was regarded as the practical application of Quranic injunctions. Unlike Western jurisprudence, which is fluid and can be modified to reflect changing times and beliefs, Islamic law was considered immutable. Derived from the divine, the interpretation by which the body of opinions and rules was developed was likewise considered divinely inspired, and therefore it could not be altered. *Sharia* also incorporated non-Islamic elements, including Bedouin tribal law, Meccan and Medinese law, and those of conquered lands.

Besides the Quran, the sunnah—or the actions, words, and silent approval *(taqrir)* attributed to Muhammad—were a secondary source of orthodox doctrine. In the second century of Islam, the sunnah were gathered and formalized as the Hadith, or accepted facts about Muhammad's words and deeds (in addition, technically, to those of his Companions and their successors). Muhammad had said, according to one hadith, "Seek ye learning, though it be in China" (Hitti 1953, 393), and thus many nascent scholars embarked on long and difficult journeys throughout the empire as a prelude to their theological studies.

Fiqh is the science of sharia, and sometimes the two terms are used synonymously. *Fiqh* covers three kinds of regulations: those relating to worship and religious observances *(ibadat)*, civil and legal law *(muamalat)*, and punishments *(uqubat)*. Legal scholars soon realized that the some 200 verses in the Quran dealing with legal issues (out of the approximately 6,000 verses it contains) did not cover all the situations that called for legal adjudication. Nor did the Hadith provide guidance for all the issues the Quran did not address. This called for scientific speculation, which created two new principles of Islamic jurisprudence: the use of analogies *(qiyas)* and consensus of opinion *(ijma)*. The practice of ijma allowed the law to be expanded (but not changed) to meet evolving realities and novel situations. *Qiyas* allowed established law to be applied to questions of justice for which no ruling existed.

A class of learned experts—authorities on the Quran and the Hadith—arose, called ulama or ulema *(alim,* singular). Meant to represent the community of Islam (ummah), they took up the role of arbiters of law. Thus, they have traditionally served as a powerful force to keep secular rulers, the caliphs, acting within the Quranic law and following the faith. Since the decision on matters of law reached by the *ummah* (or the ulama acting in their name) through consensus was thought to be divinely guided, in theory there could never be a need or a possibility to revisit a matter of sharia once it had been established. New interpretations of the text on which legal decisions were based were considered heretical. Only areas of law on which agreement did not yet exist could be a subject of debate. In practice, however, disagreement over the interpretation of the law was widespread. Over time, as more and more legal opinions were adopted, scholars lost their role as arbiters and interpreters of the law, and became its catalogers.

Punishments prescribed under sharia and sanctioned in the Quran and Hadith include amputation, the branding of foreheads, eye gouging, and stoning as a means of execution. "By Him in whose Hand my soul is!" the Prophet Muhammad is said to have exclaimed, according to the hadith *Sahih al-Bukhari* (8:81:78), "If Fatima (his daughter) stole aught I would cut off her hand." At least half a dozen hadith and a pair of verses in the Quran condone amputations of the hand for thievery. Amputations as well as beheadings are still carried out in the kingdom in public today, though statistics on their application are not made public.

Citizens in the Islamic Empire could avail themselves of courts outside the legal system officiated by *qadis* to seek redress of wrongs, called *mazalim*. In religious, and sometimes in *mazalim*, courts, a summary of any important case was given to a legal expert to solicit his opinion. Such a jurist was called a mufti. The mufti's ruling was issued in a fatwa, or statement of legal issues. Muftis generally were independent of the state, but they became part of the secular administration during the Ottoman Empire, holding a rank just below the *qadis* (Islamic judges). However, the chief mufti of Constantinople, the sheikh al-Islam, was the empire's highest religious authority.

The Four Schools of Law

The first Muslim schools, or traditions, of law were established in Mesopotamia and Syria before the end of the Umayyad dynasty in 750. During the Umayyad reign, early laws were established under Arab Islamic governors by *qadis* who melded accepted local traditions and rules with their own opinion and Quranic principles on an ad hoc basis. Governors were appointed by the caliph, and they in turn appointed the *qadis*.

During the Abbasid caliphate a uniform legal system became critical in order for uniform justice to be applied throughout the growing

Islamic world. Moreover, the laws had to win universal acceptance. Over time, four major approaches, or schools of Sunni law, developed (Shia having their own interpretation of sharia), each bearing the name of the scholar who introduced it: Maliki, Shafi'i, Hanafi, and Hanbali.

Hanafi

Some Muslims believed individual reasoning should play a role in the interpretation and definition of law. The chief advocate of this view was al Numan ibn Thabit, also known as Abu Hanifa (d. 767). A merchant and grandson of a Persian slave who lived in Kufa and Baghdad, he was Islam's first and most influential legal scholar and founder of the largest and most tolerant school of Islamic law. Abu Hanifa believed in the propriety of departing from analogy as a means of deducing law if it led to seemingly inequitable solutions, and relying on reason instead, a practice called "preference." Today, Hanafi law predominates in Turkey and Pakistan.

The Abbasids, having their capital in Baghdad, favored this school as it was developed in Mesopotamia and thus reflected the region's attitudes and practices. Abu Hanifa declined to accept the post of chief *qadi* from Caliph Abu Jafar Mansur and was sent to prison for his reticence, where he soon died. However, two of his disciples, Abu Yusef and Muhammad-Shaibini, held important positions and promulgated his teachings in their writings.

Maliki

Arabia, as noted, was relatively uninvolved in the achievements of the Golden Age, but Medina was an important literary and intellectual center of the era, particularly in its contributions to the codification of Islamic law. Here the Maliki school was founded by Malik ibn Anas (ca. 715–795), a practicing *qadi*. The Maliki school placed its emphasis on the Hadith as an interpretive tool. The past rulings of the Medinese *qadis* gathered by ibn Anas, called the *al-Muwatta* (leveled path), is one of the oldest treatises on Islamic law, codifying the sunnah and procedures used to obtain *ijma*, or consensus. Today this school is the one followed throughout north Africa. It is more conservative than the Hanafi school.

Shafi'i

Muhammad ibn Idris al-Shafi'i (767–820) founded the school that bears his name. A member of Arabia's powerful Quraysh tribe born in Gaza, al-

Shafi'i studied under Malik in Medina. He advocated a compromise between the Malik and Hanifa schools, accepting speculation, but only in prescribed manner and circumstance. The Shafi'i school blended adherence to accepted prophetic tradition (as distinct from Medinese tradition) with elements of the Hanifa school's reliance on *qiyas,* or analogical deduction. His school is today followed in parts of Egypt and East Africa, western and southern Arabia, coastal areas of India, and the Far East.

Hanbali

Another student of Malik founded the fourth of the recognized schools of Islamic law. Ahmad ibn Hanbal (780–855) took a more conservative view than Malik, espousing unwavering adherence to a literal interpretation of the Hadith. (As an extreme example, the Hadith established that urinating in a water source used for drinking was forbidden; but nothing in the Hadith specifically forbade defecating in a water source used thusly, so the Hanbali school viewed such action as permissible.) This brought him into conflict with the ruling powers in Baghdad where, under Caliph al-Mamun, Mutazalite innovations, which held that religions interpretations should be consistent with reason, found favor. Al-Mamun had Hanbal imprisoned and tortured, but Hanbal refused to recant his views. Such was his popularity that his funeral in 855 drew a crowd said to number 800,000 men. This was the school followed by Muhammad ibn Abd al-Wahhab in the 1700s, whose partnership with the House of Saud would lead to the establishment of the Kingdom of Saudi Arabia. Today, the Hanbali school forms the basis of the legal system in Saudi Arabia.

The Hanafi, Maliki, and Shafi'i schools shared the same thinking on important matters. All recognized the same sources, the Quran and the Hadith, and they accepted both the practice of *ijma* and some form of *qiya* (analogical reasoning). Also, all recognized the four systems as legitimate. However, Hanbali adherents were generally less accepting of the other schools.

The Shia, unlike the Sunni who are enjoined from further judicial development, have *mujtahids,* scholars who can speak for the sublime and perfect hidden imam and interpret his thoughts, thus allowing new religious laws to be created.

The End of Islam's Golden Age

The end of the Abbasid caliphate marked a turning point for the Golden Age. With the assumption of the caliphate by the Turkish Seljuks in 1057, the already declining central power that held the empire together further weakened. Moreover, Islam was wracked by religious schisms, accusations of heresy, sectarian violence, and assassinations. Orthodoxy was in decline, eroded by the Aristotelian logic that had been adopted as the basis for the scientific and philosophical inquiry that underpinned the advances of the Golden Age. This created a backlash that gave rise to a conservative theological movement that soon spread through Islam, one of the factors behind the hobbling of intellectual development. A theologian named Abu Hamid al-Ghazali (1058–1111) began to speak out against the value of reason. In his most influential book, *Tahaful al-Falasifa* (The incoherence, or inconsistency, of philosophy), he declared that experience that grew from reason was not trustworthy and illuminated nothing about the reality of Allah. Only direct intuition of God, he preached, which was antithetical to reason, could be trusted. (His beliefs and renown earned him the title in the West as the "St. Thomas Aquinas of orthodox Islam.") Al-Ghazali held that philosophy was a trap that led to the depths of hell. He championed the orthodox traditionalist ideas of Abu Hasan al-Ashari (ca. 873–935), creating a comprehensive ideological foundation for Sunni belief. His crusade against reason resonated with many, and by the time of his death in 1111, the scientific investigation and the philosophical and theological inquiry that had marked the Golden Age were coming to an end.

The reasons behind the stagnation of advances in the arts and sciences are complex and manifold. Clearly one is Islam's traditional reverence for the past and its ways, which began to shackle it to former glories rather than making efforts that would serve to build upon them. External pressures also helped bring the Golden Age to an end. The instability wrought by the Crusades (1097–1291) contributed to the decline, as did the political decay of the empire itself.

The Arab Islamic Empire came to an end when Baghdad fell to the Mongols in 1258. The invaders sacked the capital city and slaughtered its inhabitants. Without a central administration, the crumbling empire dissolved. Trade routes became unsafe, and even urban centers became lawless. Communities and cities withdrew into feudal isolation.

The Golden Age in Arabia

Arabia's major contribution to the Golden Age was the religious scholarship and discourse that led to the codification of Islamic law, and the school of law Malik ibn Anas developed from there. The Najd, which would play a large role in the birth of the future kingdom of Saudi Arabia, was largely uninhabited by sedentary populations, and the

Bedouin tasted little of the fruits of the Golden Age. With the decline of the caliphate in Baghdad, the road from the Abbasid capital to Mecca became less secure. Travelers sought alternative routes, further isolating Arabia's interior. This trend became more pronounced after the fall of Baghdad to the Mongols, as navigation of the Red Sea was mastered and pilgrims increasingly traveled to Arabia by ship. Though Medina had become something of an intellectual center in the eighth and ninth centuries as sharia evolved, once the rules had been established, little further scholarly examination or discussion was required, costing the city its intellectual edge. And Mecca, though noteworthy for its spiritual significance, was never a cultural or political power center of the empire.

Mecca and Hijaz did, however, gain exposure to the cultural and economic growth of the age through the annual influx of hajjis, making the region, and certainly Mecca, relatively worldly. The pilgrimage was a ceremonial occasion for which the caliph put the wealth and magnificence of his office on display. Zubaydah, cousin and wife of Caliph al-Rashid, who set the fashion for her age and was the first to decorate her shoes with precious stones, spent vast sums during a pilgrimage to Mecca, which included supplying the city with water from a well 25 miles away.

It was Hijaz's spiritual importance, the economic engine the holy cities represented, and military weakness that led to its subjugation by a series of outside regimes after the fall of Baghdad. The pilgrimage gradually became a carnival-like event, a time of licentiousness and un-Islamic behavior, and this eventually divided Arabia. To the growing population of Najd, the sinful ways of Hijaz were an abomination, feelings no doubt aggravated by classic urban versus rural antagonisms. The escalating strains would be felt in coming years, when the seeds of a reform movement that would sweep the peninsula began to grow in the harsh desert of central Arabia.

5

THE MAMLUKS,
THE OTTOMANS,
AND THE WAHHABI–AL
SAUD ALLIANCE
(1258–1745)

The razing of Baghdad by Hulagu Khan and the Mongols in 1258 marked the end of the Arab Islamic Empire. Centuries would pass before the region recovered from the depredations of the invaders. Islam ultimately vanquished its conquerors, as the Mongols converted to the religion of Muhammad. But the empire and its ruler, be he caliph or sultan, would never again have a direct connection to its Arabian roots. Nonetheless, Arabia remained a preoccupation of these leaders, as their role as *Khadim al-Haramain al-Sharifain* (protector of the two holy sites) gave their regimes legitimacy. A succession of rulers of the Mamluk and Ottoman empires claimed this mantle. After five centuries, an effort to drive out the occupiers—and to conquer and unite all of Arabia from within—commenced with an alliance between a conservative religious reformer, Muhammad Abd al-Wahhab, and a village sheikh, Muhammad Al Saud. This chapter surveys the events of these years.

Mamluk Rule in Arabia

At the time of the Mongol invasion of Baghdad, Hijaz was under the control of the Abbasid caliphate. Egypt, Syria, and Palestine had only recently come under the rule of the Mamluks, former Turkish slaves who evolved into a class of mercenaries and military leaders. Though the power they exercised in Baghdad during the Abbasid dynasty had been lost to the Seljuks some two centuries before, the Mamluks' subsequent takeover of the Fatimid caliphate in Egypt gave them a new seat of power.

By 1250 the Mamluks had conquered the Ayyubid dynasty, whose capital was Damascus. A decade later, two years after sacking Baghdad, the Mongols mounted a campaign against the Mamluks, sending an army against their forces in Palestine and Egypt. Warned of the coming attack by a chain of signal fires stretching from Iraq to Egypt, the Mamluks decisively defeated the Mongols at the Battle of Ayn Jalut (Goliath's Well) near Nazareth in Palestine. As the Mongols had inherited Arabia from the Abbasids with their victory, now it fell to the Mamluks, who retained control for more than two and a half centuries from Cairo.

Mecca

The instability in Mecca that prevailed near the end of the Abbasid era subsided with the assumption of office by Sharif Muhammad Abu Numayy (r. 1254–1301), great-grandson of Sharif Qatada ibn Idris. The shift from Abbasid suzerainty over Hijaz to that of the Mamluks early in his reign caused few ripples in Hijaz. However, Abu Numayy's uncle Idris ibn Qatada contested his rule from the beginning of his sharifate. The two periodically battled until Abu Numayy defeated ibn Qatada's forces and personally beheaded his uncle in 1270.

Before his death in 1301, Abu Numayy abdicated in favor of two sons he designated as successors, Humayda and Rumaytha. But after his

ARABIA'S SEAFARING TRADITION

For all its desert, Arabia has a rich seafaring history. Arabs' prowess as voyagers and seamen is celebrated in the legend of Sinbad the Sailor, a hero in the collection of stories known as *The Thousand and One Nights,* who, according to lore, came from the area of what is now Oman. Dhows, the traditional single-masted ships of Arabia with their triangular lateen sails, long plied the Indian Ocean, conducting extensive trade with India. The peninsula's strategic location made it an important waypoint and provisioning stop on the trade routes for ships from east Africa, Persia, and India. Yet relatively little maritime activity occurred on the Red Sea, a situation that began to change in the 13th century, when the growth of cities in Europe provided a market for luxuries that had ceased movement through the Mediterranean with the decline of the Roman Empire. Technological advances—compasses and improved ship design and construction among them—also aided the development of trade.

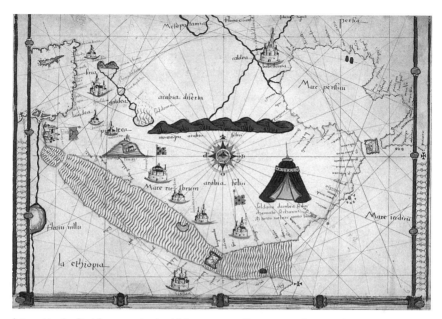

Interest in the Red Sea grew in the 15th century as European traders sought ways to circumvent Arabia. Overland trade suffered as a result. This map of the Red Sea was created by 15th-century Italian cartographer Jacopo Russo. (Courtesy of Alinari/Art Resource, NY)

passing, his sons (he reportedly had more than 30) began battling for rule. Humayda's death in 1320, at the hands of one of his slaves, temporarily ended the instability, with rule of Mecca then shared by Rumaytha and his brother Utayfa. But by 1330 these two were fighting each other and neglecting their duties as guardians of the holy sites. Sultan al-Malik al-Nasir (r. 1294–95, 1299–1309, 1309–40) summoned both to Cairo, but the two, fearful of the consequences, resolved their differences and united in defiance of al-Malik. The sultan was prepared to send his army to drive all Hashemites from Mecca, but he was persuaded by his advisers to recognize Rumaytha as sharif instead. As throughout history, the sharifs had demonstrated not only how vexing they could be to the empire's ruler but how little choice their titular sovereign had in finding a more effective partner in maintaining regional stability, the legitimacy of their regime, and a stake in the region's enterprises.

Maritime Trade

The port of Jeddah, 45 miles west of Mecca on the Red Sea, enabled Arabia to play a growing role in maritime commerce. Founded in about 646 by Caliph Uthman, the port's fortunes grew with those of the Red

Sea trade. The maritime activity also benefited from the removal of the Franks (as the Crusader forces were called), who were active up to the late 12th century, from the area. The Mamluks exercised little control over the Red Sea itself, but they regulated the ports on both the Arabian and African coasts. Large revenues came from taxes and other fees levied on goods from India and east Africa off-loaded for shipment to Cairo, and from the subsequent sale of goods to European traders. The sharif of Mecca also realized substantial income from trade passing through Jeddah. He also derived income from fees, illegal or otherwise, levied on hajjis. According to Islamic law, pilgrims were not to be taxed, a policy that the Egyptian rulers who claimed title as protectors of the holy sites typically upheld. But the sharif of Mecca was far from scrupulous about the law's observation. When forced to comply, the sharif often made up the resulting shortfall in income by adding further taxes

The port of Jeddah, established in the seventh century, enabled Hijazis and the sharifs of Mecca to benefit from the Red Sea trade as it grew some eight centuries later. The tableau of these dhows at the quay in 1950 is likely similar to port activity of centuries before. (Courtesy of the Fine Arts Library, Harvard College Library)

on the merchants of Jeddah. The share that the sharif took of all goods passing through the city became so high that in 1395 traders reportedly sought alternative ports. The taxes the sharif levied on goods became more of a point of contention with the Mamluk rulers than the taxes on pilgrims, due to the potential disruption of the lucrative trade it threatened. By 1425, the absentee landlords in Egypt had installed their own collection agents in Jeddah, handing over to the sharif his due share. This was the beginning of direct oversight of the sharifs by those in whose name they ruled. A garrison of Egyptian forces at Jeddah and a small contingent of Mamluk soldiers in Mecca ensured compliance with Cairo's decrees on commerce.

To further enforce the new rule, the Mamluk sultan Barsbay (r. 1422–38) refused to recognize Barakat as successor to his father, Sharif Hasan ibn Ajlan (d. 1425) until Barakat paid the amount the sultan claimed his father owed him. The sultan also struck down the collection of duties from Indian ships using the port of Jeddah, leading to an increase in the port traffic at the expense of Aden, on the southwest tip of the peninsula, which had previously been the dominant Red Sea port. By the end of the century, about 100 Indian ships a year were arriving in Jeddah, where prior to the elimination of the duties, a little over a dozen dropped anchor in the harbor annually.

Pilgrims who arrived by boat in Jeddah for the hajj would pass through the Gates of Mecca when leaving the port on their way to the holy city. (Courtesy of the Fine Arts Library, Harvard College Library)

FOREIGN FLEETS

During this era far-flung nations first established maritime contact with Arabia, attempting to gain influence and control over trade routes between Europe, the Far East, and Africa. The Europeans wanted to bypass the Arab middlemen and the Ottoman and Mamluk rulers who controlled access to the sources of gold, slaves, spices, and other luxury goods. But Arabia's first direct contact with states at the terminus of trade routes came not from Europe but from the East. From 1405 to 1433, the Chinese set out in fleets of giant nine-masted junks and reached Arabia. With support vessels, the crews of these armadas reportedly reached more than 27,000 sailors and soldiers. Yet less than a century later, China forbade all overseas trade, ending this intriguing chapter in both Arabian and Chinese history.

Early in the 15th century, European powers began serious efforts to establish direct contacts with the sources of commodities in east Africa and Asia. Portugal in particular began an ambitious program under Prince Henry "the Navigator" (1394–1460) to find a route around Africa. In 1487 a Portuguese ship under Bartholomeu Dias succeeded in rounding the Cape of Good Hope, the southern tip of Africa, a milestone in this effort. Ten years later, Vasco da Gama left Lisbon and reached India via this route, returning home with spices and gems.

Battles with Portugal

Following Vasco da Gama's successful voyage to India (1497–99), expeditions from Portugal were charged with converting heathens, establishing trading outposts, blockading the Red Sea, and disrupting Arab trade with India. The Portuguese seized cargoes and scuttled the Indian trading ships they found, and by 1504 the blockade and disruption of trade were affecting Cairo's fortunes. The subsequent loss of income in Arabia also lessened Egypt's power in the peninsula. A revolt in Yanbu, the Arabian port north of Jeddah, brought a local ruler to power. Egyptian forces were dispatched to deal with both the rebellious Arabians and plundering Portuguese. A force under Husayn Mushrif, also known as Husayn al-Kurdi, first suppressed the rebellion in Yanbu, then fortified Jeddah before sailing on to India to confront the Portuguese at one of their outposts.

In 1507, while Husayn Mushrif was thus engaged, a Portuguese fleet of seven ships and 500 men under Alfonso d'Albuquerque (1453–1515) seized ports and established fortified outposts on the coasts of east

Africa and Arabia. Muscat, Oman, was pillaged and plundered, and fortifications were built at the strategic Strait of Hormuz, from where
Persian Gulf traffic could be controlled.

In 1508 Husayn Mushrif, having arrived in India and allied himself
with local forces, defeated the Portuguese. But the following year the
Portuguese forces counterattacked, achieving a decisive and bloody victory. D'Albuquerque, who became viceroy and commander of all
Portuguese forces in the east in 1510, spent several years in the area trying to establish Portuguese domination along the trade routes. He
unsuccessfully attacked Aden and Mecca, and had even planned an
assault on Medina in hopes of making off with Muhammad's body to
trade for the city of Jerusalem.

In 1515 Husayn Mushrif led another Egyptian force against the
Portuguese. The Egyptians established a fort on Kamaran Island, at the
mouth of the Red Sea, discomfiting the local population, whose concern

*By the 14th century European seafarers were expanding the West's reach eastward. The
Portuguese were most active in trying to establish control over the trade routes. These
remnants of a Portuguese fortress in Hasa attest to the inroads they made. In the foreground
are Bedouin shepherds with their sheep. These animals were second only to camels in their
importance to the Bedouin.* (Courtesy of Robert Yarnall Richie/Aramco World/PADIA)

about foreign designs was not confined to the Portuguese. Indeed, the primary engagements of Husayn Mushrif's campaign devolved into unsuccessful efforts to conquer Aden. This was among the last military campaigns of the Mamluks.

The Ottomans in Arabia

The Ottomans, ethnic Turks who were also Sunni Muslims, began expanding their territory in Anatolia soon after the Abbasids fell to the Mongols. After capturing Constantinople in 1453, the Ottomans made it their capital. (The city did not officially change its name to Istanbul until 1930, but "Stambul," from the Greek meaning "in the city," was what its inhabitants had long called a major section of the sprawling metropolis.) In 1517, under Sultan Selim I (r. 1512–20), the Ottomans defeated the Mamluk armies in Syria and Egypt, and seized Cairo. Mamluks would continue to play a role in the administration of the lands they once ruled, but the defeat ended their empire. As a result of the victory, the Ottomans gained control of Hijaz, which had been under Mamluk suzerainty. Constantinople would become the center of a new Islamic Empire.

Sultan Selim assumed the title of protector of the holy sites. In Mecca, the sultan's name was mentioned during Friday prayers, an important acknowledgment of his rule. Not content to exercise hands-off control as the Mamluks had done, after their 1517 victory the Ottomans launched campaigns to subjugate Arabia. Selim's successor, Sulaiman the Lawgiver (Suleiman [or Süleyman] the Magnificent in the West, r. 1520–66), extended Ottoman power farther south along the Red Sea coast.

The Porte, or Sublime Porte, the term for the court of the Ottoman ruler, formally invested the sharif as Mecca's ruler, a position reaffirmed annually during

After millennia of isolation, the Arabian Peninsula was becoming more known in Europe, as this map by Italian cartographer Ignazio Danti (1536–86) illustrates. (Courtesy of Scala/Art Resource, NY)

the hajj. Not surprisingly, Ottoman relations with the sharifs were often strained. At times, the Ottomans appointed sharifs of their choosing to rule Mecca, but such rulers were typically unpopular, and thus often counterproductive to the Porte's strategic interests. And despite Ottoman efforts to extend their power in the region beyond Mecca, Arabia remained largely independent.

In 1534 Sulaiman's troops conquered Baghdad. The city was but a shadow of its former glory, its circumstances further reduced by the change from overland to maritime trade routes from the Orient, but it served as a point from which to extend Ottoman control over Arabia from the east, and attempt to exert viselike pressure on the peninsula's independent powers. In the last years of the 1500s the Ottomans invaded and occupied the province of Hasa, near the Persian Gulf coast, from Iraq. Fatih Pasha became the region's first Ottoman military governor following his defeat of the local dynasty in 1591. The occupation of Hasa gave the Ottomans a foothold and position of influence in central and eastern Arabia.

Some 30 years later, in 1622, Ali Pasha, the son of Fatih Pasha's successor, entertained the future sharif of Mecca, Muhsin ibn Husain ibn Hasan (1610–28) and his cousins when they visited Hufuf, Hasa's major town. Ottoman power in Hasa was dimmed in 1623 when Persian forces captured Baghdad. But after retaking the city in 1638 the Ottomans increased their presence in eastern Arabia, though their sphere of influence remained small. A series of Ottoman governors ruled over Hasa until 1669, when a local clan clashed with them, driving the outsiders from Hasa and ending some eight decades of Ottoman rule in the area. The Ottomans fared better in Hijaz. By 1700 the Ottomans had control of the entire west coast of the peninsula. Yet opposition to the foreign power and to the rising secularism that came with it sparked a reform movement that would prove to be the invaders' undoing.

Mecca

In spite of the decline of the Islamic Empire, the pilgrimage retained its importance to the faithful. In 1506, 30,000 pilgrims arrived in Mecca from Hasa in one caravan train alone. Yet the hazards of the journey remained manifold. In 1630 during the rule of Sharif Masud I ibn Idris (r. 1629–30), a flash flood swept the Holy City, almost completely destroying the Kaaba. The reconstruction took seven years. Its restoration was marked in an impressive reconsecration ceremony during the hajj season in 1636. In 1680, another flood in Mecca sent water levels reaching at least 10 feet above ground, up to the Kaaba door. Some 100 people drowned and homes and property were destroyed.

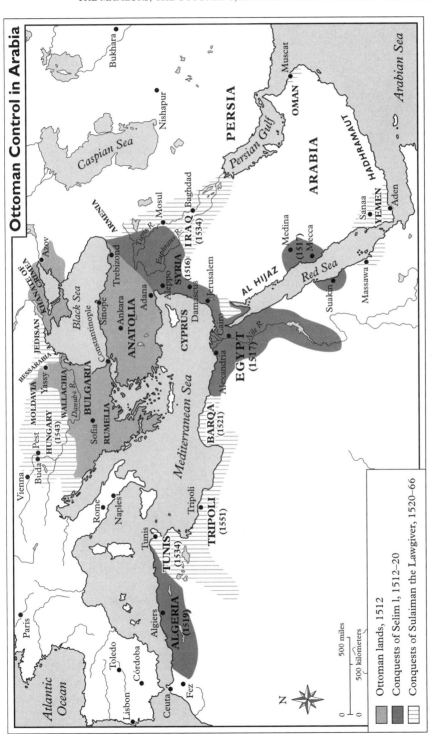

Ottoman Control in Arabia

By the mid-16th century, Ottoman control of Arabia extended over both the east and west coasts of the peninsula. Domination of the interior proved more elusive.

Ottoman lands, 1512

Conquests of Selim I, 1512–20

Conquests of Sulaiman the Lawgiver, 1520–66

The sharifs made occasional forays into the desert to plunder and punish Najdi tribes who mounted raids on oases and tribes in Hijaz. The first account of such a campaign, by historian Uthman ibn Abdallah ibn Bishr (d. 1871/72), recounts a 1578 invasion involving 50,000 warriors. (The accuracy of his figures has been questioned.) According to his record, the troops reached Riyadh, which they sacked. After appointing a new ruler and imprisoning several influential citizens, the sharif's forces returned to Mecca. The prisoners were released after a year in exchange for an agreement to pay an annual tribute. Such actions were thereafter repeated every few years by succeeding sharifs until the early 1700s, though they rarely penetrated as deeply into Najd as had the first invasion. Atrocities often accompanied the campaigns, as did the temporary banishment or imprisonment of key members of leading families of conquered settlements. Typically, after military victory, a leader allied with the sharif was installed and tribute was exacted. But control over local populations was difficult to maintain, a situation compounded by the challenge of staging campaigns in the harsh desert environment. The first definitive record of the sharifs' claim over central Arabia dates to 1667, during the reign of Sad ibn Zaid, who first ruled from 1665 until some time before 1680. However, the earlier incursions attest to the acceptance of this territorial right among the sharifs before this time.

With various branches of the Hashemite clan vying for leadership, the position of sharif was often unstable. At least four sharifs held office in the decade after Sad ibn Zaid's first reign ended in 1680. One of them was Said ibn Sad ibn Zaid (d. ca. 1728), the son who deposed him. Said himself served as sharif four different times, and one of the intervening rulers was Sad, the father he supplanted, who had regained control of Mecca by the end of the 1600s. In 1697 a large raid was led into Najd in the name of Sharif Sad. The province of Sudair, whose ongoing restiveness and lack of obeisance was deemed worthy of punishment, was the major objective. In 1699 Sharif Sad imprisoned 100 captured leaders of the Anaza tribe in Mecca. Several punitive raids were mounted against Bedouin tribes in the following two years.

Serious famine gripped Hijaz in 1702, and Sharif Sad, made unpopular by the shortage of food, voluntarily turned his rule back to Said sometime late that year or early the next, marking his son's third reign. But the famine continued, causing great unrest in Hijaz even as it decimated the population. Sensing he was losing the support of the Sublime Porte's proxy in the area, Sulaiman Pasha, the "Pasha of Jeddah," Said then abdicated in favor of his nephew, Abdul-Muhsin ibn Ahmad ibn Zaid. But Sulaiman Pasha opposed the succession, and within nine days

Abdul-Muhsin resigned and the Ottoman-backed candidate, Abdul-Karim ibn Muhammad ibn Yala, a member of another branch of the ruling family, was named sharif of Mecca. Both Said and his father Sad were exiled from Mecca.

The famine made it impossible to continue raids into the peninsula's heartland, and under the Ottomans' sharif, no military action was undertaken in Najd. But his Turkish backing made Abdul-Karim unpopular, and by 1711 Said ibn Sad had returned from exile and deposed him, becoming the sharif of Mecca for the fourth time. He retained the title until his death in 1717. Said was succeeded by Sharif Muhsin ibn Abdullah. Muhsin mounted a campaign in the Najd during the winter of 1726–27, the first such incursion from Mecca in almost a quarter century. But it was the last large-scale campaign on Najd launched by the sharif's forces.

Central Arabia and the Origins of Al Saud

Central Arabia remained in disarray throughout this period, rent by blood feuds, raiding, tribal warfare, shifting alliances, droughts, famines, and plagues of locusts. Najdi towns were said to be in a state of permanent warfare with one another, a characterization that extended to the other interior provinces. By the early 1500s, three towns—Diriya, Uyaina, and Hufuf—vied for dominance in the area.

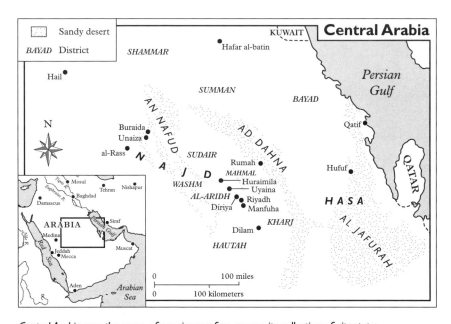

Central Arabia was the scene of ongoing warfare among its collection of city-states.

Bedouin tribes and tribal warfare all played important roles in the Arabian Peninsula's history. This map depicts the territories of major tribes.

Several large tribes also claimed territory in both Najd and the Hijaz. The Anaza, noted for their skill as riders, comprised three separate groups, each with some 60,000 arms-bearing men, representing about one-third of their people, which was a typical tribal ratio of fighters to noncombatants. The Shammar, in northern Najd, had 20,000 warriors, and the powerful and feared Qahtan tribe had 50,000. In Hijaz, the Harb tribe had 30,000.

Diriya

In Najd, the valley of Wadi Hanifa, the ancestral home of what would become the Al Saud family, drew growing numbers of settlers in the mid-15th century. In 1446 one of them, a humble migrant from Qatif, an oasis town on the Persian Gulf, visited his cousin, Ibn Dira, chief of the Duru settlers, in Manfuha, a village in the valley near Riyadh. Ibn Dira gave his relative two fiefs, Ghasiba and al-Mulaibid, undeveloped areas a dozen miles upstream from his own domain. This was the origin of the Duru settlement later known as Diriya.

The story of the village's evolution is complicated by internecine bloodshed and marred by gaps in historical records. Diriya was little noted in chronicles of the time. It is unknown if Mani al-Muraidi, who began the correspondence with his cousin, or Mani's son Rabia, who laid the foundation for the colony's prosperity, was the original recipient of the estates. But these are the earliest traceable ancestors of the house of Saud.

Rabia's son Musa usurped the chieftainship and seized control of Wadi Hanifa, though his efforts to kill his father were unsuccessful. The wounded Rabia escaped to Uyaina. Within two generations the migrants from Qatif had become the settlement's masters. By the beginning of the 1500s, Ibrahim ibn Musa had succeeded his father, and the family had assumed leadership in the valley. Ibrahim had four sons. The youngest was Markhan, who followed his father as emir of Diriya, his elder brothers having left the settlement to seek their fortunes elsewhere. Markhan's oldest son, Rabia (not to be confused with Rabia ibn Mani cited above) succeeded Markhan ibn Ibrahim. Rabia had a son, Watban, and Rabia's brother, Miqrin ibn Markhan (with whom he had gone on a pilgrimage to Mecca in 1630), had two sons, Muhammad and Markhan, the latter named after his grandfather. In 1654, Watban murdered his cousin, Markhan ibn Miqrin, to cement his claim as emir. But Watban's plan was unsuccessful, for in that same year leadership of Diriya was assumed by Muhammad ibn Miqrin (Markhan ibn Miqrin's brother). The murder did, however, set off a blood feud that would roil Diriya for three-quarters of a century.

Muhammad, who would live until 1694, abdicated the throne, and his son Nasir next assumed the title of emir, which was his by 1673. That year Nasir was assassinated as part of the blood feud begun by Watban. Watban's son Markhan ibn Watban next seized leadership, which he held until his assassination by his brother Ibrahim in 1690. It was during this time (1685) that Muhammad ibn Miqrin's son Saud, who would establish the royal lineage of Arabia that now bears his name, was first mentioned. Saud's name was recorded for his participation in an expedition against the town of Huraimila, which led to an engagement known as "the Day of the First Ambush," in which some 30 Huraimila defenders died. Saud was about 20 at the time.

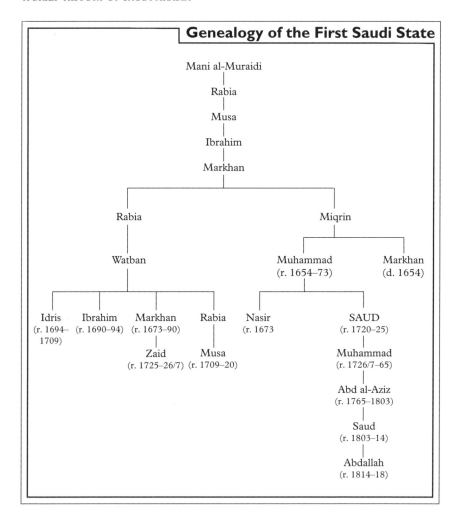

Genealogy of the First Saudi State

Mani al-Muraidi
|
Rabia
|
Musa
|
Ibrahim
|
Markhan

Rabia — Miqrin

Watban

Muhammad
(r. 1654–73)

Markhan
(d. 1654)

Idris
(r. 1694–1709)

Ibrahim
(r. 1690–94)

Markhan
(r. 1673–90)

Rabia

Nasir
(r. 1673)

SAUD
(r. 1720–25)

Zaid
(r. 1725–26/7)

Musa
(r. 1709–20)

Muhammad
(r. 1726/7–65)

Abd al-Aziz
(r. 1765–1803)

Saud
(r. 1803–14)

Abdallah
(r. 1814–18)

Ibrahim ibn Watban himself was murdered in 1694 and succeeded by his brother Idris ibn Watban. He too was assassinated, by Sultan ibn Hamad al-Qaisi from Hasa, thought to be an agent of its powerful Bani Khalid family. The sultan ruled Diriya until he was assassinated in 1708 and was succeeded by his brother Abdullah, who fell to an assassin the following year. The emirship was then taken by Musa ibn Rabia ibn Watban, a grandson of Watban, returning the city to home rule after 15 years. By 1720 Musa had been deposed and exiled by Saud ibn Muhammad ibn Miqrin, founder of the House of Saud. The following year, 1721, Saud's grandson, Abd al-Aziz ibn Muhammad, was born in Diriya to Muhammad ibn Saud. The princes of Al Saud and their retainers lived at the citadel of Turaif in Diriya. Saud died June 12, 1725, succeeded by his cousin, Zaid ibn Markhan ibn Watban.

To the north of Diriya lay Uyaina, central Arabia's grandest, or at least most vibrant city. In the winter of 1725–26 a cholera epidemic, another periodic pestilence that visited Arabia, struck Uyaina and its environs. Among the dead was Uyaina's ruler, Prince Abdullah ibn Muammar. A respected leader, his loss was acutely felt by his subjects. His grandson, Muhammad ibn Hamad, nicknamed Kharfish, succeeded him, suggesting that Abdullah's son may also have fallen victim to the cholera epidemic. Among Kharfish's first official acts was the dismissal of his grandfather's trusted *qadi,* or "judge," Sheikh Abdul-Wahhab ibn Sulaiman. The enmity this dismissal caused would have consequences for Uyaina when the cleric's son later rose to prominence in the peninsula as the progenitor of Wahhabism.

After the cholera epidemic struck, Zaid, Diriya's emir, tempted by the seemingly easy target, set off with a force to take Uyaina. En route, he was met by minions of the new ruler of Uyaina, Kharfish, offering to negotiate spoils for Zaid rather than have the poor inhabitants of the area suffer an attack. Zaid accepted the invitation to discuss the terms and set off with 40 men, including Muhammad ibn Saud. However, upon taking his seat in the reception room, Zaid was shot and killed by Kharfish's servants. Muhammad and the other men barricaded themselves in an adjoining room. Only when their safety was guaranteed by lady Jauhara, a well-known and respected daughter of Abdullah, the late ruler, and aunt of Kharfish, did they leave their refuge. Another fatality during the episode was Musa ibn Rabia, who had been living at Uyaina since he had been deposed as the emir of Diriya and banished by Saud.

Muhammad, upon his return to Diriya in late 1726 or early the next year, became emir. With the death of Musa ibn Rabia, the last of the credible claimants to the throne, Muhammad was free of the challenges that had led to so much bloodshed within the family in previous years, and he retained his position until his death in 1765. By then, the fateful partnership with the conservative cleric that led to the eventual conquest and unification of Arabia had been forged.

Uyaina

Like other rulers of these growing central Arabian settlements, the emir of Uyaina, Ahmad ibn Abdullah ibn Muammar, sought dominance in the area. He invaded Sudair province in 1642 with only minor success, and died four years later on a pilgrimage. Little further was noted of the town until 1661, when it came under the rule of Abdullah ibn Ahmad, though his tenure, which ended in 1685, was uneventful. He was succeeded by his nephew, Abdullah ibn Muammar. The succession was noteworthy in that the father of the new chief, who would have assumed the emirship under traditional custom, was still alive. Whether this marked a recognition of the son's special abilities or a reticence to rule on the part of the father, Abdullah ibn Muammar would distinguish himself as an able and respected leader. He inherited with his rule a war against the town of Huraimila. Early in his reign he joined forces with Saud ibn Muhammad of Diriya and fought in the Battle of al-Muhairis, also called the "First Ambush," noted above. Despite their defeat, the Huraimila went on the offensive and attacked the nearby territory of al-Qarina, which was allied with Uyaina. Abdullah ibn Muammar took the war back to them the following year and lured the Huraimila forces into another ambush, known as the "Second Ambush." Unready to accept defeat, the Huraimila forged an alliance with Muhammad ibn Miqrin of Diriya (who abandoned his alliance

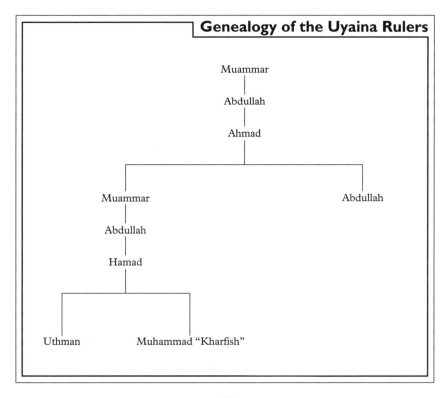

Genealogy of the Uyaina Rulers

with Uyaina) and the ruler of Kharj, and pillaged and plundered Uyaina territory. In 1688 or 1689, the war between Uyaina and Huraimila ended by treaty. This ushered in an era of peace and prosperity for Uyaina, during which the region achieved renown for agricultural development and for the civic-minded efforts to expand housing and improve amenities for its growing population. Unlike other rulers of his era, Abdullah's reputation as an able leader rested more on his civic than military achievements.

In 1709 Abdullah renewed hostilities with Huraimila, and although he had a large force, the fighting ended inconclusively. After his withdrawal from the area, forces of Huraimila, as they had before, attacked his local allies. Abdullah invaded Huraimila again in 1716 and 1718 with small-scale forces in retaliatory raids. In one of these expeditions, the enemy toll is recorded as 10 persons killed and a large number of sheep captured.

Hasa

During this era Hufuf and its neighboring oasis settlements in Hasa, east of Najd, were ruled by a prince of the Muntafiq tribe, Rashid ibn Mughamis al-Shabib, with Ottoman support. In about 1669, Barrak ibn Ghurair, sheikh of the Al Humaid clan of the Bani Khalid, one of the region's most powerful tribes, attacked and defeated Rashid's forces and killed the prince. Barrak continued his offensive, raiding the villages of the Bedouin previously loyal to Rashid and then attacking the Turkish garrison in Hufuf. He continued attacks in the region, including areas near Diriya, for several years. Upon Barrak's death in 1682, his brother Muhammad ibn Ghurair took the reins of rule and continued the raids, attacking Kharj (also known as Yamama), an agricultural town some 50 miles south of Riyadh, and territories of the Subai tribe. Muhammad died in 1691 and his successor, his nephew Thunaian ibn Barrak, son of the former ruler, was killed the same year. The chieftain's position was ultimately claimed by Sadun, son of a former ally of Barrak who had helped in his campaign against the Ottomans. Sadun allied himself with the Fudhul tribe and supporters from Hijaz, and in 1700 mounted a successful campaign against the Dhafir tribe.

In 1705 the Dhafir evicted the Anaza tribe from their summer pastures in the Sudair district. Sadun and the Bani Khalid clashed with the Dhafir again in 1709, their conflict ranging as far east as present-day Iraq, though neither side could claim victory. In 1714, Sadun joined with forces from Uyaina and the al-Aridh district for a major and ultimately successful campaign against Kharj, which they plundered before withdrawing.

Hufuf is blessed with many springs that enabled it to grow into the largest oasis town in Arabia. Its agricultural products made it one of the thriving city-states of the era. (Courtesy of the Fine Arts Library, Harvard College Library)

In the summer of 1721, Sadun invaded Najd with a large force. He used artillery to lay siege to Aqraba and al-Ammariya, and later attacked the area around Diriya, plundering its palm groves and destroying property. However, Sadun's forces were subjected to frequent counterattacks, which took a fairly heavy toll, forcing Sadun to withdraw at the end of the summer. He returned early in 1723 but died during the expedition. The claimants to his title were his two sons and the two sons of Sadun's predecessor, Muhammad ibn Ghurair, but none were of Sadun's stature. After clashes among various supporters, one of Muhammad's sons was chosen as tribal chief of the Bani Khalid, and Sadun's sons were temporarily kept in custody.

Thus, both the regions of Hasa and Uyaina lost capable and charismatic leaders who left no one of equal stature or promise to pick up their mantles. Diriya, their rival for regional hegemony, having recently concluded its own turbulent era of internecine bloodshed, was now under the hand of the ruler who would be the link to the modern kingdom of Saudi Arabia: Muhammad ibn Saud.

Assaults of nature were added to those of man. A three-year drought began in 1722, bringing famine and reducing the Hijazi populace to eating carrion. The rains that followed caused a yellow blight that ruined crops and also brought one of the periodic invasions of locusts to the land. In the winter of 1725–26 the cholera epidemic followed that struck Uyaina and killed its ruler, Abdullah ibn Muammar.

The Emergence of Wahhabism

Since the early 14th century Arabia had been awash in "heretical" movements. Pre-Islamic rites involving sorcery, idolatry, solarism, animism,

ROOTS OF RELIGIOUS REFORM

Islam developed a cult of saints, spread primarily through the Sufis, Islamic mystics who believed that the only way to know God was through intuition. They worked at inducing transcendental states in which one could become one with the deity. Sufism espoused passivity and fatalism, and some adherents drank alcohol and smoked tobacco and hashish. The Whirling Dervishes was a Sufi sect whose members spun in circles in an effort to reach union with God.

The head of the Ottoman religious hierarchy was the mufti of Constantinople, or grand mufti, but the ulama, or religious scholars, wielded considerable power. Through Sufi influence, the ulama accepted saint worship and other Sufi practices, and dervishes spread, as did the number of Sufi adherents. In the 11th century, the conservative theologian al-Ghazali, who had preached against the benefits of reason, also brought elements of Sufism and mystical love of God into Islamic orthodoxy. These ideas were anathema to the 14th-century Syrian Alim Taqi al-din ibn Taimiya (1283–1328). Ibn Taimiya was fanatical in his interpretation and application of Hanbali doctrine. He opposed all *bida* (innovations) as well as Sufism. He spoke out against popular pilgrimages to the prophet's mausoleum in Medina as contrary to the spirit of Islam, and he rejected the acceptance granted by the ulama to such practices through consensus of opinion, or *ijma*. He recorded his views in some 500 works, which went beyond the established order of orthodox Islam. Al-Ghazali, who heretofore had defined orthodox Islam, became a target for ibn Taimiya's followers. Ibn Taimiya's reactionary stance repeatedly brought him to judgment in theological courts, and he died in prison in Damascus. Some 200,000 men and 15,000 women were said to have attended his funeral. His teachings lived on, influencing small groups of conservative thinkers for the next four centuries, and eventually flowered in the harsh interior of Arabia.

and paganism were interwoven with Islam. For the most part these various forms of Islam, including saint worship, coexisted peacefully in Hijaz. Even in the oases of Najd such tolerance was practiced. Supplicants would visit the graves of saints to request favors and miracles. Many early travelers, researchers, and explorers in Arabia reported that Bedouin tribes, though professing to be Muslims, knew little about Islam. This was likely the spiritual landscape in Najd during the years when Muhammad ibn Saud came to power as well.

British Arabist H. St. John Philby noted, "Laxity in the observance of the prescribed rites of Islam, in sexual relationships and in other ways was ignored rather than approved by folk of decent standing. Superstitious belief in the efficacy of charms, offerings and sacrifices, and in the powers of trees, rocks, and certain tombs to effect or hasten the gratification of normal human desires, was but the measure of Samaritan ignorance in the masses, which the Pharisees could afford to despise or ignore amid the luxuries which their superior status assured to them." (Philby 1955, 34).

During the 18th century, economic conditions throughout the Middle East, and in Arabia in particular, deteriorated. The decay of the Ottoman Empire and its ongoing wars caused a recession in commerce as well as a decline of pilgrim traffic. This reduced the income of the Bedouin, leading to more raids on settlements to make up the shortfall. The insecurity and instability underscored the need for a centralized authority. Against this backdrop, a strong religious movement started in Najd.

Abd al-Wahhab

In about 1703 an infant who would have as great an influence on the future of Arabia as any member of the House of Saud was born in Uyaina. Muhammad ibn Abd al-Wahhab was the grandson of a respected theologian and the son of Abdullah ibn Muammar's *qadi*, or religious judge, who was dismissed by Kharfish in 1726. Abd al-Wahhab could trace his lineage back 16 generations. A devoted and precocious student, he is said to have memorized the Quran by age 10. To complete his learning, in his teens he embarked on a grand tour, studying with leading clerics as he traveled to Mecca, Medina, and Basra. In this last city his reputation for wisdom and knowledge began to spread beyond the schools. Offended by the changes that had overtaken the Islamic community, he called for a return to the principles set down by Muhammad. *Tawheed* (oneness with God) was the objective.

Abd al-Wahhab adopted an uncompromising stance against Sufism and the practices of paganism that characterized contemporary Islam, seeking to restore the strict monotheism of early Islam. He opposed all innovations, seeing them as obstacles to returning Islam to its original and pure state. He believed that there could be no intermediary between the faithful and Allah, condemning any such practice as polytheism. He likewise condemned the decoration of mosques and the visiting of the tombs of saints. Furthermore, he labeled as illegal and un-Islamic the practice of calling on any saint, prophet, or angel in prayer or supplicating them for help. His followers called themselves Muwahhidum, (Unitarians) others called them Wahhabi. His fundamentalist interpretation of the Quran drew growing opposition, resulting in his banishment from Basra.

Abd al-Wahhab went to Hasa and then Huraimila, where his father had settled. Here he wrote *Kitab at-Tawheed* (Book of monotheism, or book of unity), which laid out his austere vision of Islam. In 1740 or 1741 his father died, and Abd al-Wahhab is thought to have inherited his father's position as *qadi*. By now he was openly preaching his message of moral and spiritual regeneration through literal interpretation and application of the Quran. He reportedly alienated one of the two subdivisions of a major clan with his efforts to have some members end their debauchery and convert to the true faith. At the time, competing rulers vied for supremacy in Huraimila. Included among the followers of one claimant were agricultural workers whose habits were particularly offensive to Abd al-Wahhab's sense of propriety and religious rectitude. One night they descended on Abd al-Wahhab's home, intent on creating at least mischief if not killing him, but were driven off by his neighbors. With the situation in Huraimila unstable, Abd al-Wahhab returned to Uyaina, where Uthman ibn Hamad ibn Muammar had succeeded his brother Kharfish as the emir. Uthman welcomed Abd al-Wahhab back, even becoming one of his students.

Wahhabism Takes Root

Among Abd al-Wahhab's first acts in Uyaina was to chop down trees that had become objects of veneration. This was done without great notice to avoid arousing opposition from the citizens. Abd al-Wahhab cut down the most sacred tree himself. His next target was a tomb in the nearby village of Jubaila that drew many worshippers. Uthman accompanied Abd al-Wahhab on the mission along with a force of 600 warriors. Abd al-Wahhab personally demolished the tomb, which the idol-worshipping populace expected to result in some disaster befalling him. But when Abd al-Wahhab appeared the next morning, hale and hearty, the idolaters' opposition weakened. The most widely noted example of his strict interpretation of sharia came in the case of a woman who admitted to adultery. She refused to recant her confession, so Abd al-Wahhab sentenced her to death by stoning, a punishment that was meted out on the spot. Uthman threw the first stone. To some, this represented Abd al-Wahhab's true sincerity and rectitude, whereas to others it showed the barbarity of his teachings. Abd al-Wahhab's brother Sulaiman led opposition against him in several oases. Sulaiman objected to the intolerance of his brother's teachings, which held that all Muslims who did not agree with them were worse than pagans or the idolaters of the Jahiliyya, the time before the coming of Islam.

Word of the stoning incident spread, horrifying non-Wahhabis. Sulaiman ibn Hamad ibn Ghurayar al-Humaidi, ruler of Hasa and the area's Bedouin tribes, ordered Uthman to kill Abd al-Wahhab, threatening to withhold the annual stipend of gold, food, and material he supplied to Uyaina and other communities if his orders were ignored. Uthman was dependent on Sulaiman ibn Hamad for these subsidies and also owned properties in Hasa. Moreover, local ulama opposed Abd al-Wahhab, as he threatened their teachings and position. Instead of having him killed, however, Uthman ibn Hamad banished him, and Abd al-Wahhab set off for Diriya. The leader of the warriors, whom Uthman had sent to escort Abd al-Wahhab on his journey to exile, had secret orders to kill him. But the soldier lost his nerve at the appointed assassination place and returned to Uyaina, leaving Abd al-Wahhab to complete the journey alone.

Najdi nobility were longtime adversaries of Hijazi nobility, who followed Ottoman Islam of the Hanafi school. Wahhabi opposition was based in part on disdain for Ottoman rule, what was perceived as their haughty ways, and the corruption of Ottoman courts and administration. By labeling followers of other forms of Islam as infidels, the Wahhabi recreated the spirit that had led to the first conquests by Muslim warriors. (Subsequently the Wahhabis treated even Jews and Christians less harshly than non-Wahhabi Muslims.) By accepting Wahhabi teachings, the leader of a raiding tribe was now engaged in jihad against infidels. But adherence to Wahhabism had economic as well as religious significance. The destruction of graves and shrines of local saints deprived rulers of income from pilgrimages to the sites.

The Wahhab–Al Saud Alliance

Muhammad ibn Abd al-Wahhab settled in Diriya in 1744–45. His arrival was kept secret out of concern for the safety of the controversial cleric, but soon his supporters sought official protection for him. His supporters included two brothers and the wife of the local emir, Muhammad ibn Saud. Ibn Saud had ambitions of his own and needed religious backing for his plan to preserve an earlier taxation system that ran counter to sharia. Abd al-Wahhab needed military backing for his efforts to spread his vision of Islam. Ibn Saud sought two conditions for granting Abd al-Wahhab sanctuary: that Abd al-Wahhab stay in Diriya, and that he not oppose the tax. Abd al-Wahhab agreed to the first condition but not the second, reportedly telling Ibn Saud that the spoils of war undertaken for their cause could be far greater than what taxes would bring. Doing away with the tax also helped Abd al-Wahhab win the support of the people of Diriya. Saud extended his protection and swore allegiance to Abd al-Wahhab's vision of Islam.

Abd al-Wahhab moved to a house in the al-Bujairi neighborhood, which became the intellectual center of the city. His preaching drew large audiences of all classes, including followers from Uyaina who migrated to be near the sheikh, as Abd al-Wahhab was known. Uthman ibn Hamad, emir of Uyaina, concerned about the repercussions of his expulsion of the increasingly powerful cleric, came with a contingent of notables to plead for his return. Sheikh al-Wahhab declined the offer, saying it was Muhammad ibn Saud's decision, as he would not leave someone who befriended him. Muhammad ibn Saud declined to accommodate Uthman. The partnership that would give rise to the first Saudi state was sealed.

6

THE FIRST SAUDI STATE
(1745-1818)

The first Saudi state was conceived with the 1744/45 alliance of Muhammad ibn Saud, whose descendants now rule the Kingdom of Saudi Arabia, and religious reformer Sheikh Muhammad ibn Abd al-Wahhab. The two men shared a vision of an independent Islamic state based on a simple and austere faith. This chapter covers the span of some 75 years during which their message and might conquered Arabia, forging a politically united realm, albeit a short-lived one, an accomplishment even the prophet Muhammad had not achieved.

The Ascent of Diriya

At the time his partnership with Muhammad Abd al-Wahhab was forged, Muhammad ibn Saud was the respected leader of the tribes living in a few settlements by an oasis clinging to the Wadi Hanifa. Ibn Saud's village was Diriya, which lay between a rocky escarpment and a canal. The citadel of Turaif served as its stronghold. Before the arrival of Abd al-Wahhab at Diriya, nothing in his circumstances distinguished Ibn Saud's familial dynasty from other small fiefdoms scattered about central Arabia.

Nor was Abd al-Wahhab, as a cleric calling for Islamic reform, unique. But his reputation and deeply conservative ideals resonated among many Najdi dismayed at the laxity of religious practices and secularization of the Hijaz, and alarmed at the spread of polytheism in Najd. He provided Ibn Saud with religious legitimacy for military actions that expanded his domain, while Ibn Saud provided Abd al-Wahhab with the force to implement his vision of true Islam. Abd al-Wahhab's followers were called Wahhabis by others, which came to be considered a derogatory term by his adherents. They considered themselves simply Muslims and viewed others who professed the faith but did not hew to their interpretation of Islam as infidels. Adherents of

Wahhab's tenets prefer the terms Unitarian and Unitarianism for their form of faith. However, Wahhabi and Wahhabism being the predominate way that they and their beliefs are identified in contemporary literature, we will follow this convention. Abd al-Wahhab's religious principles would find expression in the Islamic state of Saudi Arabia.

Campaign for Najd

After making their alliance, Muhammad ibn Saud and Abd al-Wahhab commenced a campaign to conquer and unite Najd. Soon after Abd al-Wahhab moved to Diriya, a delegation of 30 Wahhabi ulama was sent to Mecca, where they requested permission for their followers to make the pilgrimage and engaged in theological debate. After hearing their arguments, the sharif proclaimed them godless and ordered them jailed.

One of Abd al-Wahhab's tenets was the need for jihad, not as a personal struggle but as a holy war, to defeat infidels, either by conversion or death. This view found favor among tribes accustomed to the time-honored practice of raiding and plundering, or *ghazu*, from which Abd al-Wahhab's jihad was essentially indistinguishable in its execution. When a village or tribe refused to submit to Diriya, they would be raided and their possessions taken. By whichever means their foes fell, all shrines, venerated tombs, and other elements of religious practices not in keeping with Abd al-Wahhab's interpretation of Islam were obliterated.

The ruler's share from raids, *khums*, was traditionally one-fifth

The worship of saints and ancestors, incorporating music and dancing, became popular religious rituals in much of Islam of the time. Muhammad Abd al-Wahhab was determined to stamp out these practices. This illuminated manuscript created in Baghdad late in the 16th century shows a Muslim leaving his ancestor's mausoleum and leading a crowd, "in ecstasy of music and dance." (Courtesy of The Pierpont Morgan Library/Art Resource, NY)

of the plunder. Under the Saud-Wahhab alliance, this went to the central treasury, which supported the offices of both the emir and the sheikh. The remainder went to the raiders, one share for unmounted, two shares for those on mounts. The raided tribe or settlement might also pay tribute, either one time or on an ongoing basis. In the aftermath of the raids a religious expert, or *alim* (pl. ulama), sent with occupational forces would provide religious instruction, teaching the articles of Islam as defined by Abd al-Wahhab and thereafter assuring compliance with its precepts.

Rule, Religion, and Revenge

The Saud-Wahhab alliance mirrored the righteous social structure preached by the 14th-century religious scholar Ibn Taimiya, whose teachings had inspired Abd al-Wahhab's struggle to reform Islam. Ibn Taimiya taught that two groups of authorities should lead a righteous society: ulama to decide matters of law, and leaders to enforce the law. Citizens were to give the leader complete obedience. Abd al-Wahhab was consulted on all matters of state by both Ibn Saud and his successors. Ibn Saud, the emir of Diriya, became known as the imam, or spiritual leader, as would all leaders of Al Saud, the House of Saud, thereafter until the reign of the founder of the modern kingdom of Saudi Arabia early in the 20th century. Signifying his position, the emir stood in front of the congregation during Friday prayers.

Uthman and the people of Uyaina, the town from which Abd al-Wahhab had been banished, allied themselves with Diriya, and Uthman became related to the Saudis through his daughter's marriage to Muhammad ibn Saud's son, Abd al-Aziz, ibn Muhammad ibn Saud. The son that union produced, Saud ibn Abd al-Aziz, born in 1748, would lead the Wahhabi to their greatest victories during the first Saudi state. But suspicion and animosity toward Uthman for his earlier treatment of Abd al-Wahhab lingered in Diriya. Uthman was accused of conspiring against Wahhabi interests, and in 1750 was murdered by Wahhabis from Uyaina. He was succeeded by a relative, but 10 years later Abd al-Wahhab replaced Uthman's kin with a ruler of his own choosing. Abd al-Wahhab then returned to Uyaina and had Uthman's family castle destroyed.

Riyadh's Rise

During this first kingdom, a fourth community joined Uyaina, Hasa, and Diriya as a growing regional power: Riyadh. This added another theater of intrigue and lethal confrontation to the ever-contentious political landscape of Arabia's interior. The emir of Riyadh at the time Abd al-Wahhab settled in Diriya was Dahham ibn Dawwas. He had taken a circuitous route to leadership. Dahham's father had been the unpopular ruler of the town of Manfuha. After the son who succeeded him was killed, Dahham and his brothers were banished from the town and settled in Riyadh, where their sister was married to its ruler, Zaid ibn Musa. In the late 1730s Zaid was murdered by a slave who then held power for three years, until rumors of an impending coup sent him fleeing to Manfuha, where he was executed. Dahham, uncle of Zaid's son, took power as regent for his minor nephew. After consolidating his rule in about 1740, Dahham exiled his nephew, as Dahham himself had been banished. By 1745 his rule of Riyadh was undisputed. Riyadh became Diriya's main rival, and their forces engaged each other annually. No record of hostilities between Riyadh and Diriya exists before this time, but the void would be filled by more than 25 years of warfare thereafter.

Early in 1746 Dahham led citizens of Riyadh and Bedouin elements from the Dhafir tribe against his hometown, Manfuha. The tide in the inconclusive battle turned when forces from Diriya arrived to reinforce the defenders. This began an alliance between Manfuha and Diriya against Riyadh. Soon after Dahham's retreat, Ibn Saud launched a nighttime attack on Riyadh, and by the end of 1746 Diriya and Riyadh were locked in a conflict that cost Muhammad ibn Saud two of his sons.

Ibn Saud continued battles against Riyadh and its allies, as they did against him, until late 1753 or early 1754, when Dahham, Ibn Saud's bitter rival, proposed a truce, swore loyalty to Muhammad and the tenets of his faith, and requested a Wahhabi teacher be sent to Riyadh. Actions against other recalcitrant towns and tribes continued, sometimes under the command of Ibn Saud's son, Abd al-Aziz.

Tribal Warfare

The years 1750 through 1753 saw attempts by several oases that had been among the first to ally themselves with Diriya to reassert their independence. All had to be confronted by Wahhabi military forces when efforts to negotiate a reconsideration failed. Abd al-Wahhab's brother, Sulaiman, who had long denounced Wahhabi teachings, engineered an insurrection as well and was defeated by forces under Abd al-Aziz. Campaigns against unsubjugated towns and tribes and errant allies continued throughout the decade. Meanwhile, Dahham, the emir of Riyadh, became restive and recommenced his campaign against Diriya, the 1754 armistice lasting less than two years. In 1758 Abd al-Aziz brought the battle to Riyadh, with inconclusive results. But in the early 1760s the Wahhabis resecured Dahham's loyalty, even extracting a large payment from him in tribute.

They also made successful advances into Hasa, which was under the rule of the Al Juaid dynasty and the chiefs of the Arayar tribe of the Bani Khalid. Hasa's tribal rulers had wrested it in 1669 from the Ottoman Turks, who had seized it from independent rulers in 1592. Ali, the fourth caliph, who gave rise to the Shia through his martyred son Husayn, had made his capital in Kufa, just over the Kuwaiti border in present-day Iraq. That had established the Persian Gulf coast and eastern Arabia as a Shia stronghold. With their rites involving veneration of saints and visits to tombs, Shia opposition to the Wahhabi was especially intense.

In the late 1750s the Bani Khalid chief of Hasa, along with allies from many Najdi districts, engaged in a series of raids against Diriya's forces. However, the battling reached a virtual stalemate, and some tribes simply gave up their fight and agreed to pay Diriya for their disloyalty. But dissatisfaction with Wahhabi rule and Saudi power continued to fester while Diriya's boundaries expanded. In 1764 a Bedouin confederation from the region around Najran, the city in southwest Arabia, rose up against the Wahhabi, attacking their stronghold, Diriya. Abd al-Aziz lost some 500 killed and more than 200 taken prisoner. The attack was instigated by the Arayar tribe in Hasa, allies of the Najrani Bedouin who had previously suffered defeat at Wahhabi hands.

Forces from the Arayar were meanwhile advancing toward Diriya under their chief, Arayar ibn Dujain. Abd al-Wahhab quickly negotiated a settlement with the leader of the Najrani Bedouin, and their forces withdrew before the Arayar could join the fray. Nonetheless when the Arayar arrived in 1765 they laid siege to the village for three weeks, but Diriya's defenses held. The defeat by the Najranis and the siege by the Arayar represented the most serious threat of Ibn Saud's reign, and the last. He died that same year.

The Reign of Abd al-Aziz

Shortly after Muhammad ibn Saud's death in 1765, his son Abd al-Aziz ibn Muhammad ibn Saud became emir of Diriya. Having withstood the threat posed by the Arayar, Diriya was now perhaps the most powerful of numerous city-states in Arabia's deserts. Even when under attack at home, Wahhabi forces continued their jihad elsewhere. The year of Abd al-Aziz's ascension saw a further expansion of Saudi-Wahhabi territory with the subjugation of the Washm and Sudair districts. The following year, Abd al-Wahhab's doctrine won recognition among the scholars of Mecca.

Throughout these years Diriya's battles with Riyadh and the mercurial Dahham continued, accompanied by shifting allegiances and shaky truces. In a campaign of 1764–65, for example, Abd al-Aziz was accompanied by forces from Riyadh, during a brief time of alliance, under the command of Dahham's son Dawwas ibn Dahham. Yet eventually enmity won out, and Dahham's two sons were later killed in battles against Wahhabi forces. In 1773, with Wahhabi troops advancing on Riyadh, Dahham fled, proclaiming himself weary of fighting, and leaving the city to Abd al-Aziz and the Wahhabi. Many citizens fled with him and perished from thirst in the desert on their way to Kharj. For years after, it was later reported, any foolish action someone committed in Najd earned comparison with Dahham's exit from Riyadh.

The 1773 fall of Riyadh to Diriya's forces under their Wahhabi banner ended the struggle for hegemony in central Najd. During the 27 years of warfare between the rival city-states, it is estimated that some 4,000 to 5,000 people were killed. Yet it took another dozen years to consolidate full control over the rest of the region, as its tribes continued to resist Wahhabi rule. Additionally, previous allies continued renouncing their ties, requiring annual campaigns to restore fealty and collect zakat, the charitable contributions mandated of all Muslims. The Wahhabi cast the payment of tribute they demanded as zakat, and themselves as merely the collection agents for a higher authority. Teams of zakat collectors went out from Diriya to collect from the Bedouin annually. The imposition of the centralized tax system that mandatory zakat represented was a key innovation wrought by the Saudi-Wahhabi regime, which helped bring a semblance of order and organization to its Bedouin followers.

Abd al-Aziz's son, Saud, led Wahhabi military campaigns beginning in 1767. Abd al-Aziz continued to lead campaigns as well, and also acted as a politician, conducting a correspondence with the sharif of Mecca. The sharif requested a visit from a Wahhabi cleric to receive instruction in Wahhabi principles. By the time of the cleric's arrival, the sharif had been deposed by opponents in his own family, and the religious leader received an unwelcome reception.

In 1774, the year after Abd al-Aziz gained Riyadh, Arayar ibn Dujain mounted a renewed threat. Leading a Bani Khalid force, he attacked

Buraida and Qasim, both allies of Diriya. The attacks drew wide support among Najdi rulers, still uneasy with the expansion of Saudi and Wahhabi power. Arayar forces proved surprisingly formidable, generating defections to his cause from several districts in Najd. But Arayar died suddenly before he could attack Diriya itself, and internecine fights over succession occupied his sons and kept them from mounting another campaign. Nonetheless, annual raids on Najd by Bani Khalid from Hasa continued, though the oases they attacked were, at best, themselves typically only lukewarm supporters of the Wahhabi cause. Still, the power and influence of the Saudi state grew. Even Abd al-Wahhab's brother, Sulaiman, his most vocal critic, was silenced when the Wahhabis captured the al-Majmaa oasis and deported him to Diriya. Only in the south, where Kharj maintained alliances with leaders of southern Najdi districts and Najrani tribes, was Diriya's expansion blocked.

Shortly after the conquest of Riyadh, a new rival appeared: Zaid ibn Zamil, the emir of Dilam and Kharj. Zaid attempted to create an alliance with tribes from Najran, who had already battled with the Wahhabis, offering to pay them to renew hostilities. Instead, they came and looted and robbed Zaid's principality. After their departure he pledged his support for the Wahhabis, a bond he later betrayed. In 1782 Zaid joined Saadun ibn Arayar, the son of the ruler of Hasa who had threatened Diriya almost a decade before. Ibn Arayar led a force of Bani Khalid, Shammar, and Dhafir tribesmen in an attack on Qasim, aimed at dislodging the Wahhabi forces, but their siege failed and the alliance fell apart. Zaid was killed the following year, and efforts of his son, Barrak, to take up his mantle, like so many others, were undermined by familial rivalries.

Diriya Consolidates Control and Expands East

In addition to the miseries of warfare, drought from the years 1783 through 1786 brought famine to central Arabia. South of Riyadh, Kharj, surrounded by Wahhabis, was desperate and became more so when Wahhabi forces attacked and conquered Dilam, its ally, in 1785. The ruler of Kharj then offered his allegiance to Diriya. Other districts were also conquered that year while nomadic tribes came increasingly under Saudi authority. The Dhafir Bedouin, for example, lost all their property to the Wahhabi in 1781, the plunder including 15,000 sheep and goats, 5,000 camels, and 15 horses.

In 1786–87 Wahhabi forces were preoccupied with countering raids on the province of Qasim, mounted by Thuwaini ibn Abdullah, the sheikh of Muntafiq. The Wahhabi repulsed his attacks, but Thuwaini next tried to conquer Basra, in present-day Iraq. He was in turn attacked and defeated in 1787 by the pasha of Baghdad. Buyuk Sulaiman (r. 1780–1802). By the late 1780s the Muntafiq, needing a strong ally, were participating in the raids with the Wahhabi forces. All of central Arabia was now under the control of Diriya. Local emirs were either dependents or appointees. Abd al-Aziz had become a respected, popular ruler, having shown courage in battle and skill in diplomacy.

In 1788 hereditary right to the emirship for Abd al-Aziz's descendants was established when Abd al-Wahhab issued the decree to all provinces and districts to acknowledge Saud as next in line of succession, that is, as the crown prince. Meanwhile the campaigns of expansion continued on multiple fronts, much of it directed against the Bani Khalid princes (that is, the sons of the emir, and the forces they controlled) of Hasa. Tribal feuds wracking the area reduced effective resistance to the Wahhabi thrusts.

In the campaign of 1791–92, Saud attacked eastern Arabian oases and occupied Qatif. But citizens of Hasa, a traditionally Shia area, revolted. In Hufuf, 30 Wahhabi officials including the governor were killed and their corpses mutilated in public. The Wahhabis' overseer in the region, Zaid ibn Arayar (son of the Wahhabi foe from Hasa who

Walled oasis towns were said to be in constant battle with each other in Najd. Qasim is typical of the walled oasis towns of Najd during the 18th century. (Courtesy of Tor Eigeland/Aramco World/PADIA)

SAUDI GOVERNMENT

Under Saudi-Wahhabi rule, the tribal justice and violence previously used to settle disputes was replaced by adjudication from Diriya. After time, as the state expanded, Diriya replaced the emirs and sheikhs of many villages and Bedouin groups with leaders from rival families of the old regimes, thereby increasing the dependence and obedience of the new rulers. As a further means of assuring loyalty, the Saudis employed the long-standing practice of taking hostages. Typically, notables from a defeated village or tribe were moved to Diriya, as were military commanders on occasion, thereby weakening the ability of the conquered to mount future opposition. It was Abd al-Aziz's custom to build a moated fortress in the oases he conquered, garrisoned with as many as 500 to 1,000 soldiers in the largest villages. Participation in jihad was one of the obligations of Bedouin groups and tribes

Safety for travelers was a great concern for the growing state. No ruler could claim legitimate dominion of his realm if he could not assure the security of hajjis on their holy journey. Abd al-Aziz worked diligently to ensure that Bedouin did not steal from travelers, sometimes becoming personally involved in the search for and punishment of thieves. Travelers no longer had to pay the tribes through whose territory they passed. Raids among tribes under Diriya's rule were drastically reduced, although both raids and insurrections continued.

Arab historian Uthman ibn Abdallah ibn Bishr (d. 1871/72) wrote, "[Abd al-Aziz] is really worthy of the title of Mahdi of his time, because one can travel with good money whenever he wants, in summer or in winter, to the left or to the right, to the east or to the west, in Najd, Hijaz, Yemen, Tihama and elsewhere. He fears nobody but God—neither a thief nor a robber" (Vassiliev 1998, 129).

died in the midst of a campaign against them) turned on the Wahhabis and supported the revolt. The Bani Khalid removed the Wahhabi-appointed sheikh, and the new ruler launched attacks on Saudi-controlled tribes and oases. Saud led a counterattack in 1793. Zaid ibn Arayar's rival and former Wahhabi adversary, Barrak ibn Abd al-Muhsin, allied himself with Saudi forces. Hasa sued for peace and submitted to Diriya. It would remain in Wahhabi control for almost 80 years, until it fell again to Ottoman occupation in 1871.

Barrak was installed as emir of Hasa. But three years later, in 1796, with insurrections in the west and southwest of the Najd occupying

Saud's attention, Barrak tried again to break away from the Wahhabi camp. Saud led an army to Hasa and put down the rebellion, then spent months eliminating adversaries. This marked the completion of the Wahhabi conquest of eastern Arabia.

A Period of Stability

During Abd al-Aziz's reign, Arabia experienced a period of stability and safety it had not witnessed in centuries. Many Bedouin tribes that had been traditional enemies encamped within sight of each other. Men throughout the state became "like brothers" in the words of more than one historian. The stability encouraged internal trade throughout Arabia. Diriya, an important oasis on the crossroads of trading routes to all points of Arabia, was well-positioned to profit from it.

Most nobility maintained a large household, with the patriarch having four wives in addition to concubines. Healthier and better fed than most of the population, the nobility had lower infant mortality rates, adding to the size of the typical nobleman's family. As much as one-third of the Saudi emir's income went to maintaining his homes, family, and entourage. He also received several hundred guests a day and was obliged, under traditions and customs of hospitality, to feed them. In contrast to the Wahhabi teachings of simplicity, Abd al-Aziz and his

Diriya, the home of Al Saud, grew into a thriving area. (Courtesy of Tor Eigeland/Aramco World/PADIA)

TITLED NOBILITY

Readers of Islamic history encounter a host of titles and honorifics claimed by or bestowed upon rulers and officials. Listed below are the more common titles:

bey   a provincial governor, high government officer, or other official or noble of the Ottoman Empire; the title follows the name

caliph   the political leader of the Islamic Empire; from the Arabic *khalifah,* "successor"

emir/amir   an independent chieftain or ruler, a military commander or governor, or a descendant of Muhammad; from the Arabic word *amir,* "commander"

imam   the spiritual leader of the community, a title traditionally claimed by Saudi rulers from the late 18th century until the reign of the kingdom's founder, Ibn Saud, who preferred the more temporal titles of sultan and king; also an honorific bestowed on eminent Islamic scholars; for the Shia, *imam* refers to Ali or any of his descendants recognized as leaders of Islam

khan   the ruler of a Mongol, Tartar, or Turkish tribe

khedive   Ottoman viceroys in Egypt in the 19th and early 20th centuries

mufti   an Islamic scholar who interprets sharia, or Muslim law, and is qualified to render a formal religious opinion, or fatwa. Under the Ottomans, the grand mufti was the chief religious authority. Most Islamic countries have a grand mufti. Saudi Arabia's last grand mufti

family lived in luxury by local standards. Abd al-Aziz was known for the magnificence of his palace, the finery he wore, and the number of attendants who escorted him in public.

Ibn Bishr recounted his visit to Diriya thusly: "If I had tried to count the people who are hurrying and scurrying about the town, pedigree horses, camels of the Amani breed and the luxurious goods of various kinds the local residents and foreigners brought there, my book would not be sufficient to embrace it. I saw a lot of wonders there" (Vassiliev 1998, 131).

The Wahhabi Army

Despite the continuous battling that characterized the Wahhabi expansion, its forces commanded only a few hundred full-time soldiers.

died in 1969. The responsibilities are now divided among the Ministry of Justice, the Supreme Council of the Judiciary, the Council of the Assembly of Senior Ulama, and other religious institutions.

mullah   a religious teacher

pasha   a provincial governor or other high official of the Ottoman Empire; the title follows the name; from the 17th-century Turkish word *pasa*

Porte, Sublime Porte   the Ottoman court at Constantinople; taken from the French for "the High Gate," the most important entrance to the city

prince   the son of an emir or other leader

qadi   an Islamic judge or magistrate

sheikh   the chief of a tribe or village; a term of respect and veneration for an older man or a senior cleric; from the Arabic *shaykh,* "old man"

sharif   the ruler of Mecca; all sharifs were members of Muhammad's clan, the Quraysh, though no formal means of succession existed

sultan   the sovereign ruler of a Muslim country, especially of the former Ottoman Empire; from the Arabic *sultan,* "rule"

suzerain   a nation that controls another's international relations but allows it domestic sovereignty; a feudal lord to whom fealty is owed

ulama or ulema (sing. *alim*)   theologians or religious scholars who interpret sharia

vizier   chief counselor; a title created during the Abbasid reign, and a position retained by Ottoman rulers

However, all men between ages 16 and 60 were eligible for military service. When planning a campaign, Abd al-Aziz sent word to each village and tribe as to the number of men needed, and where and when to meet. The men were typically drawn from areas near where the raids were to be staged. Anyone called up could send a substitute in his place, releasing many men of means from compulsory service. The troops supplied their own arms and food, as well as feed for their animals, though cavalry animals were provided fodder. Campaigns usually lasted less than a month, and the emir of Diriya was responsible for a portion of the army's provisioning for any raids lasting longer.

Before each campaign led by Abd al-Aziz, crowds gathered to see him off. After prayer at the mosque, he alighted for the meeting place astride a horse, his retinue behind him. He usually stopped between Diriya and

Uyaina to dispense alms and gifts to the poor and sick who had gathered, awaiting his arrival. At the military assembly area, the group prayed before moving out. Scouts preceded the main force. The night before battle, Abd al-Aziz would instill religious zeal in his forces with an inspirational speech. Their arms included swords, daggers, pikes, clubs, and pistols, and the infantry also used short spears. Shields, helmets, and protective clothing were worn by some. Historical accounts of their prowess vary, some avowing their fanatical boldness, others recounting how they attacked only when resistance was weak, relying on intimidation rather than force for many of their victories.

Ottoman Response

With their conquest of Hasa in 1796, Wahhabi forces stepped up their raids on areas to the north, concentrating on the nomads and villages of lower Iraq. Reports of the attacks provoked an armed response from the pasha of Baghdad, Buyuk Sulaiman. Traditionally, Baghdad depended on Bedouin allies to protect the trade routes from attacks from within Arabia, and had given them gifts and weapons to secure their allegiance. Thuwaini ibn Abdullah, the former Muntafiq sheikh exiled after his failed attack on Basra (and who had spent part of his exile in Diriya), commanded the Ottoman force sent to drive the Wahhabi from Hasa in 1797. His fighters were supplemented by Bani Khalid troops from Hasa who had fled from the Wahhabi. Abd al-Aziz sent loyal Bedouin to occupy the Bani Khalid territories and block their access to wells. Meanwhile, the best Wahhabi fighters were sent to Hasa, where they engaged in violent battles with Thuwaini's troops. During the campaign Thuwaini was assassinated by his slave, described as a fanatical Wahhabi. His army disintegrated, the Bani Khalid withdrew from the alliance, and Turkish and Bedouin fighters fled, abandoning their artillery and ammunition.

By the late 1790s, irked by the nettlesome warfare, the Porte, or Ottoman government leadership in Constantinople, brought ongoing pressure on the pasha of Baghdad to destroy the Wahhabi forces. In 1798, by the most authoritative account, a force left Baghdad for an invasion of Hasa, which took place the following year. The Ottomans' Iraqi forces, under Ali Kahya, laid siege to the Wahhabi strongholds in Hasa but were unable to conquer them. Kahya, as assistant to the pasha, concluded a truce with Abd al-Aziz. The following year a treaty was ratified in Baghdad. However, neither side put much faith in the agreement. The pasha sent a representative to Diriya to secure

The verdant oasis of Hufuf made it an attractive target, but the walls of its city kept many would-be conquerors at bay. (Courtesy of Tor Eigeland/*Aramco World*/PADIA)

Abd al-Aziz's pledge not to attack Muslim holy sites in lower Iraq, but Abd al-Aziz refused to agree.

The Battle for the Hijaz

In Hijaz during this time, Sharif Musaid bin Said II (r. 1752–59, 1760–70) held a weak grip on power, and late in his reign Mecca was threatened with the loss of autonomy granted under the Ottomans. In 1769, Ali Bey, ruler of Cairo, declared Egypt free from Ottoman rule, and proclaimed Egypt's annexation of Hijaz. But his efforts to win control of the region were unsuccessful. Diriya tried to forge closer ties to Hijaz, as well. In the early 1770s, Abd al-Aziz and Abd al-Wahhab exchanged gifts with the sharif.

Weakness persisted in the sharifate. By the time Sharif Surur ibn Musaid (1744–88; r. 1773–88) died, his eunuchs and other slaves wielded the majority of the office's power, a prerogative they retained into the rule of Surur's successor, Sharif Ghalib ibn Musaid (1750–1817; r. 1788–1813). But the slaves' policies aroused opposition, which helped Ghalib consolidate control. Seeking at least to lessen tensions with Najd, he requested Abd al-Aziz to dispatch an *alim* to explain Wahhabism to him. But like previous pedagogical expeditions, the mission failed, and soon concern about the Wahhabis' westward thrusts incited the sharif to take arms against them. In 1790 Ghalib sent a force of 10,000 soldiers and 20 artillery guns into Najd with the goal of invading Diriya and ending the Wahhabi "heresy." Joined by Hijazi Bedouins and Najdi tribes opposed to the Wahhabis, their effort bogged down in an unsuccessful siege and attacks on a small fortified town, Qasr Bassam, after which they returned to Mecca. The following year Saud ibn Abd al-Aziz attacked and defeated the sharif's tribal allies in Najd, the booty of their victory including a reported 100,000 sheep and 11,000 camels. Further attacks on allies of the sharif in western Najd followed.

In 1792 Sheikh Muhammad ibn Abd al-Wahhab, then about 89 years old, died. Little ceremony was invested in his funeral, in keeping with the traditions he had championed. The Arabia he departed was developing a far different spiritual landscape than the one he was born into, due to his efforts. His brother and major critic, Sulaiman ibn Abd al-Wahhab, took over his position as the Wahhabis' chief *alim*. No change in policy accompanied the shift, which was not surprising given that Sulaiman was living in Diriya under the watchful eye of the Saudi regime, as he had been since his capture more than a decade before and as he would until his death.

Diriya's campaign for Hijaz took a decisive step in 1795, when Wahhabi forces laid siege to Turaba, a key city on the way to Hijaz. In response, Sharif Ghalib mounted another invasion of Najd in 1795–96, but was soundly defeated by an alliance of tribes loyal to Diriya. Ghalib agreed to a truce. The rulers of Mecca, mindful of the threat posed by the Ottoman Empire, could not devote all their resources to the battle with the Wahhabi forces of the Najd. But within a year Meccan forces were again attacking Najdi Bedouin. The sharif was meanwhile losing critical support within Hijaz as tribes switched allegiance from Mecca to Diriya.

Worried about an attack by the French, who had landed forces in Egypt in 1798, the Ottomans strengthened the defenses throughout the towns of Hijaz. That same year a British squadron under Admiral Blanquet attacked Suez and later anchored in Jeddah, demanding that Hijaz end its trade with Egypt, as the commerce was seen as assisting France. Though Sharif Ghalib agreed, the trade was undisturbed.

Ghalib had by this time gathered a large force—including mercenaries from Egypt, Morocco, and Turkey—to attack the Wahhabi-controlled towns of Khura and Bisha, but the sharif's forces were defeated at Khura in 1798 with a loss of more than 1,200 men. Following this

---

FRANCE AND BRITAIN IN EGYPT

In 1798 France landed forces in Egypt and Palestine, the opening thrust in Napoleon Bonaparte's campaign to conquer parts of the British Empire. It was the most cataclysmic event for the region since the Crusades, though initially these incursions had no impact in Arabia.

The invasion commenced with Napoleon's landing at Alexandria. He proclaimed he had come to punish the Mamluks for not being good Muslims and to restore the authority of the Ottoman sultan, damaged by the Ali Bey rebellion of 1769. His true objective was not helping the Ottomans but cutting England off from India, as evidenced by his defeat of the sultan's army at the Battle of the Pyramids in July of 1798. The Porte, or Ottoman government in Constantinople, raised a massive army to oust the French forces, calling on "all true believers to take arms against those swinish infidels the French" (Nutting 1964, 219). Under Horatio Nelson the British fleet defeated the French at Abukir Bay in 1798, and Napoleon's army was defeated at the Battle of Alexandria in 1801, ending French ambitions in the area.

---

defeat, the sharif made an offer of peace to Abd al-Aziz and invited him to perform the pilgrimage. In 1800 Abd al-Aziz and his son Saud made their first hajj, accompanied by Wahhabi ulama who came to engage in theological debate. Abd al-Aziz was treated with respect and honors by Sharif Ghalib. The pilgrimage was repeated the next year, though Abd al-Aziz had to turn back, due to infirmity; he was almost 80 years old.

Ghalib's truce with Abd al-Aziz notwithstanding, the sharif was losing support of important allies. The defection of his aide and relative Uthman al-Mudhaifi was the most serious, as the Bedouin followed Uthman's urging to switch allegiance to him and the Wahhabi. Uthman led forces against the sharif, and in 1802 they easily took the town of Taif and proceeded to loot and kill its inhabitants. Ghalib turned to the Porte for help.

The Attack on Karbala

The British had displaced the French in Egypt in 1801, ending France's threat to Britain's interests in India. This eliminated Britain's need for an alliance to counter French power in the region, further marginalizing

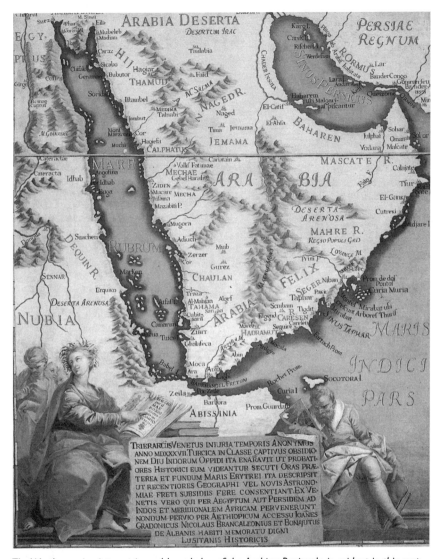

The West's growing interest in and knowledge of the Arabian Peninsula is evident in this map of Arabia made by Giustino Menescardi (fl. 1751–65). (Courtesy of Cameraphoto/Art Resource, NY)

Arabia in the minds of the European powers. But this neglect left the Saudi-Wahhabi forces unopposed externally in their efforts to establish regional dominance. With peace prevailing along the border between the Hijaz and Najd, in 1801–02 Saud set out for an attack that would have large repercussions and turn the tide against the Wahhabis. The objective was the Ottoman-controlled town of Karbala, in what is now southern Iraq, sacred to the Shia for its association with the martyrdom of Husayn. The Wahhabi were determined to take their battle for the faith's purity to the scene of the genesis of its split. The exact date has been disputed, but the most reliable accounts of Saud's attack date it to March 1802. Karbala's citizens were slaughtered and its sacred places destroyed, including the great dome of the tomb of Husayn. The wealth of the mosque of Imam Husayn, grandson of the prophet, was said by some at the time to have been the reason for the Wahhabi designs on the town. Whatever the true objectives, the attack turned the opinion of many outside of Arabia against the Wahhabi cause, which ignited the Egyptian-led and Ottoman-backed campaign that would end the first Saudi state some decade and a half hence.

Conquest of Hijaz

Hijaz became the next theater of conflict after the sacking of Karbala. Abd al-Aziz had already secured the allegiance of tribes in Asir, who had agreed to fight with the Saudi forces. Sharif Ghalib's hold on power was slipping. Autocratic rule and rising taxes had turned much of the

MUHAMMAD ALI

During Napoleon's 1798–1801 incursion, Muhammad Ali, who would have a large influence on Arabia, arrived in Egypt as part of an Ottoman-British expedition to drive out the French. A Turkish tax collector from Albania, Muhammad Ali was sent to Cairo as second in command of a detachment of Ottoman irregulars. The group was shipwrecked on their way to Egypt, and Muhammad Ali took charge when the commanding officer quit after their rescue. This was a time and place in which a ruthless, cunning, and ambitious official could make a large mark, and Muhammad Ali had all these attributes. By 1799 he had risen high enough in the command to begin plotting to take over the government and replace the administration installed by the absentee Ottoman overlords. In 1803 he instigated a revolt by Cairo's Albanian garrison on the pretext of nonpayment of salaries, an insurrection that he rode into the office of Ottoman viceroy of Egypt the following year. He would go on to play a large role in the defeat of the first Saudi state.

population against him. Ghalib asked Constantinople for arms to defend the area. In March of 1803 Saud moved on Mecca with the main Wahhabi army. The sharif fled to Jeddah, and Saud sent ulama to Mecca explaining the Wahhabi beliefs. In April, Wahhabi forces entered the city. They destroyed all mausoleums and mosques with domes (an architectural detail they deemed inherently polytheistic) and all buildings that were un-Islamic in architecture. This was obviously a challenge to the sultan's supremacy in the region, as guarantor of the sanctity and protection of the holy cities. It was a challenge for the Meccans as well, particularly when the Wahhabi began formulating rules in Mecca based on their religious principles.

As noted by Alexei Vassiliev in *The History of Saudi Arabia*, "The strict morals introduced in Mecca ran counter to its people's customs and habits. The status of the holy city made its inhabitants feel superior to all other Muslims and led them to excuse a certain lewdness of behavior. Whole blocks of Mecca belonged to prostitutes, who even paid a tax on their occupation. Homosexuality was widespread. Alcohol was sold almost at the gate of the Kaaba and drunkenness was not uncommon" (Vassiliev 1998, 138–139).

The Wahhabi had begun to restrict access to the holy sites by Ottoman pilgrims, particularly Egyptians and Syrians, beginning in 1803. They also set rules of behavior for pilgrims, many of whom had arrived with musical instruments (which were subsequently banned) and other items considered trappings of earthly pleasure or idolatrous. Restrictions grew annually, as did the fees levied on caravans and their individual travelers.

There were fears the Wahhabi would attack and conquer Syria, declare the sultan as a usurper of the caliphate, and attempt to restore the Umayyads to power. The Porte asked its governors in Baghdad and Acca (present-day Israel) for help in defeating the Wahhabis, but received none. Ultimately, the Ottomans dispatched only a small group of Turks to Hijaz. But the Wahhabi hold on Hijaz proved weak. Forces laying siege to Jeddah, severely depleted and weakened by disease, withdrew, retreating to Diriya. A small garrison the Wahhabi had left in Mecca was defeated by the Ottomans in July of 1803.

The Reign of Saud

In the fall of 1803 Abd al-Aziz was murdered at age 82 in the Turaif mosque in Diriya by a Kurdish dervish who had been living as a guest at the court. The assassin, who was killed on the spot, was thought to be a former resident of Karbala who had witnessed the attack and slaughter of his city, and his intended victim was believed to be Saud. Saud returned to Diriya and received the allegiance of all his father's allies and supporters. The great-grandson of the original Saud who established the Al Saud dynasty, Saud ibn Abd al-Aziz was 55 when he became emir of Diriya. Saud was a veteran of Wahhabi campaigns; his first had been more than 35 years before, in 1767.

In 1804, the year after his ascension, Saud attacked Basra again. The city resisted his siege, though its garrison was killed. Saud's forces also destroyed shrines and took crops. Attacks on Hijaz were also conducted. Throughout 1804, the forces of both the sharif's Bedouin supporters and Ottoman Turkish troops engaged Wahhabi forces. The following year, 1805, Sharif Ghalib's forces faced the Wahhabi in Hijaz without assistance from the Ottomans. The sharif's army of 10,000 was beaten by the Najdi invaders. With Mecca's security breached, the Wahhabis occupied the area, disrupting the pilgrimage, and during the winter of 1805–06 they blockaded Mecca. A drought that afflicted the area until the end of the decade added to the inhabitants' deprivation, and they were reduced to eating dogs.

Wahhabi ulama again arrived in Mecca to begin teaching Wahhabi theology and precepts. Ghalib tried to retain authority, but by the following year he formally surrendered. He was allowed to retain his position though his income was diminished by, among other factors, his inability to continue taxing Wahhabis living under his rule. Ottoman *qadis* and officials were exiled from Hijaz. In 1805, the autocratic and corrupt ruler of Medina surrendered the city to the Wahhabi forces with the stipulation that he remain governor. His capitulation was forced by the threat of famine after the Wahhabis gained control over Medina's caravan routes.

The pilgrimage became an annual event for Saud beginning in 1807, a rite he performed with a large entourage, his yearly exchange of gifts with Ghalib becoming an elaborate ritual.

Wahhabi Attacks in the North

After the fall of Karbala, Wahhabi armies mounted persistent attacks in Mesopotamia. Most were made on undefended villages. Effective defense was compromised after the death of Buyuk Sulaiman, pasha of Baghdad, in 1802. Rivalries, power struggles, and insurrections marked the reign of his successors Ali Kahya, who was finally stabbed to death in a mosque in 1807, and Kuchuk Sulaiman, who was murdered in 1810.

In 1808 Saud sent a letter to Damascus, Aleppo, and other Syrian cities demanding adoption of Wahhabi doctrine, submission to his rule, and payment of tribute. Concurrent Wahhabi attacks on villages in the area of Aleppo sowed widespread panic in the cities. But the Wahhabis never attacked these population centers, and their raids on Syria achieved no lasting inroads. Saud himself led several thousand troops on a raid in 1810, attacking and looting dozens of villages, but this was his last major campaign to the north.

Saud's rule now extended across almost all of the Arabian Peninsula. Even the Persian Gulf emirates paid him tribute, and the nomads of the land's northern frontier pledged their fealty. At the time, the population of the peninsula was estimated by contemporary chroniclers to number some 2.4 million people. Yet his territory was now finding its limits, heralding difficulties for his reign. As noted by historian Alexei Vassiliev, "Wars, raids, plunder and unceasing expansion were the principal bases on which the Wahhabi state was established" (Vassiliev, 1998: 113). Without these spoils, unity would have disappeared. This expansionist need sealed the fate of the first Saudi state.

Roots of Decline

Ultimately, Arabia proved too big for Diriya to govern. The vast reaches, poor communication, and rebellious local populations were too much to overcome. At the borders of the territory, abutting areas the Saudis had failed to conquer—the highlands of Yemen and the Gulf Coast emirates—local inhabitants represented an ongoing destabilizing force, one on which time and effort had to be expended in containing.

Wahhabi forces had also been unsuccessful outside of Arabia. Unlike the early Islamic armies, whose policies of inclusion encouraged cities to welcome them as liberators, the ruthless tactics of the Wahhabi armies, their slaughter of civilians, and their destruction of sacred sites stimulated active resistance to their attacks. In Syria and Iraq, the Wahhabi were unable to defeat any fortified city after the fall of Karbala. The Wahhabi forces, whose battle tactics differed little from the ones practiced in the desert for centuries, faced forces trained and equipped with modern weapons.

With the plunder decreasing, Wahhabi villages and tribes became restive. The old style of raiding made more sense as a way of enriching one's tribe or village, because spoils did not have to be shared with an absentee ruler. The Bedouin tribes especially resented the control. Throughout Diriya's fledgling empire, nomad groups would periodically revolt and stop paying *zakat,* tribute, and fines. And as the income from *ghazu,* a raid for plunder, dried up, tribes and provinces ceased making payments to Diriya. Saud waged annual campaigns to bring them back into line.

Meanwhile, a gap was growing between the nobility and the commoners. The Wahhabi teachings were at variance with the lifestyles of the nobles who profited so richly from the jihad waged in their name. The common soldiers felt that they did not get enough share of the spoils and resented the demands for their service. The ruling class itself lost interest in the state and its maintenance as growth halted. Problems were compounded by the emirate's foreign relations and economic policies. As Wahhabi power expanded, the government forbade all trade with Islamic "polytheists," that is, non-Wahhabis. The economic devastation that strict implementation would have brought was avoided by noncompliance, but nonetheless, trade with both Iraq and Syria was officially forbidden until 1810. The strictures were felt most acutely in Hijaz, where these policies drastically reduced the number of pilgrims from the Ottoman Empire.

Since the Wahhabi takeover, the Ottoman sultan no longer made an annual gift, either. While the tax levied by the sharif of Mecca had been removed, it had been replaced by the *zakat*, which even Bedouin who had been immune from the sharif's taxes had to pay. As 19th-century Arab historian Abd al-Rahman al-Jabarti wrote, ". . . the people of Mecca did not receive what they had lived on—neither alms, nor food, nor money. Taking their wives and children, they left their homeland. Only those stayed to whom these incomes were not the means of subsistence. People left for Egypt and Syria and some of them for Istanbul" (Vassiliev 1998, 138).

In Jeddah, trade declined in part because foreigners were afraid to arrive in the port, fearing they would be branded as infidels. Inhabitants left Jeddah as they did Mecca, and the city began to fall into disrepair. And for citizens of Hijaz, traditionally more sedentary than those of the Najd, embarking on jihad as a path to wealth seemed an unlikely proposition. In fact, horse owners in Medina reportedly sold their animals in an effort to evade military service.

Ali's Invasion

The Ottoman Turks were never able to establish control over central Arabia. Wahhabi attacks on caravans had been a constant vexation for the Ottomans, but their military expeditions to suppress what they viewed as heretical brigands were unsuccessful. Other regional powers were unable or unwilling to wage war against the emirate of Diriya.

In 1807 the Turkish sultan, Selim III, was assassinated. He had already been discredited for not assuring the passage of his people to Mecca for the hajj and for the inability of his proxies in Arabia to defeat the Wahhabis. Sultan Mahmud II (r. 1808–39) urged Muhammad Ali, now the viceroy of Egypt, to drive the invaders out of the holy cities. Ali had many reasons of his own to agree: Controlling trade through Jeddah would be extremely lucrative and would serve as a stepping-stone in his designs on Yemen; taking back the holy cities would enhance his stature throughout the rest of the Islamic world; and the campaign would keep his army, which was showing autonomy if not posing an immediate threat, occupied elsewhere. Moreover, his efforts to secularize Egyptian society and reduce the power of the ulama revealed an ideological opposition to Wahhabi fanaticism. In 1809 preparations for the expedition began.

Ali made contact with and solicited the support of Sharif Ghalib. He instituted a rapid ship-building effort, shipping timber and other supplies from Turkey to Cairo and over the desert to Suez. Some two dozen ships to carry an invasion force across the Red Sea were built by March 1810. The following year, Ali consolidated his power in Cairo with a massacre of Mamluks. The Hijazis saw Ali as an Ottoman ruler, and thus his possible invasion as an Ottoman liberation.

The Battle Begins

The Egyptian army was composed of Turkish, Albanian, and Maghrebi (North African) mercenaries led by battle-tested commanders who had previously fought against the British and French. In August of 1811, the forces set out. One detachment approached Hijaz by sea to take Yanbu, the port city north of Jeddah. Tusun, Ali's son, led the cavalry by land. The Egyptian sea force met no Wahhabi resistance, and it seized and sacked the town. Tusun arrived in Yanbu in November. After several weeks, the combined forces set out to attack Medina. Learning of the Egyptian designs, Saud had sent a contingent of his best fighters to Medina, and they ambushed the Egyptians near Wadi al-Safra, soundly defeating them in December. But rather than pursuing the fleeing forces, the Wahhabi fighters plundered their abandoned camp, enabling the Egyptians to retreat to Yanbu.

Instead of relying solely on a military solution, bribes were paid to win over local tribes, even as reinforcements were sent to Yanbu from Egypt. In 1812 Tusun led his army on Medina. The Wahhabi garrison in the city, consisting of some 7,000 soldiers, was weakened by disease and the inhabitants' lack of support. After starting an artillery attack on Medina, the city quickly surrendered to Tusun.

In January 1813, a small Egyptian force captured Jeddah peacefully. Meanwhile, Saud's son Abdallah brought a force to reinforce Mecca. But learning of Ghalib's treachery, and unable to count on local support, he pulled the Wahhabi troops from Mecca. The city fell to Tusun, and Taif fell a few days later. The capture of the holy cities caused great celebration in Cairo. But Wahhabi forces made counterattacks in Hijaz in the spring and summer of 1813. And tribes in Asir, who were still loyal to Saud, attacked Egyptian forces near Mecca and Medina. However, that fall the Egyptians captured the Wahhabi commander, and former ally of Ghalib, Uthman al-Mudhaifi, after his failed attempt to take back Taif. He was taken to Constantinople and executed.

Ali Takes Command

Wahhabis were now on the retreat, but their forces were still active and potentially dangerous. Ali traveled to Arabia to perform the hajj and survey the situation. He arrived in Jeddah in the fall of 1813 with a contingent of several thousand troops and quickly upset the local population. Ali strove to undercut Ghalib's power, first attempting to seize the revenues of the customs duties in Jeddah, then pressuring Ghalib to order the Bedouin under his rule to provide pack animals for the Egyptian forces. Ghalib, who retained control of several thousand soldiers and the fortress at Mecca, as well as the allegiance of many Hijazis, refused to buckle to Ali's demands. Ali had Ghalib arrested, confiscated his property, and sent him to Cairo with his family, replacing the sharif with one of Ali's own loyal relatives. Ali's heavy-handed moves, while assuring his control of Hijaz, alienated much of the population, sending many of them to support the Wahhabis. The brutality of the Egyptian forces also led some Hijazis to support Ali's foes. A string of Egyptian military defeats followed in 1813 and 1814.

To change his fortunes, Ali instituted a new tax on Egyptian peasants to pay for the war in Arabia, assuring a constant supply of reinforcements and equipment for the campaign. Libyan Bedouin loyal to Ali, who had experience in desert warfare, were also sent. To win favor with Hijazis, Ali also removed some onerous taxes, gave money to the poor and gifts to the ulama, and lowered customs duties in Jeddah.

With the holy cities again open to the hajj, the Turkish authorities resumed the payments that had ended a decade before, and the renewed wave of pilgrims likewise bolstered the economy of Hijaz, further winning

Ali local support. In 1814, Imam Saud died in Diriya. This was another blow to the Wahhabi cause, though by the time of his death, much of the land conquered outside of Najd had been lost. Saud's son, Abdallah, took command of the Wahhabi forces. He staged attacks on some of the nomadic tribes of Hijaz, but he did not have the power or support to reverse the declines.

The Wahhabi Defeat

In January of 1815, in a battle near Turaba, Muhammad Ali's forces defeated the main Wahhabi army, which numbered between 20,000 and 30,000 soldiers. They then set out to conquer Asir. Once that campaign had been successfully carried out, Ali returned to Egypt, leaving his son Tusun to continue the campaign. Tusun's first objective was Qasim, the province in central Saudi Arabia. The nobility of Rass, chafing at Wahhabi rule, promised to help Tusun, who encamped his army nearby. But months of engagements had considerably weakened Tusun, and logistical support from Medina was unreliable. Abdallah's forces were also depleted, and he recognized the potential for insurrections in Qasim. The two sides negotiated an armistice. Tusun promised autonomy for Najd and withdrew his army from Qasim. Abdallah reasserted his control in the province, purging disloyal rulers, attacking the Bedouin who had turned on him, and fortifying Diriya. To the south, hostilities continued between Wahhabi and Egyptian forces in Bisha, Turaba, and Ranya, though these engagements turned local populations against the Wahhabis.

Muhammad Ali, said to be operating under orders from the Porte to root out the Wahhabi threat once and for all, dispatched his eldest son, Ibrahim, to lead a military expedition into Najd. The force, about 8,000 troops according to one estimate, included cavalry, infantry, and artillery drawn from Turkey, Albania, and North Africa. After landing at the port of Yanbu, Ibrahim arrived in Medina in 1816. To win the support of the Bedouin, he ended the *zakat* and paid for their support against the Wahhabi forces. He also enjoined his troops from pillaging locals. Bedouin tribes in Najd began to desert Abdallah. In 1817, Ibrahim continued where his brother Tusun had left off and laid siege to Rass. Wahhabi forces, assisted by heat and disease, held off Ibrahim's forces while inflicting heavy casualties, but reinforcements replenished the Egyptians' strength. That October, the Wahhabi forces negotiated a withdrawal, allowing them to return to Abdallah with their arms.

The Fall of Diriya

By the end of 1817, all of Qasim had fallen to Ibrahim. His invasion army was supplemented by indigenous forces, some opposed to Wahhabi rule, others willing to ally themselves with the presumptive victor. Abdallah retreated farther into Najd, eventually withdrawing to Diriya, ancestral home of Al Saud, joined by supporters from throughout the region. After awaiting reinforcements, Ibrahim continued his advance early the following year. Though his force likely numbered only a few thousand, he succeeded in subduing resistance met in Najd. The Egyptian troops arrived at the gates of Diriya in April of 1818.

Though well-fortified and defended by the regime's most fervent warriors, the Saudi forces were bereft of their usual allies. The natural defenses of the desert had been breached by Ottoman supply lines. The Bedouin, who typically resisted any foreign incursion, had been so alienated by the regime that they joined outsiders. And the Egyptians had a modern, well-equipped army with artillery and superior tactics.

On September 11, 1818, following a seven-month siege that capped a seven-year Egyptian campaign, the Saudi imam, Abdallah ibn Saud, surrendered to Muhammad Ali's son, Ibrahim Pasha. The Saudi state was ended. Ibrahim looted Diriya, and on orders of Muhammad Ali, the town was obliterated. Yet almost immediately the foundation of the second Saudi state began to form within its ruins.

7

ROOTS OF MODERN ARABIA (1818–1891)

The fall of Diriya in September of 1818 marked the end of the first Saudi state. The last of its rulers, Imam Abdallah ibn Saud, who surrendered to the Egyptian commander, Ibrahim Pasha, son of Muhammad Ali, was sent to Cairo, then six months later to Constantinople. Abdallah's arrival was greeted with three days of celebrations during which he was paraded through the streets, then beheaded.

The Saudi defeat was a victory not only for the Egyptians but also for opponents of the Wahhabi who chaffed at their religious and social strictures, and for previously independent tribes resentful of their subjugation by the Saudi-Wahhabi forces. Yet despite this opposition, Al Saud and Wahhabism had united Arabia (albeit by sword) and largely halted the tribal warfare and instability that had wracked the land since before the coming of Muhammad. Their defeat at Diriya, complete as it appeared, became a mark of the resilience of their movement and the implacability of its adherents, as Saudi and Wahhabi loyalists forged a second Saudi state that would survive until the last decade of the century. This chapter surveys the resurgent Saudi state during these years.

Ashes of the First Saudi State

In Hijaz the Ottomans, who had driven the Wahhabi from Medina and Mecca in late 1812 and early 1813, had been regarded by some Wahhabi opponents as a liberating force. Strict religious doctrine and practices such as compulsory prayer and bans on music and other entertainments were vacated. Though Ottoman troops were garrisoned around the region to preserve order and establish Ottoman presence, for most in Hijaz, especially those outside of garrison towns, Ottoman rule was more transparent than Wahhabi rule had been. Not so in Najd, the birthplace and stronghold of the movement.

Following the conquest of Diriya, Ibrahim's forces fanned out across Najd. No domestic force remained to resist their advances. Many Bedouin, whose alliances were traditionally fluid and who were not deeply committed to the Wahhabi movement in any event, switched allegiances and joined with the occupying force. Ibrahim was ruthless in suppressing any remnants of the Saudi-Wahhabi rule. Leaders associated with the deposed regime were killed, and villages were plundered and then leveled, often using the inhabitants as forced labor to carry out the destruction. British captain George Forster (G.F.) Sadleir (1789–1859), on a mission to attempt to arrange an alliance with Ibrahim Pasha and the Ottomans (as we will discuss shortly), witnessed these suppression efforts and wrote of them in an official dispatch recounted in his *Diary of a Journey across Arabia*.

> *"It has unluckily fallen to my lot to have become acquainted with a leading feature of Ibrahim Pasha's character from personal observation, to which I have to add that the general history of the late campaign entrusted to his management exhibits a series of the most barbarous cruelties, committed in violation of the faith of the most sacred promises; on some occasions to enrich himself by the plunder of the very tribesmen who had contributed to his success, and in other cases to obtain the wealth of such of his vanquished enemies as had for a moment screened themselves from his rage. These unfortunate wretches, deluded by the fairest promises, have frequently fallen victims to his avaricious disposition and insatiable desire to shed human blood"* (Sadleir 1977, 158).

Ibrahim sent the ears of those killed back to his father, Muhammad Ali, in Cairo. Severed heads had originally been dispatched to Egypt, but given the great numbers killed, ears were judged more practical trophies. Despite such offerings, Muhammad Ali ordered Ibrahim to pull the forces back to Hijaz that same year. The cost of supporting the troops was high, and the problems of supplying and communicating with them across hundreds of miles of desert were great. But whether the command to pull back originated with Muhammad Ali or came from the Porte, which had ordered the thrust into Najd, is unknown. Ali also ordered Ibrahim to bring members of the Al Saud and Al Sheikh (Abd al-Wahhab's bloodline) families to Cairo for detention. After extorting protection money from them, Ibrahim seized and deported about 400, later capturing more. Before withdrawing the last of his troops, Ibrahim had Diriya completely razed. His forces destroyed all foodstocks and fortifications they came across during their pullback to Hijaz.

In the resulting power vacuum, central Arabia reverted to its pre-Wahhabi ways. Family, clan, and tribal rivalries and warfare resumed. Caravan routes were again unsafe. People abandoned the region. As anarchy and violence reigned and the enriching plunder of Wahhabi conquests gave way to poverty, the religious excesses of the Wahhabi regime doubtless dimmed in the memory of many who had welcomed their demise.

Over the next two decades, Muhammad Ali appointed a series of viceroys and governors to rule Arabia. Ibrahim was followed by his cousin Khalil Pasha, the son of Ali's sister. Khalil died soon thereafter, and his brother, Ahmad Shukri Yakan Bey, took the post. Turkish general Khurshid Pasha was given charge from 1829 into 1833 and conducted a major military campaign in eastern Arabia, a thrust that caused his removal due to British objections. After Khurshid Pasha's departure, his predecessor, Yakan Bey, was reappointed, serving until 1841. Throughout these years, opposition to the foreign occupiers rose.

Muhammad Ali also ordered a series of campaigns to subdue renewed resistance in Asir, the first of them in 1820. Several ended in decisive defeats for the invaders, and none achieved any lasting success.

Britain in Arabia

When Muhammad Ali had first mounted his campaign to bring down the Saudi-Wahhabi state under the command of his son, Ibrahim

PROTECTING INDIA'S FLANK

As the first Saudi state began to flourish at the beginning of the 19th century, India was the most precious jewel among Britain's crown colonies. The British viewed the Persian Gulf region and the east coast of Africa as India's western flank. Intent on retaining control of the sea lanes and maintaining regional dominance to protect its position in India, the British opposed efforts by other powers to establish a foothold in the region. Having exclusive access to port facilities along the Arabian coast was an important component of this policy, which was furthered by Britain's informal protectorate relationships with the controlling principalities. Two regional forces jeopardized Britain's hegemony: Pirates operating from the Gulf coast and Wahhabi attacks on the emirates both undercut British authority. British determination to suppress both activities brought them into conflict with the Saudi-Wahhabi forces.

Diriya was leveled by the Egyptians at the end of the first Saudi state. Almost immediately, efforts to rebuild it and restore the power of the Saudi-Wahhabi leadership began. (Courtesy of *Saudi Aramco World/*PADIA)

Pasha, the British had welcomed the effort. The Wahhabi demands for tribute and periodic attacks on Oman had alienated the British, whose India Office labeled the Wahhabi as "predatory" and a threat to the stability, such as it was, of the peninsula's interior. The British saw the Egyptians as potential partners in suppressing both rising Wahhabi power and piracy in the Persian Gulf, and they sought a military alliance with them. In 1819 Captain G.F. Sadleir landed at Qatif (his craft required the assistance of pilots dispatched by a local pirate lord to reach the harbor) and set off to find Ibrahim Pasha to discuss a partnership between the two governments. It took about three months before Sadleir met Ibrahim near Medina, on the opposite coast, becoming the first Westerner to cross the peninsula. After brief negotiations the Egyptians declined the British invitation and Ibrahim Pasha expelled Sadleir from Arabia.

In the absence of Egyptian assistance and on their own, British naval forces initiated successful actions against coastal emirates that were aimed at suppressing piracy. The British, with their superior firepower and tactical advantages, achieved quick success, losing only a handful of soldiers while inflicting casualties reportedly in the hundreds. The campaign concluded in the General Treaty of Peace in 1820. Bahrain and the emirs of the Trucial sheikhdoms along the coast agreed to cease acts of piracy, and Britain acquired legal rights to the area. British forces also directly engaged Wahhabi elements on land, battling the Anu Bu Ali tribe in both 1820 and 1821. Here the British suffered heavy losses in their first encounter, then returned with a larger force with which they decisively defeated the tribe and razed its town.

The Bid for Local Rule

With the occupiers gone from Najd, Muhammad ibn Mishari ibn Muammar, scion of the family that formerly ruled the town of Uyaina and a Saudi relative by marriage, sought rule of the area in 1819, soliciting Ottoman approval for his bid. Ibn Muammar returned to Diriya and began organizing reconstruction efforts, earning growing support. A rival, the sheikh of a leading Banu Khalid family in Hasa, Majid ibn Uraiir, also sought the role of emir of Najd, an effort that foundered after an unsuccessful assault on Riyadh. Two members of Al Saud sought to restore their family's leadership, as well: Mushari ibn Saud ibn Abd al-Aziz and Turki ibn Abdallah ibn Muhammad ibn Saud. Mushari was the brother of the last Saudi imam, Abdallah. Though captured by the Egyptians, Mushari had escaped and shortly thereafter established rule in the village of Washm, proclaiming himself imam. After Mushari marched on Diriya with his supporters, Ibn Muammar relinquished his rule in favor of the Saudi and left Diriya. But upon gathering more support, Ibn Muammar returned and seized Mushari, putting his own son (also named Mushari) in charge.

Turki ibn Abdallah ibn Muhammad ibn Saud, a cousin of Imam Abdallah who had evaded capture after Diriya's fall, had meanwhile taken refuge with other members of Al Saud in Riyadh. After taking Mushari, Ibn Muammar advanced on Riyadh intent on capturing Turki and other family members, removing the threat to his rule that they represented. But Turki and the others fled before his arrival. They rallied local support and soon took Diriya and Riyadh, capturing Ibn Muammar and his son. One reason given for the lack of support for Ibn Muammar among the population was his recognition by the Ottomans, a force that had few friends in central Arabia. Turki's attempts to bargain Ibn Muammar and his son's release for that of his cousin, Mushari, failed. When Turki learned Mushari had died while being taken to Cairo, he had Ibn Muammar and his son executed.

The Return of Al Saud

Concerned about renewed Saudi activity and local insurrections, Muhammad Ali had dispatched forces to Qasim, the Najdi province to the east of Medina, under Husain Bey, a commander noted for his ruthlessness. Husain Bey arrived in the late fall of 1820 with fresh Turkish reinforcements. Moving on Riyadh, he vanquished the small Saudi force, but again Turki eluded capture. Husain Bey then began a two-year terror campaign, pillaging, killing, and destroying crops and fortifications. Compounding the misery Husain Bey wrought were the ravages of a cholera epidemic that swept central Arabia. It was a time when the devil ruled the people, according to historian Ibn Bishr (Winder 1980, 56). Yet the victories were not all the Egyptians'. Several detachments were soundly defeated or fought to a standstill when they ventured out from their fortified strongholds to collect taxes around the region.

Turki, who went into hiding following Husain Bey's defeat of Riyadh, reappeared in 1821. Through a combination of what has been called "calculated bluff and courage," he brought tribes and settlements throughout the center of Najd under his control (Winder 1980, 63). In 1823 he began raids against the occupying Turkish and Egyptian forces. By then Husain Bey had been replaced by Hasan abu Zahir. But the atrocities and carnage committed in Husain's name had provoked an uprising

Riyadh, seen here in the 1930s, became Al Saud's stronghold and the Saudi state's capital in 1824 and has remained so ever since. (Courtesy of the Fine Arts Library, Harvard College Library, Twitchell Collection, Harvard Semitic Museum Photography Archives)

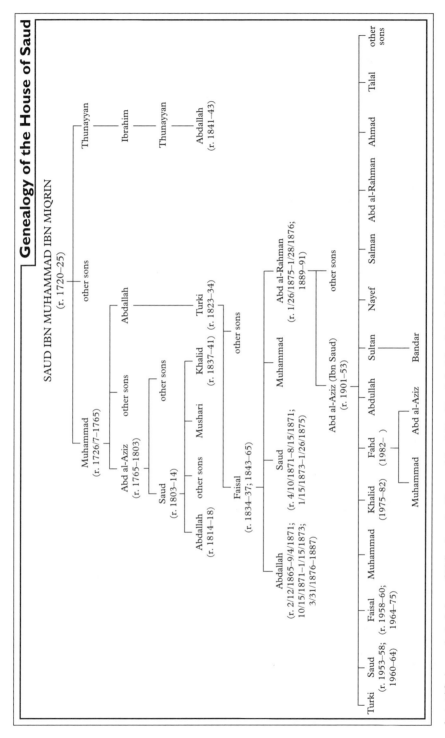

Genealogy of the House of Saud

SAUD IBN MUHAMMAD IBN MIQRIN
(r. 1720–25)

A simplified genealogical chart of Al Saud, or the House of Saud (the "Saudis" of Saudi Arabia). The family established itself in Diriya in the 15th century, and its leaders came to play a large role in central Arabia from the middle of the 18th century. Its members often battled each other for dominance.

throughout Qasim. Again unable to justify the cost of maintaining the necessary forces to control Najd in light of the growing resistance, the Egyptians largely abandoned the region once more, leaving troops only in Riyadh and Manfuha. In 1824, with a small force gathered from surrounding oases, Turki drove the occupying forces from these towns as well and made Riyadh his headquarters. Riyadh has been the capital of Najd ever since, and today is the capital of Saudi Arabia. The following year (1825) Turki conquered Kharj, the province to the south of Riyadh, concluding the first stage of the restoration of Saudi power and earning recognition as the first ruler of the second Saudi state.

Turki's Reign

Turki's reign represented a change in the ruling branch of the royal family. Muhammad, the first Saudi imam, had two sons: Abdallah and Abd al-Aziz (Turki's father and uncle, respectively). Abd al-Aziz, who succeeded Muhammad, established the line from which the following two imams—Saud and Abdallah—issued. With Turki's ascension, rule switched to the line founded by Muhammad's second son and Turki's father, Abdallah. All succeeding rulers up to the present have come from this branch of Al Saud.

Turki's rule brought brief stability to central Najd. Refugees who had fled when Diriya fell returned. Turki appointed one, his cousin Mushari ibn Abd al-Rahman ibn Mushari ibn Saud, who escaped detention in Egypt, as governor of Manfuha. But Mushari's ambitions and connections to Egypt would be Turki's undoing.

Having secured central Najd, Turki attempted to pacify the Eastern Province (Hasa), the region east of the Najd running from Kuwait in the north to the base of the Qatar peninsula in the south. Its most important center was an area of verdant oases supporting several settlements and two large towns, Hufuf and Mubarraz. Sixty miles north, on the Persian Gulf coast, was Qatif, a Shia stronghold. The primary force in Hasa was the Banu Khalid tribe. Independent as far back as the 10th century, they had resisted Saudi domination since the early days of the first Saudi state and, as previously noted, had been a major opposing force in Hasa.

From its beginning Wahhabism had been a "sedentary" movement, focused on settled populations. Bedouin like the Banu Khalid had been difficult to subdue and to force into ongoing compliance with Wahhabi precepts. Turki's campaign in Eastern Province was mounted with the goal of bringing the region's nomads into the Wahhabi community. Turki battled the Banu Khalid here from 1826 until he conquered the province in 1830. During this time at least five major tribes pledged allegiance to Turki and agreed to pay taxes—in the form of *zakat,* as during the first Saudi state—to Riyadh. These victories sealed Saudi control in the region and also demonstrated that Bedouin warriors, long celebrated for their fierceness and prowess, could not match the capabilities of military forces that could now be raised by sedentary populations.

During the eastern campaign Turki's son Faisal, who had been captured when Diriya fell a decade before, returned after escaping Egyptian arrest and was placed in charge of Hasa. He would become the greatest ruler in the second phase of Al Saud's rule. Turki, meanwhile, continued to fend off rival claimants and subdue regional resistance. He also made efforts to establish relations with the British, who responded cordially but noncommittally to his request to reach a treaty with them. Said to be a compassionate and equitable ruler, Turki lectured his commanders and representatives on the importance of showing respect and treating fairly those under them. He could also deal harshly with his enemies when necessary.

Turki's reign ended in 1834 when he was assassinated as he emerged from Friday prayers in a plot engineered by Mushari ibn Abd al-Rahman, the cousin he had appointed governor of Manfuha. Mushari ibn Abd al-Rahman had previously staged an unsuccessful revolt against Turki and been pardoned by the Saudi emir, an experience that did not deter him from his second attempt at seizing rule.

Faisal, Turki's son, rushed to Riyadh from Hasa to wrest rule from Mushari. A siege of Riyadh's citadel ensued. Abdullah ibn Rashid, a member of the Rashid family, which would play the major role in the demise of the second Saudi state, helped breach the defenses and capture Mushari ibn Abd al-Rahman, who was then executed. Faisal was quickly recognized as the new emir.

By the end of Turki's reign he had recaptured all the territories of the first Saudi state with the exception of those in Hijaz. Yet Najd would endure almost a decade of unrest and instability as several rival members of Al Saud sought rule in Riyadh.

Egyptian Rule and Faisal's First Reign

In 1831 Muhammad Ali had proclaimed his independence from his suzerain in Constantinople, Mahmud II, after the Ottoman sultan reneged on a pledge to make Ali governor of Syria in return for Ali's previous assistance in suppressing a revolt in Greece in 1827. Muhammad

Ali sent an army led by his son Ibrahim against the Ottomans in Syria and Anatolia (present-day Turkey). Ibrahim's forces came within 150 miles of Constantinople, requiring the political intercession of Britain, France, and Russia to stop the Egyptian advance. Yet Egypt's power in Arabia was already waning. Besides the military setbacks in Najd and Asir following the victory at Diriya in 1818, the defeat of the Turkish-Egyptian naval fleet at the hands of a combined British, French, and Russian fleet during the revolt in Greece had further dimmed its threat. And warfare with the Ottomans, once it began, diverted Egyptian attention and resources from Arabia. At the height of this conflict in 1832, Egyptian troops in Jeddah, angry at its conditions, switched allegiance to Turkey, requiring Egypt to send troops to subdue its own rebellious forces.

In 1837, Turki's son Faisal, now ruling Riyadh, refused to pay tribute to the Egyptian rulers in Hijaz. Egypt responded by backing Faisal's cousin, Khalid ibn Saud, brother of Imam Abdallah, last ruler of the first Saudi state, as the emir of Riyadh. Khalid had been exiled to Egypt after the fall of Diriya, where he was educated under Muhammad Ali's aegis. Cairo viewed Khalid as pliant and loyal. An Egyptian force headed by Ismail Bey, former head of the Cairo police, was sent to join with Khalid's forces and retake Najd. Faisal sent forces to confront Ismail and Khalid's army in Qasim. But Faisal's support among Najdis was weak. Khalid, after all, had a legitimate claim to rule, as the brother of Abdallah. And the firepower of the Egyptian forces, which had already been amply demonstrated in central Arabia, also made the populace reluctant to oppose them. Faisal's troops fled Qasim without fighting, with Riyadh falling to Khalid soon after. Faisal retreated south to Kharj and then Hufuf, pursued by a combined Egyptian-Arabian force estimated at 7,000 men. Yet in a decisive battle near Hilwah (from which Faisal was absent), Ismail and Khalid's army met perhaps the worst defeat of the Egyptians' repeated attempts to subdue Najd. Few besides the two leaders and a few officers escaped. Seizing the advantage, Faisal laid siege to Egyptian-occupied Riyadh. Though he was unable to dislodge the Egyptians, the two sides agreed to divide Najd. Faisal would control eastern Arabia and southern Najd, thus renouncing his claim to Riyadh; his cousin Khalid would control central Najd. But the next year, 1838, the Egyptians sent another force against Faisal under Khurshid Pasha. Khurshid, with 4,000 troops, repulsed an attack by the Wahhabi army of some 8,000 warriors near Faisal's new stronghold of Dilam. A 40-day siege of the town ensued, and in December 1838, Dilam fell. Faisal was taken prisoner and for a second time exiled to Egypt. It seemed an unpromising turn in the life of the once and future ruler of the second Saudi state.

Egypt's Last Campaigns

Though Muhammad Ali failed to dominate Najd, he nonetheless sought to extend Egyptian control over more of the peninsula. He directed Khurshid Pasha, whom he appointed as vice regent in Arabia in 1829, to lead a campaign against Bahrain. The British, hewing to their policy of blocking foreign powers from establishing a presence in the region, warned Muhammad Ali to stop his Gulf adventures. Bowing to British pressure, the campaign was halted and Khurshid Pasha recalled to Cairo.

A decade later in 1838–39, a similar scenario unfolded. During Egyptian maneuvers in the east, Khalid ibn Saud, the Egyptian-backed emir of Riyadh who replaced Faisal, attacked Oman. Britain considered blockading Egyptian-controlled Gulf Coast ports in response. Concurrently, British concerns over Muhammad Ali's campaigns in Asir were coming to a climax. In what proved to be the last attempt, Egyptian forces achieved several victories but were unable to consolidate their gains. The occupation incited a rebellion in the region in 1837, but the campaign continued. In response the British seized Aden, the strategic territory on the peninsula's southwest coast that included the port of the same name, in 1839. In March of 1840, after 11 military campaigns against Asir, Muhammad Ali ordered the Egyptian forces to withdraw from Yemen, Asir, and Najd. The retreat was one component of the sudden collapse of Ali's empire, caused in part by British efforts to contain him. The end of his ambitions was officially marked by the London Convention of 1840, in which Egypt accepted Ottoman suzerainty, thus staving off British and Russian military action against Ali's forces in support of the Ottomans. Thereafter, Egyptian influence in Arabia virtually ended.

With the Egyptians gone, the struggle for supremacy among Najdi rulers recommenced, as did warfare among the Bedouin. Raids against Shammar tribes by members of the Anaza, a tribe allied with Qasim, led to one such conflict, intensified by a rivalry between the rulers of Buraida and Jabal Shammar. Two expeditions dispatched against Jabal Shammar communities from Qasim were defeated by the Rashidi brothers.

In Riyadh, Khalid, viewed as a pawn of the Egyptians, was forced from power a year after Egyptian withdrawal by Abdallah ibn Thunayyan, the great-great-grandson of the founder of the house of Saud. After defeating Khalid in battle, Ibn Thunayyan quickly took Hufuf, in Eastern Province.

Proclaiming himself the emir of Riyadh, he courted the rulers of Hijaz with gifts, but his dealings with foes were heavy-handed, marked by executions and excessive taxes, costing him support. His authority was further undercut by his lack of control over Qasim, Jabal Shammar, and other areas of the Eastern Province beyond Hufuf.

Faisal's Second Reign

In 1843, five years after his capture at Dilam, Faisal ibn Turki escaped from Egypt. He appeared in Jabal Shammar and issued a call for support to reclaim the emirship in Riyadh, still held by Ibn Thunayyan. Given their respective records, support for Faisal quickly grew, and Riyadh was his within the year. Ibn Thunayyan was captured and imprisoned, dying soon thereafter. Faisal's return ended almost a decade of chaos in central Najd, but his military campaigns to retake territory and subdue recalcitrant tribes continued on and off for the next two decades.

Faisal first retook Hasa, which Bahrain had seized, ejecting the Bahraini garrison from the coastal city of Dammam in 1844, and winning a pledge for payment of tribute to Riyadh from the island emirate. When tribal warfare in Hasa led to an attack on a caravan of pilgrims by one of the warring tribes, the Ajman, the following year, Faisal captured and executed the tribe's sheikh. The plunder was returned and an apology issued by the sheikh's son. Insurrections, regional warfare, and blood feuds also required Faisal's intervention. Qasim proved particularly nettlesome, illustrating the challenge that faced any ruler trying to subjugate and unify the fiercely independent populations.

Qasim, a province of some 20 towns and villages east of Hijaz, resolutely resisted Faisal's control. When the sharif of Mecca invaded Najd in these years (1846–47), the population's eager assistance to the Hijazis demonstrated their antipathy for Saudi rule. After the sharif's withdrawal, Faisal replaced rulers in several of the towns, but another rebellion broke out in the winter of 1848, lasting until the following spring. Buraida and Anaza, two of the larger towns in the province with populations of about 10,000 and 20,000, respectively, both rejected Faisal's authority. He sent a force along with a message, urging inhabitants to spare him the necessity of attacking. The peace agreement subsequently concluded was soon breached by both sides, leading to a battle in which Wahhabi forces under Faisal's son defeated the forces of Qasim. Some of its leaders fled, and peace was concluded. Qasim's emir, Abd al-Aziz Al Ulayyan, though he had been left in place by Faisal, fled to Hijaz, fearing retribution. There he sought the sharif's assistance in mounting an attack on Najd. Not wanting to antagonize Faisal, the sharif declined and instead negotiated the ruler's pledge of allegiance to Faisal. However, Faisal had replaced him in the interim. Dissatisfied with the leader installed by Faisal, in 1854 a new revolt broke out in Anaza. After inconclusive battles with Faisal's troops, the revolt ended the following year, with the leader of the insurrection still in place and Faisal's appointed ruler ousted.

Hijaz: Privilege and Diversity

The Hijaz, despite its more sedentary population, was home to a diversity of tribes as was Najd, each with their area of predominance. The tribes themselves were segmented into small groups, headed by a sheikh, without any higher tribal authority and little allegiance to their brethren. Groups of Ashraf, sharifian families claiming descent from the Quraysh and Muhammad, inhabited Mecca and Medina and also lived amongst the Bedouins of Hijaz. Prominent judges and preachers in addition to political leaders came from these families.

A sizable population of nonindigenous Muslims from throughout the Middle East and Asia also lived in Hijaz, and a spectrum of Islamic beliefs were practiced here, with Shia communities, Sufi orders, and several schools of Islamic law coexisting.

Both the sharif of Mecca and the Ottoman governors in Jeddah and Medina, who typically held the title of pasha, claimed authority over central Arabia, including the right to levy tribute. The sharif used this right to send forces into Najd, reaching Qasim in 1847, but his efforts to exact tribute were only marginally successful. In Riyadh, as often happened in

Mecca's central importance to Islam and the income generated by its pilgrim traffic made rule of the city a greatly contested position, both by outside powers and by the ruling class within. This photo was taken in the late 19th century. (Courtesy of the Saudi Information Office)

A DELICATE BALANCE
OF POWER

The sharifs' power had waxed and waned since the 16th century in response to the degree of Ottoman involvement in Arabia, with whom the sharifs maintained an uneasy partnership. The representative of the Turkish sultan was responsible for issues involving commerce, administration, and foreign affairs; the sharif was responsible for matters relating to the holy cities, tribal confederations, and security outside of the urban areas. While the sultan, as the titular head of the Islamic Empire, was officially the protector of the holy sites, in practice he needed the support of the sharif to exercise his control. The sharifs, meanwhile, needed the subsidies provided by the Ottomans. This created a partnership of mutual necessity and simmering antagonism that existed for centuries, though the sharifs were usually in the subservient position. The Ottomans retained the right to appoint the sharif. Many were raised in Constantinople under the tutelage of the sultan's court, often seeing Mecca for the first time when they arrived after their appointment as the local ruler. At the same time, sharifs deemed too closely allied with the Ottomans were not accepted by Meccan citizens, limiting the sultan's ability to install leadership of his choosing in Hijaz.

such situations, Faisal paid a small sum in tribute and agreed to give more but, once the sharif's forces left, withheld additional payments.

Ottoman Designs and Actions

In addition to their assertion of dominion over central Arabia, the Ottomans also pressed their claim to Asir. Though Muhammad Ali's Egyptian forces had failed to conquer it in repeated attempts, the Ottomans continued these efforts with equal lack of success. In 1849 their forces landed by warships and were defeated in Asir and Yemen, as they were in a subsequent campaign of 1851–52. The sharif at the time, Muhammad ibn Aun, cultivated good relations with the Bedouin of Asir and Hijaz, some of whom fought against the Ottoman invasions into their territory. This friendship with their enemies led to the sharif's removal by the Ottomans, who had him and two of his sons brought to Constantinople. However, Sharif Muhammad was returned in 1855 after widespread unrest in Hijaz led to the loss of Ottoman control of

Mecca. Ottoman garrisons were driven out of Asir, and they were saved in Hijaz only by a cholera epidemic that swept the insurgents' encampments. Nonetheless, Ottoman efforts to subdue Asir continued. Two years after the Suez Canal opened in 1869, it was used to transport Ottoman troops sent to revive the occupation.

The opening of the Suez Canal in 1869 and the British occupation of Egypt in 1882 made Arabia and control of the Arabian Gulf of more concern to the British. But as already seen, Britain's interest in the region predated these events by decades.

Riyadh and Britain Joust

Britain, viewing the Arabian coast as the western flank of its empire in India, was committed to exercising dominance in the region. Riyadh, however, considered the coastal emirates within its own sphere of influence, if not under its sovereignty, and regarded Britain's protectorate relationship as interference in its domain. Riyadh's campaigns to conquer the coastal emirates and collect tribute led to ongoing conflict with Britain. Saudi forces attacked Bahrain demanding tribute in 1845 and 1846. When they repeated the incursion in 1850 a British fleet came to Bahrain's defense and Faisal made peace, though Bahrain agreed to pay tribute. In 1859 the emir of Qatif in the Eastern Province prepared an invasion of Bahrain, and a squadron of British ships again sailed to the rescue. Concerned about the stability of Bahrain's ruling family, Britain demanded the emir's rivals be exiled from Dammam, putting more distance between them and their island objective 10 miles offshore. After the emir of Qatif refused to comply, the British bombarded the city.

In 1861 Britain compelled Bahrain to agree to a treaty making it a British protectorate in the manner of the Trucial sheikhdoms. The Saudis made no further claims on the island.

As a group, the emirates skirted between compliance and defiance of Saudi demands for tribute, agreeing to and then withholding payments until Saudi-Wahhabi troops arrived in the area, with the British in the background all the while, prepared to exercise force to maintain the sovereignty of the coastal emirates, if not their freedom from paying tribute.

The Rise of Al Rashid

The power of the Saudi state ebbed during the last half of the 19th century as that of another emirship and dynasty rose in Najd: Al Rashid, or the House of Rashid. The Rashidis' power base was the province of Jabal

Shammar and its capital, Hail (a name by which the province is also known). Situated in the north-central area of Najd, it enjoyed a reputation as the most authentic and pure of Bedouin territories, celebrated for the fine pre-Islamic poetry and fierce warriors it produced. It was home of the powerful Shammar tribal confederation, known for valor and courage on the battlefield. The tribes also controlled the caravan routes—including those of smugglers—that linked the region with Iraq.

The progenitor of the Al Rashid dynasty, Ali ibn Rashid, had been a vassal of Saud, the third ruler of the first Saudi state. Following the fall of Diriya in 1818, the governor of Jabal Shammar defeated an abortive attempt to reestablish Rashidi rule in Hail mounted by Abdullah ibn Rashid, a minor member of the family. Abdullah ibn Rashid fled, ultimately receiving sanctuary in Riyadh, where he became friendly with Turki and his son, Faisal. It was in Riyadh that Abdullah helped Faisal overcome Turki's assassin, Mushari, thereby assuring Faisal the emirship and earning his gratitude.

Faisal, after withdrawing his support for the governor of Jabal Shammar who had opposed the Rashidi restoration, assisted Abdullah ibn Rashid in assuming rule in Hail, which he did in 1835. A Wahhabi *qadi* was installed in Hail, signifying the Rashidis' fealty to the Saudis.

Rashidi Expansion

In the mid-19th century during the rule of Abdullah's son, Talal ibn Abdullah Al Rashid (r. 1847–68), the Rashidis began expanding their territory north and south, attracting independent Shammar tribes and settlements predominated by Shammar to join the confederation. Intermarriage between the Rashidis and members of various Shammar tribal groups helped cement alliances. Hail, like other oasis-based settlements, had a sedentary population of farmers, merchants, artisans, and craftsmen; not all of these were Shammar, but they submitted to Rashidi rule as well. In contrast to the Saudis, expansion of the emirate did not require religious conversions of entire populations; most were already Shammar. Weaker tribes and unaffiliated settlements were subjugated by force. Upon these, the Rashidis levied a tax, but unlike the *zakat*, the religious payments of the Wahhabis, the Rashidis collected *khuwa*, or tribute, indicating a divergence of policy with Riyadh.

Tribal loyalty was the main unifying element in Jabal Shammar, but more than simple solidarity lay behind the expansion of Rashidi dominion. The Shammar had suffered at the hands of the Saudi forces at the end of the 18th century, uprooting some tribal groups to Mesopotamia

ARABIAN HORSES

The Bedouin have been passionate breeders of horses for centuries. Though less suited to desert life than camels, no animal was more highly prized or brought as much esteem to its owners as the Arabian horse. The Bedouin considered them a gift from God, and tracked bloodlines of their horses as closely as they did that of their families. Its speed made the Arabian horse an ideal raiding platform. Sometimes camels would be ridden to a point of attack and horses then mounted for the actual raid.

Europeans were introduced to Arabian horses during the Crusades. In the West, horses had been bred for size and strength to carry armored soldiers. But the introduction of firearms, whose projectiles could pierce medieval armor, made speed and maneuverability more desirable attributes, and horses from Arabia lightened the stock of equines in Europe. With their prominent foreheads, arched necks, and high tail carriage, Arabian purebreds have also long been considered the most beautiful of horses. Physiologically, they have fewer ribs and back and tail bones than all other equine species.

A large export market for Arabian horses did not develop until the 1860s, spurred by demand from British-held India. In 1863, 600 horses bred by the Shammar were reported to have been exported through Kuwait. The total number sold, given the multitude of tribes and export points, was doubtless many times that. Horses competed with dates for the honor as Arabia's top export. Such was the concern about the demand's effect on the supply of Arabian horses that a moratorium was declared on exports for four years. Today, Arabian horses remain the most coveted and ubiquitous of all purebred equines.

during the first Saudi state. The Shammar had also been attacked by the Egyptian forces who came to defeat the Saudi-Wahhabi forces in 1818 and mistook Shammar territory for that of their quarry. In vesting power in the hands of the Rashidis, the Shammar sought more power for themselves as a group. Sedentary populations supported the Rashidis because they were able to assure the security of caravans for both pilgrims and merchants, enabling trade and encouraging economic activity. As summed up by historian Madawi Al-Rasheed in *A History of Saudi Arabia*, "The centralization of power in the hands of the Rashidis stemmed from the context of political upheaval, military turmoil and foreign intervention in Arabia" (2002, 27).

Talal Al Rashid was noted for religious tolerance, allowing Shia and Jews to live and work in Hail, though he charged them large taxes. The revenues were used to build a grand palace and fortress, which Abdullah had begun, in the Barzan quarter of Hail. Talal paid an annual tribute to Riyadh, though the power of the emirate of Jabal Shammar grew while Riyadh's declined. He maintained relations with Faisal and, after Faisal's death, with his immediate successor, Abdallah ibn Faisal. In 1868 Talal committed suicide, considered a heinous sin among Muslims.

Talal's brother Mitaab (r. 1868–69) succeeded him. The following year Talal's uncle, another Saudi loyalist, died, further weakening the connection between the two emirates forged some three decades before. Mitaab was killed and succeeded by Talal's son Bandar (r. 1869–72). Bandar himself was killed by his uncle, Muhammad ibn Abdallah Al Rashid, who then dispatched Bandar's four brothers, hoping to prevent further insurrection. Muhammad ruled from 1872 to 1897, his quarter-century reign affording a period of relative stability in Jabal Shammar. By the time his reign ended, the second Saudi state had been brought down, as much by Muhammad's skillful maneuvering as by its self-destructive internal rivalries.

While the Rashidi emirate grew, exercising real control over its extended domain was difficult. Despite the unity the confederation projected, tribal intransigence among the Shammar—if not outright rebellion—was a constant, and military action, typically in the form of raids in which plunder was exacted in lieu of the tribute these recalcitrant tribes had withheld, was the sole recourse. A portion of the tribute and booty was paid out to allied tribes to ensure their loyalty. Unable to raise troops from citizens under their nominal rule, the Rashidi forces were increasingly composed of the emir's own slaves supplemented by conscripts. Concerns about potential plots hatched by apparent allies and deadly family feuds also mandated reliance on foreign soldiers. Turkish and Egyptian mercenaries served as palace guards.

Riyadh After Faisal

Faisal died in December of 1865, having reigned over a period of relative stability in Najd, ongoing military campaigns notwithstanding. He left four sons: Abdallah (the eldest), Saud, Muhammad, and Abd al-Rahman. The rivalries and competition for rule between Abdallah and Saud would reignite conflict in central Arabia and hasten the end of the second Saudi state.

Abdallah, the crown prince, succeeded Faisal. He was regarded as an able military commander and a heavy-handed administrator who reduced the independence of localities under his rule. His half-brother Saud, his primary challenger, was considered more outgoing and dashing.

In the last months of Faisal's life he had sought a larger tribute from Oman, and he sent a Saudi-Wahhabi force to back up the demand. A later Saudi-Wahhabi attack in Oman and Muscat in 1865 resulted in the death of several British subjects. Abdallah faced the repercussions soon after assuming rule. British naval forces attacked coastal towns under Saudi control, shelling forts and sinking ships. Abdallah accepted responsibility for the damages done to British interests and pledged to refrain from further attacks.

Abdallah was eager to strengthen his relations with Britain to keep them from supporting Saud. Simultaneously, he sought Turkish support to strengthen his position against the British. Saud launched a military campaign against Abdallah and forged alliances with tribal confederations, promising them autonomy upon his ascension. But Abdallah defeated his forces in 1866, though Saud escaped capture.

As in the first Saudi state, allegiance was not universal even in central Najd. As the previously cited events in Qasim and Jabal Shammar illustrate, attempts to assert control by any regional leader were resisted in many areas. The Saudi military structure remained the same, with areas under Saudi rule responsible for providing specified numbers of combat-ready fighters to take part in the Saudi-Wahhabi campaigns, be they aimed at the conquest of new areas or the reconquering of previously subdued settlements or tribes.

Saud resurfaced in Bahrain in 1870 seeking support for his cause. Nonpayment of tribute by Bahrain had by then led to more invasion threats from Riyadh, and Saud took a stand supporting the coastal emirates. That same year he forged a new alliance with Ajamn and Al-Murra tribes and captured Hasa, which had been under Abdallah's control. Abdallah's counterattack failed when key Bedouin allies defected. In 1871 Saud moved on Riyadh, and Abdallah, his forces defeated, fled. Saud soon won the allegiance of the entire Eastern Province.

Ottoman, British, Saudi, and Rashidi Maneuvers

Among those from whom Abdallah sought support following his defeat was the Ottoman governor of Baghdad. The Ottomans, eager to reverse their decline in the area, claimed Abdallah as their surrogate, justifying an invasion to save him from his rebellious brother. In 1871 the Ottomans arrived with a naval force at Ras Tanura and from there occupied Qatif, taking the Eastern Province from Saudi control. They captured Faisal's youngest son, Abd al-Rahman, and held him hostage. An attempt to take Riyadh that year failed.

The British, as had been their policy, did their best to manipulate the political situation as a way of maximizing their leverage among the various powers vying for dominance. Realizing the Ottomans backed Abdallah, the British increased aid to Saud, now the emir of Riyadh. The military actions the aid supported finally drove the Ottomans from Hasa due to the cost of occupation. Before departing in early 1874, the Ottomans named the sheikh of the Bani Khalid, Bazi Ak Arayar, as the emir of Hasa. An unpopular figure, Bazi's appointment created local support for rule from Riyadh.

Abd al-Rahman, released in 1874, led an unsuccessful revolt against the Ottomans and then retreated to Riyadh. By now the Saudis' decade of internal warfare had seriously weakened their authority. Saud's rule was tenuous in Najd and no longer recognized in Jabal Shammar or Qasim, and nomadic tribes loyal to Abdallah attacked towns. Saud died in 1875 after failing to subdue the marauding Bedouins. Now Abd al-Rahman took control of Riyadh, provoking battles with his brothers Abdallah and Muhammad for dominance. However, a larger threat was presented by the sons of Saud.

In answer to the challenge of Saud's sons, Abd al-Rahman and his warring brothers formed an alliance, ceding leadership to Abdallah to oppose their nephews. Abdallah's return to Riyadh was the eighth change of power in the 11 years since Faisal's death. Tribes and villages continued to abandon Riyadh, switching allegiance and tribute payments to the Rashidis. In 1882 the entire province of Sudair refused to recognize Abdallah's authority. When he raised a force to compel their submission, the citizens sought help from the emir of Hail. The force Muhammad Al Rashid sent drove Abdallah and his troops back to Riyadh. An unsuccessful challenge to the Rashidis by the sons of Saud, against whom Abdallah and his brothers were allied, followed. By 1884 Muhammad Al Rashid, emir of Jabal Shammar, could claim rule over all of Najd, though Abdallah remained Riyadh's emir.

End of the Second Saudi State

In 1887 Saud's sons captured Abdallah and gained control of Riyadh. Abdallah appealed to Muhammad Al Rashid in Hail for help. Advancing on the city on the pretext of liberating the city from the usurpers, Al Rashid instead seized it for himself. Saud's sons fled and Abdallah was freed from jail and taken to Hail. Al Rashid appointed a new governor, who handed the sons of Saud their final defeat the following summer. The force sent to subdue them was a mere 35 men. Three of the four remaining sons were killed.

By 1889, the increasingly powerful Shammar had extended their raids into Hijaz. That same year, Abdallah ibn Faisal, now seriously ill, was allowed to return to Riyadh, where he died. Al Rashid appointed Abd al-Rahman the new emir of Riyadh, though he served under a governor of the city appointed by Al Rashid, Salim al-Subhan. Tensions between the two rulers of Riyadh led Abd al-Rahman to incite an uprising. Al Rashid dispatched troops to quell the insurrection but, unable to breach the fortified city, called for negotiations after 40 days of siege. One of those who attended the discussions was Abd al-Rahman's young son, Abd al-Aziz, the future founder of the Kingdom of Saudi Arabia. The two sides agreed to an armistice. Abd al-Rahman retained the title of emir and agreed to recognize Rashidi suzerainty.

But discontent with Al Rashid in Riyadh and surrounding areas continued to simmer. Emboldened by the antipathy, in late 1890 Abd al-Rahman forged an alliance with Bedouin tribes and commenced a month-long battle (though Abd al-Rahman himself did not take part) against Hail's forces. In January of 1891, Muhammad Al Rashid routed the Saudi forces and their allies at the Battle of al-Mulayda. Abd al-Rahman fled to the desert with his family. He made a final unsuccessful attempt to retake Riyadh that same year, then retreated again to the desert. Al Rashid was now the ruler of Central Arabia. The second Saudi state was at an end.

8

UNITY AND INDEPENDENCE
(1891–1932)

A decade after the defeat of the second Saudi state, the seeds of the modern kingdom took root when the son of Abd al-Rahman, the last Saudi ruler, reclaimed Riyadh. Three decades after this victory the son, Abd al-Aziz ibn Abd al-Rahman ibn Faisal Al Saud, would found Saudi Arabia. In the intervening years, Saudi-Wahhabi forces battled those of the Shammar confederation under Al Rashid, along with their Ottoman backers, for dominance in Najd. Germany and Great Britain sought their own footholds in Arabia as Europe headed toward the Great War. In Hijaz, battles between the Ottomans and the sharif of Mecca culminated in the Arab revolt in the midst of World War I, finally ending Ottoman occupation. Thereafter, the forces of Al Saud and the sharif engaged in sparring that came to sustained warfare, ending with the Saudi conquest of Hijaz and the formation of the Kingdom of Saudi Arabia. These are the years covered in this chapter.

After the Fall

By the time Saudi-held Riyadh fell to the Rashidis—the rulers of the Shammar tribal confederation—in 1891, the power of Al Saud had been declining for a decade. The last Saudi ruler, Abd al-Rahman ibn Faisal Al Saud, sent his family to Bahrain and took refuge with Bedouin before establishing his residence-in-exile in Kuwait in 1893.

The emir of Kuwait was allied with Al Saud against the Rashidis and their Ottoman backers. The Rashidi defeat of the Saudis, longtime Ottoman enemies, had cemented Turkish support of the Rashidis. During his exile in Kuwait, Abd al-Rahman kept in contact with his allies in Najd. His son, Abd al-Aziz ibn Abd al-Rahman ibn Faisal Al Saud (1880–1953), came of age in Bahrain. Abd al-Aziz, known in the

Abd al-Aziz ibn Abd al-Rahman ibn Faisal Al Saud, the future founder of the kingdom of Saudi Arabia, ca. 1910, in Kuwait. (Courtesy of Dr. Michael Crocker/King Abdul Aziz Foundation)

West as Ibn Saud, would found the Kingdom of Saudi Arabia. Part of his childhood was spent among the Bedouin, where he learned of desert life and warfare. He was tutored by a religious teacher and gained military experience as a teenager alongside his father, accompanying one of Abd al-Rahman's periodic forays into former Saudi territory. Ibn Saud grew to be a tall, imposing, and charismatic figure. Like his father, he dreamed of reestablishing Saudi rule and Wahhabi faith in Arabia. Conquering Riyadh was the linchpin in his plan to reclaim his ancestral domain.

Foreign Powers in the Region

As the new century approached, several powers sought influence in Arabia. Britain's traditional regional dominance was under challenge from Germany and, to a lesser extent, from France and Russia. Germany hoped to establish a rail line across Iraq to the Persian Gulf (the "Berlin to Baghdad" rail link), bypassing British-controlled sea lanes. Thus they sought closer ties with the Ottomans. Kaiser Wilhelm II proclaimed himself "the protector of Islam," and the Ottomans rewarded German overtures in 1899 by granting them rights to build a railway from Constantinople to Baghdad and Kuwait.

Unbeknownst to either party, the emir of Kuwait, Mubarak al-Saba, fearful of the repeated Ottoman efforts to seize his territory, signed a secret protectorate treaty with Britain the same year. Mubarak, who had come to power in 1896 after killing his two brothers, became Ibn Saud's mentor and later ally (though he would ultimately betray him when Ibn Saud's power eclipsed his own). The terms of the treaty forbade Kuwait from granting concessions to any power besides Britain, thus impeding Germany's planned rail link to a Persian Gulf port.

Britain, eager to counter Turkish influence in the area, supported the Rashidis' foes and sought allies among discontented Shammar tribes, and these efforts succeeded in getting some chiefs and factions to switch allegiance. In 1901 the British and Ottomans reached an accord, agreeing to halt expansion of their regional positions.

France, also seeking to project its power, had plans to build a coaling station in Muscat, Oman, for its ships, and Russia sought a warm-water port, which drew its attention to the Persian Gulf. In 1903 Britain dispatched a naval flotilla to Arabia's Gulf Coast in a display of dominance. It was the largest foreign fleet to visit the area since a Portuguese squadron conquered Hormuz in 1515.

The Rashidis in Riyadh

Riyadh chafed under Rashidi control. Increasingly dependent on Ottoman assistance, the Rashidis were seen as tools of the Turks and as favoring

CAPTURING RIYADH

The account of Ibn Saud's retaking of Riyadh is one of the most fabled events in the kingdom's history. Leaving his brother Muhammad and a few men outside the city, Ibn Saud waited until nightfall and scaled an unguarded section of Riyadh's walls. Ibn Saud had no particular plan in mind. As he later said, "We thought to ourselves, 'What shall we do?'" (Lebkicher 1960, 59–60).

The wife of a former aide to his father told them about the daily routine of the governor installed by the Rashidis, Ajlan. Advancing across rooftops and through homes, they finally sneaked into Ajlan's house, only to learn he was in the fort he had built in Riyadh, al-Masmak. They waited to surprise him in his house, but then decided to attack when Ajlan came out of the fortress with 10 bodyguards for morning prayers. Half a dozen men led by Ibn Saud came at them. Ajlan's guards fled and he tried to run, but was cornered.

"He made at me with his sword, but its edge was not good. I covered my face and shot at him with my gun. I heard the crash of the sword upon the ground and knew that the shot had hit Ajlan but had not killed him," Ibn Saud recounted (ibid.).

After a brief fight Ibn Saud's cousin Abdullah bin Jelawi killed Ajlan with a sword. The garrison of Riyadh, thinking the attacking force was much larger than it was, was routed. Half of the 80-some soldiers were slain and the rest surrendered.

the Shammar tribes rather than the local population. Muhammad ibn Abdullah Al Rashid's death in 1897 provoked disturbances among Riyadh's restive populace. His nephew and successor, the hot-tempered Abd al-Aziz ibn Mitaab Al Rashid (known as Ibn Rashid), ruthlessly subdued the unrest, raised taxes, and plundered settlements. In these conditions of anarchy, unchecked Bedouin raids and lawlessness swept the region. In 1900 Ibn Rashid, with Ottoman support, attacked Kuwait while seeking to extend his territory to the Persian Gulf, but he withdrew after several inconclusive skirmishes. Later that year Abd al-Rahman and Mubarak mounted raids into Shammar territory from Kuwait with a force of 10,000. Ibn Saud, intent on retaking Riyadh, got his father's permission to mount a diversionary attack on the city.

Finding a warm welcome from area residents, Ibn Saud successfully entered Riyadh. He was trying to breach the city's citadel when he learned that Ibn Rashid, with the help of fresh supplies from the Turks,

The Masmak fortress in Riyadh. Here, Ibn Saud confronted and defeated the Rashidis' provisional governor in a daring surprise attack, a victory considered the first in the campaign that would end in the creation of Saudi Arabia. (Courtesy of the Saudi Information Office)

had defeated Mubarak. Ibn Saud hurried back to Kuwait. Ibn Rashid, enraged at the local support for the Al Saud and the Kuwaitis, had citizens across Qasim massacred.

The following year, 1901, Ibn Rashid attacked Kuwait again and besieged the coastal village of al-Jahra. A British warship bombarded a Shammar camp in reprisal and supplied arms to Kuwait. The Turks refrained from providing much assistance to Ibn Rashid for fear of provoking further British action. Finally the Ottoman sultan in Constantinople, bowing to British complaints, ordered an end to the siege. (Nominally, Britain and Turkey maintained friendly relations, but the latter's growing bond with the Germans drew British scrutiny.)

Birth of the Third Saudi State

During this time Ibn Saud, determined to reclaim Riyadh, set out for the city with about 40 men. He gathered many Bedouin along the way,

169

raiding tribes allied with the Rashidis, but Ibn Saud's Bedouin followers deserted at the prospect of Ottoman reprisals. Spurning his father's insistence to return to Kuwait, he spent Ramadan from December 1901 to January 1902 around the Yabrin oasis before moving on his objective, with his followers now numbering about 60. With just a fraction of these, he retook Riyadh from a much larger force in a daring raid.

Abd al-Rahman returned to Riyadh after his son's victory. Ibn Saud gathered the ulama and civic leaders and urged them to support his father. But his father declared Ibn Saud the emir, and citizens pledged their allegiance to him. Ibn Saud's grip on Riyadh was not yet firm, and the surrounding area was filled with nonallied tribes and villages, many led by sheikhs with their own designs on power. Over the next three years Ibn Saud's forces battled those of Ibn Rashid as well as lesser regional rivals. By 1904 Ibn Saud had retaken all of central Najd up to the border of Jabal Shammar, the Rashidi stronghold.

As had been the practice of previous Saudi regimes, after the capitulation of its adversaries, ulama were sent to the towns and villages to instruct the population in the Wahhabi tenets. Tombs and shrines, anathema to the simple practices of Wahhabism, were leveled.

Ibn Saud was reported to be a capable and charismatic leader, described as brave, honorable, beneficent, yet ruthless when required. British Arabist Gertrude Bell,* who met him during World War I, wrote of her impressions in *The Arab War*:

> *His hands are fine, with slender fingers, a trait almost universal among the tribes of pure Arab blood, and in spite of his great height and bredth (sic) of shoulder, he conveys the impression, common enough in the desert, of an indefinable lassitude, not individual but racial, the secular weariness of an ancient and self-contained people, which has made heavy drafts on its vital forces, and borrowed little from beyond its own forbidding frontiers. His deliberate movements, his slow, sweet smile, and the contemplative glance of his heavy-lidded eyes, though they add to his dignity and charm, do not accord with the Western conception of a vigorous personality. Nevertheless, report credits him with powers of physical endurance rare even in hard bitten Arabia (Bell 1940, 9).*

---

*Bell was the architect of the modern state of Iraq as adviser to British colonial secretary Winston Churchill after World War I and was responsible for the appointment of Faisal, of the Hashemites, as its first ruler after Ibn Saud drove him from Hijaz.

Ibn Saud's success aroused the concern of the Turks, who were aware of his friendship with the British-backed Mubarak of Kuwait. In 1904 Ibn Rashid's forces, supplemented by eight Turkish battalions with artillery, fought a series of engagements with Ibn Saud in which the Saudi leader ultimately prevailed. Ibn Saud's battles with Ibn Rashid ended only in April of 1906 when the latter was killed in an engagement near Buraida. Ibn Saud then reached an agreement with the new leader of Hail, emir Jabal Shammar, on rule in Central Arabia and compelled the Ottomans to withdraw their forces. Of the estimated 4,500 Turkish soldiers originally sent to the area, only 1,000 survived.

Despite vanquishing Ibn Rashid, Ibn Saud faced multiple threats. The Turks instigated tribal revolts against Saudi rule. His former ally Mubarak turned against him. And the Rashidis remained a regional power whose forces constantly opposed Ibn Saud. Even tribes and villages he had subdued sometimes renounced their allegiance.

The Ikhwan

Ibn Saud needed a fighting force to extend his dominion and the reach of Wahhabism. But he did not have money to pay tribes for allegiance as did the sharifs of Mecca, nor did he have control of the caravan

FAMILY RIVALRIES

In addition to facing regional rivals, Ibn Saud faced challenges from his cousins, the four sons of his paternal uncle Saud, a branch of the family that had challenged the rule of his uncle Abdallah in the 1870s. After the Rashidis ended the second Saudi state, they had confined the cousins to Ibn Rashid's court in Hail, where they could be monitored. They were freed when Ibn Saud led a successful raid on Qasim in 1904 and were hence referred to as *araif*, meaning "hostages restored on the field of battle." The Bedouin used the term to refer to a stolen camel reclaimed in a raid. (Today, in reference to contemporary members of this branch of Al Saud, *araif* means "the recognized.") But the now-liberated cousins refused to recognize Ibn Saud's rule. In 1909 and 1910 they instigated revolts in the Eastern Province. The insurrections ended only after several military forays and the marriage of two of Ibn Saud's sisters to two of the cousins.

routes to offer allies trade advantages as the Rashidis could. Instead, Ibn Saud used Wahhabi doctrine to draw recruits.

In 1912 Ibn Saud organized the Ikhwan, or "brethren," an army of Bedouin who fervently embraced Wahhabi teachings. They left their nomadic lives to settle in communities called *hijra* (pl. *hujar*), from the term applied to the Prophet's emigration from Mecca to Medina, a name meant to suggest a similar movement from a place of nonbelief to one of belief. It was part of a conservative reform movement sweeping the nomadic population of Najd. Ibn Saud provided the land, tools, and other staples to the settlers. By 1915 more than 200 *hujar* had been established, and Ibn Saud had an army of more than 60,000 men from among them.

Since the time of Muhammad, nomadic life, with its raiding, blood feuds, and tribal rivalries, was seen as less compatible with Islam than the life of sedentary populations. Settling the nomads in these communities solved several problems—religious, social, and economic—associated with their untamed existence.

Under the rules imposed by Ibn Saud, the age-old practice of raiding, or *ghazu,* was banned, replaced by state-sanctioned jihad, conducted to win converts to Wahhabism. Spoils were still collected and Ibn Saud, as was customary for tribal sheikhs, oversaw their distribution. This reduced destabilizing tribal warfare. The *hujar* were planned as agrarian communities whose crops would provide a stable income, eliminating the economic need for raiding. But the *hujar* never bore the agricultural fruits originally hoped for, later complicating Ibn Saud's efforts to end the pillage conducted by the Ikhwan in the name of their ideological commitment.

In 1913 Saudi forces comprised of both regular conscripts and Ikhwan drove the Ottomans from Hufuf, capital of the verdant Eastern Province, which had been under Ottoman control since 1871. This gave Ibn Saud control of both Najd and the Eastern Province. In the Ottoman-Saudi Treaty signed in the aftermath of the Saudi victory, Ibn Saud agreed to recognize Ottoman suzerainty in the area and the Ottomans agreed to recognize Ibn Saud as the emir of Najd, as well as compensate him with weapons and money. But the Ottomans simultaneously agreed to give Saud ibn Rashid, the new ruler of Jabal Shammar, rifles for an attack on Najd. The Ottoman duplicity made Ibn Saud open to overtures from the British.

The Ikhwan were as implacable off the battlefield as on it. They enforced public prayer, mosque attendance, and gender segregation. Music, smoking, consumption of alcohol, and any technology unknown at the time of the Prophet were condemned. They tried to convert non-

The Ikhwan, or Brotherhood, the army of settled Bedouin Ibn Saud formed, were instrumental in his military campaigns. But their fanatical devoutness would lead to a revolt against Saudi rule. Their standards bear the shahada: "There is no God but God. Muhammad is his messenger." (Courtesy of the Saudi Information Office)

Wahhabis by force. Their efforts to enforce orthodoxy almost sparked a civil war with town dwellers in 1916. Ibn Saud defused the crisis by sending religious scholars to the *hujar* to contradict the religious leaders who had approved the Ikhwan's actions. Yet the battle between Ibn Saud and the army he created would continue for more than a decade.

The Ottomans in the Hijaz

The political and social situation was quite different in Hijaz than in Najd. Compared with the desolate interior, Hijaz, containing the cities of Mecca and Medina and the port of Jeddah, was relatively cosmopolitan. It was also under the control of the Ottomans, unlike Najd where the Turks had much less of a grip on the population.

Toward the end of the 19th century the Ottomans, through their governor, slowly increased their control over caravan routes and their share of the attendant income. Relations between Hijazis and Ottomans deteriorated. These relations underwent a more stark change in 1908 with the revolution of the Young Turks in Constantinople. The

HIJAZ RAILWAY

For the most part the mechanical innovations that reshaped the world during the Industrial Revolution found little application in Arabia. But one invention held hope for vast numbers of Muslims eager to make the hajj, or pilgrimage to Mecca: the train. The hajj, one of the Five Pillars of Islam, was an impossible dream for many due to the rigors of the overland journey. The train, along with the steamship, brought many pilgrims to Arabia's doorstep, at Damascus or Cairo. But the journey's last leg was often made by caravan. It took about two months to travel from Damascus to Medina, still some 250 miles from Mecca. A rail link had been formally proposed in 1864, though nothing came of the plan for decades. It was revived by Sultan Abdul Hammad, last of the ruling Ottoman caliphs. In addition to promoting trade and encouraging hajj traffic, the Ottomans considered the railway important for moving troops and maintaining control over Hijaz.

In 1900 the sultan decided to proceed with construction. Additional funds were raised through contributions from Islamic leaders including the khedive of Egypt and the shah of Iran as well as the Turkish armed forces and civil service. Honorific titles (such as pasha and bey) were also sold to help finance construction. The challenges were great. Much of the ground was soft, shifting sand or solid rock. The parched land was subject to periodic flash floods that swept away trestles and the banks of wadis the rail traversed.

Construction began in 1904 and the rail line was operational by 1908. About 5,000 Turkish soldiers were employed in building, maintaining, and protecting the railway. The railway went as far south as Medina from its northern terminus at Baghdad. In 1912, 30,000 pilgrims used the railway. Two years later, traffic had increased tenfold, to 300,000. It also transported a growing traffic of Turkish soldiers and supplies. But local tribes whose territory the tracks traversed, along with caravan operators who

Young Turks replaced the traditional Muslim identity that had united Turks, Arabs, Persians, and other groups in the historical Muslim empires with a nationalist, secular Turkish state that sought dominance over its territories. Under the new regime, Arabs were discriminated against and persecuted politically and culturally. The use of Arabic for official communication was banned, as was its teaching in schools. This provoked a backlash of Arab nationalism and greater antipathy for the Ottoman occupation.

stood to lose their livelihood, attacked the line. Its military use also drew opposition. When World War I erupted, its strategic importance made it a military target. T. E. Lawrence, who led British efforts to support the Arab Revolt, helped destroy trains and track as part of the anti-Ottoman campaign. By war's end the rail line was unusable.

Plans to rebuild the railway were proposed over succeeding years until as late as 1971. However, road and air transportation obviated its need. Broken remnants of track and trains still lie along its route. Today the remains of the Hijaz Railway are among the few visible reminders of the many outsiders whose plans for conquest have perished in the harsh environment of Arabia.

The train stations of the Hijaz railway were built so they could double as fortresses. Note the height of the first-floor windows above the ground. (Courtesy of the Fine Arts Library, Harvard College Library)

Arabia in World War I

On the eve of World War I Hussein Ibn Ali was the sharif of Mecca. Though born in Arabia, Sharif Hussein had been forced to live in Constantinople with four sons. The Ottomans thought appointing Hussein as sharif would add credibility to their own regime.

When Germany and Britain declared war on each other, Lord Kitchener, British secretary of state for war, sent a message to Hussein asking which side the sharif would support if Turkey entered the war as an ally of Germany. If the sharif supported Britain, Kitchener promised, the British would recognize him as sharif and support him as king of an independent Arab kingdom made up of Ottoman Arab territories. Though the Ottomans, as Muslims, made them more natural allies, their continued discrimination and occupation, and his own ambitions, made Hussein receptive to British inducements.

The War in Najd

At the outbreak of the war, Ibn Saud tried to arrange a summit with Sharif Hussein, the emir of Jabal Shammar, and Sheikh Mubarak of Kuwait to develop a joint position of neutrality. But conflicting goals and alliances prevented any such agreement. Both the Ottomans and the British courted Ibn Saud, each hoping to enlist him in the battle against the other. A Turkish delegation offered him 10,000 gold liras for his support. The British dispatched Captain J. D. Shakespear, their political agent in Kuwait, to Riyadh in a successful effort to induce Ibn Saud to attack the Shammar. (In 1910, the captain had become the first Briton to meet Ibn Saud.)

In January of 1915 Ibn Saud and his allies, accompanied by Shakespear, marched north to battle the Shammar, each with a force of abut 1,500 fighters. Though the battle, fought near Jarrab, ended inconclusively, it was marked by the betrayal of some of Ibn Saud's allies, including Mubarak of Kuwait, and the death of Shakespear. Thereafter, Ibn Saud tried to remain on the sidelines of the war, despite British entreaties.

However, in December of 1915 Ibn Saud and the British, represented by Sir Percy Cox, concluded the Darin, or al-Qatif treaty, which was ratified the following July. The treaty recognized Najd and eastern provinces Qatif and Jubail as Ibn Saud's territory. This gave him tacit approval to remove the last remnants of the Rashid family from power. Ibn Saud agreed not to enter into agreements with any other power except as advised by the British, or to attack the coastal emirates under Britain's protection. He received £20,000 and 1,000 rifles from the

Sir Percy Cox with Ibn Saud. The British tried to enlist Ibn Saud to battle the Ottomans during World War I. Eager to win his cooperation, in 1915 Sir Percy Cox negotiated the Qatif treaty, in which Britain recognized Ibn Saud as the ruler of Najd, Hasa, Qatif, and Jubail. (Courtesy of Dr. Michael Crocker/King Abdul Aziz Foundation)

British. The British also agreed to give £5,000 per month to Najd beginning in 1916.

In 1917 the British dispatched another mission to Riyadh aimed in part at creating an alliance between Ibn Saud and Sharif Hussein against the Turks. Harry (H.) St. John Philby, the noted Arabist (and father of Soviet spy Kim Philby), who would play a large role as adviser to the king during the kingdom's early years, first met Ibn Saud as a member of this mission.

The War in Hijaz

Sharif Hussein did not consider Ibn Saud an equal and opposed Saudi power due in part to the brief Saudi takeover of Hijaz a century before and its disastrous results. He dismissed any proposal of a partnership. One of Hussein's sons referred to Ibn Saud as a "son of a dog," one of the harshest insults in the Arabic lexicon. The rivalry between the Saudis and the Hashemites would intensify during the war as each gained more power, Al Saud by consolidating and expanding rule in Najd, the Hashemites by defeating the Ottomans in the Arab Revolt. Hussein would proclaim himself king of the Arab countries, envisioning an independent Arab nation stretching from Syria south across Arabia to Yemen.

A few days after Turkey entered the war in 1914, the sultan called for jihad against the British. To blunt his appeal, Britain publicly declared its support for independence for the Arabs. The sharif declined to support the sultan's plea, and as a result it failed to elicit response from the Arabs. The sultan, angered, tried to have Hussein assassinated. Hussein, meanwhile, attempted to make the British define the territory the Arabs would receive in return for initiating a revolt against the Ottomans. He pressed the issue in an exchange of 10 letters with Sir Henry McMahon, Britain's High Commissioner in Egypt in 1915 (the Hussein-McMahon correspondence). Hussein stipulated that all of Syria be given independence, but finally agreed to hold final determination of borders in abeyance, accepting British assurances in their place. However, one area excluded from future Arab control was defined as "portions of Syria lying to the west of the districts of Damascus, Homs, Hamma, and Aleppo." The Arabs interpreted this as referring to Lebanon, which is due west of these cities. But the British later said it referred to Palestine, which is also west, but south of the area described.

Anti-Ottoman activity increased in the region, driven by nationalist fervor. Jemal Pasha, the ruthless Ottoman military governor of Syria and Palestine, tried to suppress the insurrection through a terror campaign. He had 21 leading citizens in Damascus hung on May 6, 1916, and starved an estimated 300,000 more already suffering from a plague of locusts by forbidding the purchase of corn and refusing efforts at intervention by the American Red Cross. Faisal, Sharif Hussein's son, was held hostage in Damascus, but he was allowed to leave on the pretext of leading a band of volunteers against the insurrectionists.

The Arab Revolt

With his son Faisal out of Ottoman hands, in June of 1916 Hussein, allying himself with Great Britain and France, began the Great Arab Revolt against the Ottomans. His sons Abdullah and Faisal commanded the Arab forces. On June 10 Hussein's forces attacked the Turkish garrison at Mecca. The Ottomans lost the city a month later after bombardment by Egyptian artillery sent by Britain, whose naval force supported the revolt. Jeddah fell a week later, followed by Taif and other cities.

That summer Hussein demanded that Ibn Saud assist in the revolt. Saud pledged to help "to the best of his power," concurrently demanding that Hussein refrain from interfering in the affairs of the Najd. Hussein replied that Saud was likely "bereft of his mind—or intoxicated," a grave insult to any Muslim, even more so to a Wahhabi (Kostiner 1993, 16). Hussein's anointing himself king of the Arab countries also angered Ibn Saud, though he spoke in support of such a kingship at an Arab congress in Kuwait.

In general the Arab Revolt failed to carry far beyond Hijaz. Jemal's harsh suppression blunted resistance. The Al Rashid of Shammar and Imam Yahya of Yemen were Turkish allies, ruling out their assistance. And Hussein's claims to kingship alienated many Bedouin tribes. However, Ibn Saud, as part of his ongoing campaign against the Rashidis, battled the Ottomans along the northern and eastern borders of Najd. By the war's end, Ibn Saud's rule extended to the outskirts of Hail, the Rashidi capital.

For most of 1916 the British provided Hussein with £125,000 per month in gold to pay for the revolt, as well as supplying weapons and military advisers. The most well-known adviser was T. E. Lawrence, the colorful, legendary adviser to Hussein's son Faisal. In July of 1917, Lawrence and Faisal's forces captured Aqaba by crossing a desert considered impassable to attack the coastal city from the rear. But though the sharif's forces defeated the Ottomans in most of Hijaz, the British decided the revolt was "a trifling sideshow worthy of only token support," and by this time had withdrawn their financial support (Nutting 1964, 282).

Later in the war, Lawrence convinced the British to outfit the Arab forces with weapons and supplies for their Syrian campaign, and led them on their advance to Damascus, racing to beat the allied armies who were intent on controlling the area after the conclusion of hostilities. On October 1, 1918, Faisal entered Damascus ahead of allied forces. But internal bickering caused the Arabs to lose control of the city. Four weeks later the Ottomans surrendered, almost exactly 400 years after Selim the Grim defeated the Mamluks, which had brought Syria and Egypt into the Ottoman Empire.

Independence Betrayed

At war's end, Britain's Arabian allies pressed for their promised independence. But Britain and France had already concluded a pact, the Sykes-Picot Agreement, struck in 1916, that effectively blocked Arab independence. The agreement divided the Middle East between Britain and France, stipulating that neither would cede their rights to any third power, "except the Arab state or confederation of Arab states." In 1920, the League of Nations put Iraq, Lebanon, and Syria under a French "mandate" and Transjordan and most of Palestine under a British "mandate" for administrative control. The British area comprised what is now Israel, the Gaza Strip, the occupied West Bank, and portions of Jordan. At the time the population of Palestine was 90 percent Arab.

In 1917 British foreign secretary Arthur James Balfour wrote a letter, now known as the Balfour Declaration, to Lord Rothschild, a leader of England's Jewish community who sought government support for a Jewish homeland in Palestine. The letter expressed sympathy for "Jewish Zionist aspirations," calling for the "establishment in Palestine of a national home for the Jewish people." However, it also stated, "nothing shall be done which may prejudice the civil and religious rights of existing non-Jewish communities in Palestine."

Postwar Conflict

With the world war over, fighting in the peninsula escalated as the rivalry pitting Ibn Saud against Sharif Hussein and the Rashidis intensified. Hussein bought the allegiance of Najdi tribes and tried to tax others under Saudi control. The sparring triggered tribal disputes that ripped through Najd in 1919 and 1920. Hussein's forces skirmished and clashed with Ibn Saud's during these years, most notably at Turaba, on the Najd-Hijaz border in 1919. Hussein sent a force of 4,000 to 5,000 troops under his son Abdullah to capture the town of Khurma. Ibn Saud's son Khalid led a force of Ikhwan to engage the sharif's army. Yet even before Khalid reached the scene, local tribesmen and Ikhwan forces mounted a surprise attack on Hussein's troops near the town of Turaba. Though Abdullah escaped, the sharif's forces were routed.

The battle at Turaba notwithstanding, Ibn Saud concentrated on defeating the Rashidis and solidifying his base in Najd, rather than battling the sharif's forces in Hijaz. The Rashidis, meanwhile, were wracked by internecine violence. In 1919 the Rashidi emir of Jabal Shammar was murdered by a member of the ambitious al-Ubayd clan. The new ruler was all of 13 years old. Rashidi notables served as his advisers. A year later the young emir sought friendly relations with Ibn Saud and drafted an agreement that gave Ibn Saud control of Jabal Shammar, but the proposed agreement was scrapped due to opposition among the Rashidi notables.

Ibn Saud faced internal threats as well, primarily from the Ikhwan, who sought a more fundamentalist Wahhabi society. They regarded themselves as missionaries for Islam, whose purpose was to impose true religion on others. In 1919 they demanded Ibn Saud speed up the settlement of Bedouin tribes.

In 1920, a Najdi delegation that came to Mecca for the hajj met with members of the sharif's family, including Hussein, several times. The two sides agreed to control movements across their boundaries and to prevent raids and encroachment from the tribes under their control. Meanwhile, the sharif and the Rashidis had been drawn together by the common enemy they faced in Ibn Saud. The Saudis saw the Hashemite-Rashid alliance as an effort to surround and weaken Najd. Ibn Saud was further worried by the installment of Hussein's sons, Abdullah and Faisal, as rulers of Transjordan and Iraq, as decided at the British-sponsored Middle East Conference in the spring of 1921. He regarded this as a "policy of engulfment" (Kostiner 1993, 50).

In August 1921, after a campaign lasting nearly a year, Ibn Saud finally defeated Ibn Rashid's forces in Hail. Surviving members of the Rashidi clan were brought to Riyadh to live as "guests" of Al Saud. This completed Saudi conquest of the Rashidis and the province of Jabal Shammar. Still Ibn Saud refrained from attacking the Hijaz, though Ikhwan armies continued trying to expand their domain. The British, concerned about Saudi incursions into Iraq and Kuwait, reached an agreement with Ibn Saud in 1922 establishing borders of the Saudi state (the Uqayr Protocol). To overcome Ibn Saud's objections to demarcating lands that Bedouin had traditionally traversed as part of their seasonal migrations, two "neutral zones" were established along Saudi territory, one in Iraq and one in Kuwait. The agreement also banned the construction of military fortifications along the borders. In a further effort to end boundary disputes, in November of

1925, Ibn Saud and Britain signed the Bahra and al-Hada agreements, establishing the borders between Najd and Iraq and Transjordan respectively. The agreements also restricted Ikhwan agitation by banning the promotion of religious beliefs across the newly defined borders.

The Conquest of Hijaz

Relations between Sharif Hussein and the British deteriorated between 1922 and 1925. His military weakness, repeated demands for assistance in his battles with the Saudi forces, continuing bids for dominance in the Middle East, and reluctance to sign a postwar treaty that acknowledged British hegemony in Palestine and Iraq led to loss of British support. Internally his support waned among his subjects due to ineffective and corrupt administration and heavy taxation. Hussein's mismanagement of the holy cities had alienated much of the Arab world, as well. When Ibn Saud announced his intention to mount a campaign against Hijaz at a 1924 meeting of Ikhwan and ulama, he cited Hussein's interference with Najdi pilgrims as a reason for the attack. Later, Ibn Saud circulated a "Green Book" explaining his decision to Muslim nations. His appeals to Muslims outside of Arabia became an element of his strategy.

Ibn Saud dispatched a main force of Ikhwan warriors to Taif. The sharif's forces under the command of his son Ali, who happened to be in Taif, left the city. The Ikhwan, after occupying the town, went on a rampage, looting and killing hundreds of inhabitants. Word of Wahhabi massacres caused many Meccans to flee and paralyzed the city's administration. Meccan notables formed a National Representative Council (NRC) and pressed Hussein to abdicate, hoping to appease Ibn Saud and retain governance of Mecca without yielding to Wahhabi rule. Hussein asked the British for aid, but in late September they declined to help. On October 6, 1924, Hussein abdicated and went into exile in Aqaba. Leaders of the NRC sued for peace and recognition of Ali, Hussein's son, as the new king of the Arab countries. Ali took his forces to Jeddah, and Mecca surrendered to Ibn Saud's forces at the end of October. Ibn Saud entered the city in early December.

After Ali sent a plane over Mecca that dropped leaflets announcing his intention to return to the holy city, Ibn Saud ordered a siege of Jeddah, where Ali and his forces were gathered. The siege lasted almost a year. Ibn Saud opened other ports to pilgrim traffic, helping solidify support for him from other Muslim nations. But Ibn Saud refused foreign offers to mediate his standoff with Ali if it preserved Hashemite rule. Ali's regime was imploding as soldiers went unpaid. From Aqaba,

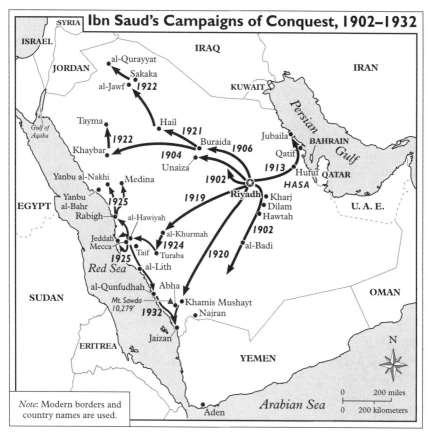

For three decades, commencing with the capture of Riyadh in 1902, Ibn Saud fought to unify Arabia under his rule. His campaign culminated in the creation of the Kingdom of Saudi Arabia in 1932.

Hussein sent Ali financial help. Ibn Saud marched on Aqaba, but withdrew after British intercession, and Hussein went to Cyprus. By the end of 1925 Medina and Jeddah were both under Saudi control, and Ibn Saud was the protector of the holy cities of Mecca and Medina.

Governing Hijaz

On January 8, 1926, the leading citizens of Mecca pledged allegiance to Ibn Saud who became king of Hijaz and the sultan of Najd and its dependencies. Ibn Saud, his brothers, and leading family members used the Islamic practice of taking four wives and the relative ease of divorce to intermarry with many leading nomadic and urban families, forging a

183

link between these families and the Saudi state. Ibn Saud also forbade internal fighting between tribes.

With his conquest of Hijaz, Ibn Saud's 25-year campaign to reestablish the Saudi state was complete. Now he faced the challenge of administering the kingdom. The pilgrimage routes had to be secured. Good relations with Muslim states had to be established and maintained. Police authority was established first in Mecca in late 1925, then throughout the realm. The League for the Encouragement of Virtue and Prevention of Vice was created to clamp down on practices incompatible with Wahhabi teachings, practices that were rampant in Hijaz. The league established public morals committees staffed by Mutawiyin, or "volunteers" (commonly called "religious police"), charged with enforcing Wahhabi doctrine. Prostitution and consumption of alcohol and tobacco were common, and all were targeted. However, the ban on tobacco was withdrawn; it was decided smoking was not expressly prohibited by the Quran, because it was not in use at the time of its writing. Additionally, cigarette sales produced large revenues for merchants and, thus, for the cash-strapped state through taxes.

The new edicts led to unrest in Hijaz, which was inflamed as the Ikhwan destroyed shrines and sought more strict enforcement of religious law. Friction between Ibn Saud and the Ikhwan intensified as well, as they pressed demands for a role in governance. They wanted to continue their raids to spread Wahhabism, ignoring borders. Various groups of Ikhwan engaged in growing mutual cooperation as their dissatisfaction with constraints imposed by Ibn Saud grew. Seeking to rally their support, Ibn Saud imposed Wahhabi principles in Hijaz. He had declared grave worship and allegiance to any being other than Allah as illegal in December of 1924. In July of 1925 he announced that sharia, holy law, would be instituted in Hijaz. During this time Ibn Saud started to implement sharia in Najd and the Eastern Province, assigning *qadis* to towns and insisting that umara (plural of *emir,* the secular rulers) enforce the religious law. The Bedouin customary law (*urf,* or *ariba,*), which previously held sway among tribal groups, gradually faded. In 1926 and 1927 a uniform system of justice based on Hanbali law—defined by six treatises written by Hanbali jurists and theologians—was adopted.

Innovations and Opposition

Before automobiles were introduced in the late 1920s, trips between Najd and Hijaz by Ibn Saud required the entire royal court to travel by camel. The kingdom had no administrative center, and all records remained in the possession of the retinue. All documents, letters, and files traveled with the court as well, shipped in huge wooden chests. Ibn Saud held weekly meetings with the ulama to discuss plans with them, ask their advice regarding innovations under consideration, and assure that his decisions met with their approval.

Under Ibn Saud's direction, telephone and telegraph systems were introduced to Hijaz. The Ikhwan, rooted in fundamentalism, opposed these innovations along with automobiles and airplanes as infidel inventions. Throughout 1926 the Ikhwan sabotaged phone lines in Mecca. The ulama met to consider the Ikhwan's complaints about these innovations, but concluded that the Quran and sunnah said nothing against the telegraph and telephone, so they could not be unlawful. Ibn Saud reportedly pointed out to the Ikhwan that their rifles were also

ADMINISTRATION IN THE NEW KINGDOM

Administering the conquered Hijaz presented new challenges to the young Saudi state. The available civil servants in the newly conquered Hijaz were holdovers from Turkish rule, whose corruption made Ibn Saud reluctant to rely on them. He was also determined to hire only Muslims, and thus turned to foreign Arabs and nonnative Muslims. He kept most family members out of government posts, though his two eldest sons, Saud and Faisal, were made his official deputies in Najd and Hijaz, respectively. (Ibn Saud's firstborn son, Turki, died in a flu epidemic of 1918–19.) A Council of Ministers was created late in his reign, and some princes held cabinet posts on the council.

Ibn Saud preferred to surround himself with associates of long-standing acquaintance. From his household staff to ministerial and administrative officials, he was reluctant to replace individuals he knew personally, which likely contributed to a stagnation in improving the administrative infrastructure.

The Ministry of Finance was essentially a one-man entity, run by Abdullah ibn Sulayman, who met daily in private with Ibn Saud to discuss the kingdom's finances. Some called him the uncrowned king, owing to his control of the treasury. Officially called "his excellency," he had an entourage of some 400 officials, slaves, and guards, which he paid for himself. Some of his wealth may have come from contracts he executed at inflated prices through figureheads.

made by infidels, and asked if they would give up their weapons in return for destruction of the telegraph.

Ikhwan Revolt

In 1927 the kingdom and Britain concluded the Treaty of Jeddah, replacing the 1915 Treaty of Qatif. The treaty recognized the independence of the dominions of the kingdom. Ibn Saud agreed to observe all treaties and cooperate in the suppression of the slave trade. But the Iraqis started building a police outpost near the Busaya oasis, close to the Saudi territory. The Ikhwan complained that this contravened the border agreement concluded in 1922. Ibn Saud tried to solve the issue diplomatically, but the Ikhwan attacked the police outpost, killing the police manning the fortification. Britain launched an air attack on Ikhwan encampments in Saudi territory in retaliation, and the Ikhwan responded by mounting raids into Iraq and Kuwait. The conflict continued for several months. Ibn Saud wanted to resolve the conflict, but Ikhwan leaders opposed the peace initiatives.

By March of 1929, Ikhwan opposition to Ibn Saud's policies and rule had coalesced into a formidable and autonomous force, and their cross-border raiding increased. Evidence suggests that three Ikhwan leaders, al-Dawish, Ibn Humayd, and Ibn Hithlayn, intended to overthrow Ibn Saud and become the rulers of Najd, Hijaz, and Eastern Province, respectively. The Ikhwan revolted and were soundly defeated by Ibn Saud's forces on the plain of Sibila. Rebellious activity continued but ended in January 1930.

The defeat of the Ikhwan was far from the end of the kingdom's battles with fundamentalists. In 1930 the nascent Directorate of Education proposed a curriculum that included instruction in technical drawing, foreign languages, and geography. The ulama objected, decreeing that drawings were the same as pictures, which are forbidden in Islam, and that knowledge of foreign languages facilitated exposure to the thinking of infidels. They also opposed teaching that the Earth is round. Ibn Saud approved the curriculum over their objections.

The Kingdom of Saudi Arabia

The suppression of the Ikhwan did not end the challenges to Ibn Saud's reign. From outside Arabia, exiles who supported the Hashemites tried to organize an armed insurrection in Hijaz, sending a small detachment into northern Hijaz to spark an uprising in May of 1932. Concurrently,

FOREIGN RELATIONS

A Directorate of Foreign Affairs was established in 1926 (renamed the Ministry of Foreign Affairs in 1930). Ibn Saud appointed his second-oldest son, Faisal, already the viceroy of Hijaz, as foreign minister.

In 1926 the Soviet Union became the first state to recognize the new kingdom, with Britain, the Netherlands, France, and Turkey establishing diplomatic relations that same year. In 1929 Persia began negotiations aimed at achieving recognition; antagonism over destruction of tombs of holy saints dear to Persia's Shia still complicated relations.

Relations with the United States were established in 1931. Egypt refused to recognize the new state because of anger over Ikhwan attacks on Egyptian pilgrims in 1926, and a dispute over the *Mahmal,* or holy carpet, the following year. The Mahmal is brought from Cairo to Mecca annually in a grand procession as part of the hajj. But in 1927, Ibn Saud banned the Mahmal from Mecca, concerned that its display might incite disorder. Relations were normalized only in 1956, after Ibn Saud's death. But no foreign embassies were established in the kingdom for more than two decades after the unification of Najd and Hijaz in 1932.

the ruler of Yemen, Imam Yahya, was maneuvering to seize territory in Asir, an action that had already led to armed conflict with Saudi forces along the border. Responding to the former threat, Ibn Saud had opponents in Hijaz arrested, routed the invaders, and banned all political parties, which were formerly permitted in Hijaz. By that summer, Ibn Saud's control over Najd and Hijaz was complete. That September, 18 officials of the Hijazi government sent Ibn Saud a petition requesting that he proclaim Hijaz and Najd a single nation in recognition of their unity of faith, history, and traditions. It is presumed that their request was engineered by Ibn Saud himself.

On September 18, 1932, Ibn Saud issued a decree proclaiming the merger of Hijaz and Najd. All obligations and treaties signed by the previous governments were to remain in force. On September 23 Ibn Saud proclaimed the foundation of the Kingdom of Saudi Arabia. The land was now united in both name and deed. But the prospects for the future did not appear to warrant the hardship and sacrifice it had taken to create the kingdom.

9

BIRTH OF A KINGDOM
(1932–1953)

At the kingdom's birth, Saudi Arabia's situation and prospects were bleak. The new state was in debt, payments to creditors had ceased, and further loans were unobtainable. Additionally, the worldwide depression reduced pilgrimage revenues, its main source of income. Whereas 129,000 pilgrims made the hajj in 1926, the number had fallen to 29,000 in 1932 and 20,000 the following year. Many state employees had not been paid in months, and a border dispute with Yemen was blistering into warfare. King Abd al-Aziz, or Ibn Saud as he was known in the West, who had assembled the kingdom using the skills of a desert warrior, now had to become an international statesman. And the nation and its people, little changed from medieval times, had to join the 20th century. The two decades of his rule witnessed a wrenching transformation, precipitated and made possible by the discovery of massive petroleum resources beneath the kingdom's desert sands, years and events that this chapter surveys.

The New Kingdom

Upon its official founding on September 23, 1932, now celebrated as independence day, the Kingdom of Saudi Arabia was little less isolated or more worldly than the first Saudi-Wahhabi state at its birth in the mid-1700s. By one account, fewer than 50 non-Muslims lived in the kingdom. Tribal alliances, feuds, and flexible loyalties still shaped the political landscape. Though Najd and Hijaz were united in name, the inhabitants viewed each other with suspicion. The worldliness of Hijaz, exposed as it was to Western and European influences, was a shock to the sensibilities of the sheltered and more conservative Najdis.

Ibn Saud retained the title of imam, as had all Saudi rulers since the end of the 18th century, though in his official functions he was more commonly addressed as king. Common allegiance to the imam and the Wahhabi cause he led unified the disparate tribes within the kingdom. The title also signified his leadership of the jihad under which the kingdom had been created. But with the consolidation of its territories and the defeat of the Ikhwan, Ibn Saud ended the military offensive component of his titular role of imam. The symbolism of the title was carried through in the flag of the new state.

The flag, though it has been slightly modified over the years, represents the two forces that united the country: Islam and armed jihad. The Arabic script proclaims the *shahada,* or "witnessing," whose recitation is one of the five religious responsibilities of all Muslims: "There is no God (Allah) but God (Allah), Muhammad is His Messenger." The sword, lying horizontally across the lower portion of the banner, symbolizes holy war, which had established Saudi rule and the Wahhabi form of Islam throughout the land. The background of green, the Prophet Muhammad's favorite color, symbolizes heaven and the verdant paradise awaiting those who lead their lives as good Muslims in the parched temporal world they inhabit.

Ibn Saud had long exhibited an interest and appreciation for international affairs. The year after taking Riyadh in 1902, he initiated contact with Arab leaders and with Britain, Russia, and other foreign governments. Thus, by the time the kingdom was officially established it had received recognition from several countries. Fittingly, the first crisis the kingdom faced was international in nature. Saudi efforts to establish control over southern Asir, whose territory had historically been claimed by both Arabian and Yemeni rulers, ignited a border war.

Yemeni Border War

In an agricultural area in the south of Asir, the Idrisi family, descendants of a 19th-century Sufi teacher, Ahmad ibn Idris, ruled a loose tribal confederation that had fought Ottoman occupation since the late 1800s. With the Ottomans gone, control over the area had been contested by the rulers of Hijaz and of Yemen. Ibn Saud, too, had mounted a campaign in Asir before his conquest of Hijaz in the mid-1920s, winning the allegiance of tribes in the area. Yemen's ruler, Imam Yahya, who had united the southern end of the peninsula as Ibn Saud had unified Arabia, refused to recognize Ibn Saud's claim. Imam Yahya took over parts of Asir, straining relations with Ibn Saud. In 1926 the emir of Asir, worried about further Yemeni conquests, signed a treaty making his territory a Saudi protectorate. But in 1930 Ibn Saud imposed a new treaty on the Idrisi ruler, al-Hasan al-Idrisi, taking most of his power. That led Al Idris to secretly seek alliances with both Imam Yahya and the Hijazi liberals, a group seeking to expel Ibn Saud from Hijaz.

In 1932 a plot to attack Hijaz and oust Ibn Saud was uncovered. The plotters were led by a Hijazi tribal chief and notables who had fled to Yemen after the fall of Hijaz seven years before. The plot made the Saudis wary of the trouble their enemies were fomenting from their sanctuary. In November of that same year Al Idrisi commenced a revolt against Saudi rule. Saudi forces quickly put down the insurrection, and Al Idrisi and his followers fled to Yemen.

In 1933 Imam Yahya's son Prince Ahmad occupied Najran in southern Asir, citing its inhabitants' (a branch of a Yemeni tribe) assistance to a rebellion against Imam Yahya. Ibn Saud sent a delegation to Sanaa to settle the rebellion. But the imam had support from the Italians, who wanted more influence in the region, and the British, who sought to offset the tension caused by their presence in Aden. The peace negotiations floundered. Yemeni forces marched into Asir and occupied al-Badr. The Idrisis instigated an uprising against the Saudi governor of Asir. Ibn Saud sent Imam Yahya an ultimatum to withdraw. In response, the imam signed a treaty with Great Britain, securing protection for his forces. Meanwhile, Ibn Saud sought arms from the British to confront the Yemenis. The British rebuffed his request and tried to dissuade him from military action.

Subsequent negotiations between Saudi and Yemeni delegates were unsuccessful. In March of 1934 Ibn Saud, having bought weapons with a loan from Standard Oil of California (Socal), launched an invasion of Yemen led by his sons Saud and Faisal. But naval forces from Great Britain, France, and Italy steamed toward the Yemeni port of Hodeida, which Saudi forces had captured. With the conflict reaching a stalemate, an armistice was concluded in May of 1934. The peace agreement was formalized in the Treaty of Taif, signed later that month. Imam Yahya waived his claim to the Idrisis' territories, and Saudi forces relinquished the Yemeni territories they occupied. The treaty failed to end the dispute over the border location, but Ibn Saud won the release of hostages taken in the conflict and the formal recognition of Ibn Saud's authority over Asir. Thereafter, relations between the two countries warmed.

The Oil Concessions

The world financial crisis of 1929–33 had reduced pilgrimage traffic, cutting state revenues from fees and taxes. The war against the Ikhwan and the expenses of Ibn Saud's court had already put the monarchy in

AN EARLY OIL CRISIS

In 1920 W. Fairish, the future president of Standard Oil Company of New Jersey, warned that oil deposits in Texas and Oklahoma were being depleted. Concurrently, a leading U.S. geology expert concluded the United States would run out of domestic petroleum resources in less than 20 years. Meanwhile, Senator Henry Cabot Lodge voiced concern over Britain's growing domination of the world's oil supply, and U.S. naval officials worried about the adequacy of domestic reserves. These concerns galvanized the U.S. government to assist oil companies in their quest for international growth. At the San Remo Conference in April 1920, convened to discuss the future of the lands formerly in the Ottoman orbit, the U.S. government demanded an open-door policy on commercial activity and access for U.S. oil companies. This countered a British and French plan to monopolize the territories for their own interests.

debt. The new government's expenditures—construction of several radio stations, improvements to Jeddah's water supply, the purchase of several automobiles—had raised its deficit to £300,000.

A U.S. citizen, Charles Crane, a well-connected Chicago philanthropist and former ambassador, played a large role in reversing the government's budget deficit (perhaps a misnomer, as the early kingdom was operated without the benefit of a budget). Crane had first come to Arabia at the invitation of Sharif Hussein, and after, so impressed by the displays of religiosity he observed, he went on to study Islam at Al Azhar University in Cairo. Ibn Saud's adviser, H. St. John Philby, claimed to have suggested the king meet Crane to discuss his possible assistance in searching for water or other sources of wealth beneath the kingdom's sands. Crane first attempted to meet the king in 1928, setting off in a car caravan from Basra, Iraq, for Riyadh. But the travelers were attacked along the way, with one of their party killed, and they returned to Basra. The king and Crane finally met in 1930, after which Crane arranged for Karl S. Twitchell, a geologist and mining engineer who had been doing work in Yemen, to conduct a survey of the country. Twitchell arrived in the spring of 1932. If the survey was offered as a favor, finding a rich source of oil was also of interest to the United States, where concerns about the depletion of domestic oil deposits had already been expressed.

Efforts to find oil in Arabia began in 1922 when a New Zealander, Major Frank Holmes, negotiated a concession, or right to explore for oil, covering 30,000 square miles in Eastern Province, for an annual fee of £2,000 to Ibn Saud. In 1925 Holmes negotiated for a concession in Bahrain, as well. He eventually sold the Bahrain concession to U.S.-based Gulf Oil after failing to interest British firms in a deal. The British did not think oil was in the area but were nonetheless opposed to U.S. activity in the region. Gulf Oil subsequently sold the concession to Standard Oil of California (Socal) due to preexisting agreements in Turkey and Iraq that effectively precluded Gulf Oil from working in Bahrain.

The Search for Oil

Twitchell, who would spend some 20 years in Saudi Arabia, found a geological structure indicating the presence of oil in the area and returned to the United States to report his findings. Socal was eager to have its geologists explore Saudi Arabia's Eastern Province. The Anglo-Persian Oil Company was also interested in the region. However, when the Saudis demanded $100,000 in gold for the concession, or rights for exploration and extraction, the Anglo-Persian Oil Company dropped out of contention, and Socal offered $50,000 in gold for the 60-year concession. Philby, who was being paid by Socal for his assistance, urged the king to accept the agreement. Ibn Saud preferred the United States over Britain, as the United States had no history of colonialism in the region. The agreement, signed on May 29, 1933, included an "anti-imperial" clause forbidding the company's influence on internal affairs, a clause that would be difficult for both sides to rigorously observe, given the fluid dynamics of the evolving relations and the needs of the parties. The annual rental fee was £5,000 in gold. Socal also

In 1938, commercial quantities of oil were discovered. This well, Dammam No. 7, near Dhahran, was the first to strike oil. (Courtesy of the Nestor Sander Collection/Aramco World/PADIA)

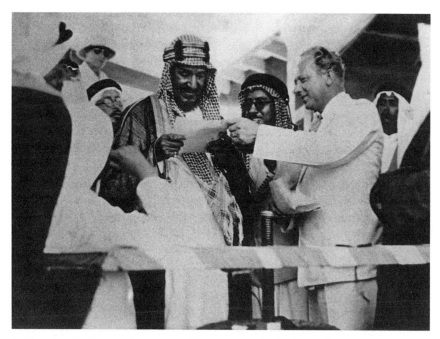

In May of 1939, King Ibn Saud came to Ras Tanura, on the Persian Gulf, to mark the first commercial shipment of Saudi crude oil. Here, Abd al-Aziz is briefed by a U.S. official of Casoc at the company's facilities at Ras Tanura. (Courtesy of the Saudi Information Office)

loaned the king £20,000. Socal created a wholly owned subsidiary, the California Arab Standard Oil Company (Casoc), the predecessor to the Arabian American Oil Company (Aramco) that was formed in 1944.

Within four months Socal geologists were prospecting, using camels to transport their equipment. Trucks arrived some months later. By the end of 1933 eight oil experts were in Saudi Arabia. Prospectors found a promising geological structure in 1935 and drilling began. After several unproductive wells, Dammam No. 7 struck oil, ultimately producing 1,500 barrels per day.

Commercial production commenced in 1938, and the following year the king came to inspect extraction station No. 39 in Dhahran, setting up an encampment of 350 tents and remaining for several days of celebration. On May 1, 1939, the first tanker filled with Saudi Arabian oil sailed from Ras Tanura. (The oil terminal at Ras Tanura, which would become the kingdom's major oil transfer facility, did not begin operations until 1945.) Half-a-million barrels were shipped that year.

The development of the oil industry required an influx of infidels. Ibn Saud found justification for their presence in the Quran: "Say: O ye

The U.S. tanker Scofield *takes on the first shipment of Saudi crude oil at Ras Tanura for transport to refineries abroad in May 1939.* (Courtesy of the Saudi Information Office)

that reject faith. I worship not that which he worship, nor will ye worship that which I worship. And I will not worship that which ye have been wont to worship, nor will ye worship that which I worship. To you be your way and to me mine" (Quran 109: 1–6).

State Administration

When the kingdom was first declared, matters of state were attended to by the king, a small circle of princes, and an eight-member "political committee" of foreign advisers from Egypt, Syria, Libya, and Lebanon, as well as British Arabist H. St. John Philby. The leadership, only lately removed from the isolation of the peninsula's interior, was slow to abandon its disdain for the ways of the outside world, and failed to establish the administrative framework a modern state required. Government needs were addressed on an ad hoc basis. In the 1930s Ibn Saud appointed members of the kingdom's leading merchant families to serve as Saudi Arabia's representatives abroad. Over time, members of these families came to form the core of the government's civil service. The minister of finance, al-Sulaiman, retained control of the treasury. (He retired in 1954, the year after Ibn Saud's death.)

An agency was established to manage the kingdom's military forces upon the kingdom's formation, but throughout the 1930s and into the

FAMILY AND SEXUAL POLITICS

While Ibn Saud had employed alliances, threats, rewards, and other inducements to expand his power, the majority of his domain was subjugated by force. But as a member of the modern family of nations, he would have to keep the kingdom united without resorting to the internal warfare that had convulsed the peninsula for centuries.

After consolidating power in Arabia and declaring the kingdom, Ibn Saud sought to solidify the continuity of his own lineage, limiting succession to his sons. Yet he faced threats to his designs from within his extended family. Between 1922 and 1943, his brother Muhammad challenged Ibn Saud's power and positioned his own son Khalid to vie for rule. Muhammad and Khalid were opposed to Ibn Saud's harsh treatment of the Ikhwan. Muhammad also opposed the 1933 appointment of Ibn Saud's eldest surviving son, Saud, as crown prince, and refused to affirm allegiance to the king. The threat ended in 1938 when Khalid died under circumstances that have been called mysterious. Muhammad, his father, died in 1943. This left Ibn Saud with no rivals of his generation. Throughout this time he relegated brothers and nephews to the periphery of power in favor of his many sons.

Ibn Saud took multiple wives and concubines. By 1953 he had 43 sons and more than 50 daughters. He admitted, according to several accounts, to having married more than 100 and as many as 235 women. In keeping with Islamic law, he kept only four wives at a time, divorcing one when he took a new wife. As noted by Al-Rasheed, ". . . Ibn' Saud's marriages were perceived as extraordinary even in a society that allowed a mixture of both polygamy and concubinage" (Al-Rasheed 2002, 76)

The reasons behind this proclivity have been attributed to both overindulgence and efforts to create alliances by marriage, though the strength of bonds created by such wholesale marriages has been questioned. Doubtless some alliances were strengthened or created by the blood ties resulting from the progeny of these unions. Ibn Saud also married off daughters and arranged unions for his sons that served to strengthen his power by diluting threats of family members and others.

1940s, there was virtually no formal military force. Remnants of the Ikhwan formed the core of the national guard.

As noted, Ibn Saud preferred to surround himself with associates of long-standing acquaintance, from ministerial and administrative officials to his household staff, and was disinclined to recruit replacements. This hindered the development of an effective administrative infrastructure.

World War II

Though officially neutral at the outset of World War II, Saudi Arabia was a theater of intrigue and espionage between the Allies and Axis in the early days of the conflict. Adolf Hitler, Germany's leader, saw Saudi Arabia as a springboard to Russia's southern flank. He secretly promised Ibn Saud the title of king of all the Arabs if he attacked British forces. But Ibn Saud tacitly backed the British with whom, despite their quarrels, Saudi Arabia had a far larger economic relationship. Though Ibn Saud allowed Germany to station an agent who conducted clandestine operations from Jeddah, the operative was expelled in 1941 after the British complained about his activities. Hitler's interest in Saudi Arabia ebbed as the tide of war turned against Germany.

Growing Ties with the United States

The United States had long regarded Saudi Arabia as under Europe's, and particularly Great Britain's, sphere of influence. Though the United States recognized the kingdom in 1931, no American diplomat made a formal visit until 1940, when the U.S. envoy to Egypt, Bert Gish, received accreditation to represent the U.S. government in the Kingdom (of the Hijaz and Najd and Its Dependencies, as it was known at the time). Despite seeming U.S. indifference to the relationship, the Saudis saw the Americans as a counterbalance to British regional influence, and one with less imperialistic ambitions in the area.

Aramco, with its American roots, was eager to strengthen U.S.-Saudi ties, particularly in the heat of wartime when other powers were vying for its favor. The company briefed U.S. policymakers on Saudi Arabian oil reserves and handled travel arrangements for Saudi royalty visiting the United States. The U.S. government, as it came to recognize the strategic importance of oil, also appreciated the need for a stronger relationship. President Franklin Roosevelt declared the kingdom vital to the defense of the United States, qualifying it for American Lend-Lease assistance and for foreign-aid loans and grants.

Ties with the United States drew closer in 1942 with the appointment of a chargé d'affaires to Jeddah. In October of the following year, Crown Prince Saud paid an official visit to Washington during a month-long trip. That same year, Prince Faisal and his brother Khalid visited the United States and met President Roosevelt, congressmen, and other members of the government, while two delegations led by U.S. Army generals visited Saudi Arabia. The first aimed to assess the oil situation as it affected the United States. The second, in December, led by General Roys, commander in chief of U.S. forces in the Middle East, sought arrangements for construction of a military airfield in Dhahran.

Britain's influence in Saudi Arabia, long strained over its competing regional alliances, began to rebound during the war years. Attempting to counter the thaw, the United States demanded that part of a $425 million loan it had provided to Britain be given to Saudi Arabia. The money was funneled through Britain because the Roosevelt administration believed Congress would not approve direct aid to Saudi Arabia. After U.S. oil companies complained the indirect funding diluted U.S. influence, aid was dispatched directly to the kingdom.

The King Meets the President

The new Saudi-U.S. relationship was underscored on February 14, 1945, by a meeting between Ibn Saud and President Roosevelt, who was on his way back to the United States from the Yalta Conference. They met aboard the Navy cruiser USS *Quincy* in the Great Bitter Lake along the Suez Canal. Ibn Saud's desire to find a powerful ally to guarantee the kingdom's independence and the United States's need for oil and military reach yielded what seemed a mutually beneficial relationship. But the two leaders disagreed on a major issue. Roosevelt attempted to win the king's support for the plan to allow Jews displaced in the war to settle in Palestine. The king believed Germany, not Palestine, should be responsible for providing relief, arguing that the Arabs had done nothing to the Jews and expressing determined opposition. However, Ibn Saud agreed to give U.S. ships access to Saudi ports and confirmed the agreement to allow construction of a U.S. Air Force base at Dhahran. In granting permission for building an air base, however, Ibn Saud stipulated that Saudi Arabia would not be occupied as other Arab states had been; the property would be leased for only five years and then transferred back to Saudi Arabia with all its buildings and structures. (By its completion in 1946 the war was over. It was used as a training installation for Saudi army personnel taught by U.S. and British military advisers.) Roosevelt

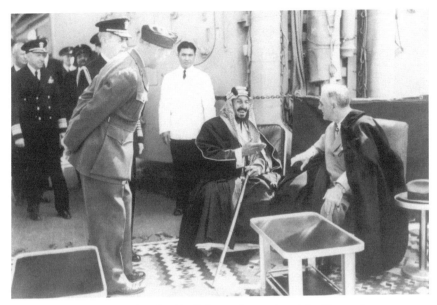

In 1945 Ibn Saud and President Franklin D. Roosevelt met aboard the Navy cruiser USS Quincy. (Courtesy of Dr. Michael Crocker/King Abdul Aziz Foundation)

also agreed to provide light weapons to Saudi Arabia, and the king also agreed to declare war on the Axis, which he did in March of 1945, a declaration that eased Saudi Arabia's entrance to the United Nations.

The agreement reached aboard the *Quincy*, according to historian Al-Rasheed, marked the first area outside the Western Hemisphere where U.S. influence supplanted Great Britain's. The meeting was kept secret, but Britain learned about it shortly beforehand. Prime Minister Winston Churchill met with the king immediately after but was unable to change the basic agreements with the United States. In April Roosevelt sent Ibn Saud a letter promising that as president he would never undertake actions hostile to the Arabs and that the United States would not change its policy toward Palestine without full and prior consultation with both Arabs and Jews.

The Growing Power of Oil

U.S. influence in Saudi Arabia grew at the expense of Britain's in the postwar years, the relationship powered by oil. Even though production development all but stopped during World War II, production had risen from the 500,000 barrels pumped in 1939, the first year of commercial production, to more than 21 million barrels in 1945.

In the last half of the 1940s more oil was discovered, and demand for oil surged. In postwar years, the switch to liquid fuel from coal, global industrialization, and the rise of plastics and consumerism created an unprecedented demand for oil. By the end of the 1960s, oil consumption in the United States rose 250 percent, while usage in the rest of the world, driven by the modernization of undeveloped countries, increased more than eightfold. The kingdom, or more properly its rulers, were growing rich, though not realizing all the profits due them; oil companies undercalculated payments through accounting irregularities often perpetrated by collusion with Saudi administrators.

In Syria, Husni al-Zaim came to power in March 1949. He was supported by the United States and Saudi Arabia, primarily because of his backing for the proposed Tapline oil pipeline, which would traverse Syria in its route from eastern Saudi Arabia to the Mediterranean. A second military coup brought an opponent of the proposed pipeline to power. But yet a third coup brought a pro-U.S. ruler to power who approved the project. The Tapline, a massive construction project and engineering feat, was built and put into operation in 1951. However, the pipeline suffered periodic disruptions in service due to damage, and shipment by sea ultimately proved more cost-effective. In the early 1980s the Trans-Arabian Pipeline Company (an Aramco subsidiary) announced that the Tapline would cease operations.

Stirrings of Labor Problems

Aramco was becoming a much more powerful force in the country, taking on responsibilities for public projects, including waterworks (Ibn Saud demanded that a water well be drilled along with every oil well) and a railway. Aramco was also responsible for training the bulk of the kingdom's first generation of an educated class, the domestic technocrats and administrators needed to run the company. But as the kingdom began granting concessions to independent oil companies, the more favorable terms it received indicated that its arrangements with Aramco were inequitable. In addition, Aramco's treatment of Arab workers, particularly foreigners imported for unskilled labor, resulted in labor unrest. The majority of them came Egypt, Yemen, Jordan, Syria, and Kuwait, and large numbers of imported laborers also came from Pakistan, India, and the Philippines. Low wages, poor housing and food, racial discrimination, inadequate training, and lack of workers' rights were among their complaints. The first strike by Aramco workers

THE AL-BURAIMI DISPUTE

As with Yemen, the undefined borders with the Gulf States, which were British protectorates, led to disputes. The location of boundaries with Oman, Qatar, and the Trucial States became increasingly important in the 1930s and 1940s, when the value of desert parcels soared as oil companies sought concessions in the area. One of the most bitter disputes revolved around a traditional crossroads on the caravan routes of southeast Arabia, the Buraimi Oases. Comprising nine villages spread over some 2,000 square kilometers, the area had been claimed by the first Saudi state in 1795. Ibn Saud authorized Aramco geologists to begin exploring the area in 1949. But Britain objected, asserting that historically the oases belonged to Abu Dhabi and Muscat and demanding that exploration be halted until ownership was established. The following year the predecessor of British Petroleum (the Anglo-Arabian Oil Company) began exploring islands and other areas under British control that Saudi Arabia claimed, leading to Ibn Saud's objections. The British dismissed the claims as unfounded, and tensions rose. A 1951 conference in Dammam attended by representatives of all countries involved, with Prince Faisal leading the Saudi delegation, failed to reach any resolution.

After the British sent an agent to establish an administrative presence in the oases in 1952, the Saudis did the same, using local citizens, some armed, to supplement their contingent. An armed British detachment was dispatched to the area, and British aircraft buzzed the Saudi-occupied

occurred in 1945. Aramco was forced to accede to temporary concessions, including an eight-and-a-half-hour working day, a six-day week, and two weeks of paid leave. The government then deported the striking workers. Both Aramco and Saudi Arabia remained aggressively opposed to labor activism. However, Saudi Arabia adopted a labor code in 1947 mandating standards including an eight-hour workday and a six-day week in all companies with more than 10 employees.

Labor unrest continued to fester. In 1953, 20,000 Aramco workers went on strike, and martial law was declared in the oil fields. The strikers found support among the population of the Eastern Province, who viewed Aramco's American managers unfavorably. Soldiers that were brought in to quell the disturbances were reluctant to take action. The strike gained sympathy in other Arab countries, forcing Aramco officials to accede to many worker demands, including a raise in pay, bet-

village of Khamasa, while on the diplomatic front they demanded Saudi withdrawal. The U.S. ambassador, acting as mediator, recommended a return to negotiations while maintaining the status quo of Saudi and British occupation. This was the situation upon Ibn Saud's death in 1953. It would be another two decades before the dispute was settled.

In 1954 Saudi Arabia and Britain agreed to submit the dispute over ownership of the Buraimi Oases to a court of arbitration. Britain withdrew from the arbitration the following year before a decision was rendered, fearing an adverse judgment. That October, troops from Abu Dhabi and Muscat, in whose name Britain was furthering the border dispute, were sent to the oases under British command. Saudi Arabia filed a protest with the UN Security Council. Again the United States offered to mediate. The British engaged in direct negotiations with the Saudis, led by Faisal. Progress was ended by the Egyptian seizure of the Suez Canal. When the British, French, and Israelis attacked Egypt, Saudi Arabia severed diplomatic relations and cut off oil exports to both Britain and France. It was only in 1963, after mutual interest in blocking the nationalist and socialist movements in the Arab world renewed their bond, that diplomatic relations were restored and negotiations over the dispute resumed, though with little progress.

In 1971, Abu Dhabi became one of the seven Trucial states that joined in the United Arab Emirates (UAE). The ongoing border dispute prevented Saudi Arabia from recognizing the UAE. Saudi Arabia and Abu Dhabi finally concluded an agreement settling the dispute in 1974 and leading to the establishment of diplomatic relations with the UAE.

ter working conditions, and the release of workers who had been arrested for their part in the strike.

The monarchy took a hard-line stance against demonstrations, unionization efforts, and workers' rights organizations. Whatever its outward policies, the behind-the-scenes struggles and debates within the ruling family and the powerful elite that shaped them remain unknown. Scholars and historians call the policymaking apparatus of this time "opaque." But it is accepted that bitter internal disputes wracked the ruling elite composed of branches of Al Saud.

Palestine and Israel

The future of Palestine and growing Jewish immigration to the area became a defining issue for Saudi Arabia as for all Arab states. At the end of World War I the population of Palestine was 90 percent Arab. Jews claimed Palestine as their historical homeland, citing their forced eviction from the area in Roman times. They began resettling in Palestine in increasing numbers as Hitler rose to power in Germany in the early 1930s.

During this time Palestine was only a peripheral issue for Ibn Saud. Though the mufti of Jerusalem, Hajj Amin Al-Husseini, complained to him about Britain's Zionist bent—an issue that galvanized Palestinian and Syrian activists—Ibn Saud remained uninvolved. Britain, meanwhile, treated policies within its mandate as its business alone. During the British mandate, the Balfour Declaration, discussed in the last chapter, was cited as a British commitment for a Jewish national home in Palestine. Arab resistance to British control and the influx of Jews led to the Arab Revolt of 1936–39. Led by Hajj Amin Al-Husseini, it resulted in the deaths of thousands of Arabs and Jews. The British army,

Confrontations between old and new became increasingly common after the discovery of oil. This 1947 photograph shows a Bedouin and his camel crossing paths with modern machines in the midst of road building near Hufuf. (Courtesy of Robert Y. Richie/Aramco World/PADIA)

Exposure to the outside world brought benefits as well as displacement. This 1931 photograph from the collection of surveyor Karl Twitchell identifies the subjects as pilgrims on their way to Mecca, a journey made easier by the automobile in which they are traveling. (Courtesy of the Fine Arts Library, Harvard College Library, Twitchell Collection, Harvard Semitic Museum Photographic Archives)

Jewish militias, and Arab governments worked to suppress the violence. Al-Husseini fled to Iraq and later to Nazi Germany.

In 1937, the British promoted a plan to divide Palestine into Arab and Jewish states. Ibn Saud's primary concern for the future of Palestine revolved around the designs of Abdullah, the Hashemite ruler of Transjordan, who hoped to absorb Palestine into his realm. Ibn Saud's lack of enthusiasm for getting involved was also due to concerns about encouraging the emerging ideals identified with the nascent Pan-Arab Palestinian cause, which included secularism and political reforms antithetical to the Saudi state. Nonetheless, Ibn Saud was opposed to establishing a Jewish state, fearing Zionist intentions in the area. Indeed, he had explicitly made his views known to President Roosevelt during their historic meeting in 1945.

The First Arab-Israeli War

Britain turned the issue of Palestine's future over to the United Nations in 1947. In May of that year the UN General Assembly annulled the British mandate and divided the territory into the states of Israel and Palestine. The Palestinian leadership rejected the plan, noting that the

THE ARAB LEAGUE

In 1943 representatives of Saudi Arabia and other Arab countries met in Egypt to discuss establishing what would become the League of Arab States, commonly called the Arab League. The original goals of the organization were threefold: to gain independence for Arab states; to stop Jewish immigration to Palestine; and to block the creation of a Jewish state. However, for Saudi Arabia these issues were secondary to concerns for the kingdom's continued existence. The Egyptian leadership and Hashemite influence in the proposed organization dampened Saudi Arabia's support, and the kingdom demanded recognition of its territorial integrity as a condition for joining.

When formalized in Cairo on March 22, 1945, the charter members were Egypt, Iraq, Lebanon, Saudi Arabia, Syria, Transjordan, and Yemen. The goals of the league evolved to incorporate mutual defense and economic cooperation, formalized in 1950 with the signing of a Joint Defense and Economic Cooperation Treaty. This agreement was also a response to the members' perception of the threat posed by the existence of Israel.

Belying the impression that Arab interests are typically in alignment, the Arab League has historically exhibited disunity and inaction, and has often highlighted its lack of agreement. Today its membership comprises 21 independent countries and Palestine, stretching from Africa to Asia. Member countries must have Arabic as their dominant language.

Jews were to receive most of the land, though they made up a far smaller percentage of the population. When the British withdrew their forces, Jewish leaders proclaimed the state of Israel on May 15, 1948. This was referred to as Nakba—the catastrophe—in the Arab world. On May 16, 1948, the first Arab-Israeli war, also called the 1948 War and the Israel War of Independence, erupted. Saudi Arabia, along with Egypt, Syria, Iraq, Lebanon, and Jordan, declared war on Israel. Egyptian, Jordanian, and Syrian forces mounted an invasion of the Jewish state. Saudi Arabia remained largely on the sidelines, though Ibn Saud dispatched a battalion to assist the Egyptian army.

During the conflict about half of the Arab inhabitants of Palestine, or 700,000–800,000 people, were displaced from their homes and became refugees. No peace agreement was ever signed, but four successive armistice agreements ended the conflict. The armistice agreement of

April 3, 1949, divided what had been Palestine into three parts. Israel received 77 percent of the territory (about 50 percent more than it had been allotted under the UN Partition Plan); Jordan took control of East Jerusalem and central Palestine, which became known as the West Bank; and Egypt gained control over the coastal area around Gaza, which became known as the Gaza strip. More Palestinians were expelled from what was now Israel, swelling the population of displaced persons.

Hashemite Designs

Ibn Saud's concerns with Hashemite designs in northern Arabia, which colored his response to the Palestinian issue, were not unfounded. King Abdullah, the ruler of Transjordan, harbored dreams of creating a unified Arab nation, Greater Syria, under Hashemite control, stretching from Lebanon and Palestine across Iraq, and including Transjordan as well as Syria. Ibn Saud viewed these ambitions as the major threat, in part because the Hashemites, unlike the Al Saud, could claim a genealogical link to the Prophet Muhammad and thus to leadership of the Islamic Nation.

King Abdullah also sought restoration of sharifian rule in Hijaz, which would enhance his influence. In 1947 Abdullah hosted a congress on Hijaz that was attended by opponents of Saudi rule from the region. But after Saudi Arabia threatened to challenge Transjordan's borders, specifically Aqaba and Maan, which Saudi Arabia considered Hijazi territory, Abdullah ended his open support for the cause.

During these years Saudi Arabia's relations with Syria hinged on whether its leader of the moment supported Syrian independence (which Saudi Arabia favored as a hindrance to Hashemite intentions) and on his stance regarding construction of a trans-Arabian pipeline across the nation.

In late 1949, after the Arabs' defeat in the first Arab-Israeli war, Abdullah annexed the Arab areas of Palestine (the West Bank) over strong protests from Saudi Arabia and Egypt. Despite the prodding of these two member states, the Arab League avoided dealing with the issue. Abdullah was assassinated in 1951, ending the movement for a greater Syria and the perceived Hashemite threat to Saudi Arabia. Abdullah was succeeded by his son, Talal, whose mental problems quickly brought Abdullah's grandson, Hussein, to the throne of Transjordan.

State Institutions Under Ibn Saud

The king regarded the state coffers as his personal treasury. The majority of its contents had traditionally been spent on maintenance of the king's household, payments to loyal rulers under his suzerainty, and *zakat*, or "charitable donations." The concept of spending money on things to benefit the public was largely alien. No infrastructure existed to make and oversee such expenditures. As oil revenue grew, this lack of programs and the administrative capability to implement them continued. Almost no funds were spent on public works such as roads or utilities, or for social services like education and health care.

As the 1950s dawned, a government capable of running a modern state still had not been established. The two ministries (Ministry of Foreign Affairs and Ministry of Finance) employed fewer than 4,700 people, the majority receiving no regular salaries. Agencies kept no formal records of their operations. The country lacked even a state currency. British gold sovereigns, Indian rupees, Austrian talers, and Egyptian pounds were among the common currencies in use. Early in the decade, more formal government institutions were created. In 1951, the Ministry of Interior and the Ministry of Health were created. The Saudi Arabian Monetary Agency (SAMA), predecessor to the kingdom's Central Bank, was also formed and the Saudi Arabian riyal and halala were introduced.

In the kingdom's first years, government funds were spent on maintenance of the royal household (Ibn Saud would host as many as 2,000 people a day at meals) rather than public projects, a fact reflected in the rough appearance of the kingdom's capital, Riyadh. (Courtesy of the Fine Arts Library, Harvard College Library, Twitchell Collection, Harvard Semitic Museum Photographic Archives)

The currency was pegged at 3.75 riyals to the U.S. dollar. The Ministry of Communication, Ministry of Agriculture and Water, and Ministry of Education were created in 1953 under Ibn Saud's successor, King Saud.

As the structure of the nascent state was erected, Ibn Saud also undertook the repair and expansion of the mosque at Medina, the most extensive renovation of the holy site since the time of the Umayyads more than 1,200 years before. He also approved the extension of the square surrounding the Kaaba (although the project did not begin until 1955, two year after his death) and funding for a search for underground water in central Arabia.

The Sunset of Ibn Saud

Ibn Saud grew detached from matters of governance at a time when their complexity and demands were growing. Beset by infirmities of age, Ibn Saud largely withdrew from public life. Because of an old leg wound, he needed an hour of massage on his knee nightly before he could sleep. President Roosevelt had sent him a wheelchair, an exact duplicate of the president's own, but Ibn Saud's overreliance on it may have contributed to his physical decline.

Near the end of his life Ibn Saud spent most of his time among close relatives, particularly his youngest sons whom he had fathered with beloved ex-concubines in the 1930s and 1940s. Talal ibn Abd al-Aziz Al Saud was one such prince. Because his mother was from neither a branch of the Saudi family nor Arabian nobility, Talal was not affected by the family rivalries that sometimes tainted relationships involving Ibn Saud's sons borne by his wives. The power and attention Ibn Saud gave to Talal and his full brothers created rifts within the royal family, though divisions did not emerge until after his death.

Ibn Saud was well aware of the danger of internecine conflict and its power to bring down Saudi rule. It had done exactly that during the second Saudi state, when feuds ripped the family apart after the death of his grandfather, Faisal ibn Turki. Ibn Saud made his eldest sons, Crown Prince Saud and Faisal, promise to pursue a harmonious path in their future relations. In one of his last official acts, in October of 1953, Ibn Saud issued a decree reorganizing the Council of Ministers (*majlis al-wuzara*) and extending its authority beyond Hijaz to the entire country. The reorganization was also meant to reduce the tensions likely to follow his death by giving more insiders a voice in decision making, and so soften potential disputes between the king and crown prince. The council comprised the king, who also served as prime minister; the crown

Near the end of his reign Ibn Saud took pleasure in spending time with the young sons he sired later in life with favorite concubines. Here Ibn Saud is with, from left to right, Prince Mishal, Prince Talal, Prince Nawaf, and Prince Mirab. (Courtesy of Dr. Michael Crocker/King Abdul Aziz Foundation)

prince, who was deputy prime minister as well; the second deputy prime minister; and cabinet ministers.

Ibn Saud died on November 9, 1953, in Taif, outside of Mecca, where he had spent summers hunting gazelles. Some 100 princes—sons, grandsons, and nephews—were in attendance. All pledged their loyalty to Saud as king and Faisal as crown prince. (Thirty-four sons were said to be alive at the time of his death. His total number of sons, daughters, and sons' children was close to 160.) He was buried in Riyadh in a simple grave in accordance with the Wahhabi teachings he had dedicated his life to upholding.

10

A PATH TO WORLD POWER
(1953–1973)

The two decades following the death of Ibn Saud, the kingdom's founder, were marked by rivalries that threatened the monarchy from within and nascent opposition that began to challenge it from without. Despite the pledge made to their father not to undermine each other, the first two monarchs who followed him—Saud and Faisal—fought battles for control of the government that lasted a decade and threatened the survival of the state. This era also saw the beginning of a massive coordinated national development and construction program as revenue from oil began to rise.

Crumbling colonialism seen in many parts of the world was mirrored by the kingdom's appropriation of ownership of Aramco. These years also saw relations with Egypt turn hostile, as the two countries came close to warfare while backing opposing sides in a civil war in Yemen. But the most significant conflicts of this era were the 1967 Arab-Israeli War and the 1973 Arab-Israeli War. The latter led to the Oil Embargo that would bring Saudi Arabia unprecedented wealth and influence, and alter the world's balance of power. This chapter chronicles the events of these two decades.

The Change in Leadership

Following King Ibn Saud's death the scores of princes gathered for his passing pledged allegiance to Saud (b. 1902) as king and Faisal (b. 1906) as crown prince. King Saud then confirmed Faisal as deputy prime minister and minister of foreign affairs. Though the half-brothers promised their father before his death not to undermine each other, the rivalry between them and the resulting instability dominated state politics for the next decade.

Three camps arose within the royal family: that led by Saud; the faction headed by Faisal and loyal half-brothers (called the "Sudairi

Seven" in the West, after their matrilineal link to the Sudairi clan, an important Najdi family) along with paternal uncles; and a faction of Ibn Saud's younger sons headed by Talal. The young princes in this last group shifted their support between Saud and Faisal, though they grew independent and increasingly critical of both during these years.

The government was formally inaugurated on March 7, 1954. In his first address, made at the reorganized *majlis al-wuzara,* the council of ministers, King Saud proclaimed his intention to carry on the traditions and principles his father espoused, and to retain a strong anti-Israeli policy. He set forth goals including strengthening the army; combating famine, poverty, and disease; improving the nation's health; and establishing ministries of education, agriculture, and communications. To create goodwill among citizens, he reduced customs duties on food, clothes, and a range of goods.

The involvement of council members in decision making in the reconstituted council was intended to lower friction between the king and crown prince. But the council became a battleground for Saud and Faisal's rivalry; its authority was limited, and it could issue ministerial decrees only with the king's approval.

Saud's Reign

Saud had shared his father's responsibilities since he had been named crown prince 20 years before, but during that time a government barely existed. Soon after taking office Saud undertook a round of visits to foreign capitals and receptions at home with neighboring leaders to reassess and reaffirm the kingdom's international relations. He met with the leaders of Egypt, Pakistan, Jordan, Bahrain, Kuwait, Qatar, and Yemen. He gave political refuge to the toppled dictator of Syria, and "reviewed" relations with Syria as well as Lebanon. Crisis over the contested Buraimi Oases with Abu Dhabi remained an ongoing source of strain and discussion with Britain.

In his first year in power Saud established several new ministries: Ministry of Agriculture and Water, Ministry of Education, and Ministry of Communication. Several more were created during his first decade of rule, including the Ministry of Petroleum and Natural Resources and the Ministry of Pilgrimage and Islamic Endowments (1960), the Ministry of Labor and Social Affairs (1962), and the Ministry of Information (1963). These were joined by the Ministry of Defense and Aviation, the Ministry of Post, Telephone and Telegraph, the Ministry of Finance and the National Economy, the Ministry of Health, and the Ministry of Foreign Affairs.

King Saud, who succeeded King Abd al-Aziz (Ibn Saud), at the UN in 1957. Saud's profligacy and mismanagement created problems that eventually forced him from the throne. His ongoing battles with Prince Faisal for control of the government almost brought down the House of Saud. (Courtesy of the Saudi Information Office)

The powers of the Ministry of Finance, previously under the autocratic control of Sulaiman, were dispersed among various departments, and Sulaiman retired in 1954. Two more of Saud's brothers were nominated as ministers. The king and crown prince remained president of the Council of Ministers and vice president, respectively. Seven of the 10 cabinet positions were occupied by princes. Saud also eliminated the position of prime minister, which Faisal considered part of his portfolio.

Unchecked Spending

King Saud lived as potentates of the past had. He entertained lavishly, gave expensive gifts, and maintained a court of some 5,000 people along with a large harem and many slaves. The government had banned the importation of slaves and slavery in 1936, but both slavery and slave markets remained in existence into the 1950s.

As his father had, Saud viewed state revenues as the royal family's property. But Saud did not have his father's authority, piety, or strong personality. Members of the family had begun traveling abroad in the 1940s and 1950s, where they acquired a taste for luxury. Vast amounts were spent at their whim. As recounted by historian Alexei Vassiliev, "A mad race for luxuries started in the country. Hundreds of the most expensive cars, including gold Cadillacs, were imported. . . . King Saud built twenty-five palaces for himself. . . . Colossal sums were spent on women's garments and jewelry and on the maintenance of slaves, servants, drivers, bodyguards and mere spongers. Generous emoluments were paid to the poets who panegyrized the Sauds, to the 'scholars' who made up a semilegendary history of the kingdom and to the 'journalists' who created its contemporary political mythology" (Vassiliev 1998, 333–334).

Control of the treasury became the major point of contention between Saud and Faisal. Faisal sought to end Saud's authority over state finances as a necessary step in establishing a sound economy. Saud wanted to retain his prerogatives as monarch, even as his spending drove the kingdom deeper into debt. The two also had conflicting personalities. Faisal was regarded as the more pious, more worldly, and mere pragmatic of the two.

With oil dollars flowing, businessmen descended on Riyadh from throughout the Middle East, eager for a share of the vast sums changing hands. Bribery, corruption, and illegal currency transaction were common. H. St. John Philby, Ibn Saud's expatriate British adviser, criticized the corruption in the country and the royal court. Among his attacks, he wrote, "The traditional anarchy of the Badawin tribes now yields pride of place to the selfish irresponsibility of a new bureaucracy, whose thin veneer of education has done in a couple of decades more harm to the reputation of a great country than the wild men of the desert ever did in thousands of years" (Philby 1955, xviii). Philby was expelled from Saudi Arabia for his candor, though eventually he was allowed to return.

Opposition Movements Take Root

In the 1950s an anti-Western movement began to sweep the Arab world, driven by anticolonialism, nationalism, and pan-Arabism. Calls for reform were amplified in Saudi Arabia by the sharp division between the wealth and power of the ruling elite and the lack of freedoms among the populace. Opposition groups, illegal in the kingdom, began to appear. The Front of National Reforms (FNR) was the first. Its founding coincided with a 1953 strike by oil workers in the Eastern Province. The FNR espoused an end to foreign and oil company domination, a constitution, free press, elections, the right of assembly, abolition of slavery, and improved education.

Among the kingdom's responses to calls for reform was to encourage a return to traditional values and curtailment of modernization. In 1954 Saud, noting that some youth were neglecting studies of the Quran, posted a 2,000-riyal prize to anyone who memorized the holy book. The following year all students studying abroad were recalled to Saudi Arabia. Newspapers critical of the government were pressured to modify their stance, and security forces sought out activists. The government claimed victory over the FNR in 1956 with the arrest of some of its leaders. But Egypt, under Gamal Abd al-Nasser, allowed Saudi dissidents to make radio broadcasts into Saudi Arabia criticizing the regime.

The Eastern Province, with the presence of Aramco, the U.S. air base at Dhahran, and its population of oppressed Shia, who made up the bulk of unskilled oil workers, was a natural breeding ground for reform groups and protest. King Saud came to Dhahran in July of 1956 and was confronted by large-scale protests demanding closure of the Dhahran air base and workers' rights. Two days later the king banned all strikes and demonstrations, with a penalty of three years imprisonment for violators. Activists, whose names were provided by Aramco, were arrested and beaten.

That same year students in Najd, birthplace of Wahhabi tradition, founded the kingdom's first student organization. They demanded the dissolution of the League for the Encouragement of Virtue and Prevention of Vice and clashed with authorities. But the government's impulse to clamp down on the students' calls for reform was offset by the state's need for specialists to run its expanding infrastructure. Additional secular schools were opened, and students of well-off Saudis went to study abroad.

In the 1950s the first generation of foreign-educated Saudis began returning home with their degrees. Many found employment in the growing administrative and military branches of the government, but tribal affiliation often counted for more than education and capability in social position and career achievement. This created resentment that percolated in the ranks of civil servants and members of the military as their numbers grew, and some became key voices in the growing opposition movements in Saudi Arabia.

To ensure the kingdom could meet internal and external threats, a regular army and national guard were expanded and formalized from existing forces. The national guard descended from the Ikhwan. Not all the Ikhwan tribes had been rebellious, and under Ibn Saud members of loyal tribes had been absorbed into a force known as the White Army, after the Ikhwan's traditional white garb. This army became the national guard. A permanent, standing force whose loyalties and ties were closely allied with the ruling family, the national guard served as a balance to the regular army at a time when coups were toppling monarchs in nearby kingdoms.

Changing Relations with the United States

In the United States, Vice President Harry Truman was elevated to president when Franklin Roosevelt died in office in 1945. Truman did not abide by Roosevelt's promise of equivalence and consultation with the Arabs and Israelis on U.S. policy in Palestine, which took a more pro-Israel turn. This strained Saudi-U.S. relations, as well as relations with other Arab countries. To U.S. diplomats posted in missions throughout the Arab world who expressed concern about the policy shift, Truman responded, "I'm sorry, gentlemen, but I have to answer to hundreds of thousands of people who are anxious for the success of Zionism. I do not have hundreds of thousands of Arabs among my constituents" (Howarth, 1964: 253).

The Baghdad Pact

Cold War politics dominated U.S. foreign policy considerations of the era and were the basis of a mutual defense assistance pact the kingdom and the United States signed in 1951. But strains in the relationship occurred early in the presidency of Dwight Eisenhower, Truman's successor, when Eisenhower sought additional regional partners for an anti-Soviet alliance. Ultimately a coalition of five countries—Britain, Iraq, Iran, Pakistan, and Turkey—united in what was called the Baghdad Pact, which was supported by the United States. This allied the United States with some of Saudi Arabia's opponents, irking Saud. He dismissed a U.S. aid mission to the kingdom in February of 1954, and the following year Saud signed a mutual defense agreement with Nasser, who was perceived in the West as being pro-Soviet. (Nasser turned to the Soviets after the West rejected his requests for financial aid to help build the Aswan Dam.) The agreement allowed Egyptian military advisers into the kingdom to train Saudi forces. In another sign of the kingdom's turning from the West, that same month (February 1954) Saud approved an agreement with Greek shipping magnate Aristotle Onassis. It gave Onassis the right to transport all the country's oil shipped by sea with the exception of oil transported by tankers owned by companies with oil concessions and their affiliates and oil buyers. This was to be the first step in creation of a transport company co-owned by the kingdom and Onassis. The agreement triggered protests from competing shipping companies and their governments. Britain called it "a most flagrant example of flag discrimination and a grave interference with normal commercial practice" (Vassiliev 1998, 333). Oil companies boycotted Onassis's ships. Within a few months Onassis withdrew from the contract.

Relations with Egypt and the Suez Crisis

In 1952 a group of military officers in Egypt, the Free Officers Committee led by Col. Gamal Abd al-Nasser, staged a coup. Nasser declared Egypt a republic and King Farouk abdicated. Farouk had been Ibn Saud's friend, and both reform and the antimonarchist Nasser were both threats to the kingdom. But Ibn Saud maintained good relations with Nasser, a policy Saud initially followed.

In 1956 Nasser nationalized the Suez Canal, which was owned by an international consortium including the British government. (Egypt, which pledged to repay the titleholders for their property, as it later did, had lost its share soon after the canal's completion in 1869, when it defaulted on loans taken for construction amidst falling cotton prices.) Saudi Arabia supported the seizure and pledged military aid to Egypt. Two months later Britain, France, and Israel attacked Egypt in an effort to retake the canal. Saud severed diplomatic relations and halted oil exports to Britain and France. The kingdom had no diplomatic and

Prince Faisal with Egyptian president Gamal Abd al-Nasser in Mecca, 1956. When the Arab world hero—and antimonarchist—arrived in Saudi Arabia for the hajj, the tumultuous welcome he received from the public caused the royal family concern. (Courtesy of Bettmann/CORBIS)

economic ties with Israel to cut. The UN ultimately supported the nationalization, and the episode made Nasser even more popular in the Arab world. The effusive public reception Nasser was accorded on a state visit to Saudi Arabia in 1956 alarmed the royal family. Nasser had come to discuss a union of Arab states, incorporating Egypt, Syria, and

Saudi Arabia. But the ruling family was disinclined to see Nasser as a partner when he continued to allow expatriate Saudi dissidents to beam anti-Saudi radio broadcasts into the kingdom. Ultimately Nasser's pan-Arab socialist ideals and reform efforts were not compatible with the monarchist rule of Saudi Arabia, to say nothing of the peninsula's long tradition of independence. Relations between the two countries grew strained and deteriorated further when a plot to overthrow the monarchy, planned by Egyptian-trained army officers, was uncovered.

To counterbalance Egypt's growing power and in defiance of Nasser's opposition, Saud established ties that same year (1956) with Jordan and Iraq, whose Hashemite rulers were the Saudis' traditional enemies. These newfound allies, Jordan's Hussein and Iraq's Faisal II, were, respectively, the nephew and grand-nephew of Ali, the last Hashemite ruler of Hijaz, whom Saud's father had driven from Saudi Arabia. Now the common threat to their monarchies posed by nationalism brought these former enemies together.

King Saud supplied financial and military support to Jordan in 1957, when Hussein dismissed his government, citing its leftist leanings. Saudi Arabia also felt the threat of exported nationalism when Palestinian terrorists, allegedly sent by the Egyptian government, were arrested in Riyadh with explosives. Soon after, the Saudis launched an internal campaign equating Arab nationalism with communism, an ideology the Saudis had long associated with Zionism and atheism, and which they thus staunchly opposed.

The Eisenhower Doctrine

Eisenhower had taken a strong stance against Britain, France, and Israel's attempt to retake the Suez Canal, fearing it would give more leverage to the Soviets in courting regimes in the region. Eisenhower's forceful opposition had restored the United States' reputation in the region and its relationship with Saudi Arabia. But with the defeat of Britain and France in the Suez War, the United States was concerned about the lack of a military power in the area to counter Soviet influence. Nasser was already demonstrating a leftward tilt. This concern was the basis for the Eisenhower Doctrine. Proclaimed in 1957, it guaranteed U.S. defense of the territorial integrity of any country in the region attacked by a communist-supported nation. King Saud visited Washington at Eisenhower's invitation to discuss the doctrine. On the way he met in Cairo with the leadership of Egypt, Syria, and Jordan, all of whom were against the plan and who bid Saud to convey their opposition. But once in Washington, Saud got a U.S. commitment to supply Saudi Arabia with military aid and a loan in exchange for his suspending all aid to Egypt. Saud also granted the United States a five-year extension on the Dhahran airbase lease. Back in the Middle East, Saud tried to win support for the doctrine but finally abandoned it himself, bowing to Nasser's opposition and public opinion in Saudi Arabia.

That same year (1957) Saud traveled to Baghdad to bolster the relationship with the Hashemite king, Faisal II, the grandson of Faisal who had fought the Ottomans in Hijaz during World War I. But this newfound alliance, meant to counter Egypt's growing influence, would be short-lived.

The UAR and Repercussions

The year 1958 was a traumatic one on several fronts for the kingdom. Egypt and Syria merged into the United Arab Republic (UAR), a union that Saud opposed. The United States and Great Britain, concerned about the leftist tilt of the newly formed UAR, promoted the unification of Jordan and Iraq as a counterbalance, but Saudi Arabia, fearing the strength that such a union would give to the Hashemites, refused to join or endorse the union, and relations with Jordan again soured. In July of 1958 Iraq's Faisal II was deposed and executed in yet another military revolt staged in the name of nationalism and self-determination.

Soon after the UAR's formation, an assassination plot aimed at Nasser and financed by King Saud was revealed. A Syrian intelligence officer—hired to carry out the assassination by having Nasser's plane shot down—made the conspiracy public and produced proof of a payment of £1.9 million made by the king.

Given Nasser's popularity, the episode provoked public anger and grave concern among members of the royal family. Saud had already alienated many in the ruling circle. His profligacy and policy of appointing his sons to ministerial posts and giving them privileges denied other royals had created resentment within the ruling family. Saud was unpopular with the army, as well. His ongoing disputes with Faisal had also nurtured opposition to his monarchy. Saud's opponents used the assassination plot as leverage to pry him from the throne.

Leaders of the royal family and the ulama agreed that power should be transferred to Crown Prince Faisal, who had already solicited the support of key Bedouin sheikhs. In March of 1958, a group of princes gave Saud an ultimatum to step aside in favor of Faisal and dismiss the advisers involved in the conspiracy to assassinate Nasser. Lacking support, Saud agreed.

Faisal Succeeds Saud

On the last day of March 1958, Faisal took control of the kingdom and began making changes in the ruling structure and state policies. To garner support, Faisal had publicly presented himself as a reformer eager to reconcile with Nasser, which made his ascension cause for concern among Western powers. However, Faisal demonstrated himself to be a staunch ally of the West.

In an address in April, Faisal stated a desire to establish relations with all friendly governments and remain unaligned with any military bloc, invoking the principles of both the United Nations and Islamic law. In May he reformed the Council of Ministers in an effort to end rampant corruption among its members. Ministers were henceforth prohibited from appropriating state property and sitting on the boards of commercial enterprises.

Saud's lack of attention to the finances—combined with corruption and wasteful spending—had plunged the kingdom deeper into debt. At the time of Ibn Saud's death in 1953 the kingdom owed $200 million. By 1958 the figure reached $480 million, and the riyal had lost half its official value against the dollar. At the urging of the International Monetary Fund, Faisal instituted a series of harsh financial reforms: Imports of all goods except food, medicine, and textiles were banned; car imports were suspended for a year; social, educational, and health-care expenditures were slashed; and construction on several palaces was halted. Currency reforms instituted in 1959 further dropped the value of the riyal. But by the next year the reforms had reversed the kingdom's fortunes, and most import restrictions were lifted.

Yet Saud, the former king, was not reconciled to his abdication and mounted efforts to have a strong role in state affairs and even to regain the throne.

The Free Princes

Before Saud's abdication, a third faction of the royal family began to vie with Saud and Faisal's familial allies for a voice in the kingdom's rule. This group was composed of Ibn Saud's younger sons, the progeny of his unions with beloved concubines consummated in his later years. Headed by Talal ibn Abd al-Aziz, their calls for reforms gave this group the name of the Free Princes. In seeking support for their goals during the 1950s, the Free Princes shifted their allegiance between Saud and Faisal, though ultimately they grew critical of both. The reform-minded Free Princes also had the support of intellectuals and foreign-educated members of the royal family.

During Saud's reign Talal had proposed creating an advisory national council as a first step toward establishing a constitutional monarchy. Saud, seeking cover for withholding assent, gave the proposal to the ulama to determine whether it was compatible with sharia. In 1960 Talal presented a draft constitution for a constitutional monarchy to Faisal, who rejected the proposal, antagonizing the Free Princes. Saud exploited the schism; when Faisal sought to appoint an acting prime minister so that he could travel to Europe for medical treatments, Saud refused to agree to the choice. Thus, Faisal remained in Saudi Arabia, and the division between Saud and Faisal loyalists widened. Saud also demanded the right of approval of all matters of government and refused to approve the kingdom's budget. In response, Faisal sent Saud a letter stating that he was unable to continue governance in such circumstances.

Saud Reclaims Rule

Saud seized on the missive as Faisal's resignation, though Faisal denied it was offered as such. Nonetheless, Saud reassumed the throne in December of 1960, appointing several of the Free Princes to ministerial posts. That same month the state radio announced that a series of reforms would be implemented, including the adoption of a constitution and limited elections. Reflecting behind-the-scenes disarray, three days later the same outlet denied that any such reforms would occur. Struggles for power consumed the leadership during 1961. Talal's efforts to enhance his power led to growing opposition from both Saud and Faisal's supporters. Talal's problems were compounded when the economy weakened and his efforts to stimulate it through public works were marred by poor planning, insufficient funds, and embezzlement. Moreover, the ulama, at Faisal's instigation, protested Talal's reform efforts, claiming that they were un-Islamic and asserting their right to examine all laws for their compliance with sharia. In September of 1961, Talal and the other Free Princes were removed from the government as Saud tried to settle his differences with Faisal. Nevertheless, Talal continued pushing for reform. Facing growing pressure to soften his efforts, Talal instead moved to Beirut, Lebanon, in 1962 with his full brothers and Saudi intellectuals. Here the Free Princes became a formal opposition group, committed to establishing a constitutional monarchy in Saudi Arabia.

As noted, the Free Princes was one of many groups seeking reform. To give the state a stronger hand in dealing with its opponents, Saud adopted an ordinance making anyone who plotted against the regime liable to capital punishment. In this climate the protection offered by the presence of U.S. forces on Saudi soil was seen as more problematic than beneficial. In 1961 the government informed the United States that its lease on the Dhahran air base would not be renewed, and in April of 1962 ownership of the base was transferred to Saudi Arabia, as called for in the lease agreement.

Faisal's efforts to seek medical attention outside the kingdom had precipitated Saud's restoration; now Saud's declining health set the stage for Faisal's return to the throne. In March of 1961 Saud went to the United States for medical treatment after appointing Faisal as regent in his absence. The next March, after his treatment, Saud's declining health led to Faisal's appointment as acting head of state. Faisal brought his half-brothers Fahd and Sultan into the government and purged several ministers from the council, consolidating his control.

In September of 1961, following another coup, Syria declared its independence from the UAR, effectively dissolving the confederation. Saudi Arabia immediately recognized the new regime, further raising tensions with Egypt. At the same time, Saudi Arabia also renewed its friendship with Jordan. In 1962 Faisal and Jordan's Hussein signed the al-Taif Pact, pledging cooperation on foreign policy and the development of economic, military, and cultural ties.

Revolution in Yemen

In September of 1962 Imam Ahmad, Yemen's ruler, died and was succeeded by his son, Muhammad al-Badr. A week later an Egyptian-backed military officer, Abdullah al-Sallal, staged a coup, declaring Yemen a republic. The new nation, the Yemen Arab Republic (YAR), was immediately recognized by Egypt and, soon thereafter, by more than two dozen other states.

The YAR represented the first state in the Arabian Peninsula not led by a monarch, and thus posed a threat to the Saudi leadership. Underscoring the internal threat, some of Saudi Arabia's military pilots defected while on missions to supply the royalists, flying their planes to Egypt and asking for asylum. One of the pilots claimed that an underground organization was in place in Saudi Arabia, waiting for the right moment to mount an insurrection. Saudi officials temporarily grounded all of their military aircraft.

The Yemeni republicans failed to completely subdue royalist supporters, and the conflict developed into a civil war and a proxy conflict between Saudi Arabia and Egypt. King Saud and King Hussein of Jordan sent aid to the royalist forces, and Saudi Arabia broke off diplomatic relations with Egypt in November. Faisal declared a general mobilization and asked for military support from the United States. Both the United States and Britain were concerned about the YAR's Soviet-backed leadership, and the British were also concerned about the impact on Aden, their protectorate in Yemen's southwest corner. Responding to Faisal's request, the United States dispatched warships and aircraft to the kingdom. By October, Egypt was dispatching troops to Yemen.

The revolution was supported by Yemeni intellectuals, workers, and students energized by the same issues confronting previously toppled Arab monarchies: dynastic rule, corruption, religious rather than civil law, and a lack of social programs for the impoverished majority. These were the same conditions existing in Saudi Arabia. Yet the new regime in Yemen failed to generate widespread support beyond these progressive elements.

Saudi Arabia gave al-Badr and his supporters sanctuary along the Yemeni border, where he established a government in exile. Saudi Arabia also provided arms and money for the war. The royalist forces, numbering some 40,000 troops, regularly infiltrated Yemen and attacked the republican and Egyptian forces, and the Yemeni civil war increasingly turned into a conflict between Saudi Arabia and Egypt.

Faisal Retakes Leadership

Saudi officials and upper classes were divided on whether to back the royalists or recognize the YAR. The Saudi cabinet included six commoners who represented the nascent middle class and who favored the republicans. Faisal's brother Prince Khalid and his faction supported the royalists. Saud's characteristic indecisiveness proved dangerously paralytic in dealing with the disagreement. The royal family and the ulama pressured Saud to give up his power, if not his title, a second time. On October 25, 1962, Saud appointed Faisal prime minister and minister of foreign affairs.

Faisal then purged Saud's sons from key posts and removed most of the royal guard, which was loyal to Saud, from Riyadh, sending the majority to the Yemeni border area. The following month Faisal issued a 10-point program aimed at demonstrating his commitment to reform. Its promises included freedom of speech ("within the framework of the Islamic faith and general law and order"); reform of the Committees of Public Morality; improved health-care, education, and social services; economic reform; and the complete abolition of slavery. It promised to loosen the austerity demanded by the current application of sharia and "make the means of entertainment available to its citizens." It also affirmed the Quran, the Hadith, and the sunnah as the kingdom's foundation. Yet the reform pledges were vague and seemed aimed more at undercutting the demands of the Free Princes than at promoting real reform.

Reform Movements

The war in Yemen had given the Free Princes' movement a new opening, positioning reform as the way to avoid the fate of the monarchies in Egypt and Yemen. The same month Faisal took control of the government, Talal formed the Arab Liberation Front to seek democracy in Saudi Arabia. Supporters of the movement also sought an overhaul of the oil concessions, the abolition of slavery, and Arab unity against imperialist pressures. Another reform group, the Federation of the Sons of the Arabian Peninsula (FSAP), with a membership of mostly commoners, appeared in Cairo. The FSAP changed its name to the Union of the People of the Arabian Peninsula and moved to Yemen's capital, Sanaa, to mount attacks against Saudi Arabia. Talal opposed the actions and created yet another organization, the Arab National Liberation Front (ANLF), seeking to marginalize the FSAP. But the Free Princes became increasingly estranged from Nasser, their ideological leader, a split that was underscored when Radio Yemen, an Egyptian-controlled organ, urged listeners "to kill all members of the Al Saud royal family without exceptions," the Free Princes obviously included (Vassiliev 1998, 369). In August of 1963 Talal withdrew his group from the ANLF and announced that his criticism of Saudi policy had been "entirely wrong" and expressed admiration for Faisal's reforms (ibid). By early 1964 the Free Princes had all returned to Riyadh from Beirut, ending their movement.

U.S. president John Kennedy, who succeeded Eisenhower in 1961, pledged U.S. support in preserving the kingdom, but also advanced a peace plan subsequently rejected by Saudi Arabia and Egypt. (Kennedy had also used his office to push for reforms in the kingdom. In a 1962 meeting with Faisal, he promoted a reform plan that included participatory democracy, civil rights, free speech, and the abolition of slavery. Faisal told the president of plans to create an

Crown Prince Faisal and U.S. president John F. Kennedy at the White House in 1962. Kennedy reaffirmed the U.S. defensive commitments to the kingdom and made efforts to secure Saudi Arabia's observance of human rights. (Courtesy of the Saudi Information Office)

assembly of appointed deputies to advise the throne, though without lawmaking power, a reform that was enacted 30 years later.) When the YAR threatened to close the missions and embassies of nations that refused to recognize the new regime, the United States reluctantly established relations.

End of Dual Power: Faisal Becomes King

While war split Yemen, turmoil threatened the home front, from within the royal family and without. In December of 1962, 40 officers were arrested for conspiring to stage a coup, and martial law was declared on January 1. A former Saudi diplomat and several military officers were arrested and charged with antigovernment conspiracy. That April, after Saud returned from Europe, where he had gone for medical treatment, his 39 brothers demanded all power be transferred to Faisal. Saud yielded, retaining only his title as king.

In March of 1964 Saud again tried to retake power. Ignoring the ulama's recommendation that he step down, Saud attempted to rally support among loyal units of the royal guard. Only when Faisal had Saud's palace surrounded by the national guard did Saud capitulate. The ulama issued a fatwa transferring absolute power to Faisal. That fall, princes, tribal sheikhs, and ulama met in Riyadh and proposed that Saud abdicate the throne. The Council of Ministers later approved a fatwa declaring Faisal as king, and the entire royal family signed a letter swearing allegiance to Faisal. Saud, however, refused to pledge fealty until threatened with house arrest and the loss of his property. Saud abdicated and left Saudi Arabia for Europe in January of 1965. Khalid ibn Abdul was appointed crown prince.

However, Saud continued interfering with Faisal's rule and asserting his claims to the throne. In late 1966 he moved to Cairo from Europe and, with Nasser's help, mounted an effort to restore his authority. Calling Faisal an "agent of imperialism," Saud stated his intention of returning to Saudi Arabia (Vassiliev 1998, 370). In April 1967 he visited Sanaa, the capital of YAR, where the president proclaimed him "the legitimate king of Saudi Arabia" (ibid).

Labor unrest also simmered throughout the decade, heated by dissatisfaction with work-related grievances. Antigovernment plots were also periodically uncovered, but rigorous internal security and the arrests of hundreds of individuals for subversive activities kept the threat level low. In 1967 a group of non-Saudi "saboteurs" was arrested and charged with plotting to blow up government offices and other targets. Seventeen were beheaded, the sentences meted out in public as customary. In 1969 a plot to assassinate Faisal involving a large number of Saudi military officers was uncovered. Almost 2,000 people connected to the alleged conspiracy were estimated to have been arrested in the aftermath, including oil workers and other dissidents. Another monarchy fell that same year when Libya's King Mohammad "Idris" al-Sanousi was ousted by the Free Unitary

225

Officers, whose leader, Col. Muammar al-Qadhafi, announced the coup to citizens of the new Libyan Arab Republic on national radio.

Meanwhile, the war in Yemen continued. By 1965, 15,000 Egyptians and thousands of Yemenis had been killed. Seeking an end to the conflict, in August of that year, Nasser and Faisal signed the Jeddah agreement, named for the city in which they reached its terms, which called for an immediate cease-fire, Yemeni self-determination, and withdrawal of foreign troops. A conference was convened in Harad, Yemen, with royalist and republican leaders to discuss forming a provisional government. But the conferees reached a stalemate and hostilities resumed.

By 1967, 50,000 to 70,000 Egyptian troops were in Yemen. A series of royalist victories created growing republican opposition to the war, already fanned by Egypt's use of the country as its battlefield. Yet Nasser proclaimed that Egypt would stay until the YAR could defend itself. Saudi Arabia closed branches of Egyptian banks, and Egypt confiscated property belonging to Saudi royalty in Egypt.

Development Plans

While internal intrigue and external clashes roiled the kingdom, the 1960s also saw the beginning of state funding for public works. Agriculture, health care, education, irrigation projects, and settling the Bedouin were among the beneficiaries. The largest sums were spent on the military, which consumed 40 percent of the state's budget and 10–13 percent of the gross national product (GNP). This was higher than the defense expenditures of the United States or any NATO country, though below the percentage spent by so-called front-line Arab states—Syria, Jordan, and Egypt—that were consumed with their conflict with Israel.

After assuming the throne, Faisal engaged in an aggressive state-building effort to repair the effects of Saud's neglect and mismanagement. He instituted an elaborate welfare system, with guaranteed free health insurance and free education for all Saudi citizens. In 1965 he formalized the state's financial and budgetary plans. Under Faisal's direction the Central Planning Organization was established and the first five-year plan unveiled in 1970, covering defense, education, transport, and utilities. Under the plans, massive national projects were initiated to build the nation's infrastructure of airports, ports, roads, power stations, and communication networks. The plans also provided for the construction of schools and the provision of free education for all children. The education of females, introduction of television, and other modernization efforts required the acquiescence of the ulama. Television created the largest outcry from fundamentalists. Violent demonstrations against the opening of a television station in Riyadh in 1965 led to the death of the king's nephew, a leader of the opponents.

Women, despite modernization reforms and access to education, were still bound by tribal laws. In Najd women were forbidden to marry men from Hijaz or Asir. Likewise, fathers in Najdi tribal groups would not allow their daughters to marry men of sedentary, nontribal backgrounds. Hijazi women of aristocratic sharifian background would not marry Najdi nobility or Hijazi commoners. Upper-class men, meanwhile, began taking second and third wives, while men from the common classes who studied abroad sometimes took foreign wives. The trend became so worrisome to officials that in the mid-1970s the government required permission from the Ministry of Interior for Saudi men to marry non-Saudi women, and made it illegal for Saudi women to marry non-Saudi men.

In 1970 Faisal established the Ministry of Justice. The ulama appointed to the ministry became state officials. This gave Faisal the power to hire and dismiss the religious authorities whose permission was required for his reforms. He kept the most liberal and removed those most conservative and resistant to change.

Also that year 23 foreign ministers met in Jeddah to establish the General Secretariat of the Muslim League, and agreed to meet annually to "promote cooperation" among Muslim states. The World Muslim League had its genesis in a conference sponsored by Faisal in Mecca in 1962. At the league's second meeting, in 1972, the conferees agreed to create "a fund for the holy war" against Israel. The conflict had been the dominant concern of the Arab world since the 1967 war with Israel.

The 1967 Arab-Israeli War and Its Aftermath

In June of 1967, the Arab states and Israel engaged in the brief but decisive 1967 Arab-Israeli War, also referred to as the Six-Day War. Unlike Egypt, Jordan, and Syria, which committed large military contingents to the war, Saudi Arabia had little direct involvement. Israel captured the Sinai Peninsula and the Gaza Strip, the Golan Heights, and the West Bank. This last region included East Jerusalem, site of the Al-Aqsa Mosque, the third holiest site in Islam. Israeli occupation here represented a sacrilege to Muslims. The United Nations, in response to the territorial appropriations, adopted Resolution 242, which called for Israeli withdrawal from land it captured in the war and peaceful coexistence of all states in the region.

Nasser, in the wake of the war with Israel—with the loss of income from the Suez Canal and the need to rebuild the military—could no longer afford the conflict in Yemen. Meanwhile, a surge in anti-Israeli sentiment and sympathy for Egypt engulfed the Arab world. Past differences were subordinate to the threat seen posed by Israel.

Faisal and Nasser met at the Arab summit conference in Khartoum, Sudan, in August of 1967. The primary purpose of the conference was to discuss Arab strategy in response to the war. Delegates affirmed a staunch anti-Israeli position, summed up in their policy statement: "No peace, no direct negotiations, no recognition." During the conference Faisal and Nasser concluded an agreement ending the conflict in Yemen. It called for removing Egyptian troops and ending Saudi support for royalist forces. Saudi Arabia also agreed to contribute $140 million per year to a fund to help Egypt, Jordan, and other Arab combatants defray costs associated with the war with Israel.

The rapprochement of Saudi Arabia and Egypt also ended Saud's efforts to reclaim the throne, as he lost Egypt's support. The former king died in February of 1969. By then, Egypt's military was on its way to being rebuilt, and Saudi Arabia's relations with its neighbor across the Red Sea were growing strained again.

But even after Egypt's withdrawal, the battles between republicans and royalists in Yemen continued until mid-April of 1970. A conservative republican government, which Faisal supported, was installed, and that summer Saudi Arabia officially recognized the YAR. In 1973 the two nations extended the Treaty of Taif, originally signed by Ibn Saud and Imam Yahya in 1934, that recognized Saudi Arabia's rule in southern Hijaz.

THE PLO

The Arab League had established the Palestine Liberation Organization (PLO) in 1964 as a vehicle for coordinating efforts to win Palestinian rights. Palestinians gained control of the PLO from its founding sponsors after the 1967 war, and a liberation movement arose to wage a political and military struggle for Palestinian independence. An umbrella organization, the PLO includes such member groups as Fatah (from *fath,* "conquest") and the Popular Front for the Liberation of Palestine. Saudi Arabia became a major benefactor of the PLO, through both government funding and contributions from wealthy Saudi citizens.

The Islamic Conference Organization

Seeking to counter the influence of the Nasser-dominated Arab League, Saudi Arabia proposed formation of the Islamic Conference Organization, an alternative association of Arab states. But the proposal received a cool welcome from secular regimes. Nasser condemned the organization as ". . . created by imperialism and reactionaries . . . spear-headed against the national liberation movements" (Vassiliev 1998, 386). But after the Al-Aqsa Mosque in Jerusalem was set afire in 1969, Faisal convened an Islamic summit in Rabat, Morocco. Twenty-five of 35 Islamic countries invited attended, and 10 of the delegations were led by heads of state. Though marred by disagreements, the meeting did establish a network beyond the Arab League for countries in the region to work together.

Nasser's death in November of 1970 changed the dynamic of Egypt's relationship with Saudi Arabia as well as with the region and the world. For the royal family, it removed a large and often ominous shadow. Nasser's successor, President Anwar Sadat, sought to restore relations with Saudi Arabia and invited Faisal to Egypt. Faisal's tumultuous welcome in Cairo in 1971 likely brought back memories of the greeting Nasser had received in Riyadh 15 years before. This marked Egypt's turn from its Soviet sponsors. Soviet-style economic restrictions were lifted, and Nasserites were purged from positions of power. In July of 1972, Sadat expelled all Soviet military personnel from the country. Sadat also sought to end Egypt's standoff with Israel, but he was rebuffed by both the United States and Israel.

British Regional Withdrawal and Its Fallout

Britain's withdrawal from Aden in 1967 brought Saudi Arabia into conflict with another state on its southern border, the independent state of South Yemen that replaced Britain's Eastern Aden Protectorate. An anti-monarchist group, the National Front, took power and set out to suppress tribal rule within its borders. In 1969 South Yemen, or the People's Democratic Republic of Yemen (PDRY), began implementing Soviet-style reforms.

Saudi Arabia sent troops to attack the regime and supported opposition forces in the country. The YAR, with its conservative republican leadership, also opposed the PDRY's Marxist orientation. The YAR began repeated invasions in 1971 that escalated into a large-scale month-long border war the following year. The two Yemens then agreed to a truce, but Saudi Arabia, still displeased with the government, did not establish diplomatic relations with the PDRY until the 1980s.

In 1971 Britain ended its protectorate treaties with the Gulf States, which consisted of Bahrain, Qatar, and the Trucial States. The latter consisted of Abu Dhabi, Ajman, Dubai, Fujaira, Ras al-Khaima, Sharja, and Umm al-Qaiwain. By the end of 1970 almost all British troops were gone. After political initiatives and intrigues over their future by Britain, Saudi Arabia, and Iran (which claimed islands in Gulf States' territories), in 1971 Bahrain and Qatar declared their independence, and the Trucial States united in a federation, the United Arab Emirates (UAE). Saudi Arabia did not establish diplomatic relations with the UAE until a long-standing boundary dispute with Abu Dhabi was settled in 1974. But unofficial relations were close, motivated in part by Saudi Arabia's desire to counter Iran's influence in the Gulf States.

Saudi Arabia and OPEC

Though the kingdom had been resistant to using its oil as a political tool since Ibn Saud's reign, it was not shy about seeking to gain economic control over this resource. The effort was spurred first by a postwar glut that led Aramco to cut production (as did oil companies operating in other oil-producing nations), reducing the kingdom's income. A drop in world oil prices that began in 1954 exacerbated the revenue slump. Furthermore, it became apparent that despite profit-sharing agreements, Aramco was making more money on Saudi oil than Saudi Arabia was, a situation seen in other producing nations. Concerns about this state of affairs led to the first Arab Petroleum Congress, held in Cairo in April 1959.

At the congress, Saudi Arabia's minister of petroleum and mineral resources, Abdullah al-Tariqi, a protégé of Ibn Saud's minister of finance, Sulaiman, proposed periodic renegotiation of oil contracts, saying that the original contracts had taken advantage of the producing nations' inexperience and lack of knowledge about the oil business.

The congress led to the formation of the Organization of Petroleum Exporting Countries (OPEC) in Baghdad in September of 1960. OPEC's goal was to stabilize markets by having members work in concert, or as a cartel as it was popularly called in the West. Iran, Iraq, Kuwait, Saudi Arabia, and Venezuela were the founding members, and Abu Dhabi, Algeria, Equador, Gabon, Indonesia, Libya, Nigeria, and Qatar subsequently joined. Initially OPEC was unable to achieve its objectives because, under the terms of their contracts, concession holders determined how much oil to produce in some countries.

Nonetheless, in Saudi Arabia the new assertiveness resulted in a revised agreement with Aramco that increased the kingdom's income from oil exports more than 50 percent. Recognizing a commonality of interest, in 1968 the Arab OPEC member states joined in the Organization of Arab Petroleum Exporting Countries (OAPEC).

The organization's initial objectives have been called "modest," but its demands and tactics changed following a confrontation between Libya and its concessionaires in 1969. Libya sought an increase of a few percent in its royalty fees, a nominal figure but enough to give the country the majority of the income instead of splitting it evenly with the oil companies. The companies refused, and the following year Libya, which supplied almost 20 percent of Europe's oil at the time, decreased production quotas. The oil companies, unable to ensure alternative supplies, finally agreed to the revised financial arrangement. With the precedent set, the Gulf States soon negotiated similar arrangements. At the same time, growing demand for oil on the international market was turning what had been a buyer's into a seller's market. The Tehran agreement of 1971, which gave the Gulf States virtual control over "reference prices," demonstrated that OPEC had achieved its initial goals. But by now the exporting countries' demands had evolved to include ownership, not just majority participation, in the oil companies. In 1972 OPEC began negotiating with oil companies toward this final objective. The same month that Faisal became king in 1962, he had appointed Sheikh Ahmad Zaki Yamani to replace Al-Tariqi as the oil minister as part of his consolidation of control of the state apparatus. Yamani became OPEC's chief negotiator and public face. The agreement concluded between OPEC and the oil companies gave Saudi Arabia an ownership stake that would rise annually, reaching majority ownership by 1983. However, due to the huge price increases of 1973–74, implementation of the agreement was accelerated; by 1976 the Saudi government had a majority stake, and achieved 100 percent ownership by the early 1980s.

The Oil Embargo

King Faisal had continued his father's policy that oil not be used as a weapon, proclaiming that "oil and politics should not be mixed" (Al-Rasheed 2002, 136). In April of 1973, indications of a shift in policy emerged; Saudi Arabia's minister of petroleum and mineral resources, Sheikh Yamani, first linked an increase in Saudi oil production to U.S. pressure on Israel to negotiate a political solution to the Palestinian issue. King Faisal stated that Saudi–United States cooperation would be difficult to maintain if the United States continued its support for Israel.

In July of 1973 OPEC raised the price of oil 11.9 percent. Yet Saudi Arabia remained a moderating voice and was not among members pressing for an increase. Faisal hoped that this stance would help maintain the friendship with the United States and give the kingdom greater leverage in its dealings. Throughout the summer of 1973, as tensions with Israel grew, Saudi Arabia continued threatening to reverse its oil policy and reduce supplies if a war with Israel occurred. On August 31, King Faisal reiterated his warning. Both the United States and Europe ignored him.

The 1973 Arab-Israeli war began on October 6, 1973, with a coordinated surprise attack launched by Egypt and Syria. (The conflict is also referred to as the Yom Kippur War, for the Jewish "Day of Atonement" holy day on which it began.) The day after hostilities began U.S. secretary of state Henry Kissinger asked King Faisal to call on Egypt and Syria to cease fighting. Faisal, however, vouched his support for the two countries and called on Kissinger to persuade Israel to leave the occupied territories.

At an OPEC meeting in Kuwait later that month, the 10 Arab members agreed to reduce production by 5 percent and raise prices by 17 percent each month until the Middle East conflict was resolved. (Iraq, having advocated more forceful measures, refused to join the action, then increased production to take advantage of the high prices resulting from the boycott. Iran also ignored the boycott.) U.S. president Richard Nixon assured Faisal that the United States would show no favoritism between the Arabs and Israelis during the war. Shortly thereafter Israel made an emergency request to the United States for replacement arms, and Nixon gave the Israelis $2.2 billion in aid. Faisal felt betrayed by the agreement, though the wide publicity accorded the assistance may have been more upsetting to him than the arms airlift itself. Saudi Arabia unilaterally declared an embargo on oil shipments to the United States and the Netherlands for their support of Israel, and on shipments to oil refining facilities that supplied the United States, a boycott some other Arab OPEC members soon joined. Some OAPEC members also agreed to raise oil prices, and by December the cost of oil had more than tripled.

11

OIL AND ARMS
(1973–1990)

Saudi Arabia's fortunes underwent a profound change in the two decades following the 1973 Oil Embargo. The reluctant reversal of the kingdom's long-standing policy against using oil as a weapon would bring it unprecedented power, influence, and wealth. But these riches could not stop a tide of dissent from both liberal secular and fundamentalist religious opponents. The Soviet Union's invasion of Afghanistan diverted some critics' attention while bringing Saudi Arabia and the United States together in creating an army of Islamic fighters, the mujahideen, to battle the Soviets. These years also saw the creation of large public works and generous social services within the kingdom, as the state made efforts to develop its infrastructure and diversify its economy. Meanwhile, the pursuit of its own military capability became an overriding concern for the kingdom as all around it monarchies fell and the protection of powerful allies proved illusory. These boom years were succeeded by an era of declining revenues and fiscal, political, and social problems, an era capped by an invasion of Kuwait by Saudi Arabia's erstwhile ally, Iraq. The invasion threatened the kingdom's independence even as it exposed the hollowness of the defensive capabilities it had paid so dearly to acquire. The most effective solution, military intervention by a U.S.-led coalition, would prove almost as dangerous to the monarchy as had the Iraqi invasion. These are the years covered in this chapter.

The Oil Embargo's Aftermath

In the wake of the 1973 Oil Embargo, Saudi Arabia's oil revenues soared. The gross domestic product of 1973 (of which about 90 percent was represented by oil) rose almost 150 percent over the previous year, from 40.5 billion to 99.3 billion riyals. The Arab world saw the embargo

233

as a huge victory, a liberating defiance of the West, and a salve for the humiliating defeat in the 1967 war with Israel. In the West the embargo raised concerns about "oil dependency" and stoked anti-Arab sentiment. King Faisal, who played a reluctant role in its implementation, and Saudi Arabia were admired throughout the Arab world for their leadership. The increased revenue enabled the kingdom to spend freely on causes of its choice around the Arab world, giving Saudi Arabia unprecedented influence in the Middle East. Faisal also used the burgeoning wealth to fund an ambitious modernization program, grand public works, and an ambitious buildup of Saudi military forces.

The Central Planning Organization (CPO), officially established in 1965, set the development agenda in a series of five-year plans. The first five-year plan, covering the years 1970–75, focused on projects involving defense, education, transportation, and utilities development. Planned in a time of relative austerity, the unanticipated increases in production capacity and oil prices that occurred in the midst of the first plan's execution enabled the budget to more than double, from $9.2 to $21 billion.

To outsiders, it looked like the only challenge the country faced was how to spend its unprecedented wealth. In the second five-year plan,

Under a series of five-year development plans that began in 1970, the country spent large amounts to build its infrastructure, as well as diversify the economy and provide generous social programs. The refinery at Jubail was a major industrial development project. (Courtesy of the Saudi Information Office)

The Ghazlan steam-powered generator plant was a major project designed and implemented as part of a five-year development plan. (Courtesy of B.H. Moody/Aramco World/PADIA)

total expenditures were budgeted at more than $140 billion, and actual spending was about $200 billion. But the massive influx of goods and materials that the expenditures paid for overwhelmed the kingdom's transportation system. At Saudi ports, ships waited four to five months to unload cargo. (Not coincidentally, development of roads and ports was a priority of the second plan.) The influx of development dollars also created a shortage of workers and annual inflation rates estimated by some at 50 percent. More problematic, the oil wealth created a two-tier social system and exacerbated concerns about the secularization of the regime and the country.

The first three plans (1970–84) focused on developing the kingdom's infrastructure. During this time 100,000 miles of roads, 25 airports (three of them international), and 21 seaport facilities were built.

Rapprochement with the United States

Paradoxically, Faisal used his new leadership role gained through defiance of the West to promote Egyptian-U.S. reconciliation and to encourage anti-Soviet activities in the region and around the world.

Saudi relations with the United States warmed in 1974 with the United States's involvement in efforts to end the Arab-Israeli war that began in October of 1973. American secretary of state Henry Kissinger negotiated the cease-fire agreement between Egypt and Israel and between Syria and Israel by engaging in shuttle diplomacy, flying between the three countries. Faisal's sincerity about the kingdom's relationship with the United States was signaled when Saudi Arabia threatened to withdraw from OPEC in March of 1974 because of the organization's anti-Western stance, a threat that succeeded in persuading the organization to keep oil prices low. Despite the thaw, the United States considered Iran (under the rule of its shah) and Israel as its two principal regional allies in the Middle East.

In the post-embargo period, Saudi Arabia increased its oil production to make up for shortfalls of supplies in the West. In June of 1974, President Nixon visited Jeddah, the first visit to Saudi Arabia by a U.S. president. Another highlight of this month was Saudi Arabia's assumption of majority ownership of Aramco, implementing an agreement that gave the nation 60 percent ownership of the company's assets and concessions.

Faisal's stature spread beyond the Arab world. For all his concern about making a break with the United States in 1973, at the end of 1974 *Time* magazine proclaimed Faisal its "Man of the Year." Faisal was a universally respected figure, regarded as a pious and devout Muslim by the ulama and traditionalists, and as a progressive and pragmatic ruler by others.

Assassination and Succession

On March 25, 1975, at Faisal's weekly *majlis,* or "public audience," his nephew, a young prince who had recently returned from spending several years at school in the United States, shot and killed King Faisal. The motive is presumed to have been revenge for the death of the assassin's brother, a fundamentalist religious activist killed by Saudi police in the 1960s during protests against a new TV station that was preparing to begin operations in Riyadh. The assassin was said to be mentally unstable. The ulama approved his beheading, and the sentence was carried out in Riyadh's public square.

Three days after Faisal's death Crown Prince Khalid succeeded King Faisal. His brother Muhammad, who would have been the heir apparent by virtue of being the eldest of the remaining sons of Ibn Saud, was deemed by the royal family to have a drinking problem and a violent temper, and therefore passed over. Fahd was named crown prince with responsibility for domestic and foreign policy. With Prince Sultan serving as minister of defense and aviation (a position he still occupied in

King Khalid (right) with Prince Abdullah. Khalid became king after Faisal's assassination in 1973, but he soon became a figurehead, ceding authority to Crown Prince Fahd. (Courtesy of the Saudi Information Office)

2004), the reorganization represented the ascension of the so-called Sudairi Seven, Faisal's full brothers, maternal sons of the Sudairi clan. They were Fahd; Sultan; Nayef, the minister of the interior; Salman, the governor of Riyadh; Abd al-Rahman, vice minister of defense and aviation (since 1962); Ahmad, vice minister of the interior; and Turki, vice minister of defense until 1978.

As king, Khalid continued Faisal's efforts to expand the economy, social programs, and educational system while also stressing orthodoxy and conservatism within society. But Khalid, an avid sportsman, preferred spending time in the desert, often hunting with his falcons, and he increasingly became a ceremonial figure while Fahd became the de facto head of government.

The kingdom also used the oil revenues to try to diversify its economy. Agriculture expanded greatly during these years. From 1970 to 1989, production of fruit and vegetables grew almost 40 percent; dairy products increased by more than 45 percent; egg production jumped from 5,000 to more than 100,000 tons; and poultry production surged from 7,000 tons to 226,000 tons. However, this expansion came at great cost, in terms of government subsidies and depletion of the underground aquifer used to provide water for the kingdom's agronomy. The wheat grown in Saudi Arabia, for example, was produced at a cost seven times the world price.

Government Largesse

As a result of its burgeoning oil wealth, Saudi Arabia became a world financial force during this period. The kingdom extended billions of dollars in credit to the International Monetary Fund (IMF), and it became a permanent member of the IMF board in 1978. By 1979 it had a reported $133 billion in foreign investments, a figure believed to have grown by at least $100 billion by 1981.

As its revenues increased, Saudi Arabia became a major donor to developing countries (primarily Islamic nations). The kingdom also provided support to political organizations and resistance groups, including Palestinians through the PLO, Muslims in Bosnia, and the Contras in Central America. The kingdom also sponsored the spread of the Wahhabi interpretation of Islam through the madrassas, or Islamic schools, that it established and funded throughout the Muslim world. From 1973 through 1991, Saudi aid to developing nations and organizations was more than $60 billion. The financial aid proffered by Saudi Arabia in these years was among the highest in the world in dollar figures as well as in the proportion to the donating nation's gross national product. In 1991 it spent 1.5 percent for such purposes, contrasted with the U.S. figure of 0.2 percent. The king and crown prince stated in 1994 that they had provided, presumably in toto up to that time, $106 billion

CAMP DAVID AND EGYPTIAN-ISRAELI PEACE

In September of 1978, at the invitation of President Jimmy Carter, Egypt's president Anwar Sadat and Israeli prime minister Menachem Begin came to Camp David, the presidential retreat in Maryland, to reach a peace agreement. On September 17, after 13 days of negotiations, the two sides signed what became known as the Camp David Accords, laying out the basic agreement for normalizing their relations. The accord led to the Egyptian-Israeli Peace Treaty, signed at the White House on March 26, 1979. The terms called for the mutual recognition of UN Security Council Resolution 242, whose key provision was the illegitimacy of territorial acquisition by war. The resolution had been adopted in 1967 following the Arab-Israeli war in which Israel captured the Sinai from Egypt, the West Bank from Jordan, and the Golan Heights from Syria. The accords provided for Israeli withdrawal from all Egyptian territory taken in the 1967 war (the Sinai Peninsula), mutual diplomatic recognition, and the replacement of Israeli military forces and civilian authorities in still-occupied areas with self-governing authorities.

The accords were a watershed in the modern history of the Middle East, countering a century of adamant and complete Arab opposition to a Jewish state in the region. The agreement would earn the Nobel Peace Prize for Sadat and Begin, but it was seen as an act of betrayal in the Arab world. Saudi Arabia denounced the agreement and, along with all the other Arab states, severed diplomatic relations with Egypt on the day after the Egyptian-Israeli Peace Treaty was signed. All financial aid to Egypt from the kingdom was suspended.

in aid to Islamic nations and $14.6 billion to other developing countries. Seventy countries in all were beneficiaries. But the largesse distributed to its people, to other Arab states, and to political organizations did not shield the regime from threats, both internal and external.

Seizure of the Great Mosque

As the decade drew to an end, signs of unrest grew. In 1979 cells of anti-monarchists in the military were found. Illegal arms imports had already been uncovered. In Hijaz, tribal relations were roiled by the seizure of lands by Saudi princes, which was a prerogative of the royal family. Rumblings of discontent also came from younger princes themselves, angry about shrinking allowances and the grip on power their elders held. In September, a new type of threat announced itself with the appearance of antigovernment leaflets. Distribution of such tracts was of course illegal and was troubling to a regime that was accustomed to effectively policing the opposition through its General Investigations security agency. More troubling to some was the message, calling not for liberalization and modernization but for a return to rigid religious orthodoxy. Defense forces were put on high alert.

In mid-November during the hajj, small armed rebel units totaling some 3,500 men seized positions on roads leading to Medina. Soon the forces of an obscure group, the Movement of the Muslim Revolutionaries of the Arabian Peninsula (MMRAP), controlled a significant area between Mecca and Medina. They were mostly members of a former Ikhwan tribe who now served in the national guard. Some were students, both Saudi and foreign, from the Islamic University of Medina who were active in the Muslim Brotherhood, an organization that had been suppressed by Nasser and whose members had been given refuge by Faisal. Dividing in two, the group moved on Mecca and Medina. Government troops in Medina engaged and defeated the rebels. Though no casualty figures were released, unofficial estimates put the number of those killed in the engagement at 250. In Mecca, however, defense forces were caught by surprise, and on November 20, the first day of the 15th century in the Muslim calendar, the revolutionaries, variously estimated at between 200 and 1,000 rebels, seized Mecca's main mosque.

Government Response to the Threat

Deputy Prime Minister Prince Fahd ordered an assault on the shrine, which went on for two weeks. The last rebel was captured on December 3. No casualty figures were released, but estimates ran into the hundreds, including more than 100 rebels and 27 Saudi soldiers killed. The group's spiritual leader, Muhammad bin Abdullah al-Qahtani, was among those killed. The insurrectionists' commander, Juhayman al-Utaybi, was captured and publicly beheaded along with 63 other rebels. In the aftermath of the rebellion several senior officials were dismissed and thousands of foreign workers expelled. In December, an opposition leader who had escaped to Beirut was kidnapped and disappeared. The Saudi security services were overhauled with help from the CIA and the French and West German intelligence agencies.

To placate reform-minded citizens, Fahd pledged to create a "Fundamental Law" that would give the middle class a voice in government. To shore up support among the ulama, many of whom were concerned by the modernist drift of the kingdom, hairdressing salons were closed, female announcers dismissed from TV, and girls were no longer allowed to attend schools outside the kingdom. The conservative shift continued. In 1984, a respected member of the ulama condemned travel agencies that promoted trips by young Saudis to Western Europe and the United States because such journeys exposed them to evil influences, a position the king publicly supported. That same year importing dolls was made a punishable offense. Western or foreign women who declined to wear a veil in public were harassed by the morality police. The public defenders of propriety also broke windows of photography studios, shut mixed-use beaches, and attempted to

THE MAHDI

The political leader of the group that seized Mecca's Grand Mosque was Juhayman al-Utaybi. Their spiritual leader, Muhammad bin Abdallah al-Qahtani, called himself the Mahdi (one who guides), or messiah. Al-Qahtani claimed their goal was the "purification of Islam" and the dissolution of the "infidel clique" of the royal family and corrupt ulama (Vassiliev, 1998: 396). The MMRAP presented a list of demands, including the dismissal of some senior princes from their posts, the termination of oil sales to the West (which would have drastically reduced the kingdom's income), and a return to "genuine" Islam. Al-Utaybi called for a return, under the Mahdi's guidance, to the society of the first centuries of Islam, which he described as a golden age of justice and equality.

The seizure drew support from manual laborers and students of tribal origin, from the lower classes, and from foreign laborers who hailed from Egypt, Yemen, and Pakistan. But the political discontent that led to the uprising was temporarily eclipsed by the claims of the self-proclaimed Mahdi. While the insurrectionists held the Grand Mosque, senior ulama engaged in debate over the nature of the true Mahdi and concluded that al-Qahtani could not possibly be that individual. A fatwa of 30 leading ulama in late November branded the group as rebels. The government used the finding to discredit the movement and detract attention from the grievances that led to the uprising. The ulama issued a fatwa in support of the royal family, permitting military action in the holy site.

keep foreigners from celebrating Christmas. The majority of citizens did not share the extremist views of those on either end of the spectrum, but a lively debate was conducted in the media and across society about the threat that modernization posed to traditional ways of life that had existed for centuries in the peninsula.

Eastern Province Uprising

Two weeks after the takeover of the Grand Mosque was ended, a Shia insurrection erupted in Eastern Province (Hasa), site of the kingdom's major oil fields and a Shia stronghold, where some 300,000 to 350,000 of the Shia minority lived. The unrest coincided with the observance of Ashura, the mourning rituals honoring the death of the martyr Husayn. The Wahhabis had long suppressed this and other Shia celebrations as heretical, and banned them from being performed in public since recapturing Hasa from the Ottomans in 1913. The Shia themselves had been discriminated against as well, prohibited from attending educational institutions and from serving in the army or employment in several professions. The government dispatched 12,000 to 20,000 national guard troops to the area after demonstrations occurred in late 1979. In February of 1980, Shia in Hasa took to the streets to perform their observances in public but were blocked by the Saudi forces. This sparked three days of antigovernment riots throughout the Eastern Province. Army barracks and banks were set afire. In all, more than a score of people are thought to have died in the unrest that fall and winter.

Iran, as we will see, was now under the control of a Shia regime headed by Ayatollah Khomeini, and was believed to have had a role in fomenting the demonstrations, in part by sponsoring radio broadcasts into the kingdom attacking the monarchy. More demonstrations and strikes occurred in Qatif that year (1980) to mark the first anniversary of Khomeini's return to Iran. In addition to its military crackdown, the Saudi government announced plans for reforms to pacify the Shia, pledging to improve educational, economic, and social opportunities, but these initiatives failed to still the dissent.

Defense Spending

With threats seen just across its borders and within them, and the commitment or ability of the United States to guarantee the security of the Saudi government in question, the kingdom spent heavily on defense in the post-embargo years. Large defense expenditures continued into the 1980s, even after oil revenues began a long decline. During these years Saudi Arabia spent $14–24 billion on defense annually. This represented 20 percent of the gross domestic product (GDP) throughout the 1980s, reaching more than a third of GDP (36 percent) in 1988. The United States was the major arms supplier. The relationship the two nations pursued during this time has often been reduced to one of "weapons for oil," a policy whereby the Saudis provided a stable supply of oil at a reasonable price, and the U.S. government and private sector provided for the defense and arming of the kingdom. With their ample resources, the Saudis sought sophisticated weapons. But concerns about their potential offensive use against Israel increasingly complicated the purchases. The Saudis worked quietly and directly with the leadership of the successive administrations of presidents Gerald Ford, Jimmy Carter, and Ronald Reagan to facilitate arms transactions.

But matters of diplomacy went beyond oil and arms. The Saudis saw their relationship with the United States as a way to influence policy toward Israel, attempting to convince the United States to increase its pressure on Israel to negotiate a peace agreement with the Palestinians. Yet the closer the Saudis drew to the United States, the more they angered governments and the public throughout the Arab world. This heightened security concerns, driving Saudi Arabia's rulers closer still to the United States.

In 1976 the kingdom sought 60 F-15 aircraft and armaments. The sales were opposed by members of the American Jewish community and supporters of Israel. The following year King Khalid reportedly reached an agreement with U.S. president Gerald Ford. The king promised not to increase oil prices by more than 5 percent until 1984 (a pledge later abrogated) and to invest the bulk of the income from oil sales in the United States. Ford promised to defend the kingdom from military attack, regardless of its source. The king also wanted the F-15s. By that year, according to one analysis, the number of weapons already purchased by Saudi Arabia would have taken another six years to fully deploy.

In 1978 Ford requested authorization to sell the aircraft to Saudi Arabia, and other military aircraft to Egypt and Israel. But Congress balked, due to American-Jewish and Israeli opposition. The Saudis enlisted Bandar, a young prince in the Saudi air force stationed in Washington and an experienced fighter pilot, for assistance. Bandar ibn Saud ibn Abd-al-Aziz went on to have a direct role in virtually all high-level exchanges between the kingdom and the United States. He became Saudi ambassador to the United States in 1983, a position he still held in 2004, along with the honor of being dean of the diplomatic corps. Congress ultimately approved the sale.

In total, Saudi Arabia bought more than $34 billion in military equipment from the United States alone during the 1970s. But at the end of the decade three events further spiked arms sales: the Iranian Revolution in 1979, the Soviet invasion of Afghanistan the same year, and the Iran-Iraq war the following year.

Iranian Revolution

During the 1960s leftist and radical movements spread throughout the Arab world, trends that alarmed the Saudi leadership. Strong opposition to these antimonarchist trends led the kingdom to supply troops during the 1970s to help suppress leftist uprisings in North Yemen and Oman. These trends also brought the Saudis and the shah of Iran into an agreement to oppose secular and radical regimes in the region. But Shah Mohammad Reza Pahlavi himself was overthrown on February 11, 1979, replaced by Ayatollah Khomeini as head of a Shia regime, a branch of Islam antithetical to Saudi Arabia's Wahhabi doctrine. The fall of the shah also made the Saudis question the security guarantees given by the United States. After all, the shah was the United States's staunchest ally in the Arab world, and the failure to protect his regime reduced Saudi confidence in its partnership with the United States. This made the ruling family even more determined to provide its own security.

Seeking to reassure the Saudis, in his January 1980 State of the Union address, President Carter pledged that any Soviet aggression in the Gulf would be viewed as an assault on the vital interests of the United States, a policy that became known as the Carter Doctrine. (In late 1980, at Saudi Arabia's request, U.S. Air Force AWACS [airborne warning and control system] aircraft were dispatched to the kingdom to guard against penetration of Saudi airspace by Iranian aircraft.) Throughout the 1980s Saudi-U.S. relations became stronger as the Saudis bought more arms, while refusing to host U.S. troops on their soil.

The Islamic Republic of Iran's anti-Western stance extended to allies of the West, which included Saudi Arabia. The Iranians hoped to inspire revolutions in Islamic countries with Shia populations, especially Kuwait, Bahrain, and Saudi Arabia. These efforts helped ignite the unrest in Eastern Province in 1979 and 1980 already discussed. Additionally, the pilgrimage brought thousands of Iranians to Saudi Arabia where they often staged demonstrations in protest of Israel, the West, and its Arab allies. In 1987, these protests became violent and resulted in more than 400 deaths, of which 275 were Iranians. After, Saudi Arabia set a quota system, in part to limit the number of Iranians and to clamp down on the protests. Iran announced that it would boycott the hajj because of the deaths and the quota system. This incident, combined with Iranian naval attacks on Saudi ships in the Persian Gulf, led Saudi Arabia to sever diplomatic relations with Iran.

The Iran-Iraq War

In late 1980, Iraq, led by President Saddam Hussein, attacked Iran. With the shah's military machine smashed from within by the forces of Khomeini's Islamic revolution, Hussein calculated that his campaign to acquire Iranian territory and gain better access to the Persian Gulf would be quick and successful. But the war soon bogged down. Hussein's secular Baathist regime was regarded as a threat to the Saudi kingdom, but Iran, with its goal of spreading its Shia Islamic revolution throughout the region, was judged as the greater evil. Thus, Saudi Arabia and its neighbors in the Gulf States backed Iraq in the conflict.

Yet there was concern among the peninsula's states that their support of Iraq would invite attack from Iran. In May 1981, in Abu Dhabi, Saudi Arabia joined in the formation of the Gulf Cooperation Council (GCC) with Kuwait, Bahrain, Qatar, the United Arab Emirates, and the Sultanate of Oman. The strategic objectives listed in GCC's charter included promoting regional security, keeping the region free from intentional conflicts, and respect for member states' national sovereignty. The organization also established agreements that promoted free trade and funded regional development projects. The council's security agreements were downplayed in order to avoid the appearance of undercutting the Arab League. Yet, led by Saudi Arabia, the GCC loaned billions of dollars to Iraq to finance the war. By the time the war ended in 1988, Saudi Arabia had contributed more than $25 billion to Iraq, some provided as loans and some as gifts, according to King Fahd, who had succeeded Khalid in 1982. These war debts, which totaled $160 billion, created resentment in Iraq and would be a factor in its invasion of Kuwait in 1990.

The increased oil production necessary to raise the needed capital eventually depressed prices, hampering Iran's ability to fund the war. In retaliation, Iran launched missile attacks on ships of the GCC states in the Persian Gulf, prompting the United States, already at odds with Iran for its seizure of U.S. diplomatic personnel and anti-Western policies, to support Iraq. But the closest cooperation of the era between Saudi Arabia and the United States was triggered by the Soviet Union's invasion of Afghanistan.

The War in Afghanistan

In late December of 1979, by order of Leonid Brezhnev, president of the USSR, the Soviet Union invaded Afghanistan. The date is often given as December 24, 25, or 26, but Soviet combat forces had entered the country at least several days before. The invasion was staged to prop up the Soviet-allied regime of Hafizullah Amin (1929–79), president of the Democratic Republic of Afghanistan, which was under attack from Muslim resistance groups. The invasion was to be a quick, surgical operation aimed at securing Kabul, the Afghan capital, and primary communication lines linking the country and the Soviet Union. However, the Soviets had no interest in propping up Amin himself. On December 28, Amin was assassinated and Babrak Karmal (1929–96), a Soviet protégé and puppet, was installed as president.

A communist government in the previously Islamic nation had already aroused Saudi concern and opposition, and the Soviet invasion underlined the affront. The United States, engaged in the cold war, was likewise opposed to the Soviet action. Saudi Arabia and the United States became close allies in organizing, funding, and supplying opposition efforts.

President Jimmy Carter quickly canceled U.S. participation in the 1980 Summer Olympics, to be held in Moscow, in protest. Carter had already taken more forceful steps to counter Soviet designs in Afghanistan. Covert U.S. aid began six months before the invasion with a secret directive he had signed authorizing assistance to opponents of the pro-Soviet regime in Kabul. After the invasion, the United States initiated a large-scale covert program to support anti-Soviet Islamic mujahideen, or "freedom fighters."

The United States supported efforts to recruit Muslims from around the world for the war to demonstrate the unity of Islamic opposition to the communist occupation of Muslim land, and to harness the religious fervor of those who viewed the battle as a holy war against invading infidels. Estimates on the amount spent by the United States and Saudi Arabia in support of the mujahideen range as high as $40 billion over the decade of the conflict. Throughout this time, the United States and the kingdom organized Islamic fundamentalists with ties to some of the Saudi elite. Osama bin Laden was a key figure among them.

The Soviet Defeat

Pakistan's Inter-Services Intelligence Directorate (ISI) was also involved in recruitment. Training camps in Afghanistan and Pakistan prepared the holy warriors for battle against the Soviets. As many as 100,000

THE RISE OF BIN LADEN

Born in 1957, Osama bin Laden was the youngest of some 20 surviving sons of Sheikh Mohammad bin Laden, an emigrant from southern Yemen. A close friend of Ibn Saud, Mohammad was the founder of the Bin Laden Group (BLG), a construction company that grew into one of Saudi Arabia's largest private enterprises, thanks to the patronage of the king. The BLG also diversified into agriculture, financing, investments, and other ventures.

Mohammad's children and those of the king were close in their youth, as the company became the primary contractor in the country, building many public buildings and several palaces. Ibn Saud gave Mohammad the contract for the restoration of the holy sites in Mecca and Medina and exclusive right to all contracts for construction of religious-oriented structures, a concession that lasted until 1967. The 1979 seizure of the Grand Mosque was accomplished in part by the rebels' use of BLG trucks to transport weapons into the site. Because of the company's exclusive repair contract, the trucks were admitted without inspection. In planning the counterattack, Saudi and Western forces used company maps of the underground passageways to mount their assault; no one else had such documents. One of the sheik's sons had been subsequently arrested for ties to the extremists, but he was later released when it was determined that the trucks were used without his knowledge. The fact that the government continued to do business with the company after this lapse underscores the close ties the bin Ladens enjoyed with the ruling family.

The sheikh died in a helicopter crash in 1968, leaving 13-year-old Osama an $80-million inheritance. Bin Laden earned a civil engineering degree from King Abdul Aziz University in Jeddah in 1979. The following year he went to Afghanistan, bringing funds raised from members of the Saudi ruling class, as well as his own. He established guest houses and training camps in Afghanistan and Pakistan, and he sponsored Saudis and other Muslims who traveled to Afghanistan to become mujahideen.

Muslims from dozens of countries may have undergone training in the camps after 1982. Using the rugged terrain as a cover for their lightning attacks and ambushes, the mujahideen turned Afghanistan into what became called the Soviet Union's Vietnam. Osama bin Laden founded Al Qaeda (the base) there in 1988 or 1989, an umbrella organization that gave support to a variety of militant Islamic groups.

The Saudi government funded the construction and operation of madrassas, or religious schools, primarily in Islamic countries around the world. Without alternative educational opportunities in many of these locations, the schools have been welcomed, providing a basic education as well as food and shelter for students. These institutions also ground students in Wahhabi interpretation of Islam, and have been accused of perpetuating an intolerant view of the world. During the 1980s and after, the madrassas also served as conduits to help graduates join the mujahideen fighting in Afghanistan, first against the Soviets, then against Afghani forces battling the Taliban for supremacy in the country. When hostilities with the United States appeared imminent in the wake of 9/11, additional madrassa graduates and foreign volunteers traveled to Afghanistan to join what was seen as jihad against the infidel invaders.

The Soviets withdrew in 1989, having suffered casualties of 15,000 dead and 17,000 wounded, and leaving behind a shaky regime barely in control of Kabul. More than 1 million Afghans died in the war and 5 million became refugees. With the Soviets gone, the mujahideen turned on each other. Warlords with private armies fought for dominance. Bin Laden, disillusioned by the infighting, returned to Saudi Arabia in

THE CONTRA CONNECTION

Despite the ups and downs of Saudi relations with the United States, ties between the two nations had grown closer during the 1980s, strengthened not only by oil and arms but by mutual interests in opposing the forces of communism. This mutual concern (along with a desire to maintain close ties) led the kingdom to finance anticommunist contra forces fighting a civil war in Nicaragua at the request of the Reagan administration.

Following Reagan's approval of the sale of Stinger missiles to Saudi Arabia in 1984, Prince Bandar began making monthly deposits of $1 million to a bank account in the Cayman Islands controlled by the contras, deposits that continued for several months. Congress had blocked U.S. spending in support of the contras that same year, but the Reagan administration saw the Saudis as a conduit for circumventing the prohibition.

After King Fahd visited President Reagan in Washington in 1985, the Saudis made a $5 million deposit in the Caymans that went to the contras, with monthly payments of $2 million thereafter. Also in 1985, the

1990. When the government in Kabul fell in April of 1992, it was regarded as a grand victory for Islam by the mujahideen and as a major defeat for communism by the West.

As the Saudi Arabian mujahideen returned home, they brought along the idealism for a pure form of Islam that had fired them in Afghanistan. Many soon came to view the state and society they returned to as corrupt. Osama bin Laden, who had helped raise funds and organize resistance to the Soviet occupation, founded a welfare organization for veterans of the war, some 4,000 of whom had settled in Mecca alone, and dispensed money to families of those killed.

Stockpiling Arms

As regional threats proliferated in the 1980s, Saudi Arabia sought more arms, even as its oil revenues declined. The procurement efforts generated more battles in the United States as opponents concerned about Israel's security tried to block the sales. When the Saudis were unable to overcome this opposition, they bought weapons elsewhere. The large sums involved in these transactions also provided opportunities for

Reagan administration orchestrated a secret arms sale to Iran through Israel, brokered by Saudi Arabian arms dealer Adnan Khashoggi. Though Iran was an enemy of the United States and arms sales to Iran were prohibited, Reagan authorized a secret program to supply arms. The transaction was aimed at securing the release of six Americans kidnapped by Iranian-sponsored terrorists in Lebanon and possibly improving relations with the regime in Tehran. In the first half of 1986, 180 tons of military equipment was shipped from the United States, with Iran as its final destination.

After the sales were disclosed by the press in 1986, first by a Lebanese newspaper, U.S. government officials testified in Congress that Saudi Arabia had contributed more than $32 million to the contras through Cayman banks. (Additionally, the Reagan administration gave $18 million of the $30 million raised by the weapons sales to the contras.) Whatever motives may be ascribed to their contributions, the assistance provided by the Saudis strengthened their relationship with the Reagan administration even as the Saudis indulged in the customary tribal code in which they were raised, where comrades stand up for comrades.

commissions, kickbacks, and bribery, further enriching members of the ruling elite.

In 1984, with the war in Afghanistan raging and Saudi- and U.S.-backed mujahideen battling the Soviet forces, President Reagan ordered the sale of Stinger antiaircraft missiles to Saudi Arabia over the objection of Congress. When the Saudis sought more F-15s the following year, Congress blocked the sales. The Saudis turned to British suppliers and, over the course of the decade, concluded several major weapons purchases with them.

After Saudi Arabia was blocked from buying short-range missiles to counter the Iranian missile threat, King Fahd sent Bandar (who had been named ambassador to the United States in 1983) to China to find an alternative source. Secret negotiations in 1986 and 1987 resulted in a Saudi order for intermediate-range nuclear-capable missiles and mobile launchers. The following year, when U.S. satellite surveillance photos revealed the presence of such missiles in Saudi Arabia, the Saudis maintained that the purchase was necessitated by the U.S. refusal to sell it missiles.

After fence-mending by the Reagan administration, Saudi Arabia signed the UN Treaty on the Non-Proliferation of Nuclear Weapons. Following Iran's attack on shipping in the Persian Gulf, Saudi Arabia

King Fahd. When Fahd succeeded King Khalid in 1982, he had been the de facto head of the state for several years. (Courtesy of the Saudi Information Office)

severed diplomatic relations with the regime in Tehran, as previously noted, and the United States approved sales of missiles to the kingdom to counter the Iranian threat.

The Reign of Fahd

In June of 1982 King Khalid died and was succeeded by his half brother, the crown prince—Fahd ibn Abd al Aziz (b. 1921). Fahd had already taken on much of the king's responsibilities as Khalid became more figurehead than ruler. The kingdom's policies remained unchanged. King Fahd and his six full brothers (the Sudairi Seven) solidified their control over the government. Their half-brother Abdullah, commander of the national guard, was named crown prince. In 1986 Fahd adopted the title "protector of the two holy sites," which he assumed in order to underscore the religious significance of his role as the kingdom's leader.

Falling Revenues

Declining oil revenues played havoc with the kingdom's finances during Fahd's first years on the throne. From 1938, when commercial extraction began, to 1981, when it peaked, revenues grew from $0.5 million to more than $116 billion. But revenue fell precipitously in subsequent years, declining almost 85 percent to $18.4 billion by 1985. This resulted in part from a collapse in oil prices, which fell from $32 per barrel in 1981 to $15 per barrel by the middle of the decade, dropping to $8 per barrel in 1986. The collapse, in turn, was spurred by overproduction driven by the need to fund Iraq's war against Iran. Concurrently the GDP, which peaked at more than 415 billion Saudi riyals ($110.7 billion) in 1982, declined to 271 billion in 1986 before it began to rebound. That same year Sheikh Yamani, who had served as oil minister from 1962, was removed as the head of the Ministry of Petroleum and Minerals Resources.

Fahd stated that the price decline "made it impossible to formulate meaningful revenue and spending guidelines" (Vassiliev 1998, 453). Government spending had to be cut drastically, though spending by the royal family remained unchecked. In many cases the government refused to pay private contractors for work already finished. Of 1,200 companies that had such contracts, one-third went bankrupt or had serious financial problems in the years 1984 and 1985. When construction companies went bankrupt, their foreign workers were often left stranded. In some cases the Saudi government assumed responsibility and arranged for payment and transportation home. But workers who engaged in public protest were deported immediately.

Public Projects

The fourth five-year development plan, covering the years 1985–89, focused on economic and social programs rather than grand infrastructure and construction projects, as had previous plans. What large projects had been proposed were suspended or scrapped, including refineries, a petrochemical plant, and an international airport. Yet even social programs were beyond the kingdom's means due to the drop in revenues. The state was reluctant to impose taxes to make up for the budget shortfall, fearing popular opposition. Likewise, it was hesitant to reduce the free health-care and other social services the populace had come to expect as a result of the oil wealth. The high birth (3.68 births per 100 persons in the population, annually) and fertility rates (6.48 children per woman, one of the highest in the world) further strained the costs of these services to the treasury. Utility rates were raised, but this led to complaints.

Another goal of the fourth plan was "Saudization" of the workforce, putting Saudi workers in positions held by foreign workers. The government remained the main employer, and there were not enough jobs for all the Saudis now graduating and looking for work. Meanwhile foreigners, who numbered about 4 million, were estimated to hold more than 71 percent of the jobs in 1985. Undocumented immigrants were deported and immigration tightened as part of this effort, with an estimated 300,000 being sent home in 1985 and 1986. But the Saudization program realized only marginal success. Saudi nationals had neither the training for the skilled jobs nor the inclination to accept menial positions.

Thanks to the educational system that had been put in place, the population was becoming more educated, but opportunities were still limited, particularly for those without connections to the ruling elite, either by birth or through familial social ties. Also, foreign-educated Saudis received better positions and opportunities than those educated within the country, and attending schools in the United States and Europe was not an option for many without such connections. This led to growing class division and resentment among those shut out. The increasing discontent was exploited by clerics who preached against corruption and Western influence. Their message found resonance in the middle class and especially in the lower classes. While liberal would-be reformers pushed for moderation in application of religious law, more worrisome to the leadership was the criticism of conservative religious leaders who rejected all *bida* or innovations, and thus opposed the Saudi rule.

Women were also denied employment opportunities due to restrictions on their activities, such as on driving. Although no formal law against driving by females existed, those who did were routinely stopped by the religious police, taken to police stations, and forced to wait until a male relative came to retrieve them.

Yet all the kingdom's plans and problems were thrown into sharp relief when its very future was called into question after Saddam Hussein commanded the Iraqi army to invade Kuwait, leaving Saudi Arabia more exposed and vulnerable than it had ever been.

12

THE GULF CRISIS AND
ITS AFTERMATH
(1990–2001)

Despite decades of tumultuous dissent, armed disputes with neighbors on all sides, and internal rifts that almost destroyed the monarchy, the Iraqi invasion of Kuwait presented the gravest threat to modern Saudi Arabia's future. The kingdom could be saved, but the now-apparent inadequacy of its military force and the necessity of relying on the United States for its rescue would have far-reaching consequences of their own. Once the Persian Gulf War ended, citizens questioned the vast sums previously spent on defense, and the stationing of "infidel" troops on Saudi soil likewise provoked intense criticism from conservative clerics and many others. Reforms enacted in the wake of the war were unable to quell the dissent. Though the government tried to discount the extent of the organized opposition and the threat it represented, this position would become untenable after the events of September 11, 2001, in which 15 of the kingdom's citizens took part in a coordinated terrorist attack on the United States, thrusting the world into a new era. This tumultuous decade and the events leading up to that day in September are the subjects of this chapter.

The Invasion of Kuwait

With the economic devastation wrought by Iraq's war with Iran, Kuwait and its rich oil fields made an attractive target to Iraqi president Saddam Hussein. On July 17, 1990, Hussein charged Kuwait and the United Arab Emirates with driving down oil prices by overproduction, and he accused Kuwait of pumping oil from a field whose ownership Iraq contested. Iraqi military units moved to the Kuwaiti border. As the two nations negotiated, the UN sought to ease tensions. Secretary General Javier Pérez de

Cuéllar called for restraint from both sides. On July 25, the U.S. ambassador to Iraq, April Glaspie, met with Hussein. It was subsequently reported that Hussein misinterpreted the ambassador's remarks, construing them as signaling U.S. indifference to an Iraqi invasion of Kuwait. On August 1 negotiations between Kuwait and Iraq collapsed, and the following day Iraq invaded, sending 100,000 troops over the border and driving the emir, Sheikh Jabir Al-Ahmad Al-Jabir Al Sabah, into exile. Iraqi troops looted and pillaged, burning buildings and brutalizing civilians. Several weeks later Iraq claimed Kuwait as its 19th province.

The invasion toppled one more monarchy and raised grave concerns about Iraq's intentions toward Saudi Arabia. The kingdom regarded both its own defense and the liberation of Kuwait as imperatives. But Saudi forces, despite the country's vast expenditures for defense, could do neither. The Iraqis had overwhelming forces, whose growth had been financed by the kingdom itself, other GCC (Gulf Cooperative Council) states, and the United States. Kuwait alone had spent about $10 billion on Iraq's war against Iran. Hussein had been pressing the emir for months to forgive his war debts, and some speculate that his pique at the emir's refusal helped trigger the invasion. The Saudi government suppressed news of the invasion for several days while it determined its options and how to respond publicly.

On August 5, U.S. president George Bush forcefully declared that the invasion "will not stand." The following day, U.S. secretary of defense Richard Cheney, on an international diplomacy mission to rally support against the invasion, presented King Fahd with evidence of Iraqi forces massing on his border. The following day Saudi Arabia formally requested U.S. military assistance, and U.S. president George Bush announced plans to deploy U.S. forces to defend the kingdom. International outrage at Iraq's invasion and its brutality in Kuwait was growing.

Saudi Response to the Invasion

On August 9, 1990, Fahd publicly announced that U.S. military forces would temporarily be garrisoned in the kingdom. Additionally, he requested assistance from other Arab countries. Egypt, Syria, and Morocco eventually supplied troops for the coalition forces. The United States provided the majority of the troops, basing more than 500,000 in the theater during the Persian Gulf War. This was not the first time U.S. troops had been stationed on Saudi soil; the United States had an air base at Dhahran until 1962, and in 1963 U.S. F-100 fighters were briefly stationed in the kingdom to defend against Egyptian incursions during

THE INVASION'S ROOTS

Since its creation after World War I, Iraq had claimed Kuwait as its 19th province, citing a historical link the two states shared with Mesopotamia. During the Ottoman Empire, some had regarded Kuwait as part of the province of Basra, though it operated as an independent principality long before Iraq's creation. Al Sabah rule in Kuwait extends back to the 1700s. Britain recognized Kuwait in 1899 when it signed a protectorate treaty with its sheikh. When the Ottoman Empire was divided amongst the victors after its defeat in World War I, Britain assured Kuwait's independence in part to have access to the Kuwaiti port for its naval fleet, which Britain had been using for more than a century. Many Iraqis were angered by the division. When British troops pulled out of Kuwait in 1961, giving the sheikhdom its independence, Iraq again claimed all of Kuwait as its territory, and Iraqi troops massed on the border. In response, British troops returned, and after an appeal to the Arab League by Kuwait, forces from Saudi Arabia, Egypt, Jordan, and Sudan were also sent to the new state, and the Iraqis withdrew. But in 1973, Iraq seized a border station near the port city of Uum Qasr, claiming it as part of "occupied Iraq." After another Kuwaiti appeal to the Arab League, Saudi Arabia mediated Iraq's withdrawal. A similar episode occurred a decade later.

the Yemeni civil war. But this time the population was more aware, educated, and angry. The request for U.S. protection incensed many Saudis, both because it allowed outsiders into the kingdom and revealed that the vast sums spent on military equipment had been wasted. While many other Saudis saw the necessity of the military arrangement, however distasteful, young religious scholars denounced having "infidels" protect the home of Islam. In September a leading Islamic scholar concluded that the enemy Saudi Arabia faced was not Iraq but, rather, "an evil greater than Saddam, that is the USA" and the West, as he wrote in a letter to the head of the Council of Higher Ulama and the Institution of Ifta' and Scholarly Research (Al-Rasheed 2002, 166).

Given the magnitude of the crisis the government could not stifle the dissent as imperiously as was its custom. The issues were discussed in the media and among the public, generating an unaccustomed atmosphere of openness (*infitah*). Advocates of reform and liberalization raised their voices along with the conservatives. Even women used the opportunity to press for rights. In the kingdom's first public protest staged by women, 45 of them drove into Riyadh to show opposition to the prohibition against women operating automobiles. Fahd later met with four of them and publicly backed their cause, though all initially were dismissed from employment and had their passports taken away for their actions. Their jobs and passports were restored along with back pay six months later.

Operation Desert Shield, a defensive effort to protect Saudi Arabia from invasion, was launched as troops arrived in preparation for possible military action. The unprecedented number of foreign journalists (about 1,500) admitted to the country to cover the crisis amplified the internal debate as they sought Saudis to express their views on the unfolding events. Journalists also reported on the conflicts and contradictions they observed within the society, providing rare glimpses of life and people in the kingdom. The openness and exposure to foreign influences also provoked increased vigilance and enforcement of religious rules by the morality police. Some of these police were transferred by the government away from the Eastern Province, where the majority of foreign troops were based, to minimize their contact with outsiders.

Operation Desert Storm

The January 15 deadline set by the UN for withdrawal from Kuwait passed without Iraqi compliance. Under the command of General H.

UN RESOLUTIONS

Subsequent to the invasion, the UN passed 12 resolutions against Iraq's action. The last, UN declaration 678, of November 29, 1990, called for an Iraqi withdrawal by midnight of January 15, 1991, and authorized the use of "all means necessary" to eject Iraq from Kuwait. In early January 1991, with the UN-mandated deadline for Hussein's withdrawal approaching, Saudi Arabia's supreme religious leader, Sheikh Abd al-Aziz ibn Baz, issued a fatwa permitting jihad against Saddam Hussein, even if necessitating the use of infidel forces. Rather than stifling dissent, the edict further undercut the credibility of the king and the ulama, who gave the monarchy its legitimacy among conservative and radical religious figures. After last-minute diplomacy between the United States and Iraq failed to avert the crisis, the U.S. Congress voted to support United Nations resolution 678 and authorized the use of U.S. forces in the war on January 12, 1991.

Norman Schwarzkopf, Jr., the coalition's military offensive, dubbed Operation Desert Storm, began on January 17 with an intensive air campaign targeting Iraqi forces and assets in Kuwait and Iraq. Saudi Arabia served as the staging area and committed most of its 160,000 troops, both the regular army and the national guard, to the war effort. A Joint Arab-Islamic Force under the command of Lt. General Khalid bin Sultan was a major component of the coalition, joined by the Gulf Cooperation Council's (GCC) 10,000-strong Peninsula Shield Force. Britain, France, and Italy were also coalition partners. A ground assault followed the aerial bombardment and quickly outflanked and overcame Iraqi forces in Kuwait. Incursions by coalition forces into Iraq followed, and a cease-fire took effect on February 28. Meanwhile, President George H. W. Bush urged the Iraqi people to rise up against Hussein. A revolt spread in the heavily Shia southern region, but the United States made no effort to support the Shia revolt, and the remnants of Hussein's army brutally suppressed the uprising.

Kuwait had been liberated and Saddam Hussein defeated, but the ruling family could hardly claim victory. Criticism intensified over the vast sums spent on defense, the basing of infidels in the kingdom, and the impotence of the government in the face of the threat. Many of the

As the military buildup to the Persian Gulf War continued, U.S. president George H. W. Bush traveled to Saudi Arabia and met with King Fahd to discuss the liberation of Kuwait in November 1990. (Courtesy of the Saudi Information Office)

During the Persian Gulf War, coalition forces included veteran mujahideen soldiers who battled the Soviets in Afghanistan. Here Afghan mujahideen consult with a U.S. Marine in eastern Saudi Arabia in February of 1991, discussing battle strategies and their knowledge of fighting in the region's harsh terrain. (AP/Wide World Photos)

elite and members of the royal family had fled the country, further reducing public confidence in the regime.

Exact figures are difficult to ascertain, but the war is estimated to have cost Saudi Arabia $60 billion. That figure is in addition to the $25 billion it contributed to Hussein's 1980–88 war against Saudi Arabia's enemy, Iran. The expenditures were enough to keep the kingdom stuck in the recession that began with the steep decline in oil prices of the mid-1980s. In the 1990s, with oil at about $18 or less per barrel, budget deficits approached $20 billion annually. By 1995, GDP per capita had declined from $17,000 in the early 1980s to slightly more than $7,000.

Pressure for Change

The debates the crisis provoked intensified in its aftermath, producing what has been called "the age of petitions," as reform proposals from both the left and right were promulgated and presented to officials. In 1991 a liberal opposition group of 43 prominent figures from the government, business, and academia submitted a petition to King Fahd proposing 10 reforms. These included establishing a Consultative Council (Majlis Shura) as a means of introducing a more representative government; the restoration of municipal councils; modernization of the judicial system; equality for all citizens; use of merit-based standards instead of family ties for government appointments; more freedom for the media; reforms for the Committee for the Propagation of Virtue and the Prevention of Vice; and a greater role for women in public life. At the same time, they pledged allegiance to the state and government. The signatories and their followers became identified as Secularists.

On the other side of the ideological spectrum were conservative clerics and their adherents known as Islamists. In May, after presentation of the liberals' petition, 52 leading religious leaders sent a petition to King Fahd, the "Letter of Demands." It also listed 10 demands including greater adherence to sharia, or "religious law," singling out areas of the judicial system, the army, the economy, social institutions, and public administration as those needing more rigorous application of Islamic justice. It also demanded the removal of restrictions on clerics, preachers, and religious scholars and a greater role for the ulama in all government agencies. The 10 points were expanded upon in a longer pamphlet, "Memorandum of Advice," signed by more than 100 Islamists and submitted to Abd al-Aziz ibn Baz, the kingdom's chief religious authority and head of the council of leading ulama, in 1992. It advocated transforming the kingdom into a more fundamental Islamic state. Additionally, the memorandum objected to the prohibitions against preachers discussing issues relating to politics and current events, and criticized the government's failure to support Islamic causes outside its borders. The media were criticized for promoting Western values and diverting youth from their religious obligations. It called for banning unveiled women from television and for using the media to promote Islamic principles, and it advocated creating an Islamic foreign policy and a strong army. It also called for increased spending on social programs, health care, and education, and the withdrawal of all aid to governments that failed to comply with Islamic principles.

The "Memorandum of Advice" was published outside Saudi Arabia, giving it widespread attention throughout the Islamic world (and shielding its publishers from efforts to stifle its printing), embarrassing the kingdom's leadership. The government demanded an apology from the ulama for the memorandum. Ibn Baz condemned the pamphlet's publication though not its message.

The government answered with "Explicit Reading of the Memorandum of Advice," a booklet refuting the clerics' tract. It detailed Saudi financial contributions to Muslim governments, programs, and education around the globe in an effort to blunt the memorandum authors' claims that the Saudi leadership failed to support Islamic causes.

Government Reforms

Despite disagreements with critics, in its vulnerable state the government felt compelled to accede in some form to calls for change. In March of 1992 Fahd announced three major reforms: the Basic Law of Government, the Law of the Consultative Council, and the Law of the Provinces.

The Basic Law of Government reaffirmed the religious principles and monarchical rule on which the kingdom was built, as if laying a foundation for, and perhaps limiting, the reforms that would follow. The law emphasized Saudi Arabia's status as an Islamic monarchy, with rule limited to the royal family. The rules of succession were also addressed: "The King chooses the Heir Apparent and relieves him of his duties by Royal order. . . . The Heir Apparent takes over the power of the King on the latter's death until the act of allegiance has been carried out" (Vassiliev 1998,

The Consultative Council in session. After the first Persian Gulf War, the government felt obliged to make some concessions toward reform. The long-promised revival of the Consultative Council was one of them. (Courtesy of the Saudi Information Office)

466–467). Article six mandated allegiance to the king and submission to his rule. It placed the family at the center of Saudi society and stressed the importance of proper Islamic upbringing and training. The state's duty to protect Islam and its holy places was also recognized. Access to the king and the crown prince's courts to seek redress for injustice was guaranteed.

The Basic Law also decreed the formation of the Consultative Council, which had been agreed upon in 1980 in response to the seizure of the Grand Mosque and unrest in the Eastern Province, but never implemented. Created to balance the monarchy's absolutism, the rules defining the council and its role were spelled out in the Law of the Consultative Council, published in March of 1992. The council would have a chairman and 60 members, all Saudi men over the age of 30, who served at the invitation and pleasure of the king. It could interpret law and "examine" reports at the behest of government ministers and agencies. Yet is was simply an advisory council with no powers to make law on its own. The Consultative Council was finally established in 1994. Reflecting the government's desire to create a progressive body, over 60 percent of the appointees were educated at Western universities. Only nine were specialists in religious law.

The Law of the Provinces was meant to correct the lack of oversight and control exercised over regional administrations. Prior to its promulgation in 1992, local rule was largely autonomous and responsibilities were undefined, determined mostly by the relationship between the leading provisional authority, the governor or emir, and the king. The 13 provinces were put under the control of "governorates" and subdivided into districts and precincts.

In the aftermath of the war the government also took steps to improve relations with its long-restive Shia population in the Eastern Province.

Action Against the Opposition

Concurrent with the announcements of reforms, a campaign against dissidents began, marked by increased surveillance, intimidation, and enforcement of bans on subversion and criticism. Islamists rather than secularists were the primary targets from 1992 to 1994. Public relations was also employed, with the government arranging for publication of positive articles about religious moderation. The government put the number of those arrested during the campaign at about 110, while opposition groups claimed the number was more than 1,000. The number ultimately held in custody beyond initial questioning is likely closer to the official figure.

Saudi Arabia has 13 provinces. Following the Persian Gulf War, administration of the provinces was restructured in an effort to ensure proper governance.

The crackdown intensified after the Buraida Uprising, a large protest against government corruption and immorality in September of 1994. Two prominent dissident clerics, Safar al-Hawali and Sheikh Salman al-Oudah, were arrested along with other preachers and a reported 1,300 followers in the provincial capital of Qasim. This was the homeland of the Al-Saud, and thus represented a dangerous disaffection with its traditional loyalists. Ibn Baz issued a fatwa decreeing that unless the two recanted they would be banned from lecturing, meetings, and recording their sermons. In October Fahd established a Supreme Council of Islamic Affairs and the Council for Islamic Call and Guidance. The two groups were given responsibility for overseeing the behavior of Saudis abroad and of those involved with operating mosques, which were regarded as potential breeding grounds for dissident activities. Yet opposition continued to grow, leading to the arrest of senior ulama like Safar al-Hawali and Salman al-Oudeh. Ultimately the government's practice of meting out severe punishments to opponents while showing leniency toward those who retracted their criticisms seemed to succeed in silencing an already fractious conservative opposition. But the silence ended after the government executed a conservative activist in August of 1995. Opponents answered with attacks against the government and U.S. military installations and personnel within the kingdom.

Many opponents had fled the country and continued their criticism from abroad. They settled in the Western countries they attacked rather than the Arab capitals of Cairo, Beirut, and Baghdad that had been the sanctuary of secular-minded reformers such as the Free Princes during the 1960s. Groups like the Committee for the Defense of Legitimate Rights (CDLR) and an offshoot, the Movement for Islamic Reform in Arabia (MIRA), press their reform agenda using e-mail, Web sites, and the media. The CDLR was formed by Muhammad al-Musari in Riyadh in 1993 and moved its operations to London the following year. In addition to its reform agenda, the CDLR publicized information about governmental abuses, serving as a source of information on activities within the kingdom to outsiders and expatriates. Saudi Arabia pressured England to deny asylum to the CDLR leadership, but this led to negative publicity for both the kingdom and Britain when reports of the campaign exposed links between English arms manufacturers and the British government.

From Hero to Foe

Even before the government commenced its crackdown, Osama bin Laden, who had helped the kingdom pursue its policies in Afghanistan during the previous decade, began assuming the mantle of the monarchy's greatest foe. His opposition was precipitated by the government's response to the Iraqi invasion of Kuwait. Bin Laden had proposed raising a force of veteran mujahideen from the war in Afghanistan to defend the kingdom. He regarded the royals' decision to allow instead infidels onto holy soil to take arms against Muslim brothers as a sacrilege, and loudly denounced the decision. His criticisms led to travel restrictions confining him to Jeddah. He left Saudi Arabia in 1991, settling in the Sudan, where he established several businesses and, according to intelligence reports and later indictments, organized and financed terrorist activities. These included a hotel bombing in Yemen in 1992 and the training and arming of the militants in Mogadishu,

Somalia, who killed 18 U.S. soldiers in 1993. Also in 1993, one of the towers of New York's World Trade Center was car-bombed, an attack for which an Egyptian cleric, Sheikh Umar Abd-al Rahman, who shared bin Laden's philosophy, was convicted.

In 1994, Saudi Arabia stripped bin Laden of his citizenship and his family disowned him. (The Bin Laden Group built a $150 million facility to house 4,300 U.S. troops in Kharj, south of Riyadh, in 1998.) Under pressure from Saudi Arabia and the United States, the Sudan expelled him in 1996. Bin Laden returned to Afghanistan and was welcomed by the Taliban, an ultraconservative regime influenced by Wahhabi teaching that had formed two years before.

Though Islam allows only trained clerics to issue fatwas, bin Laden took it upon himself to pronounce edicts. In a February 1998 fatwa "Declaration of the World Islamic Front for Jihad against the Jews and the Crusaders," he declared that "to kill Americans and their allies, both civil and military, is an individual duty for every Muslim who is able, in any country where this is possible." The United States launched

STATE FINANCES

The slide in oil revenues that began in 1982 would worsen as the decade progressed. An era of budget deficits began in 1983, along with a recession, and continued into the 1990s. In 1991 deficits totaled 19 percent of GDP. The deficits began to drop in succeeding years, as strong oil prices boosted revenues. In 1992 the deficit was almost 15 percent, and in 1993 it was still more than 14 percent. It dropped to 8 percent in 1994 and fell to 5 percent or less over the next three years. One goal of the sixth five-year development plan, which began in 1995, was to eliminate the deficits by the year 2000. But at the time, it was estimated that deficits of 3 percent or more of GDP would persist into the new century. And despite diversification efforts, oil still underpinned the economy. Officially oil accounts for about one-third of total GDP, but it makes up 90 percent of export earnings and 75 percent of budget revenues. And the kingdom was still vulnerable to the reverse shock of oil prices. When prices dropped in 1998 the deficit rose to more than 8 percent.

Through it all, arms purchases continued. From 1992 through 1995, the kingdom purchased $22.3 billion in arms, $15.6 billion of it from the United States.

a cruise missile attack against one of his training camps in Afghanistan that August, and in November the U.S. Justice Department named bin Laden in a 238-count indictment for conspiracy to kill Americans, involvement in the embassy bombings in Nairobi and Dar es Salaam, and other terrorist crimes.

Support for Islamic Struggles Abroad

Saudi Arabia remained active in supporting Muslim causes, armed and otherwise, throughout the period. In Bosnia, where ethnic Muslims were under attack by the Christian majority and their Serbian and Croatian backers, a contingent of 400 volunteers from the Arabian Peninsula joined the fight, with the majority coming from Saudi Arabia. The government contributed $120 million to the cause, while wealthy citizens gave an additional $200 million, according to the government, along with 150,000 tons of relief supplies. Money was also spent on repair and rebuilding of mosques destroyed in the conflict. These were built in a style consistent with Wahhabi doctrine, eliminating the ornamentation and frescoes that had adorned many of them, as part of an effort to convert Bosnian Muslims to the Saudis' more conservative brand of Islam. Reports alleged that Saudi Arabia additionally funded a $300 million covert operation to supply arms to the Muslim-led government of Bosnia.

In early August of 1995 NATO began a bombing campaign against Serbia in defense of the Muslims, which brought an end to the war. The Saudi fighters left Bosnia after the 1995 Dayton Peace Accord was signed, which mandated the withdrawal of all foreign forces from Bosnia.

Attacks on U.S. Interests

Following the Gulf War some 20,000 U.S. troops remained in the region, with about 6,000 stationed in Saudi Arabia at the middle of the decade. Their presence remained a source of bitter opposition from conservative elements. In November of 1995, a Saudi Arabian National Guard facility in Riyadh, in which U.S. military personnel also worked, was bombed. Seven people—five U.S. citizens—were killed, and 60 others, 37 of them from the United States, were injured. Four Saudi nationals were arrested and executed in 1996 after confessing their involvement on television.

The month after their execution, on June 25, 1996, a blast in an oil tanker truck loaded with an estimated 55,000 pounds of explosives parked just outside the Khobar Towers near the King Abdul Aziz Air Base in Dhahran, Saudi Arabia, killed 19 U.S. soldiers and injured more than 500 people. The compound of 50 high-rise buildings housed some 2,000 troops. The sophistication of the bomb led U.S. investigators to suspect a foreign government of orchestrating the attack. Saudi authorities believed Iran was responsible and reportedly detained some 40 suspects, Saudi Shia affiliated with an Iranian-backed Hezbollah group. U.S. investigators were reportedly frustrated by Saudi refusal to make suspects available for interrogation, and for their perceived determination to deny the possibility that the attack was the work of a larger, internal opposition group. FBI director Louis Freeh traveled to Saudi Arabia three times during the investigation, though he and other U.S. officials denied reports of any rift surrounding the probe.

The October 2000 bombing of the USS *Cole* in a Yemeni port, which killed 17 U.S. sailors, was linked to al-Qaeda and was also connected to the kingdom. The rubber dinghy used in the attack was purchased in Saudi Arabia and smuggled into Yemen.

Israeli and Palestinian Issues

During the postwar period Saudi Arabia softened its opposition to Israel. Perhaps it was a show of gratitude toward the United States; a display of its anger toward the PLO, which under Chairman Yasir Arafat had supported Iraq in the Persian Gulf War; or because old rigid models of friend and foe were being reassessed. In one sign, in July of 1991 Saudi Arabia threw its support behind Egypt's proposal to end the Arab Boycott of Israel in exchange for a freeze on Israeli settlements in the occupied West Bank and Gaza. The Arab Boycott had predated Israel itself, being adopted by the Arab League Council in December of 1945, soon after the organization's inception, as the conflict between Arabs and Jews in Palestine escalated. Under its terms, which gained stronger application after Israel declared its statehood in 1948, all Arab governments and people were to refuse any economic dealings with Israel or Jewish-owned businesses or those who did business with them, directly or indirectly. Many nations, Japan and France among them, observed the boycott to protect their trade interests with Arab states, of which Saudi Arabia was by far the biggest spender.

Not all the steps toward some form of normalization of relations were forward. In September of 1991 the Gulf Cooperation Council, which often reflected Saudi views, supported continuing the Arab Boycott until Israel withdrew from all occupied territories.

A wider rapprochement had gathered momentum at the 1991 Madrid Peace Conference sponsored by the United States and Soviet

Union, which brought together Israel and its neighbors Lebanon, Egypt, and Syria as well as a joint Jordanian-Palestinian delegation. In 1987 an intifada, or "uprising," had erupted in the Palestinian territories as disaffected, rock-throwing youths, representing the rage of the population, engaged in daily battles with Israeli forces. The uprising continued into 1993. The international community sought a diplomatic solution. The year after the intifada began, the Palestine National Council agreed to a UN partition plan, recognized Israel's right to exist, and renounced terrorism. The agreement led to discussions that eventually produced the Madrid conference.

This led to further discussions among the parties that began the following year in Moscow. Saudi Arabia strongly supported the dialogue. In 1993 Israel and the PLO announced that they had reached a peace agreement after months of secret negotiations in Oslo, Norway. This was the basis of the Oslo Agreement, also known as the Gaza-Jericho Agreement, which granted autonomy to Palestinians in the West Bank and Gaza after a five-year transition that began upon signing the agreement's Declaration of Principles that September.

Saudi Arabia strongly supported the agreement, and Arafat needed to regain Saudi support himself. During the decade before the Gulf War, Saudi Arabia is estimated to have provided $1 billion to the PLO. In the aftermath of the war, Saudi government funding ended because of Arafat's backing of Hussein. After Arafat signed the agreement, Saudi Arabia pledged $100 million to support implementation of the peace plan during its first year. These annual payments are thought to have continued at least through the middle of the decade. But while the Saudi government was supporting the peace process, a U.S. State Department report of 1993 reported that "private benefactors" in Saudi Arabia were funding Hamas, which was carrying out attacks against civilians in Israel.

Control of the Gaza Strip was turned over to the PLO on July 1, 1994, but the peace process soon bogged down amidst growing violence. On September 30 of that year, Saudi Arabia and the Gulf States ended support for the secondary and tertiary phases of the Arab Boycott. The secondary phase was directed against companies that did business with Israel or Jews, and the tertiary boycott targeted companies that did business with those covered by the secondary boycott. The primary boycott, against direct economic dealings with Israel or those linked by religion, remained in place.

In 1995 the U.S. Congress passed the Jerusalem Embassy Act of 1995, mandating the relocation of the U.S. embassy in Israel from Tel

Aviv to Jerusalem by May 31, 1999. Saudi Arabia vigorously protested, citing the city's importance to Muslims; the Al Aqsa Mosque, third holiest site in Islam and location of the first *qibla,* or the direction Muslims face when praying, is in Jerusalem. Presidents Clinton and George W. Bush both subsequently invoked waivers written into the legislation to avoid moving the embassy.

Fahd's Incapacitation, Abdullah's Succession

In 1995 King Fahd suffered a stroke and Crown Prince Abdullah, his half brother, assumed day-to-day rule of the kingdom. At the time Abdullah was commander of the Saudi National Guard and first deputy prime minister. A rift was said to have existed between Abdullah and the seven Sudairi brothers, one of whom was Fahd, the stricken king, when he first took the reins of government. (Abdullah's mother was a member of the Rashid clan, the Sauds' longtime rivals.) That November Prince Sultan, minister of defense, publicly described Fahd's incapacitation as a "slight ailment." This was interpreted by some as undercutting Adbullah's authority and signaling Sultan's opposition to his assumption of the throne.

Abdullah's status as a caretaker ruler limited his ability to make independent decisions. However, his practice of building consensus and considering others' views, along with his reputation for piety, made him more popular among the public than Fahd had been. Outside observers also viewed him as more nationalistic and less friendly to the United States, though more open and worldly than preceding monarchs (with the exception of King Faisal [r. 1964–75]). He has been described as blunt, emotional, and decisive as well as the most popular Saudi ruler among his subjects since Faisal. His popularity did not shield the state from ongoing opposition, as demonstrated when Buraida was again wracked by protests in 1998, requiring the national guard to quell the unrest.

The monarchy's stewardship of the holy sites, its most sacred obligation, was also called into question in this period as hundreds of pilgrims died in accidental calamities in Mecca. During hajj in 1997, fire killed 343, and the next year 119 pilgrims died in a stampede.

Foreign Relations under Abdullah

Confounding suppositions of an anti-U.S. stance, under Abdullah the kingdom repaired its relationship with U.S. oil companies, relations that had first been ruptured when the kingdom nationalized their assets in 1975. During a visit to Washington in 1998, Abdullah's first since becoming caretaker of the throne, Prince Bandar, ambassador to the United States and son of Sultan, hosted a gathering of CEOs of major U.S. oil companies at his residence in Maclean, Virginia. At the gathering Abdullah offered to accept proposals from them for gas and oil development activities in the kingdom. Stimulating the push for renewed ties was the kingdom's need for foreign investment and more jobs. A proposal from Exxon-Mobil ultimately led to its selection as lead developer in two of three major projects initially valued at $20 billion, though the projects were later scrapped after the two sides were unable to agree on terms.

Regional unity was another theme pursued at the end of the decade. During the late 1990s Abdullah normalized relations with Iran, bringing greater stability to the Gulf region. At the GCC summit in December of 1999, members agreed to establish a customs union, to take effect in 2005. It exempted all goods from GCC members from import taxes in GCC states if at least 40 percent of the value was added in a member state, and the company was majority owned by citizens of a GCC nation.

In 2000, Saudi Arabia and Yemen reached an agreement delineating the border between the two countries, sections of which had been in dispute since the 1930s. In February of 2001, Saudi Arabia and Syria signed a bilateral free-trade agreement. On June 11, the kingdom took ownership of the Iraqi pipeline that traversed Saudi Arabia to its Red Sea coast, citing continued Iraqi threats and provocations.

Relations with the United States

During this period outgoing president Clinton tried to broker a new peace agreement between the PLO and Israel, bringing PLO chairman Yasir Arafat and Israeli prime minister Ehud Barak to Camp David for intensive negotiations. But Arafat ultimately rejected the terms proposed by Israel. Hopes for Palestinian statehood and peace for Israel again seemed unattainable. In September of 2000 the second intifada began in Palestinian territories.

Yet as the new millennium dawned, outwardly the signs of stability and continuity in the Saudi-U.S. relationship appeared propitious. Clinton's successor, President George W. Bush, had expressed a desire to remain active in promoting peace in the region. Moreover, he was the son of a former president revered by many Saudis for his role in defending the kingdom during the Gulf War. And in a land where power tra-

PRIVATIZATION AND GLOBALIZATION

Economically, the end of the decade saw recognition that privatization and globalization were two trends with which the country needed to align itself. In 1999 King Fahd proclaimed that "globalization" was the way of the future to which the country would adhere. That same year the government formed a Supreme Economic Council to help attract foreign investment, create jobs for Saudi nationals, and promote privatization. Wide access to the Internet was also allowed, having been previously restricted out of concern for the unfiltered influences it allowed into the kingdom.

In January of 2000 a Supreme Oil Council was formed to take charge of the country's oil and gas policies. Also that year the Supreme Economic Council eased restrictions on foreign businesses operating in the country. Taxes were lowered (to a maximum of 30 percent from 45 percent), and enhanced protection for rights of investors against expropriation were adopted.

ditionally flowed from father to son, George W. Bush's ascendance was viewed positively in its own right. But policy and technology soon combined to cast the United States in a negative light within the kingdom and in the Arab world. While the intifada raged, the Bush administration was perceived to have a laissez-faire attitude toward the violence against Palestinians. Arab cable television networks such as al-Jazeera brought images of the violence home to millions of Saudis, further inflaming attitudes about Israel and its protector, the United States. The Saudis sent a series of letters and messages to the president urging a more active involvement in peace efforts and a more even-handed approach in condemning violence in the region. But the Bush administration had pulled back from the failed mediation efforts of the Clinton administration.

Abdullah was shaken by the president's unwavering support for Israel and its new prime minister, Ariel Sharon. In late August of 2001, with images of the intifada filling the screens of TVs in the Arab world, Abdullah recalled a high-level Saudi military delegation that had just arrived for talks at the Pentagon and instructed Ambassador Bandar to deliver a message announcing a fundamental break in the countries' relationship. Saudi Arabia prepared to convene an emergency summit of Arab leaders to offer complete support for the Palestinians. On August 27, Bandar informed U.S. national security adviser Condoleeza Rice at the White House that the kingdom was prepared to rethink its military relationship and its cooperation on law enforcement and intelligence operations with the United States. In response the Bush administration went to extraordinary steps over the next two days to repair the damage. In an August 29 letter delivered to Abdullah in response, Bush stated in part, "I firmly believe that the Palestinian people have a right to self-determination and to live peacefully and securely in their own state in their own homeland." This was the first public statement of support for an independent Palestinian state by a U.S. president. Abdullah shared the letter with the leaders of Egypt, Jordan, Syria, Lebanon, and Yemen, in addition to Arafat, informing Bush on September 7 that all viewed the letter as the beginning of a resumption of the peace process. Abdullah urged Bush to take charge of its revival. Hope for peace in the region was renewed, and the ever stormy relationship between the two world powers appeared back on track. In the United States, the Bush administration prepared to make public its support for a Palestinian state.

13

THE CHALLENGES AHEAD

As the 100th anniversary of Ibn Saud's 1902 capture of Riyadh approached, the challenges facing the kingdom may have seemed minor compared with those that confronted the founder of Saudi Arabia a century before, but they were nonetheless formidable. (Due to its use of a lunar calendar, whose years are shorter than those of the solar-based Gregorian calendar, the kingdom celebrated its official centennial in 1999.) These included political and religious opposition to the regime, a stagnating economy, a soaring birthrate, and an ever-expanding royal family that placed a large drain on the state. Yet these challenges were balanced by opportunities represented by the vast wealth of its energy reserves, its position of power and influence in the Arab world, its modern infrastructure, and an aggressive and efficient security force that minimized internal threats to the regime. Moreover, Al Saud's rule, though not unbroken, extended back more than two and a half centuries, an important precedent in a land that placed great importance on tradition and custom. The status quo of the regime—and the world—was severely shaken by the events of September 11, 2001, which were planned and perpetrated in the main by Saudi-born terrorists. Given the special nature of the Saudi-U.S. relationship, the aftershocks were felt deeply in the kingdom, leading many in both countries to question the basis and legitimacy of their long-standing alliance. The aftermath of the attack and a survey of what the challenges cited above portend for Saudi Arabia's future are the subject of this chapter.

September 11, 2001

A new world was born in the ashes of the terrorist attacks conducted on September 11, 2001, when hijackers flew four U.S. airliners into New York's World Trade Center towers, the Pentagon in Washington,

273

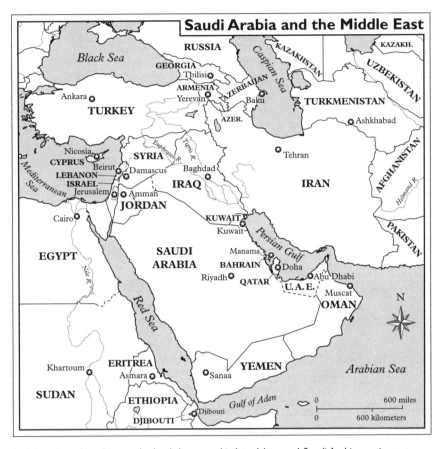

As it has throughout history, the land that gave birth to Islam and Saudi Arabia continues to play a pivotal role in the Middle East, and now the world. Modern infrastructure, transportation, and communication have eased the peninsula's historic isolation, though official policies keep it closed to most outsiders.

D.C., and a field in Pennsylvania. The day after the attack CIA director George Tenet informed the Saudi Arabian ambassador, Prince Bandar, that 15 of the 19 hijackers appeared to be Saudi Arabian citizens. On September 13, Osama bin Laden, the fugitive Saudi terrorist, was named by U.S. secretary of state Colin Powell as the prime suspect in masterminding the attacks. The hijackers were soon linked to al-Qaeda, the terrorist organization bin Laden had founded.

The attacks, given the kingdom's connection to them, presented the greatest challenge the Saudi-U.S. alliance had yet faced. Yet the initial Saudi response seemed emblematic of the secrecy and denial that, critics claimed, allowed the Islamic extremism blamed for the attacks to grow. Saudi officials downplayed the significance of the fact that most of the hijackers were its citizens. Information about the hijackers and their origin was initially kept out of Saudi newspapers. Not until early 2002, after months of denial, did the government acknowledge the involvement of Saudi citizens. Subsequently, almost no newspaper in the kingdom delved into the hijackers' backgrounds or examined the paths that led them to their mission.

The hijackers were not unschooled fanatical youths or the angry products of a refugee camp; they came from the middle class and were well-educated. Twelve were from leading tribes in southern Hijaz and Asir, the picturesque mountainous region the government has been positioning as the centerpiece of its nascent tourism industry. For the few Western journalists granted visas to visit Saudi Arabia in the wake of the events, however, access to Asir was often restricted.

Few of the hijackers had strong links to militant Islamic movements. What they seemed to share was lack of opportunity or meaningful employment, which led several of them to mosques presided over by a few well-known conservative clerics, and later to Afghanistan to train for the war in Chechnya. Some outsiders have seen the hijackers more as disaffected youth than fundamentalist fanatics. The government does not tabulate unemployment figures, but early in the century private estimates put the rate as high as 30 percent of those under the age of 25, a demographic that comprises almost 70 percent of Saudi Arabia's population. And Asir has traditionally been a neglected corner of the kingdom, bereft of the grand buildings and large public works found in most other settled regions.

At first no expression of contrition or concern over this link came from the kingdom. Crown Prince Abdullah in a later interview explained that Saudis never thought Americans would doubt the kingdom's friendship. However, shortly after the events, Saudi Arabia condemned the attacks. On September 14, King Fahd sent a cable of condolence to President Bush in which he conveyed the kingdom's great sorrow and grief over the attacks.

During a meeting at the White House on September 20, 2001, Minister of Foreign Affairs Prince Saud Al-Faisal assured President George W. Bush of Saudi Arabia's full cooperation in the fight against terrorism.

Growing Antagonism

To the Saudi government, bin Laden's use of Saudi citizens in the attack was a calculated, cunning effort to drive a wedge between it and the

As crown prince, Abdullah assumed leadership after King Fahd's stroke, and by the new century he was the de facto ruler. (Courtesy of the Saudi Information Office)

United States. As bin Laden's goal was toppling the ruling family, ending U.S. support for the Saudi regime was critical, and anything that created a rift was a victory in its own right. But in the United States, the large percentage of Saudis involved was viewed as proof of the kingdom's true anti-Americanism.

The attack brought long-festering antagonisms between the two nations to the fore. The Saudis were blamed for exporting an intolerant brand of Islam and donating large sums to groups that supported ter-

276

rorism. The United States was blamed for its unbending support for Israel, which was seen as the root cause of the attacks. Prince Alwaleed bin Talal, son of the founder of the Free Princes movement, came to New York to express his sympathy and offered a $10 million donation for the victims, along with advice for the United States to rethink its Middle East policy. New York mayor Rudolph Giuliani rejected the advice and the $10 million donation, and the episode came to represent the vast gulf that had suddenly opened between the two longtime allies.

War in Afghanistan

On September 14, the day after U.S. secretary of state Colin Powell named Osama bin Laden as the prime suspect in masterminding the attacks, the U.S. Congress approved the use of military force against those responsible. Less than a week later U.S. troops began deploying to the Persian Gulf region, Diego Garcia, Uzbekistan, and Tajikistan, all within striking distance of Afghanistan, where bin Laden was known to be based under the protection of the Wahhabi-styled Taliban. On September 20 Bush demanded that the Taliban turn over bin Laden to U.S. authorities. Saudi Arabia, one of only three nations still maintaining diplomatic relations with the regime, used its contacts within the Taliban to press, unsuccessfully, for their surrendering of the fugitive terrorist. Saudi Arabia severed diplomatic relations with the Taliban by the end of the month.

In some quarters in Saudi Arabia, years of resentment and anger directed at the United States, and fed primarily by its support for Israel, found outlet in feelings of justification and satisfaction in the attack. In November a survey of educated Saudis aged 25 to 40 conducted by the Ministry of the Interior found 90 percent of respondents expressed some degree of support for bin Laden. Yet at the same time, the great majority did not believe bin Laden was responsible for the attack. The lack of public condemnation of bin Laden or support for the United States was cited as one reason the regime did not support U.S. intervention in Afghanistan.

On October 7 the United States commenced Operation Enduring Freedom with a bombing campaign directed against Taliban and al-Qaeda positions in Afghanistan. Though publicly the kingdom refused to allow its facilities to be used in the operation, or for attacks on any Arab state, the air campaign was directed from a newly completed Combined Air Operations Center at Prince Sultan Air Base. Five weeks later, November 12, the Northern Alliance, an opposition Afghan force with which the

United States was allied, captured Kabul. On November 18, with punishing air strikes continuing, the Taliban announced it would no longer provide sanctuary to bin Laden. With the December 6 capture of Khandahar, the Taliban stronghold, by Northern Alliance forces, the regime and organized resistance ended. Hamid Karzai was sworn in as the interim prime minister of Afghanistan on December 22. In the aftermath of the fighting in Afghanistan, relations between Saudi Arabia and the United States were further strained by U.S. detention of Arab prisoners of war, many of whom were reportedly Saudi nationals, at Camp X-ray, a prison camp constructed at the Guantánamo Bay Naval Station in Cuba.

Financial Control, Damage Control

Oversight of charitable organizations and contributions became a key issue between the Saudi government and agencies concerned about the use of charitable contributions to fund terrorist activity. In Islam, charity is one of the pillars of faith, and giving money to Islamic causes has long been seen as a sign of piety. Wealthy Saudis were suspected of supporting extremist activity through charities that served as front organizations or as conduits to fund terrorism. These charges were denied or played down by the Saudi Arabian government.

In March of 2002, Saudi Arabia and the United States blocked accounts of the Somali and Bosnian branch offices of the Saudi-based Al-Haramain Islamic Foundation, which was believed to be supporting terrorist activities and organizations. In a difficult battle for hearts and minds, the kingdom also funded a public relations effort in the United States through Qorvis Communications that included TV and radio advertisements urging the public to keep an open mind about the kingdom. The United States, meanwhile, tried to develop a public relations campaign to change opinions about America in Saudi Arabia, a campaign that floundered and saw the resignation of the advertising executive hired to lead the project in 2003.

In August of 2002 a group of some 600 family members of victims of the September 11 attacks filed a $1 trillion lawsuit in the United States against the Bin Laden Group, various Saudi government officials, members of the royal family, the government of Sudan, and other parties, accusing them of complicity in the deaths through their alleged financial support of terrorists. The legal action brought strong condemnation from within the kingdom.

In October of 2002, NATO-led troops in Sarajevo raided the Saudi High Commission for Relief, a charitable foundation of the Saudi

Arabian government that had spent more than $560 million in Bosnia. The organization was founded in 1993 by Prince Salman, one of Ibn Saud's sons. Authorities found photos of U.S. military installations and government buildings as well as computer files with information on crop-dusting aircraft and on producing fraudulent State Department ID badges. A Saudi government spokesman denied the charity was involved in any illegitimate activity.

In December of 2002 the government established a high commission for oversight of all charities and unveiled measures aimed at stopping the flow of funds to terrorists. It required all Saudi charities to undergo audits and created a financial intelligence unit to investigate money laundering. Additionally the government froze 33 bank accounts containing some $5.5 million. At the height of public attention on this issue it was reported that part of a $2,000 charitable contribution from Prince Bandar's wife had gone to two of the September 11 hijackers. No evidence of her knowledge of the misappropriation of the donation was found; the check had apparently been signed over by its recipient. To Saudis, the incident demonstrated the difficulty of policing all funds made in good faith. In the United States many saw it as further proof that Saudi Arabia's elite funded terrorism.

The Saudi government also mandated that banks and departments participate in international seminars and symposia on combating terrorist financing activities. As part of the Financial Action Task Force (FATF) created by the G-7 nations in 1988, Saudi Arabia has implemented the 40 FATF recommendations on preventing money laundering and eight special recommendations on preventing the financing of terrorists. The Saudi Arabian Monetary Authority (SAMA) shares information with other financial authorities and law enforcement agencies. Saudi Arabia is also a signatory of the International Convention for Suppression and Financing of Terrorism based on UN Security Council Resolution 1373.

In other steps, the Saudi government questioned more than 2,000 individuals, many veterans of fighting in Afghanistan, Bosnia, and Chechnya, about their activities. Saudi Arabia also extradited suspected al-Qaeda members from the Sudan and Iran and asked Interpol to arrest 750 people, 214 of them Saudi nationals, for suspected involvement in terrorist activities, money laundering, and other illegal activities.

Abdullah's Peace Plan

The seemingly intractable Palestinian-Israeli conflict had spun even more out of control in the wake of President Clinton's failed final effort to broker a peace agreement between the two sides and the second intifada, which began in September of 2000. A resolution of the situation became more important when viewed as a critical element of the global terrorism equation. After years of refusing to consider establishing relations with Israel, Prince Abdullah led an Arab policy reversal, advancing a plan for peace that included recognition of Israel. At a summit of the Arab League in Beirut in March 2002, Prince Abdullah proposed a plan for peace, calling for Israel's withdrawal to its pre-1967 war borders in return for full peace and security guarantees from Arab League states. The basic plan was first advanced in a column by *New York Times* reporter Thomas L. Friedman. In a later interview with the reporter, prior to the Arab League meeting, Abdullah said that he had been working on a proposal that was "virtually identical" to Friedman's, and an account of their conversation became a trial balloon of sorts by which the prince's peace plan was first floated.

However, the plan Friedman had suggested included no provisions for Palestinian refugees. After negotiations regarding Abdullah's plan among Arab League members at the Beirut gathering, the resulting Beirut Declaration called in part for Israeli agreement to deal with the refugee issue in accordance with UN General Assembly Resolution 194. Arabs generally regard this resolution as allowing for the right of return of the refugees to their homeland, which Israel has consistently opposed. Also, due to pressure from Syria, Abdullah changed his initial proposal for the "normalization" of relations, with its connotation of trade and tourism links, to simply "normal" relations.

Before the Arab League gathering ended, a series of terrorist bombings in Israel and reprisals conducted in the West Bank derailed the peace initiative. By the time the meeting concluded, PLO chairman Yasir Arafat was under siege in his headquarters in Ramallah, surrounded by Israeli tanks. The United States asked the Saudis to press Arafat to rein in the suicide attacks and agree to concessions for the sake of peace.

In April 2002 Crown Prince Abdullah traveled to Crawford, Texas, to visit President Bush at his ranch. He presented an eight-point plan to achieve a cease-fire between the Israelis and Palestinians and restart the peace process. But the lack of a joint statement from the two heads of state at the conclusion of the talks evidenced the large divide between them.

War in Iraq

As the War on Terror took primacy in U.S. foreign policy, Washington focused new attention on regimes held to support or sponsor terrorism,

REFORMING "THE ARAB CONDITION"

When viewed against a panorama of the community of nations, those in the Arab world suffer by comparison. A report commissioned by the United Nations, the Arab Human Development Report 2002, concluded that a lack of political freedom, repression of women, and isolation from free inquiry were leading to stagnation of Arab societies. Stagnant economies, lack of basic freedoms, little recourse to due process, and woefully backward cultures and societies were endemic. While Saudi Arabia's fortunes were much better than most, the litany of problems resonated even in the kingdom among those with a clear-eyed view of the situation. The crown prince had already spoken out publicly and forcefully about the kingdom's own need for self-examination. Now he addressed needs of the Arab world as a whole. In January of 2003, Saudi Arabia published a "Charter for Reform of the Arab Condition," outlining a suggested course of action for Arab League member states to end the stagnation of their societies and economies. The proposals called for, among other things, representative governments. The Saudis have proposed implementing them in the monarchy by allowing elected representatives in the Consultative Council.

Other regimes in the peninsula were taking similar action. Kuwait has long had a parliament, and Bahrain had recently restored its parliament. Qatar was drafting a constitution that would lead to the creation of a parliament. Oman established a consultative council chosen in part by local elections.

epitomized in President Bush's declaration of an "Axis of Evil" comprising Iraq, Iran, and North Korea. His aggressive efforts to confront Iraq's president Saddam Hussein for his defiance of the UN further damaged Saudi relations with the United States. Under the terms of surrender that ended the first Persian Gulf War, Iraq had agreed to allow UN weapons inspectors to search for and ensure the removal of weapons of mass destruction, believed to be primarily biological and chemical agents. But in 1998 Iraq announced it was ending cooperation with UNSCOM, the United Nations Special Commission, which conducted the inspections, and later that year Iraq took down the monitoring devices deployed at potential production sites. Inspections resumed in 1998, but inspectors left in December of that year, citing lack of cooperation from the Iraqis.

Under renewed U.S. pressure, Iraq allowed the inspectors to return in 2003. After charging the Iraqis with continuing to conceal weapons, the United States sought support for military action from the UN. Failing to gain international backing, the United States forged a coalition with partners including Britain, Australia, Spain, Poland, and Bulgaria. Under a new policy of preemptive engagement, Bush, citing the threat posed by the weapons and acquisition programs, announced his intention to remove Saddam Hussein's regime from power.

Unlike the first Persian Gulf War, which caused division among Saudis regarding the need for a foreign military presence, war against Iraq was universally condemned in Saudi Arabia and throughout the Arab World. The Bush administration's disengagement from the peace process and support for Israel and its right-wing prime minister, Ariel Sharon, stoked opposition from a public already inflamed by daily images of the Intifada and convinced that anti-Muslim sentiment and thirst for oil drove U.S. policy. Additionally, in the eyes of the patriarchal societies of the Middle East, George W. Bush was seen as hungry to vanquish the foe, Hussein, who had tried to kill his father, George Bush, after the first Gulf War failed to dislodge him from power.

On March 19, 2003, Operation Iraqi Freedom was launched with an air strike on a complex where Saddam Hussein and his sons were believed to be. An invasion by U.S. and British ground forces soon followed. The war as seen in Saudi Arabia was carried on Arab television networks such as Al Jazeera, Abu Dhabi TV, and Arabiya, which concentrated on civilian casualties, often captured in graphic footage. An editorial in a Saudi newspaper complained that U.S. television coverage was focused only on military movements instead of the casualties of their operations.

By April 9 most of Baghdad was under the control of U.S. forces, and on April 15 U.S. Marines claimed control of Tikrit, the last stronghold of Saddam's loyalists. On May 1, aboard the aircraft carrier USS *Lincoln,* the president declared that the major combat was over. The warfare and subsequent looting left the country ravaged, and no weapons of mass destruction were found after offensive operations ended. As insurgency and terrorist actions took a rising toll on both foreign and Iraqi targets during this time, the Bush administration made efforts to hasten the transfer of authority from U.S. to Iraqi leadership. The final impact of the war on Iraq, Saudi Arabia, and the region remains to be determined. However, in an indication of the estrangement of the alliance with the United States and the Saudi public's opposition to it, following the war the United States announced that all its military forces would leave Saudi Arabia.

Terrorists Strike the Kingdom

Saudi Arabia itself became a terrorist target in May of 2003, when four car bombs driven by suicide attackers were set off in Riyadh. Though the targets were primarily apartment complexes housing foreign workers, many of the 34 killed were Muslims and Saudi citizens. The investigation revealed that several of the perpetrators had escaped a raid staged a week before the attacks in which Saudi security forces seized hundreds of pounds of explosives along with weapons. In the wake of the bombing the government exhibited an increased determination to grapple with the problem. This included promulgating pictures of suspects, a tactic the regime, ever eager to present the kingdom as stable and without internal security problems, had never taken. Clerics were instructed to condemn the attacks, the perpetrators, and terrorism conducted in the name of Islam at Friday prayers.

The attacks further strained relations with the United States when it was disclosed that the Saudis had failed to enhance security at the residential compounds sufficiently, despite requests and specific warnings from U.S. intelligence services that these sites were targets.

In November of 2003, a suicide car bomb attack believed orchestrated by al-Qaeda killed 17 people and injured hundreds at a residential compound in Riyadh catering to non-Saudi Arabs working in the kingdom. The attack signaled that even Muslims were fair game in the view of the terrorists, whose goal was thought to be the destabilization and destruction of the Saudi regime.

Domestic Issues

Going forward, Saudi Arabia's economy, educational system, stance on the rights of its citizens, and even issues of succession within the monarchy, all present significant challenges for the kingdom.

The Economy Today

Oil continues to drive the Saudi Arabian economy. Some 90–95 percent of export earnings, 70–80 percent of state revenues, and 40–55 percent of the state's gross domestic product (GDP) come from oil. The oil income, which in the 1970s and early 1980s produced revenues of almost $24,000 per person annually, had fallen to $6,000–7,000 by 2001.

Seeking to exploit its underdeveloped natural gas resources, in March of 2004, the kingdom announced an agreement with Russian and Chinese energy companies (Lukoil and Sinopec, respectively) for limited

Many Saudis try to retain connection to a past that seems threatened on all sides. These national guard soldiers in traditional dress wield their swords at a heritage festival. (Courtesy of the Saudi Information Office)

natural gas exploration in Saudi Arabia, the first such contract signed with foreign companies in three decades. This followed the collapse of a tentative agreement with U.S. company Exxon Mobil the preceding year.

Agriculture accounts for about 6 percent of GDP. Government spending, which includes utilities, health care, education, and the national airline, accounts for some 24 percent of economic activity. About 40 percent of the country's economy is classified as in the private sector. Economic reform and privatization are viewed as essential, but the state has not moved aggressively in this area. State-owned entities have not yet been privatized, as had been advocated in the late 1990s.

Between 1999 and 2001 world oil prices rose, helping boost the kingdom's economic outlook. But the events of September 11 also delivered a blow to the sputtering economy as a worldwide economic downturn brought lower oil prices and revenues.

With the age of the population declining (as of 2002, 50 percent of the population was under age 18), real economic growth fell behind population growth, presenting large risks for the future stability of the country. Unemployment among 20- to 24-year-olds was 28 percent and at least 10 percent among those aged 25–29, according to estimates. Since the economy was growing more slowly than the population, new jobs could not keep pace with young graduates seeking work. For those with jobs, salaries were half of what they were during the boom years in the early 1980s, and only one-quarter of the level when adjusted for inflation.

The government has also had limited success in raising the number of Saudi nationals employed in both public and private sector jobs, which have typically been filled by foreign workers.

With no minimum wage, many jobs are taken by foreigners willing to work for little money. Saudis, furthermore, have shown a reticence for blue-collar jobs. Under the government's "Saudization" plan, by the end

EDUCATION REFORM

The curriculum of Saudi schools, developed under the supervision and approval of the ulama, has been criticized for its emphasis on inculcating Wahhabi doctrine. A 10th-grade textbook entitled *Monotheism,* from the Ministry of Education, contains anti-Christian and anti-Jewish diatribes along with bellicose interpretations of Quranic verse. On the subject of Judgment Day the book teaches, "The Hour will not come until Muslims will fight the Jews, and Muslims will kill all the Jews" (Sennott 2002).

Such texts have been taken as proof of the kingdom's anti-Western stance. But they are more a reflection of the power exercised by the ulama in shaping the educational system. Educational reforms had begun in the late 1990s, according to the government. The Saudi connection to the events of September 11 brought more external, if not internal, pressure for change. Equally troubling to some critics is the emphasis placed on rote learning, by memorization of religious passages, instead of on critical reasoning skills. The education minister, a supporter of reform, noted that this style of teaching was producing "parrots." The author of the aforementioned textbook, a noted conservative cleric, Shah Saleh Al Fawzan, responded in an interview in a Saudi newspaper, saying in part, "They say we create parrots, but they are the real parrots repeating what our enemies say of Islam" (Sennott 2002).

Whatever its failings, the system has taken a country that two generations ago had a literacy rate of 25 percent and brought the rate up to more than 75 percent today. At the post-secondary level, in 1970 some 2,500 students graduated from Saudi universities. Today some 200,000 graduate annually. Tuition is free and financial assistance is available for textbooks and other expenses.

Protection of the holy sites remains a major responsibility for the Saudi monarchy. An average of 2.3 million of the faithful make the pilgrimage to Mecca every year, making it the largest annual religious gathering on Earth. (Courtesy of Samia El-Moslimany/*Saudi Aramco World*/PADIA)

of 2002, Saudis were mandated to compose at least 30 percent of the employees of companies with 20 or more workers. The percentage was supposed to increase by 5 percent each year. Yet with fewer than 300,000 people employed in the approximately 10,000 companies of this size, the plan was not expected to have a large impact on the economy. Barring foreign workers or mandating a minimum wage were deemed too risky to the economy, which could ill-afford higher labor costs at the time.

Labor unions are prohibited in Saudi Arabia. However, in 2001 the government approved the formation of "labor committees" in companies employing more than 100 Saudi citizens. Consisting of three to nine members, the committees can make recommendations on work conditions and processes, health and safety, and training. Foreign workers may not form or be members of such committees.

Human Rights

Human rights continue to be denied to Saudi citizens. Because the government views its version of Islamic law as the only legal code to which it is answerable, Saudi Arabia does not recognize internationally accepted definitions of human rights. Nonetheless, in 2000 the government initiated small steps to address issues that fall under the purview of such standards. On October 1, 2001, the Council of Ministers approved a law aimed at protecting detainees from mistreatment and allowing those accused of crimes to hire a lawyer or legal agent. However, implementation has been far from vigorous.

Yet, during 2001 the government tolerated a wider range of debate and criticism in the press regarding domestic issues than previously allowed. In 2000 the kingdom established a committee to investigate allegations of torture under the Convention against Torture and Other Cruel, Inhuman, or Degrading Treatment or Punishment.

The government has taken steps to rein in the power of the Committee for the Propagation of Virtue and the Prevention of Vice (*Mutawwain*), whose minister holds cabinet rank. The government promulgated guidelines for the *mutawwain* in conducting its duties in order to protect the public from the group's excesses. However, compliance has not been universal. During the first year of the new regulations, the government neither publicly criticized abuses by *mutawwain* and religious vigilantes nor sought to curtail them. The actions of the *mutawwain* included the closing of commercial establishments during the five daily prayer observances, dispersing gatherings of women in public places designated for men, as well as preventing men from entering public places designated for families.

In 2002 the *mutawwain* prevented girls from fleeing a fire in their school because they were not covered in the traditional *abaya* garb, the full body-covering garment. Fifteen girls died in the fire. In the aftermath, newspapers took the unprecedented step of criticizing the *mutawwain* in print. The tragedy also led directly to restructuring the control of girls' education, infuriating conservatives.

Women's Rights

Women have the right to own property and are entitled to financial support from their husbands or male relatives. However, they are not regarded as equal to men in the eyes of the law or society. Daughters receive half the inheritance given to sons. In a sharia court, the testimony of one man is equal to that of two women. The maternal mortality rate is twice that of Latin America and four times higher than in East Asia. Women cannot be admitted to a hospital for medical treatment without the consent of a male relative. Women may not drive and must obtain written permission from their closest male relative before they

STATE OF THE MONARCHY

King Fahd remained the titular head of state at the beginning of the 21st century. Crown Prince Abdullah retained control during his brother's infirmity. Fahd periodically appeared in newspapers and on TV, but his ability to participate in governance was unknown. Abdullah was said to consult with him regularly. Crown Prince Abdullah turned 80 in 2003. Prince Sultan ibn Abd al-Aziz, the minister of defense and aviation, is next in line for the throne after Abdullah. A conservative, he heads the Sudairi branch of the royal family. Prince Salman, the conservative governor of Riyadh who helps arbitrate disputes among the more than 5,000 princes in the royal family, is also seen as a potential successor to Abdullah, but he would not displace Sultan. Other princes discussed as possible heirs to the throne include Prince Nayef, the minister of the interior; Muhammad ibn Fahd, the governor of Eastern Province and son of the stricken king; and another son of the incapacitated monarch, Abd al-Aziz ibn Fahd, the minister of state. The selection of the ruler to follow Crown Prince Abdullah—or who takes the throne in his stead— will likely be a contentious decision, pitting conservative members of the royal family against those with a more secularist agenda, and it will have enormous implications for both the state and all those who have dealings with Saudi Arabia.

can travel inside or leave the country. In November of 2001 the government began allowing women to obtain their own identity cards, but they must first receive written permission from their nearest male relative. Under Saudi divorce laws, fathers have automatic custody of their children after infancy.

Religious Freedoms

Religious divisions continue to cause unrest. In April 2000, in Najran near the Yemeni border, members of the Makarama Ismaili Shia rioted, and an armed group of Shia attacked the hotel housing the office of the regional governor. Gun battles with security forces ensued. The government, while denying the unrest was caused by religious tension, reported that five members of the security forces were killed. No casualties among the public were reported, though local opposition put the number at 40.

The Hanbali interpretation of the sharia holds that judges may discount the testimony of non-Muslim witnesses or of Muslims not adhering to prescribed doctrine. Shia in Saudi Arabian courts have had their testimony ruled inadmissible as a result. The government discouraged travel of Shia to Iran, requiring government permission for such trips. However, it has been reported that the government has lifted the requirement for prior permission for such trips. Travel to Iraq requires government permission.

Public displays of non-Muslim religious practices are prohibited. The government has publicly stated its policy of protecting the right of non-Muslims to worship privately, but guidelines defining public and private worship do not exist, and instances of arbitrary enforcement have been reported. The government claims any such instances as acts contrary to its policy.

A religious movement within the already austere Wahhabism of Saudi Arabia is demanding an even more conservative religious shift. The conservatives have a powerful voice that constrains the government. This partly explains the government's reluctance to take stronger action against charities identified as supporting terrorism. Calls from the United States for stronger action give more power to the conservatives, who criticize the government for being subservient to the United States.

The Coming Years

Some members of the royal family see more openness and public participation in government as an antidote to the religious fundamentalism and militancy that afflict the kingdom. In October of 2003, Saudi Arabia announced it would hold its first elections, with candidates running for seats on local councils. Though no date for elections was set, Crown Prince Abdullah ordered the government to complete preparations for the voting within a year. This was not the first time the government had promised democratic reforms. In 1975, for example, the government issued a law to allow the formation of municipal councils, but these representative bodies were never instituted. Whether more dramatic moves toward democracy lie ahead, and how these changes may affect the monarchy and its opposition, remains unknown.

But even as it moves toward the future, Saudi Arabia's tribal roots are clearly visible. The allegiance to one's clan as the defining social unit of society is exemplified by the royal family. The patriarchal society of its past is seen in the strictures that prevent women from driving and hinder their employment and educational opportunities. So, too, is the historical wariness of outsiders, which today keeps foreigners out through laws that restrict access to the kingdom by those who would come for business or pleasure and that at times frustrated investigators trying to work with Saudi officials to combat terrorist activities. The countervailing current of the culture's famed hospitality can be seen in the warm welcome visitors receive within Saudi homes. The pre-Islamic ideal of the heroic and noble Bedouin is also still strong, seen in the huge crowds that attend heritage festivals celebrating the kingdom's ancient traditions. Perhaps it is this code of honor and the famed ability of its desert dwellers to endure hardships and travail that holds the most promise for the kingdom's tomorrows, for surely the path ahead will be rough and fraught with obstacles.

Whatever challenges the kingdom faces and whatever configuration the state takes in years to come, it is likely to wield power and influence for the foreseeable future due to its role in the world energy market, the influence of its wealth, and the moral authority it continues to enjoy among Muslims as the homeland of their religion. The nature of its future relationship with the United States and the West is less certain. The outcome of the internal struggle between voices of conservatism and modernization is also unknown. However, a greater understanding of the complexities and realities of the political and social structures underpinning the state will enhance the prospects for mutually beneficial ties with Saudi Arabia among all those seeking its cooperation in securing peace and stability in the Middle East and around the world.

Appendix 1

Glossary

abaya   a black garment worn by women that covers the entire body. It is expected to be worn in public

adhan   the call to prayers, performed by a muezzin

A.H.   after the Hegira; the reference used in the Islamic calendar, marking Muhammad's emigration from Mecca to Medina

Allah   Arabic for "the God"

Amir al-Muminin   "commander of the faithful"; the title of the caliph, in his role as leader of the Islamic community

Ansar   the "helpers"; the name for those citizens of Yathrib who first accepted Muhammad and Islam when he and his followers moved to their city, which was later renamed Medina

bida   innovation, or departure from custom (sunnah) in Islam; regarded as heresy

caliph   the leader of the Islamic Empire; from *khalifa*, Arabic for "successor"

emir (amir)   a chieftain or ruler; from the Arabic word *amir*, meaning "commander"

fatwa   official ruling by a religious authority

fiqh   jurisprudence, the study of sharia, or Islamic law

Five Pillars of Islam   five practices that define the duties of the faithful Muslim: *shahada* (testimony of faith), *salat* (daily prayer), *zakat* (almsgiving), *sawm* (fasting during Ramadan), hajj (pilgrimage to Mecca)

ghazu   raid or warfare between Bedouin tribes

hadith   the sayings of Muhammad, upon which much Islamic law is based

hajj the pilgrimage or rite of going to Mecca; one of the Five Pillars of Islam

Hegira the year of Muhammad's emigration from Mecca to Medina; the Muslim calendar begins at this date

hujar the settlements created by Ibn Saud to house formerly nomadic Bedouin communities from which his military forces were drawn

Ikhwan "the brotherhood"; the Bedouin army that Ibn Saud created, drawn from the formerly nomadic tribesmen who settled in *hujar*

imam the spiritual leader of the community, a title traditionally claimed by Saudi rulers from the late 18th century until the reign of the kingdom's founder, Ibn Saud, who preferred the more temporal titles of sultan and king; also an honorific bestowed on eminent Islamic scholars. For the Shia, *imam* refers to Ali or any of his descendants recognized as leaders of Islam

Jahiliyya time of ignorance before Muhammad

jihad striving; refers to both the personal struggle for holiness and holy war against infidels

madrassa a school for Islamic studies

majlis traditional gathering where leaders meet their subjects and visitors, who come for mediation and supplication

mosque a place where Muslims gather for communal worship

Muhajirun the "emigrants," who came to Medina with Muhammad after his move from Mecca in 622

Muslim an adherent of Islam; literally, "one who submits" to the will of Allah/God

mutawwain the "volunteers"; the name given to those on the Committee for the Propagation of Virtue and Prevention of Vice, who assure compliance with Wahhabi strictures in public. In non-Islamic countries they are referred to vernacularly as religious police

qadi an Islamic judge or magistrate

qibla the direction or orientation toward Mecca that Muslims face during their daily prayers

qiyas a practice of Islamic law, using analogy to determine answers to legal issues not defined by existing Islamic law

Quran the book of Allah's revelations as brought forth by Muhammad; literally, the "recitation"

salat   prayer performed five times daily; it is one of Islam's Five Pillars

sawm   fasting performed during the month of Ramadan

shahada   the Muslim profession of faith: "There is no god but Allah, Muhammad is his Messenger"; one of the Five Pillars of Islam

sharia   Islamic law; based on the Quran, the hadith, and tribal and customary law

sharif   the ruler of Mecca; all sharifs were descendants of Muhammad's family, the Quraysh, though no formal means of succession existed

sheikh   the chief of a tribe or village; a term of respect and veneration for an older man or a senior cleric; from the Arabic *shaykh,* old man

Shia   one of the two major branches of Islam (Sunni being the other); the Shia recognize descendants of Ali, Muhammad's cousin, as the rightful leaders of the Islamic community

sultan   the sovereign ruler of a Muslim country, especially of the former Ottoman Empire; from the Arabic *sultan,* which means "ruk"

sunnah   custom, conduct, or practice as determined by the words and deeds of Muhammad as related by those who knew him

Sunni   the larger of the two major branches of Islam; the Sunni reject Shia claims of the divine right of Ali's descendants to leadership of the Islamic community, believing that they are the true followers of the sunnah, or customary behavior called for by Muhammad; Wahhabis, the followers of Saudi Arabia's conservative form of Islam, are Sunni

tafrah   upswing or leap; in Saudi Arabia it refers to the post–Oil Embargo boom years

ulama or ulema (sing. *alim*)   religious scholars who rule on points of law

ummah   the Muslim community, either local or global

urf   common law or custom

Wahhabi   a follower of the teachings of Muhammad ibn Abd al-Wahhab, a cleric who founded a conservative school of Islamic observance upon which the kingdom's theocracy is based; Wahhabi regard themselves as simply Muslims

zakat   alms; the tithing of one's money for the poor; one of the Five pillars of Islam

Appendix 2

Basic Facts About Saudi Arabia

Official Name
Kingdom of Saudi Arabia (Al Mamlakah al Arabiyah as Saudiyah)

Geography

Area	757,000 square miles (1,960,582 sq km); slightly more than one-fifth the size of the United States. It occupies about 80 percent of the Arabian Peninsula, the world's largest such landmass.
Land borders	Yemen, Oman, Qatar, United Arab Emirates, Jordan, Iraq, Kuwait.
Coastal borders	Red Sea, Persian Gulf
Elevations	Highest: Jabal Sawda', 10,279 feet (3,133 m)
Terrain	Mostly uninhabited, sandy desert. Mountains along west coast, broad plains on the east coast. No rivers or navigable waters exist within the country.

Government
Founded on September 23, 1932, Saudi Arabia is a hereditary monarchy. The king leads the executive branch and serves as both chief of state and head of government. There are no elections and no political parties are sanctioned. The kingdom is governed in accordance with sharia (Islamic law). A Basic Law adopted in 1993 defines the government's rights and responsibilities, and formalizes the Quran and the Sunna (traditions of the prophet Muhammad) as the kingdom's constitution. A Council of Ministers, formed in 1953, whose members are appointed by the monarch and include many royal family members, oversees the drafting and implementation of state policies and legislation. A Consultative Council (Majlis Al-Shura) established in 1993,

made up of 120 members and a Speaker appointed by the monarch to four-year terms, advises the king on matters of governance. A religious council headed by a Supreme Council of Justice also advises the king on proposed laws and legislative issues. Commercial disputes are settled by special committees. There is no suffrage.

Political Divisions

Capital	Riyadh (Population: 4.5 million)
Other Cities	Mecca, Medina, Jeddah, Dhahran
Subdivisions	13 provinces

People

Population	24,293,844 (includes 5,576,076 non-nationals, July 2003 est.)
Growth rate	3.27 percent
Ethnic groups	Arab, 90 percent; Afro-Asian, 10 percent
Languages	Arabic
Religions	Muslim 100 percent
Literacy	(Ability to read and write at age 15) 78 percent
Age structure	0–14 years: 42.3 percent (male 5,245,413; female 5,028,595); 15–64 years: 54.8 percent (male 7,700,121; female 5,622,099); 65 years and over: 2.9 percent (male 393,173; female 304,443)
Median age	total: 18.8 years
	male: 20.9 years
	female: 16.8 years (2002 est.)
Population growth rate	3.27 percent
Birth rate	37.2 births/1,000 population
Death rate	5.79 deaths/1,000 population
Sex ratio	At birth: 1.05 male(s)/female
	under 15 years: 1.04 male(s)/female
	15–64 years: 1.37 male(s)/female
	65 years and over: 1.29 male(s)/female
	Total population: 1.22 male(s)/female (2003 est.)
Infant mortality rate	Total: 47.94 deaths/1,000 live births
	female: 45.67 deaths/1,000 live births (2003 est.)
	male: 50.1 deaths/1,000 live births

Life expectancy at birth	Total population: 68.73 years
	Male: 66.99 years
	Female: 70.55 years
Total fertility rate	6.15 children born/woman (2003 est.)

Economy

Petroleum is the foundation of Saudi Arabia's economy, accounting for roughly 75 percent of budget revenues, 45 percent of gross domestic product (GDP), and 90 percent of export earnings. About 25 percent of GDP comes from the private sector. The government exercises strong control over major economic activities but is expected to seek increased private-sector growth to lessen the kingdom's dependence on oil and provide employment for the rapidly expanding Saudi population. In 1999 an 11-member Supreme Economic Council was formed, charged with overseeing and regulating the kingdom's economy. That same year the government announced plans to begin privatizing electricity companies. Privatization of the kingdom's telecommunications company was also undertaken. The government is also involved in efforts to build the kingdom's agricultural industry. However, shortages of water and rapid population growth constrain its ability to increase self-sufficiency in agricultural products. Some 4 million foreign workers play an important role in the Saudi economy, primarily in the oil and service sectors.

GDP	$242 billion purchasing power parity (2002 est.)
GDP real growth rate	0.6 percent (2002 est.)
GDP per capita	$10,500 purchasing power parity (2002 est.)
Natural resources	Petroleum, natural gas, iron ore, gold, copper
Arable land	1.72 percent
Permanent crops	0.06 percent
Irrigated land	16,200 square kilometers (1998 est.)
Economic sectors	
Agriculture	5.6 percent of GDP
Industry	51.2 percent of GDP
Services	43.6 percent of GDP
Agriculture	Wheat, barley, tomatoes, melons, dates, citrus, mutton, chickens, eggs, milk
Industries	Crude oil production, petroleum refining, basic petrochemicals, cement, construction, fertilizer, plastics

Services	Financial
Major exports	Petroleum and petroleum products
Labor force	7 million
By occupation (1998 est.)	
Agriculture	12 percent
Industry	25 percent
Services	63 percent

Environmental Issues

Desertification, depletion of underground water resources, coastal pollution from oil spills

Transnational Issues

Nomadic groups on border region with Yemen resist demarcation of boundary; Kuwait and Saudi Arabia have been negotiating a long-contested maritime boundary with Iran; the treaties not having been made public, the exact alignment of the boundary with the UAE is still unknown and labeled approximate

Data, except where otherwise noted, reflect information as of August 2003

Sources: *CIA World Factbook,* 2003, and the government of Saudi Arabia

Appendix 3

Chronology

Arabia: The Land and Its Pre-Islamic History

ca. 20–25 million B.C.	formation of the Arabian Peninsula
pre 13,000 B.C.	human settlement of Arabian Peninsula
ca. 8000 B.C.	agriculture and permanent settlements develop in Arabia
ca. 3200–1600 B.C.	Dilmun civilization in eastern Arabia
ca. 2000–1500 B.C.	first form of writing in Arabia
ca. 1500–1000 B.C.	domestication of camel
ca. 900 B.C.–A.D. 542	Sabaean civilization in southern Arabia
ca. 420 B.C.–A.D. 105	Nabatean kingdom in northern Arabia
853 B.C.	first reference to the Arabs in an inscription of the Assyrian Shalmaneser III
44 B.C.	assassination of Julius Caesar destabilizes Arabian frontier
24 B.C.	Roman Aelius Gallus mounts expedition to South Arabia
A.D. 542	collapse of the Marib dam

The Birth of Islam (571–632)

ca. 570	Muhammad born in Mecca
595	marriage of Muhammad to Khadija
610	Muhammad's first revelation at Mount Hira
ca. 613	Muhammad begins preaching the message of Islam
615	persecution of Muslims by Quraysh
619	death of Muhammad's wife Khadija and uncle, Abu Talib
620	Muhammad's Night Journey

622	Hegira, Muhammad's emigration from Mecca to Yathrib (later renamed Medina)
624	Muslim victory at the Battle of Badr
627	Battle of the Ditch; Muslims withstand Meccan siege at Medina
628	Muhammad reaches Truce of Hudaibiya with Mecca
630	Muhammad's conquest of Mecca
632	death of Muhammad

The Islamic Empire and Arabia (632–1258)

632–661	reign of the four "rightly guided" caliphs at Medina
632–634	Abu Bakr caliphate
634–644	Umar caliphate
636	Battle of Yarmuk; Muslims defeat Byzantines
644–656	Uthman caliphate
ca. 653	Uthman standardizes the Quran
656–661	Ali caliphate
656	Muslim civil war; Battle of the Camel; Revolt of Muawiya in Syria
657	Ali moves caliphate to Kufa; Ali and Muawiya battle at Siffin
661	assassination of Ali by Kharijites
661–750	Umayyad caliphate in Damascus
680	martyrdom of Ali's son Husayn at Karbala
687–691	Dome of the Rock built in Jerusalem
750	defeat of Marwan II at the Battle of Great Zab; end of the Umayyad dynasty
750–1258	Abbasid caliphate at Baghdad

The Golden Age of Islam (ca. 750–1258)

ca. 750–850	Epoch of Translation reintroduces classical works to the world
832	Mamun founds House of Wisdom in Baghdad
ca. 850	Al Khwarizmi publishes astronomical tables
786–809	reign of Harun al-Rashid, high point of Islamic Golden Age
ca. 861	Mamluks control the caliphate
866	oldest paper Arabic manuscript

930	Carmathians attack Mecca and steal the Black Stone from the Kaaba
ca. 942	"Thousand Nights and a Night" appears in Arabic
ca. 967	sharifs gain leadership of Mecca
969	Fatimids take control of Cairo, gaining authority over Hijaz
1037	Seljuks become the power behind the Abbasid caliphate
1107–1291	a succession of European armies attack the Holy Lands under the banner of the Crusades
1250	Mamluks seize power from Ayyubid dynasty
1258	Mongols destroy Baghdad; end of the Abbasid caliphate and the Arab Islamic Empire

The Mamluks, Ottomans, and the Wahhabi-Al Saud Alliances (1258–1745)

1260	Mamluks defeat Mongols
1270	Abu Numayy consolidates rule of Mecca
1425	Mamluks establish direct oversight of Meccan rule
ca. 1446	Al Saud ancestors found Diriya, capital of the first Saudi state
1507	Portuguese fleet captures Hormuz, establishes Arabian outposts
1517	Ottomans defeat Mamluks, establish authority in Hijaz
1541	Portuguese attack Jeddah
1550	Ottomans capture Hufuf
1578	the sharif dispatches forces against Najd
1591	Ottomans establish authority in Hasa
1669	Banu Khalid revolt and drive Ottomans from Hasa
1744	Muhammad ibn Abd al-Wahhab moves to Diriya

The First Saudi State (1745–1818)

1744	Abd al-Wahhab and Muhammad ibn Saud form alliance
ca. 1744–1800	Saudi-Wahhabi forces fight for control of Najd
1762	Muhammad dies, succeeded by son Abd al-Aziz ibn Saud

1773	Saudi-Wahhabi alliance gains control of Riyadh
1792	Abd al-Wahhab dies, Saud becomes imam
1794	Al Saud forces capture Hasa
1798	Al Saud forces defeat Sharif Ghalib forces near Khurmah
1798	Ottomans launch offensive against Saudi-Wahhabi forces; French invade Egypt
1801–1802	Saudi-Wahhabi forces attack Karbala
1802	Saudi-Wahhabi emirate expands in Hijaz
1803	Abd al-Aziz ibn Saud assassinated, succeeded by son, Saud
1804–1805	Medina recognizes Saudi authority
1811	Muhammad Ali's Egyptian forces land in Hijaz
1813–1814	Egyptian forces end Saudi-Wahhabi rule in Hijaz
1814	Saud dies, succeeded by son Abdullah
1815	main Wahhabi army defeated by Egyptians
1818	Egyptian forces sack Diriya, ending the first Saudi state

Roots of Modern Arabia (1818–1891)

1818	British try to form alliance with Egyptians against Saudi-Wahhabi forces
1820	Egyptian force arrives in Najd to suppress renewed Saudi activity
1824	Turki ibn Abdullah reestablishes Saudi rule in Riyadh
1830	Saudi rule expands into Hasa
1834	Turki assassinated; Turki's son Faysal becomes amir/imam in Riyadh
1835	Faysal appoints Abdullah ibn Rashid as governor of Hail
1837–1838	Faysal captured by Egyptians and sent to Cairo
1840	Egyptian forces leave Najd
1843	after escape, Faysal returns to Riyadh and regains control of Najd
1864–1865	Faysal dies; his sons battle for leadership
1868	appointment of Midhat Pasha as governor-general of Baghdad leads to Ottoman expansion into Arabian Peninsula
1871	the Ottomans occupy Hasa and Asir

1871	Muhammad ibn Rashid captures Hasa from Al Saud
1889	Abd al-Rahman ibn Faysal assumes leadership of Al Saud, ejects Al Rashid from control of Riyadh
1891	the Rashidis (Muhammad ibn Rashid) defeat the Saudis and end their rule in Riyadh and of the second Saudi state

Unity and Independence (1891–1932)

1893	Saudis receive sanctuary in Kuwait
1902	Ibn Saud captures Riyadh
1903	Ibn Saud takes the title, "Sultan of Najd"
1906	Ibn Saud conquers Qasim
1908	Ibn Saud challenged by his cousins, the Araif; Ottomans "appoint" Hussein ibn Ali sharif of Mecca
1910	British political agent Capt. J. D. Shakespear meets Ibn Saud
1912	Ikhwan brotherhood founded; Ibn Saud establishes the first Ikhwan settlement
1913	Ibn Saud conquers Hasa
1915	Great Britain recognizes Ibn Saud as ruler of Najd and Hasa under Anglo-Saudi treaty
1916	Sharif Hussein proclaims Arab Revolt and declares himself king of the Arabs
1918	forces of Ibn Saud and sharif clash at Khurmah
1921	Ibn Saud takes title, "Sultan of Najd"
1922	Uqayr Protocol establishes borders between Najd, Iraq, and Kuwait
1924	Ibn Saud takes Mecca
1926	Ibn Saud is declared "King of Hijaz and Sultan of Najd and Its Dependencies"
1927	Anglo-Saudi Treaty of Jedda gives British recognition to Ibn Saud, while he recognizes their bond with gulf coast states
1927	Ikhwan revolt against Ibn Saud
1929–1930	Ibn Saud defeats the Ikhwan at Battle of Sibila
1932	Ibn Saud establishes the Kingdom of Saudi Arabia

Birth of a Kingdom (1932–1953)

1933	oil concession signed with Socal; United States and Saudi Arabia establish diplomatic relations
1934	border war with Yemen ends with Treaty of Taif that same year
1938	commercial oil production begins
1939	oil export by tanker begins
1944	California Arab Standard Oil Co. is renamed Arabian American Oil Company (Aramco)
1945	Ibn Saud and President Franklin D. Roosevelt meet; League of Arab States formed
1946	Ibn Saud visits Cairo; American air base established at Dhahran
1947	King Abdullah in Transjordan convenes Congress of Hijaz
1948	State of Israel declared; first Arab-Israeli war begins
1951	government ministries created; Tapline, oil pipeline across Saudi Arabia, completed
1952	Free Officers revolt brings Nasser to power in Egypt
1953	Council of Ministers established; first strike by Aramco workers; Ibn Saud dies

A Path to World Power (1953–1973)

1953	Saud succeeds Ibn Saud; demonstrations by Aramco workers
1954	U.S. aid mission ejected, Saud signs treaty with Nasser
1955	coup plot against King Saud uncovered
1956	Nasser nationalizes Suez Canal; riots by Aramco workers in the Eastern Province
1957	King Saud makes effort to promote Eisenhower Doctrine in the region; King Saud University, Saudi Arabia's first, opens in Riyadh; King Saud visits United States
1958	Saudi plot against Nasser revealed; Faisal takes government's reins
1960	OPEC formed; King Saud regains control over government from Crown Prince Faisal
1961	Free Princes movement begins

1962	Yemeni civil war begins; United States leaves air base at Dhahran
1964	Saud abdicates; Faisal becomes king; Palestine Liberation Organization formed
1966–1967	a series of bombs set off in Saudi Arabia by opposition groups
1967	second Arab-Israeli war; Khartoum summit ends Egyptian-Saudi differences
1969	plot against government discovered
1970	first five-year development plan inaugurated
1973	fourth Arab-Israeli war; Arab Oil Embargo; oil prices quadruple

Oil and Arms (1973–1990)

1974	Saudi Arabia threatens withdrawal from OPEC; rapprochement with United States
1975	Faisal assassinated; Khalid becomes king
1976	Saudi Arabia seeks purchase of U.S. F-15 fighter aircraft
1978	Congress approves sale of F-15 combat aircraft to Saudi Arabia
1979	siege of the Grand Mosque at Mecca; Saudi Arabia severs diplomatic relations with Egypt for signing peace agreement with Israel; Ayatollah Khomeini returns to Iran; Soviets invade Afghanistan
1979–1980	Shia unrest in Eastern Province
1980	"Fundamental Law" unveiled to give the public a greater voice in government; Iran-Iraq war begins; Aramco becomes 100% Saudi owned
1981	Gulf Cooperation Council (GCC) formed
1982	King Khalid dies; succeeded by King Fahd
1984	Saudi government provides funds for the contras in Nicaragua
1985	Saudi government participates in U.S. "arms for hostages" weapons sales
1986	oil prices decline; Fahd takes title, "custodian of the two mosques"
1987	diplomatic relations with Egypt restored; 400 Iranians die in riots during hajj

| 1988 | explosions set off at refinery in Ras Tanura and petrochemical plant in Jubayl |

The Gulf Crisis and Its Aftermath (1990–2001)

1990	Saddam Hussein invades Kuwait; Saudi women protest ban on women driving
1991	Persian Gulf War; King Fahd petitioned by both liberals and conservatives seeking reforms; government calls for end to secondary boycott of Israel
1992	Consultative Council created; "Memorandum of Advice" promulgated
1993	reform movement, Committee for the Defense of Legitimate Rights, formed in Riyadh, is declared illegal, and members lose their jobs
1994	"Buraida Uprising" protests government corruption; Osama bin Laden stripped of Saudi citizenship
1995	King Fahd suffers a stroke; Crown Prince Abdullah takes charge of the government; bombing of National Guard facility in Riyadh kills five Americans
1996	bombing of U.S. forces at Khobar Towers kills 19 U.S. soldiers
1997	fire during hajj kills more than 340 pilgrims
1999	GCC nations establish a customs union
2001	President George W. Bush's support for Israel strains U.S.-Saudi relations

The Challenges Ahead

September 11, 2001	hijacked airliners used in suicide attacks in the United States; 15 of the 19 terrorists are Saudi nationals; death toll is 2,976.
October 7, 2001	Operation Enduring Freedom begins to dislodge Taliban from power in Afghanistan
October 2001	law approved to respect judicial rights of detainees
March 2002	Crown Prince Abdullah unveils plan for Arab peace with Israel

April 2002	Abdullah meets with President Bush in Crawford, Texas
2002	Saudi government establishes high commission to stanch terrorist funding
2002	confrontation between United States, United Nations, and Iraq strains Saudi relations with United States
January 2003	Saudi Arabia publishes "Charter for Reform of the Arab Condition"
March 2003	Operation Iraqi Freedom launched
May 2003	terrorist bombings in Riyadh linked to al-Qaeda kill 35, most of them Muslims
November 2003	terrorist bombing linked to al-Qaeda targeting Muslims in Riyadh kills 17
March 2004	Natural gas exploration contracts signed with foreign firms, the first such agreements in three decades
April 2004	A suicide bombing in Riyadh leaves four people dead and 148 wounded

APPENDIX 4

BIBLIOGRAPHY

Abir, Mordehai. *Saudi Arabia: Society, Government and the Gulf Crisis.* London: Routledge, 1993.

Aburish, Said K. *The Rise, Corruption and Coming Fall of the House of Saud.* London: Bloomsbury, 1994.

Almana, Muhammed. *Arabia Unified: A Portrait of Ibn Saud.* London: Hutchinson Benham, 1980.

Al-Ali, Jasin. *An Analysis of the Financial Structure and Economic Development in Oil-Producing Countries: The Case of Saudi Arabia.* London: Gulf Centre for Strategic Studies, 1992.

Anscombe, Frederick F. *The Ottoman Gulf: The Creation of Kuwait, Saudi Arabia, and Qatar.* New York: Columbia University Press, 1997.

Beling, Willard A., ed. *King Faisal and the Modernization of Saudi Arabia.* London: Croom Helm; Boulder, Colo.: Westview Press, 1980.

Bell, Gertrude L. *The Arab War; Confidential Information for General Headquarters from Gertrude Bell.* London: Golden Cockerel Press, 1940.

Bishai, Wilson B. *Islamic History of the Middle East: Backgrounds, Development, and Fall of the Arab Empire.* Boston: Allyn and Bacon, 1968.

Bligh, Alexander. *From Prince to King: Royal Succession in the House of Saud in the 20th Century.* New York: New York University Press, 1984.

Burton, Sir Richard F. *Personal Narrative of a Pilgrimage to Al Medinah and Meccah.* London: George Bell and Sons, 1907.

Cave, Anthony Brown. *Oil, God, and Gold: The Story of ARAMCO and the Saudi Kings.* Boston: Houghton Mifflin, 1999.

Citino, Nathan J. *From Arab Nationalism to OPEC: Eisenhower, King Sa'ud, and the Making of US-Saudi Relations.* Bloomington: Indiana University Press, 2002.

Clark, Arthur C., et al., eds. *Saudi Aramco and Its World: Arabia and the Middle East.* Houston: Aramco Services, revised ed., 1995.

Dahlan, Ahmed Hassan, ed. *Politics, Administration and Development in Saudi Arabia.* Brentwood, Md.: Dar al-Shorouq, 1990.

Diodorus of Sicily. 12 vols. Loeb Classical Library. English translation by C. H. Oldfeather. New York: G.P. Putnam and Sons, 1933–67.

Doughty, Charles M. *Travels in Arabia Deserta*. London: Jonathan Cape and the Medici Society, 1926.

Doumato, Eleanor Abdella. *Getting God's Ear: Women, Islam and Healing in Saudi Arabia and the Gulf*. New York: Columbia University Press, 2000.

Dunlop, D. M. *Arab Civilization to AD 1500*. London: Longman, 1971.

Elgood, Robert. *The Arms and Armour of Arabia in the 18th, 19th and 20th Centuries*. London: Scolar, 1994.

Fandy, Mamoun. *Saudi Arabia and the Politics of Dissent*. New York: St. Martin's Press, 1999.

Friedman, Thomas L. *Longitudes and Attitudes: Exploring the World after September 11*. New York: Farrar, Straus, Giroux, 2002.

George, Linda S. *The Golden Age of Islam*. New York: Benchmark Books, 1998.

Gibb, H. A. R. *Islam*. Oxford: Oxford University Press, 1949.

Goldberg, Jacob. *The Foreign Policy of Saudi Arabia. The Formative Years, 1902–1918*. Cambridge, Mass.: Harvard University Press, 1986.

Golub, David B. *When Oil and Politics Mix: Saudi Oil Policy, 1973–1985*. Cambridge, Mass.: Harvard University, Center for Middle Eastern Studies, 1985.

Guillaume, Alfred. *The Life of Muhammad: A Translation of Ishaq's Sirat Rasul Allah*. London, New York: Oxford University Press, 1955.

———. *Traditions of Islam: An Introduction to the Study of the Hadith Literature*. Beirut: Khayat, 1966.

Hart, Parker T. *Saudi Arabia and the United States: Birth of a Security Partnership*. Bloomington: Indiana University Press, 1998.

Haykal, Muhammad Husayn. Translated by al Ismail Faruqi. *The Life of Muhammad*. 8th ed. Plainfield, Ind.: American Trust, 1995.

Henderson, Simon. *After King Fahd: Succession in Saudi Arabia*. Washington, D.C.: The Washington Institute for Near East Policy, 1994.

Hitti, Philip K. *History of the Arabs: From the Earliest Times to the Present*. London: MacMillan & Co., 1953.

———. *The Origins of the Islamic State*, a translation of *Kitab Futuh al-Buldan*. Vol. 1. New York: AMS Press, 1916, 1968.

Hodgson, Marshall G. S. *The Venture of Islam*. Vols. I, II, III. Chicago: University of Chicago Press, 1974.

Holden, David, and Richard Johns, with James Buchan. *The House of Saud: The Rise and Rule of the Most Powerful Dynasty in the Arab World*. New York: Holt, Rinehart and Winston, 1982.

Hourani, Albert. *A History of the Arab Peoples*. London: Faber, 1992.

Howarth, David A. *The Desert King: Ibn Saud and His Arabia*. New York: McGraw-Hill, 1964.

Hoyland, Robert G. *Arabia and the Arabs*. New York: Routledge, 2001.

Ibn Hishani, Abd al-Malik. *The Life of Muhammad: A Translation of Ishaq's Sirat Rasul Allah*. London: Oxford University Press, 1955.

Ibn Khaldun. *The Muqaddimah: An Introduction to History*. Translated by Franz Rosenthal; abridged and edited by N.J. Dawood. Princeton, N.J.: Princeton University Press, 1969.

Ibn Ishaq. Translated by A. Guillaume. *The Life of Muhammad*. Oxford: Oxford University Press, 1978.

Ide, Arthur Frederick. *Jihad, Mujahideen, Taliban, George W. Bush & Oil: A Study in the Evolution of Terrorism and Islam*. Garland, Texas: Tanglewild Press, 2002.

Johnson, Paul. *Civilizations of the Holy Land*. London: Weidenfeld and Nicolson, 1979.

Klein, Misha, and Adrian McIntyre, eds. *September 11: Context and Consequences; An Anthology*. Berkeley, Calif.: Copy Central, 2001.

Kostiner, Joseph. *The Making of Saudi Arabia 1916–1936*. Oxford: Oxford University Press, 1993.

Kurpershoek, P. Marcel. *Oral Poetry and Narratives from Central Arabia*. Vol. I. New York: E. J. Brill, 1994.

Lacey, Robert. *The Kingdom: Arabia and the House of Saud*. New York: Harcourt Brace Jovanovich, 1982.

Lawrence, T. E. *Seven Pillars of Wisdom, a Triumph*. Garden City, New York: Doubleday, Doran & Co., 1935.

Lea, David, ed. *A Political Chronology of the Middle East*. London: Europe Publications Limited, 2001.

Lebkicher, R., G. Rentz, M. Steneke, et al. *Aramco Handbook*. New York: Arabian American Oil Co., 1960.

Leick, Gwendolyn. *Who's Who in the Ancient Near East*. London and New York: Routledge, 1999.

Lewis, Bernard. *The Muslim Discovery of Europe*. New York: McLeod, 1982.

Maalouf, Amin. *The Crusaders through Arab Eyes*. London: Al Saqi, 1984.

Maher, Joanne, ed. *The Middle East and North Africa, 2003*. London: Europa Publications, 2002.

Mansfield, Peter. *The Arabs*. New York: Penguin Books, 1992.

McGloughlin, Leslie J. *Ibn Saud: Founder of a Kingdom*. New York: St. Martin's Press, 1993.

McNeill, William H., and Marilyn R. Waldman, eds. *The Islamic World*. New York: Oxford University Press, 1973.

Mez, Adam. *The Renaissance of Islam*. New York: AMS Press, 1937.

Moomen, Majoon. *An Introduction to Shi'a Islam*. New Haven, Conn.: Yale University Press, 1985.

Munro, Alan. *An Arabian Affair: Politics and Diplomacy behind the Gulf War.* London, Washington: Brassey's, 1996.

Myers, Eugene. *Arabic Thought and the Western World in the Golden Age of Islam.* New York: Ungar, 1964.

Nicholson, Reynold A. *A Literary History of the Arabs.* London: Cambridge University Press, 1969.

Nutting, Anthony. *Arabs, a Narrative History from Mohammad to the Present.* New York: New American Library, 1964.

Ochsenwald, William. *Religion, Society and the State in Arabia: The Hijaz, under Ottoman Control, 1840–1908.* Columbus: Ohio State University Press, 1984.

Osborn, Robert D. *Islam under the Arabs.* London: Longmans, Green, and Co., 1876.

Peters, F. E. *Allah's Commonwealth: A History of Islam in the Near East, 600–1100 A.D.* New York: Simon and Schuster, 1973.

————. *The Hajj: The Muslim Pilgrimage to Mecca and the Holy Places.* Princeton, N.J.: Princeton University Press, 1994.

————. *Mecca.* Princeton, N.J., Princeton University Press, 1994.

Peterson, J. E. *Historical Dictionary of Saudi Arabia.* Metuchen, N. J. and London: The Scarecrow Press, 1993.

Philby, H. St. John. *Sa'udi Arabia.* New York: Frederick A. Praeger, 1955

Pickthall, Marmaduke. *The Meaning of the Glorious Koran.* New York: Alfred A Knopf, 1930.

Potts, Daniel T. *The Arabian Gulf in Antiquity.* Oxford, New York: Oxford University Press, 1990.

Rahman, Fazlur. *Islam.* 2d ed. Chicago: University of Chicago Press, 1979.

Al-Rasheed, Madawi. *A History of Saudi Arabia.* Cambridge: Cambridge University Press, 2002.

————. *Politics in an Arabian Oasis: The Rashidi Tribal Dynasty.* London: I. B. Tauris, 1991.

Rashid, Nasser Ibrahim. *Saudi Arabia and the Gulf War.* Joplin, Mo.: International Institute of Technology, 1992.

Rashid, Nasser Ibrahim, and Esber Ibrahim Shaheen. *King Fahd and Saudi Arabia's Great Evolution.* Joplin, Mo.: International Institute of Technology, 1988.

Riley, Carroll L. *Historical and Cultural Dictionary of Saudi Arabia.* Metuchen, N.J.: The Scarecrow Press, 1972.

Ronart, Stephen, and Nancy Ronart. *Concise Encyclopedia of Arabic Civilization.* New York: Frederick A. Praeger, 1960.

Sadleir, George Forster. *Diary of a Journey across Arabia (1819).* Cambridge, Mass.: Oleander Press, 1977.

Saudi Arabia Ministry of Planning. *Achievements of the Development Plans, 1390–1405 (1970–1985): Facts and Figures.* Riyadh: 1406/1986.

Schippmann, Klaus. Trans. by Allison Brown. *Ancient South Arabia: From the Queen of Sheba to the Advent of Islam.* Princeton, N.J.: Markus Wiener, 2001.

Schneider, Seven A. *The Oil Price Revolution.* Baltimore: Johns Hopkins University Press, 1983.

Schwartz, Stephen. *Two Faces of Islam.* New York: Doubleday, 2002.

Sennott, Charles M. "Driving A Wedge: Saudi Schools Fuel Anti-US Anger." *Boston Globe,* March 4, 2002. Available on-line. URL: http://www.boston.com/news/packages/underattack/news/driving_a_wedge/part2.shtml. Downloaded November 15, 2002.

Shimoni, Yaacov, ed. *Biographical Dictionary of the Middle East.* New York: Facts On File, 1991.

Skeet, Ian. *OPEC: 25 Years of Prices and Politics.* Cambridge, Mass.: Cambridge University Press, 1988.

Susser, Asher, and Aryeh Shmuelevitz, eds. *The Hashemites in the Modern Arab World, Essays in Honour of the Late Professor Uriel Dann.* London: Frank Cass, 1995.

Titelbaum, Joshua. *The Rise and Fall of the Hashemite Kingdom of Arabia.* London: Hurst and Co., 2001.

Turner, Louis. *The Political and Economic Impact of Saudi Arabia's Industrialization Policies.* Oslo: Norwegian Institute of International Affairs, 1980.

Twitchell, K. S. *Saudi Arabia, with an Account of the Development of Its Natural Resources.* 3rd ed. New York: Greenwood Press, 1969.

Vassiliev, Alexei. *The History of Saudi Arabia.* New York: New York University Press, 2000.

Vogel, Frank E. *Islamic Law and Legal System: Studies of Saudi Arabia.* Leiden and Boston: Brill, 2000.

Watt, W. Montgomery. *Early Islam: Collected Articles.* Edinburgh: Edinburgh University Press, 1990.

Winder, R. Bayly. *Saudi Arabia in the Nineteenth Century.* New York: Octagon Books, 1980.

Woodward, Peter N. *Oil and Labor in the Middle East: Saudi Arabia and the Oil Boom.* New York: Praeger, 1988.

Yahya, Ahman Ibn. *The Origins of the Islamic State.* Part I. Translated by Philip Hitti. New York: AMS Press, 1968.

Young, Arthur N. *Saudi Arabia: The Making of a Financial Giant.* New York: New York University Press, 1983.

APPENDIX 5

SUGGESTED READING

Arabia: The Land and Its Pre-Islamic History

Hoyland, Robert G. *Arabia and the Arabs*. New York: Routledge, 2001.

Johnson, Paul. *Civilizations of the Holy Land*. London: Weidenfeld and Nicolson, 1979.

Potts, Daniel T. *The Arabian Gulf in Antiquity*. Oxford and New York: Oxford University Press, 1990.

Schippmann, Klaus. Translated by Allison Brown. *Ancient South Arabia: From the Queen of Sheba to the Advent of Islam*. Princeton, N.J.: Markus Wiener, 2001.

The Birth of Islam (571–632)

Haykal, Muhammad Husayn. Translated by Ismail al Faruqi. *The Life of Muhammad*. 8th ed. Plainfield, Ind.: American Trust, 1995.

Ibn Hishani, Abd al-Malik. *The Life of Muhammad: A Translation of Ishaq's Sirat Rasul Allah*. London: Oxford University Press, 1955.

Peters, F. E. *Mecca*. Princeton, N.J.: Princeton University Press, 1994.

Pickthall, Marmaduke. *The Meaning of the Glorious Koran*. New York: Alfred A Knopf, 1930.

The Islamic Empire and Arabia (632–1258)

Hitti, Philip K. *The Origins of the Islamic State*, a translation of *Kitab Futuh al-Buldan*. Vol. 1. New York: AMS Press, 1916, 1968.

Hourani, Albert. *A History of the Arab Peoples*. London: Faber, 1992.

Nutting, Anthony. *Arabs, a Narrative History from Mohammad to the Present*. New York: New American Library, 1964.

Peters, F. E. *Allah's Commonwealth: A History of Islam in the Near East, 600–1100 A.D.* New York: Simon and Schuster, 1973.

The Golden Age of Islam (ca. 750–1258)

George, Linda S. *The Golden Age of Islam*. New York: Benchmark Books, 1998.

Myers, Eugene. *Arabic Thought and the Western World in the Golden Age of Islam*. New York: Ungar, 1964.

Nicholson, Reynold A. *A Literary History of the Arabs*. New York: Kegan Paul International, 1998.

Vogel, Frank E. *Islamic Law and Legal System: Studies of Saudi Arabia*. Leiden and Boston: Brill, 2000.

The Mamluks, Ottomans, and the Wahhabi-Al Saud Alliance (1258–1745)

Hitti, Philip K. *History of the Arabs: From the Earliest Times to the Present*. London. Macmillan, 1953.

Nutting, Anthony. *Arabs, a Narrative History from Mohammad to the Present*. New York: New American Library, 1964.

Peters, F. E. *Mecca*. Princeton, N.J.: Princeton University Press, 1994.

Vassiliev, Alexei. *The History of Saudi Arabia*. New York: New York University Press, 2000.

The First Saudi State (1745–1818)

Philby, H. St. John. *Saudi Arabia*. New York: Frederick A. Praeger, 1955.

Vassiliev, Alexei. *The History of Saudi Arabia*. New York: New York University Press, 2000.

Winder, R. Bayly. *Saudi Arabia in the Nineteenth Century*. New York: Octagon Books, 1980.

Roots of Modern Arabia (1818–1891)

Anscombe, Frederick F. *The Ottoman Gulf: The Creation of Kuwait, Saudi Arabia, and Qatar*. New York: Columbia University Press, 1997.

Elgood, Robert. *The Arms and Armour of Arabia in the 18th, 19th and 20th Centuries*. London: Scolar, 1994.

Ochsenwald, William. *Religion, Society and the State in Arabia: The Hijaz, under Ottoman Control, 1840–1908*. Columbus: Ohio State University Press, 1984.

Rasheed, Madawi al-. *Politics in an Arabian Oasis: The Rashidi Tribal Dynasty*. London: I. B. Tauris, 1991.

Sadleir, George Forster. *Diary of a Journey across Arabia (1819)*. Cambridge, Mass.: Oleander Press, 1977.

Unity and Independence (1891–1932)

Almana, Muhammed. *Arabia Unified: A Portrait of Ibn Saud.* London: Hutchinson Benham, 1980.

Kostiner, Joseph. *The Making of Saudi Arabia 1916–1936.* Oxford: Oxford University Press, 1993.

Lawrence, T. E. *Seven Pillars of Wisdom, a Triumph.* Garden City, N.Y.: Doubleday, Doran and Co., 1935.

McGloughlin, Leslie J. *Ibn Saud: Founder of a Kingdom.* New York: St. Martin's Press, 1993.

Titelbaum, Joshua. *The Rise and Fall of the Hashemite Kingdom of Arabia.* London: Hurst and Co., 2001.

Twitchell, K. S. *Saudi Arabia, with an Account of the Development of Its Natural Resources.* 3rd ed. New York: Greenwood Press, 1969.

Birth of a Kingdom (1932–1953)

Bligh, Alexander. *From Prince to King: Royal Succession in the House of Saud in the 20th Century.* New York: New York University Press, 1984.

Holden, David, and Richard Johns, with James Buchan. *The House of Saud: The Rise and Rule of the Most Powerful Dynasty in the Arab World.* New York: Holt, Rinehart and Winston, 1982.

Lacey, Robert. *The Kingdom: Arabia and the House of Saud.* New York: Harcourt Brace Jovanovich, 1982.

A Path to World Power (1953–1973)

Cave, Anthony Brown. *Oil, God, and Gold: The Story of Aramco and the Saudi Kings.* Boston: Houghton Mifflin, 1999.

Citino, Nathan J. *From Arab Nationalism to OPEC: Eisenhower, King Sa'ud, and the Making of US-Saudi Relations.* Bloomington: Indiana University Press, 2002.

Holden, David, and Richard Johns, with James Buchan. *The House of Saud: The Rise and Rule of the Most Powerful Dynasty in the Arab World.* New York: Holt, Rinehart and Winston, 1982.

Oil and Arms (1973–1990)

Aburish, Said K. *The Rise, Corruption and Coming Fall of the House of Saud.* London: Bloomsbury, 1994.

Al-Ali, Jasin. *An Analysis of the Financial Structure and Economic Development in Oil-Producing Countries: The Case of Saudi Arabia.* London: Gulf Centre for Strategic Studies, 1992.

Al-Rasheed, Madawi. *A History of Saudi Arabia.* Cambridge, Mass.: Cambridge University Press, 2002.

Beling, Willard A., ed. *King Faisal and the Modernization of Saudi Arabia*. London: Croom Helm; Boulder, Colo.: Westview Press, 1980.

Golub, David B. *When Oil and Politics Mix: Saudi Oil Policy, 1973–1985*. Cambridge, Mass.: Harvard University, Center for Middle Eastern Studies, 1985.

Hart, Parker T. *Saudi Arabia and the United States: Birth of a Security Partnership*. Bloomington: Indiana University Press, 1998.

The Gulf Crisis and Its Aftermath (1990–2001)

Fandy, Mamoun. *Saudi Arabia and the Politics of Dissent*. New York: St. Martin's Press, 1999.

Munro, Alan. *An Arabian Affair: Politics and Diplomacy behind the Gulf War*. London and Washington: Brassey's, 1996.

Al-Rasheed, Madawi. *A History of Saudi Arabia*. Cambridge: Cambridge University Press, 2002.

Rashid, Nasser Ibrahim. *Saudi Arabia and the Gulf War*. Joplin, Mo.: International Institute of Technology, 1992.

Vassiliev, Alexei. *The History of Saudi Arabia*. New York: New York University Press, 2000.

The Challenges Ahead

Doumato, Eleanor Abdella. *Getting God's Ear: Women, Islam and Healing in Saudi Arabia and the Gulf*. New York: Columbia University Press, 2000.

Friedman, Thomas L. *Longitudes and Attitudes: Exploring the World after September 11*. New York: Farrar, Straus, Giroux, 2002.

Ide, Arthur Frederick. *Jihad, Mujahideen, Taliban, George W. Bush & Oil: A Study in the Evolution of Terrorism and Islam*. Garland, Tex.: Tanglewild Press, 2002.

Schwartz, Stephen. *Two Faces of Islam*. New York: Doubleday, 2002.

INDEX

Page numbers followed by the letter *f* indicate illustrations; the letter *m* indicates a map; the letter *g* indicates an item found in the glossary.